The Cross-Dressed Caribbean

New World Studies

J. Michael Dash, *Editor*

Frank Moya Pons and
Sandra Pouchet Paquet,
Associate Editors

The Cross-Dressed Caribbean

Writing, Politics, Sexualities

Edited by
Maria Cristina Fumagalli, Bénédicte Ledent,
and Roberto del Valle Alcalá

University of Virginia Press
Charlottesville and London

University of Virginia Press
© 2013 by the Rector and Visitors of the University of Virginia
All rights reserved
Printed in the United States of America on acid-free paper

First published 2013

9 8 7 6 5 4 3 2 1

Library of Congress Cataloging-in-Publication Data

The cross-dressed Caribbean : writing, politics, sexualities / edited by Maria Cristina
Fumagalli, Bénédicte Ledent, and Roberto del Valle Alcalá.
    pages   cm. — (New World Studies)
  Includes bibliographical references and index.
  ISBN 978-0-8139-3522-5 (cloth : alk. paper) — ISBN 978-0-8139-3523-2
(pbk. : alk. paper) — ISBN 978-0-8139-3524-9 (e-book)
  1. Caribbean literature—History and criticism. 2. Transvestites in literature.
3. Sex in literature. I. Fumagalli, Maria Cristina, editor of compilation. II. Ledent,
Bénédicte, editor of compilation. III. del Valle Alcalá, Roberto, editor of compilation.
  PR9205.05.C76 2013
  810.9′9729—dc23

                                                                2013022154

Contents

4 Symptoms and Detours

Acknowledgments

FIRST OF all we would like to express our gratitude to our contributors—it has been a long journey but we have always been able to count on their commitment to the project. The three anonymous readers who read the manuscript should also be thanked for all their work and for their incisive feedback which made our collection a much better and more significant one. We are also very grateful to Cathie Brettschneider at Virginia who has been a very patient, understanding and supportive editor: it has been a privilege working with her.

Two essays in this collection first appeared elsewhere: Mayra Santos Febres's "The Caribbean and Transvestism" was originally published in Spanish as "Caribe y travestismo" in *El artista caribeño como guerrero de lo imaginario,* edited by Rita De Maeseneer and An Van Hecke (Frankfurt/Madrid: Vervuert Iberoamericana, 2004), 37–44; Shani Mootoo's "On Becoming an Indian Starboy" was published in *Canadian Literature* 196 (2008): 83–94. A slightly different version of Roberto Strongman's "The Body of Vodou: Corporeality and the Location of Gender in Afro-Diasporic Religion" was published as "The Afro-Diasporic Body in Haitian Vodou and the Transcending of Gendered Cartesian Corporality" in *Kunapipi: Journal of Postcolonial Writing & Culture* 30, no. 2 (2008): 11–29, and as "Transcorporeality in Vodou" in *Journal of Haitian Studies* 14, no. 2 (2008): 4–29. A few pages from Odile Ferly's "Defying Binarism: Cross-Dressing and *Transdressing* in Mayra Santos Febres's *Sirena Selena vestida de pena* and Rita Indiana Hernández's *La estrategia de Chochueca*" first appeared in Odile Ferly, *A Poetics of Relation*, published in 2012, and are reproduced here with permission of Palgrave Macmillan. We wish to thank Shani Mootoo and *Canadian*

Literature; Roberto Strongman and *Journal of Haitian Studies;* Odile Ferly and Palgrave Macmillan; Mayra Santos Febres, Rita De Maeseneer, and An Van Hecke, for granting us their permission to republish these essays.

Introduction

ON 23 JUNE 2010, Christopher "Dudus" Coke, Jamaica's most wanted fugitive, was arrested along the Mandela Highway in St. Catherine. When he was apprehended, he was clean-shaven and wearing a woman's wig; in the car in which he was traveling, the police found a pink wig, a pair of female glasses, and a hat. Also wanted by the United States to answer drug–trafficking and gun-running charges, "Dudus" had escaped from his stronghold of Tivoli Garden, West Kingston, when the police had tried to arrest him on 17 May. It was suggested that he might have been able to stay at large for more than one month because he was wearing women's clothes.[1]

Dudus's masquerade was aimed at eluding surveillance rather than attracting attention, but it nevertheless echoes Johnny Depp's camped-up performance of ambidextrous sexuality as Captain Jack Sparrow in the film *Pirates of the Caribbean.* The image of Caribbean pirates was shaped by histories such as the seventeenth century's *Bucaniers of America,* a protean and influential account which emphasized the pirates' homosocial tribalism, their cruel yet chivalrous behavior, and their predilection for aristocratic, old-fashioned, and extravagant clothes.[2] As the cases of Dudus and Jack Sparrow exemplify, cross-dressing has always had multiple functions, so it is not surprising that the pirates' subversive sartorial extravagance has paved the way to Carmen Boullosa's *They're Cows, We're Pigs* (1997), a contemporary rewriting of *Bucaniers of America* that features a young girl who, wishing to end a life of exploitation as a prostitute, decides to wear male clothes and board a ship bound for Tortuga to become one of the "Brethren of the Coast." In a similar vein, in *Kingston by Starlight* (2005), the Jamaican-born writer John Farley combines facts and fiction in his retelling of the story of Anne Bonny, a real-life Irish woman who traveled to Jamaica, dressed as a man, became a pirate, had a relationship with another cross-dressing woman, and was then put on trial in London in 1721 for piracy. Anne Bonny's life echoes in important ways the life of Enrique/Henrietta Faber, who cross-dressed as a man to study medicine at the University of Paris, served as a military surgeon in Napoleon's army, and went to Cuba, where she also practiced medicine. In 1823 Enrique/Henrietta was accused by his estranged wife of being a woman and was sentenced to serve four years in the Havana Women's Hospital. Her story is reimagined by the Cuban novelist and theorist Antonio Benítez-Rojo in *Mujer en traje de batalla* (2001; Woman in battle dress), a novel that exposes the colonial origins of heteronormativity and, as Kerstin Oloff argues in this volume, exemplifies how racial, patriarchal, and class oppressions converge in the white conjugal family, the bulwark of colonial values. The rejection of heteronormativity, Oloff insists, is posited as a crucial step toward the full decolonization of contemporary Caribbean discourse and society.

In the geography of the imagination, therefore, Enrique/Henrietta Faber's and Anne Bonny's adventures, the aspiring "Bucanier" girl's cross-dressing in Boullosa's novel, and Captain Sparrow's camp excessiveness powerfully realign the Caribbean, a region only too often associated with machismo and homophobia, with daring transgressions of colonial values predicated upon gender binarism, patriarchy, and race and class division. Fictional scenarios are nevertheless informed by specific power relations, and these "piratesque" subversions of gender allocations are, like Dudus's strategic performance, just one component, perhaps a symptom, of broader power struggles that comprise, but are not limited to, the sexual sphere. Not unlike Jack Sparrow's, Boullosa's pirate girl's, Enrique/Henrietta's, and Anne Bonny's, Dudus's cross-dressed body becomes a complex emblem of queerness, vulnerability, and *badness;* it challenges dominant gender norms but also reminds us of the complex history of disenfranchisement and emasculation that has characterized the Caribbean since the fifteenth century and is still playing out in contemporary collective spaces of (dis)identification such as Jamaican dancehalls. It is intriguing that in Jamaican dancehalls, a space generally associated with that country's culture of homophobia, it has become popular for men to bleach their skin and to wear a stylized coordination of branded clothes, expensive jewelry, tight jeans, and intricate and flamboyant hairstyles.[3] Of course, these men's obsession with attire does not necessarily imply that they are not sexist and/or homophobic and that they do not support, or even practice, violence against women and gay people. Dancehalls, however, are important sites where the politics of clothing still play a crucial role in the ongoing contestation of Caribbean sociopolitical, gendered, racial, and class-bound hierarchies. In her reading of Ebony Patterson's recent series of paintings inspired by dancehall culture, Lizabeth Paravisini argues that dancehalls have the potential to become places where traditional gender allocations and social norms can be challenged.

Caribbean Cross-Dressing and the Politics of Clothing

In this volume the Caribbean is understood as a cultural, regional, multilingual area made up of former plantation societies, whose contours have always suffered from a form of indeterminacy.[4] Signifiers such as "Antilles," "West Indies," and "Caribbean" tend to denote geographical zones that overlap but are not synonyms: denominations, in fact, often reflect colonial empires that have mapped, divided, renamed, and remapped the area according to political supremacy. Caribbean thinkers have tried to go beyond colonial and linguistic subdivisions in different ways: they have affirmed that "the unity is submarine" (Edward Kamau Brathwaite) and that the Caribbean is "the sea" (Derek Walcott), "a multiple series of relationships" (Édouard Glissant), and "an island that 'repeats' itself, unfolding and bifurcating until it reaches all the seas and lands of the earth" (Antonio Benítez-Rojo).[5] The essays in this volume chart the Caribbean, developing and investigating a series of submarine trajectories and multiple relations that connect Cuba and mainland Surinam passing by Haiti, the Dominican Republic, Puerto Rico, Jamaica, Guadeloupe, Martinique, Saint Lucia, and Trinidad. Our contributors also follow the unfolding and bifurcation of Benítez-Rojo's "repeating island" and include in their analyses fantastical and imaginary settings that, however, maintain strong connections with the region and, implicitly or explicitly, take into account different diasporic locations, which Evelyn O'Callaghan has controversially indicated as being fundamental to Caribbean diasporic authors' "daring" to bring to the fore "the troubling consequences of the heterosexual imperatives which operate in the Caribbean."[6] Residents of the Caribbean, however, are becoming more and more vocal about gender and sexuality issues and forcefully demand the abolition of laws that criminalize non-heteronormative behaviors and sexual orientations: among other things, for example, Caribbean lawyers are spearheading an ongoing legal battle challenging the constitutionality of the ban against cross-dressing in Guyana, which could have far-reaching effects region-wide.[7]

The politics of clothing have always had a strong symbolic function in the Caribbean. Ever since Columbus's arrival in the New World, clothing has been instrumental to the production and (re)definition of race, color, class, and ethnicity. Quite significantly, the indigenous population's nakedness or semi-nakedness was strategically re-encoded as a sign of primitiveness, savagery, and passivity.[8] The New World itself was re-qualified as a tabula rasa, a female "nude" ready to be possessed by the powerful and fully (albeit not always appropriately) dressed colonists.[9] Later, the slaves' paucity—or complete lack—of clothing became a powerful marker of their animal-like status: "Why not also ask us to put clothes on our cows, mules and dogs?" a colonist of Saint-Domingue replied to a visitor who asked him why his slaves were left completely naked.[10] Despite the fact that a Royal Ordinance of 1784 prescribed that every slave should be provided with two changes of clothing per year, in travel writing about the eighteenth-century French colony, slaves are frequently referred to as wearing "tattered rags" or nothing at all.[11] Nudity is still a problematic signifier in contemporary Caribbean societies. In an insightful analysis of the controversy caused by Laura Facey's *Redemption Song,* a monument comprising two naked figures (one male and one female) created to celebrate Jamaica's emancipation from slavery, Carolyn Cooper identifies their nudity as the core of the problem because, in a Caribbean context, it can still suggest vulnerability, impotence, and lack of dignity.[12] In a 2007 study of the politics of gender in Trinidadian Carnival, however, Pamela Franco shows that women's nudity can also be seen as subversive: when women began to participate more actively and in greater numbers in the street parade of Carnival Monday and Tuesday, it was their intense *wining* (a highly sexualized dance) and the scanty costumes they were wearing in what became known as "skimpy *mas*" that provoked public outrage.[13] Far from being a stable signifier, nudity has always had multiple functions. Also, dressing in a particular way and cross-dressing can have a multiplicity of meanings depending on specific conjunctures of place and time, and the essays that follow try to do justice to transvestism's shifting connotations.

During slavery, in the plantation areas, much of the profit derived from the sale of provision grounds' produce went into self-fashioning, and in the cities, tailors assisted the ambitious house servants partial to personal ornamentation. Their limited resources notwithstanding, some slaves worked hard to improve their appearance; and for the slaves who could afford it, clothing developed into a crucial indicator of social status, an individual signature and a signifier of resistance. In his *Description topographique, physique, civile, politique et historique de la partie française de l'Isle Saint-Domingue* (Topographical, physical, social, political and historical description of the French part of the island of Saint-Domingue), Médéric Louis Élie Moreau de Saint-Méry explains that there were varying degrees of "luxury" among male slaves: "if they were not lazy," they possessed several changes of shirts and pants, hats, and shoes and donned expensive kerchiefs on the head, around the neck, and in their pockets. Often, he continues, such a wardrobe could cost as much as forty or fifty French louis.[14] As for female slaves, Saint-Méry insists that it is hard to believe how much they were ready to spend for a fancy garb. This could include a chemise, a skirt, ten or twelve handkerchiefs for their hair, necklaces and gold rings, beaver hats or hats with gold embroidery, corsets, camisoles, mules, and even stockings.[15] Free blacks and enfranchised mulattoes (especially women) were also extremely conscious of dress. Their proud ostentation of luxury items initiated "the war of lace and clothing" that engaged the White and Colored inhabitants of the colony in a fierce competition. White colonists found it imperative to legislate on clothing in order to restrain what they considered a dangerous display of individuality on the part of the Black and Colored people. In 1740 and 1779, for example, very specific and detailed ordinances enjoined house slaves and freedmen/women to restrain from ostentation in dress.[16]

Given the importance that clothing had acquired as an instrument of repression and, concomitantly, as a means of resistance, it is not surprising that a valuable weapon in the arsenal of one of the legendary leaders of the 1791 Saint-Domingue slave rebellion, Romaine Rivière or Romaine the Prophetess, was his impressively non-normative appearance. The father of two children, married to a mulatress, Romaine the Prophetess was well known for his cross-dressing practices and his appropriation of the Virgin Mary symbol. He set up quarters in an abandoned church near Trou-Coffy, preached mass before an inverted cross with a saber in his hand, and proclaimed to the slaves that God was black and that all the whites were to be exterminated.[17] According to some sources, Rivière's religious practices testify to the variety one finds among Vodouisant cults of the time, and his appropriation of Mariology could identify him as Kongolese, that is, from a part of Africa that had been exposed to and had freely adapted Catholic symbolism for three hundred years.[18]

Catholic symbolism is also at the core of Lee Easton and Kelly Hewson's essay on Lawrence Scott's *Aelred's Sin* (1998), in which they highlight the instability of the gendered meanings of ecclesiastic vestments—here the monk's robe—and explore the ambiguities and liberating possibilities generated by a cultural encroachment rooted in the Catholic past of colonial Europe. *Aelred's Sin* is structured around two cross-dressed fictional figures. Jean Marc de la Borde is a West Indian man who, in the 1960s, enters Ashton Park Monastery as Brother Aelred but subsequently rejects Catholic sexual morality, embraces his own homosexuality, and becomes a scholar of the Black Atlantic. Significantly, when he dons the ambiguously gendered robe of the monk, Jean Marc/Aelred begins to feel anxious about his racial identity. The second crucial cross-dresser in the novel is the African slave-boy Jordan, a captive at Ashton Park in the eighteenth century, who appears next to a "gentleman of wealth" (probably the previous owner of the estate) in a portrait hanging in the stairway of the monastery. Kneeling at the gentleman's feet, the black boy is dressed in silks, satins, and taffetas, mimicking his master's attire. While revealing how clothing was employed to enforce the white master's ideas about race, class, and gender, this portrait and the visual tradition it encapsulates also disclose how colonial discourse contained the seeds of its own destruction: as Homi Bhabha would put it, in the slave-boy Jordan's cross-dressing, one can detect "at once resemblance and menace."[19]

However, if Catholic symbolism and the politics of clothing are crucial in Scott's *Aelred's Sin* and played their part in Romaine the Prophetess's subversive cultural, class, racial, and gender cross-dressing, it is noteworthy that, as Roberto Strongman insists in his comparative study of novels by René Depestre and Franketienne, and Anne Lescot and Laurence Magloire's film *Des hommes et des dieux* (2002; Of men and gods), the transcorporeality of the Afro-diasporic religious tradition of Vodou greatly facilitated the assumption of cross-gender subjectivities. Romaine the Prophetess's transvestism, therefore, is a thoroughly complex reinvention which reveals that Caribbean cross-dressing has always been part of broader struggles against colonial oppression and cannot be reduced to sexual politics alone. It is noteworthy that the law that bans cross-dressing in Guyana, and which is currently being contested, comes from a section relating to "Minor Offences, Chiefly in Towns" and is the product of old vagrancy laws promulgated in the late nineteenth century when Guyana was a colony. Such laws were designed to restrict access to public spaces by the working poor and to control the behavior of black and brown people in the urban center.[20]

The legacy of Romaine the Prophetess is evident throughout this collection, but the link between political militancy and cross-dressing is addressed in particular by Kerstin Oloff, Paula K. Sato, Roberto del Valle Alcalá, Chantal Zabus, and Michael Niblett. Oloff, as already mentioned, analyzes Benítez-Rojo's revisitation of the life of Enrique/Henrietta Faber through a

Foucauldian lens. Organizing his protagonist's self-understanding around a queer sexuality, Oloff argues, Benítez-Rojo puts the nineteenth and twentieth centuries in dialogue and invites us to apply Enrique/Henriette's transgressive vision to revolutionary Cuba, redirecting his critique toward Cuban discourse on the nation and on the post-revolutionary institution-alization of homophobia in the 1960s and 1970s.

It was José Martí, in 1889, who defined the Cuban male as possessing the "happy faculty" of allying opposing signs of race and gender. Not only was the Cuban both black and white, he also concealed beneath the delicate appearance and poetic temperament of a woman the fighting nature of a man. Martí's vision of racial inclusiveness became the ideal of all Cuban governments in the twentieth century, including that of the rev-olutionary government, which recycled the multiracial, military side of Martí's construction in its symbolic figure of the new Cuban man. How-ever, this image reclaimed the masculine, military side of Martí's Cuban through his abjection of the Cuban male of effeminate appearance as anti-Cuban and counter-revolutionary. Sato argues that Severo Sarduy's 1967 novel *De donde son los cantantes* (Where the singers are from) recuperated Martí's description of Cuban man in all its queerness and reinstated the "effeminacy" of Cuban identity as an occasion for agency and autonomy rather than passivity and defenselessness. The Sino-Cuban transvestites of Sarduy's novel manage to deflect the heteronormative and Orientalist gaze of the imperialistic "West," while reclaiming a gendered inclusivity that the hypermasculine archetypes of 1960s revolutionary Cuba had rejected and proscribed.

The logic of immanent resistance as developed by Reinaldo Arenas in his autobiography *Antes que Anochezca* (1992; Before night falls) is investigated by del Valle Alcalá. Set against the normalizing instincts of bureaucratic consolidation in the Cuban revolutionary process, Arenas's libidinal masquerades and equivocal gender types offer to constantly de-stabilize the binary inscription of desire within well-policed discursive frames. Cross-dressing, in this context, takes on a nonliteral and conse-quently explosive dimension in the constant shuffle of internal dissidence. The proliferating cast of pansexual figures, *locas,* "real men," and poets confirms a radically "other" existence haunting the very core of the disci-plinary projection and threatening to subvert it from within at every turn.

The instability of gender, complicated by the vagaries of nationalism, is also the focus of Zabus's contribution. Through the "split" characters of Clare Savage, the tragic mulatta, and the glamorous and exuberant Harry/Harriet, Zabus argues, Michelle Cliff's *No Telephone to Heaven*

(1987) documents the growth of the Jamaican nation under Michael Manley (in his first term [1969–80]) up to the disillusionment with his "politics of participation," and "flaunts" a concern with *passing*, both racial and sexual. While making a necessary detour through conceptions of drag, cross-dressing, and camp in the 1970s, this chapter rehearses recent theories on transgender to reflect on Cliff's uses of camouflage (in its military sense and in terms of cross-dressing and cross-gendered identification). H/H's move from tokenistic "under-dressing" (that is, wearing the underwear appropriate to the opposite sex) to becoming a non-surgical male-to-female transgendered passing subject is mediated via an excessive "over-performing." This reaches bathetic levels when H/H and Clare Savage camouflage themselves as armed resisters against Jamaica's "sodomy-rape" by American imperialism and futilely aim to engender a nation-in-drag.

The importance of gender politics to a rethinking of strategies of resistance is also at the core of Niblett's essay on Patrick Chamoiseau's *Biblique des derniers gestes* (2002; Biblical register of final deeds). It takes as its starting point the assertion by Balthazar Bodule-Jules, *Biblique*'s protagonist, that his participation in various struggles against oppression was compromised by his not being "Palestinian enough in Israel. Not Jewish enough in Germany. Not Zapatista enough in Mexico. Not Black enough in South Africa. . . . Not gay enough in San Francisco. . . . Not woman enough everywhere."[21] The essay considers the ways in which the destabilizing of traditional gender roles intersects with a reformulation of the politics of rebellion, liberation, and national identity, and suggests that Chamoiseau has shifted his conception of gender, and its codification in the narration of the nation, over the course of his novels. In *Biblique*, it is argued, the emphasis on cross-dressing and the sexual dimorphism of many of the characters are central to the book's problematization of individual and collective identities.

Caribbean Cross-Dressing, Masquerading, and Carnival

The slaves and rebels of Saint-Domingue, as we have seen, resorted to clothing in order to make, both explicitly and implicitly, a political point. But they were not the only ones. In Isaac Mendes Belisario's truly wonderful *Sketches of Characters, in Illustration of the Habits, Occupation, and Costume of the Negro Population in the Island of Jamaica*, published in 1837, we are presented with twelve hand-colored lithographs, some of which represent black actors, musicians, and dancers richly and extravagantly dressed and performing in several traditional masquerades such as the Jonkonnu—a feature of Jamaican culture since the early days of slavery—and the "Set-Girls"—which, incidentally, might have arrived in Jamaica from Saint-Domingue after the 1791 revolt.[22] The "Queen/Maam" of the "Set-Girls" wore rich ornaments, which were "probably the loan of their mistress," while "the remainder of the dress was invariably purchased by herself, and at the cost of several pounds."[23] The dresses of the Set-Girls "correspond in color, &c. agreeably to establish rule, those of their Queen, and other Leaders, differing only in the *superior texture* of the materials. These latter also display a greater profusion of Jewellery than their young followers can boast."[24] The Queen/Maam also held a whip in her hands, which was "highly necessary," Belisario explains, "for the preservation of order in her *corps de ballet*" but also "in mockery of the purpose to which it is not infrequently applied,"[25] thus enacting a sharp parody of the (male) slave-driver and a profound subversion of colonial strategies of reinforcement of social and gender hierarchies. These masquerades originally came from Africa, and the decisive role played by clothing in the survival of such African traditions in the New World is testified to by the various elements of multiple African cultures that have been identified in the costumes and attitudes of the masqueraders.[26] In point of fact, the Jonkonnu performance, invariably referred to by Europeans in the anglicized "John-Canoe," was constituted by a central figure who wore a distinctive headdress, generally in the shape of a houseboat, which had a clear conceptual connection with those used by the Ijo, Ibo, Ibibio, Yoruba, and Agoni people in the Cross River delta in Nigeria.[27] Although African in derivation, the headdress had become creolized by the late eighteenth century and assumed by that time the shape of a colonial house.[28]

Obviously, Caribbean masquerades and transvestism derive from an ongoing process of creolization, which brings together different traditions in a syncretism that is typically Caribbean and that also blurs the boundaries between categorical subdivisions: gender, race, and class are simultaneously interrogated, problematized, and challenged. The white masters strove to control and homogenize the politics of clothing, notions of sex and gender, and behavioral codes of their slaves and indentured laborers who came from different cultures and functioned according to different rules. The Indian indentured workers who crossed the Kala Pani to work on the sugar cane estates of the Caribbean, for example, came from a tradition where *hijras* (physiological males with feminine gender identity, women's clothing, and other feminine gender roles) have a long recorded history, and Sean Lokaisingh-Meighoo has brought to the fore the homoerotic subtext of Indo-Caribbean identity by focusing on the *jahaji bhai* ("ship brother") culture.[29] In this volume, Trinidadian writer Shani Mootoo recounts that on a recent trip to India, she observed that many ordinary men on the streets sport earrings and slippers and wear stylish and colorful scarves and kurta down to their knees. "They all looked, in Western terms, gay," she concludes, but then adds, "I bet few were." She also laments that the gentle and reluctant-to-fight Bollywood starboy she used to admire at the Metro Cinema in San Fernando, Trinidad, when she was a child and with whom she controversially identified, has now been replaced by a tougher and more aggressive hero because Hollywood's convention made the old starboy's ways look effeminate and "fey." Indians were not the only indentured laborers who arrived in the Caribbean after emancipation. As exemplified in Sato's essay in this volume, there were Chinese migrants too, mostly males, whose presence in the Americas was surrounded with specific gender stereotypes, in particular a questioning of their masculinity.[30] Interestingly, this is addressed in Jamaican Patricia Powell's novel *The Pagoda* (1998) through a Chinese woman, Lau A-yin, who dresses up as a man to be able to migrate to Jamaica and lives there as a shopkeeper called Mr. Lowe. Being "'between' and outside, neither black nor white," Powell's cross-dressing character is an alienated individual whose complex identity clearly "disrupts processes of colonial heteropatriarchy."[31]

Creolized figures such as the shape-shifter Pitchi Patchi from the Jonkonnu tradition and the West African Spider Anancy, the folk hero and trickster of the *Anansesem*, which, incidentally, is often represented as a hermaphrodite,[32] are effectively revisited in the Jamaican Sistren Theatre Collective's play *Muffet Inna All a Wi* (1986) where, as Karina Smith explains in this volume, actresses from an all-female cast reverse the gender parody found in the Jamaican pantomime and cross-dress to perform male characters. In Sistren's retelling of the nursery rhyme "Little Miss Muffet," in which a garden spider, descending from its web, frightens a little girl, the Jamaican Miss Muffet is empowered because the spider forces her to fight for her rights. While exposing the gender binary system as a fraudulent construction, Sistren, far from simply caricaturing Jamaican men, make an explicit political statement about the treatment of Jamaican women in the machinery of the State. The play comments specifically upon the exploitation of women in the home, in the media, and in Jamaica's Free Trade Zone in addition to portraying the everyday violence many Jamaican women endure on the streets and in their communities.

Masquerade and cross-dressing are also at the heart of carnival, a crucial component of Caribbean culture and history and a powerful instrument of political opposition. One of the constitutive elements of carnival is the notion of "the world turned upside down," which manifests itself through different forms of cross-dressing. If, in Europe, the (mis)rule of carnival had a person of low rank impersonating someone of high status, in the Caribbean it is not difficult to imagine that slaves cross-dressed as slaveholders and other powerful figures of the colonial administration. Belisario thus comments on a masquerade that took place during the Earl of Mulgrave's administration: "His Lordship with several other distinguished characters were personated by negroes in full costume, as closely imitating their models in *this* respect as possible; but, alas! they had lost sight of one grand requisite to complete the resemblance, viz—ease of manner, and consequently their deportment being strangely at variance with that of their originals, rendered such mimic actions truly amusing."[33]

The accuracy and seriousness with which the enslaved population embarked in cross-dressing is evident, but what is equally clear is the anxiety that such practices created in the white ruling classes and the latter's resulting urge to contain the challenge implicit in such performances—an urge undiminished by the fact that, as Gerard Aching has controversially suggested, what were originally spiritual practices might have been transformed into mere marketplace activities.[34] As a matter of fact, both residents and visitors to Jamaica had a tendency to exorcistically diminish and patronize masquerades by describing them as naive folkloric expressions and picturesque manifestations while they were in reality alarmingly subversive acts and transgressive assertions of resistance and autonomy.[35]

Carnival cross-dressing, as we have seen, concerned itself mainly with the subversion of color and class relations, but gender subversion also played its part in the general questioning and undermining of social hierarchies and power relations. In nineteenth-century Trinidad, for example, the "Baby Doll" and the "Pissenlit" were among the most outrageous masquerading traditions. For the "Baby Doll," a man in drag held a doll that was supposed to be the "bastard baby" of some bystander and made a big scene while his companion, impersonating a policeman, was called in to force the victim to pay child support. In the "Pissenlit" (literally the "bed-wetter"), a man walked around sporting bed sheets or linens stained red in imitation of menstrual blood.[36] Interestingly, in the 1880s the "Pissenlit" was banned because it was considered too destabilizing for the colonial order and its gender allocations. In more recent, post-colonial times, the "Pissenlit" character has been conveniently left out from the project of preservation of "traditional" carnival culture by the National Carnival Commission, a state-sanctioned governing body that oversees carnival activities in Trinidad.[37] However, the attempt to appropriate (and neuter) the subversive potential of carnival is not directed exclusively at cross-dressing performances. We have already seen how women's exhibition of flesh and defiant display of sexuality during carnival have met with intense disapproval in Trinidad, and Richard Fleming and photographer Leah Gordon warn us that the spontaneous, surrealist, anarchic, and "whorish" happenings and masquerading that characterize Mardi Gras in Jacmel, a coastal town in southern Haiti, might be under threat because of their incompatibility with "corporate sponsors, ticket sellers and travel agents who prefer the pomp and organisation of a one-day parade, or *defile,* along a main street stretched with seating and banners promoting mobile phones and beer."[38]

Gender-bending performances also feature in other carnivalesque forms of artistic expression and public arts such as the "Paille-banane," a traditional Boxing Day dance that takes place in Castries, the capital city of the island of Saint Lucia, and that is described by Derek Walcott in *Omeros* and analyzed by Paravisini in this volume. The *Paille-banane* dance—whose central purpose is that of reliving the trauma of the Middle Passage—signifies simultaneously the commitment to maintaining African-derived traditions and to altering binarism and those race-, gender-, and class-based identities imposed by colonialism.

Cultural practices such as carnival and masquerade are strictly related to Caribbean (especially diasporic) experiences of hybridity, de-essentialization, or re-essentialization that register important connections and continuities with recent developments in gender studies. The role played by Caribbean performative traditions such as carnival and dubbing in the reconstruction of gender/sexuality, particularly in response to the legacies of slavery, is explored by Wendy Knepper in her essay on Nalo Hopkinson's queer science-fiction novel *Midnight Robber* (2000). Knepper argues that in this coming-of-age story, which takes place in alternative worlds and where the queering of space and time intersects with the queer experiences of the developing child and transgender hero(ine) Tan-Tan, carnival and cross-dressing operate in complex ways: both can serve hegemonic interests, but both can also serve a more radical function in terms of personal and self-transformation. Hopkinson's work is approached here also as an opportunity to rehearse a specific concern with in-betweenness and multiple contextuality that is common to both queer theory and Caribbean diasporic dynamics and that refuses to inscribe itself in a unitary or monolithic frame of reference.

Caribbean Cross-Dressing, Biopolitics, Mimicry, and Performance

The political theorists Michael Hardt and Antonio Negri, inspired by Michel Foucault, tentatively define "biopower" as a disciplinary, if sometimes diffuse and porous, "power over life" through which domination is made effective. This is contrasted to a notion of "biopolitics," which refers to the converse, resistant capacity of life to "determine an alternative production of subjectivity" beyond the frameworks of dominance (or "normality") and oppression.[39] This schematic opposition suggests a fundamental split within the regulatory function of discursive and categorical thinking, and, in the particular context of potentially subversive practices such as cross-dressing, a very specific mode of immanent resistance undermining the geometries of the power relation: "biopower," viewed from the hybrid waters of Caribbean responses to the problematic of gender, names those manifestations of an organizing logic of colonial and heteronormative provenance which the jocular, but serious, modes of cross-dressing might effectively counter and transform. What the subject positions charted by the essays in this collection effectively instantiate is the enduring commitment of gendered life to the irreducible multiplicity and productivity of biopolitics, to the unrelenting and liberating creation of new subjectivities that different power forms induce in various institutional and social contexts. The disruptive life of gender subversion is therefore a privileged setting for the exploration of Caribbean history.

More poignantly, in her contribution to this collection, Mayra Santos Febres declares that she found her way to represent the Caribbean in the figure of an adolescent transvestite, going as far as suggesting that the Caribbean *is* transvestism. Once again, the problematic history of the Caribbean can provide an explanation for Santos Febres's provocative analogy. After all, Christopher Columbus, who found himself in the Caribbean when his intended destination was the "spice islands" of the East, does say in his journal that the Caribs or "canibales" or "Caniba" are "nothing else than the people of the Grand Khan,"[40] thus paving the way for the subsequent patronymic "cross-dressing" of the area as the West *Indies* and to the nineteenth-century "Levantinization" of the Caribbean.[41] Unsurprisingly, the literature from the area has often thrived on rewriting, intertextuality, and literary ventriloquism, techniques that can all be seen as forms of creative textual cross-dressing.

The Caribbean and transvestism, moreover, have traditionally been associated with, or, rather, erroneously or strategically reduced to, mimicry. Bhabha, however, has demonstrated how in colonial and post-colonial settings mimicry complicates the relation between colonizer and colonized and is always potentially destabilizing to colonial discourse.[42] Similarly, Marjorie Garber has pointed out that cross-dressing is an index of category crisis, "a failure of definitional distinction, a borderline that becomes permeable."[43] Enabling border crossing from one category to another, transvestism powerfully reveals the discursive constructedness of all categories and of their (alleged) distinctiveness and discloses the fact that, as Judith Butler has insisted, to a certain extent, all identities are unstable and imitative.[44] Concomitantly, the ability not only to mimic but, most important, to "master" the practices, gestures, and attitudes of the (alleged) "original" has been recast by Caribbean writers and theorists as a truly creative act of the imagination, not as mere imitation. As the Saint Lucian poet, playwright, and essayist Derek Walcott has argued in his revisitation of the relation of the steel drum and calypso with the xylophone and the group chant, what originated in imitation ended in invention.[45] In this volume Santos Febres claims transvestism as the ploy through which the Caribbean signifies itself in a permanent process of *reinvention* that privileges the logic of transversality and what Édouard Glissant calls "opacity" and "relation."[46] The cultural specificity of the Caribbean is located here in its protean human worlds—embodied by the unruly figure of the cross-dresser—and in its irreducibility to the imported taxonomies of Euro-Atlantic sexual politics.

Cross-dressers, hermaphrodites, transgendered people, and transsexuals haunt Caribbean literature, where sexual "eccentricities" often become a key to understanding the Caribbean and its "mongrelized" identity; and, as we have seen, the central role played by clothing in the Caribbean and, by extension, the challenge to the social and racial hierarchy and to the binary construction of gender that it entails, appear to be foundational, ongoing, striking, and intriguing. Giving the figure of the transvestite in Caribbean literature pride of place and foregrounding the productive transformation that cultural and, in particular, literary forms can impose on inherited power relations, this collection offers a distinctive contribution to debates on biopolitics, biopower, and the formation of imagined collectivities in the postcolonial world that are currently unfolding both *within* and *without* the Caribbean and its diasporas.

The central role that performance and performativity play in cross-dressing is acknowledged by most essays in the collection, and the theatrics of transvestism are revealed as instrumental to undermining or reinforcing the naturalized hierarchies of power—as we have seen, Smith highlights this aspect particularly forcefully in her article on the Jamaican Sistren collective. However, *The Cross-Dressed Caribbean: Writing, Politics, Sexualities* also brings to the fore the dispersal or reinforcement of social conventions, norms, and discourses latent in literary texts that are often more ambiguous and fluid than embodied and specific performances, and points therefore to the fact that cross-dressing is not always liberatory. The discursivity of the marked body, for example, plays an important role in the establishment and debunking of such conventions and is the focus of Carine M. Mardorossian's essay on Maryse Condé's *Célanire cou-coupé* (2000; *Who Slashed Célanire's Throat?* [2004]). In this unorthodox tale, Mardorossian insists, the fantastical functions as the literal and dramatic embodiment of the workings of hegemonic identity construction, and, more specifically, as the dramatization of how norms of gender identity are given meaning via configurations of crossing. Indeed, gender in the narrative gets paradoxically naturalized not through an essentialist rhetoric of biological fixity but through its association with other identities such as race, nationality, and sexuality, which stabilize gender *by default*.

In "Tales Told under the San Fernando Hill," Trinidadian Lawrence Scott suggests instead an imaginative scenario where cross-dressing takes place in the context of young boys from a well-off family experimenting with their sexuality. Their playful crossing over, with its transformative and liberating potential, becomes a metaphor for various transgressive behaviors and desires, which are viewed as sins and therefore repressed in a colonial society where a moralizing Catholic Church seems to play a prevalent role. The boys' erotic performance, inspired in part by Hollywood films, is echoed in different narrative strands, alluding in turn to transvestite boys from Venezuela, a transracial love story between a white girl and an Indian yard boy, as well as an affair between the parish priest and one of his parishioners. Through these secret tales of crossing over, Scott presents the soul of a community whose passions have been smothered under an imposed veneer of respectability and normativity and for which transgression is a major element of their identity quest.

The experience of Indian indentured laborers is the point of departure for Mootoo, who revisits this dislocation by emphasizing its transformative potential and by characterizing this moment in which one left behind language, family ties, community, religion, and cultural traditions and embraced a new way of being as "a queerness of no return." Such "queerness" has been reenacted by subsequent generations who have responded to the restlessness engendered by that earlier dislocation by migrating elsewhere yet again and/or by continuing to reinvent themselves. Mootoo identifies this primal rupture as the how and the why of the stories written. From a personal perspective, Mootoo reveals how the figure of the soft-hearted Indian starboy with whom she identified still informs her writing and her creative artwork and assists her in the creation of new spaces where the multiplicity of genders is celebrated.

Caribbean Cross-Dressing: Repetition with a Difference

As Antonio Benítez-Rojo has famously pointed out, the Caribbean archipelago presents "the features of an island that repeats itself," but he also insists that "every repetition . . . entails a difference."[47] This is true also of the trope of cross-dressing, which is indeed "repeated" in all the texts analyzed by our contributors but, crucially, "with a difference." Furthermore, much like nudity and wearing (particular) clothes (for example, the master's clothes), the practice of cross-dressing signposts different possibilities for subversion but also for reinscription of traditional and repressive values: "differences" in "repetition," therefore, are to be contextualized and historicized. *The Cross-Dressed Caribbean: Writing, Politics, Sexualities* is the first critical text focusing on representation of cross-dressing in Caribbean literature that attends to both "repetition" and "difference" by putting side-by-side texts from the Anglophone, Francophone, Hispanophone, and Dutch-speaking Caribbean and from the Caribbean diasporas.[48] All the texts in question have, in different ways, the trope of the transvestite at their heart; but, far from fitting into an overarching argument about transvestism and its implications, they powerfully demonstrate that there is no transparent interpretation of cross-dressing, which has multiple manifestations in Caribbean literature. Transvestism is here put in dialogue, but never conflated, with transsexuality (to be understood here as a form of gender reassignment, not of gender violence),[49] transgendered identities (characterized by the irreducible social contradiction of sex and gender expression in the same individual),[50] intersexuality and hermaphroditism, and the "open mesh of possibilities" represented by the term "queer."[51] Cross-dressing practices, in fact, are often concomitant with, and at times instrumental to, all these non-heteronormative forms of sexuality. Rejecting the distinction between transvestism and cross-dressing as, respectively, a compulsive disorder and a choice of lifestyle,[52] the following essays use both terms to signify oppositional strategies with manifold, at times contradictory, potentialities.

As we have seen, alongside gender cross-dressing, the contributors to this volume explore class, cultural, and racial cross-dressing, and Santos Febres in particular identifies transvestism as an empowering and opaque strategy for survival and as a compelling metaphor for Caribbean culture. Sato's study of the work of Severo Sarduy analyzes transvestism as a narrative strategy for the inclusion of sexual and racial difference through a simulation of cultural and geographic otherness; under-dressing and over-performing, as we have seen, are discussed by Zabus in her essay on Cliff, and *transdressing,* a peculiar form of "posthumous" cross-dressing practiced by a real-life eccentric of Santo Domingo, is recounted by the novelist Rita Indiana Hernández and analyzed here by Odile Ferly. Ferly's essay explores how Santos Febres's *Sirena Selena vestida de pena* (*Sirena Selena* [2000]) and Hernández's *La estrategia de Chochueca* (1999/2003; Chochueca's strategy) dismantle the binary mind-set that underlies common understandings of identity. Ferly argues that in these novels the cross- or *trans*dressed figure functions as a third position, *neither* male *nor* female. Yet, rather than putting forward a single alternative or third gender that would be static, these millennial texts propose a gamut of genders. Indeed, the protagonists shift gender identifications and/or sexual orientations, deflating any essentialist approach to selfhood. Both novels unsettle dichotomous conceptions of self to consider instead the multitude of intermediate positions available on the identity spectrum, while simultaneously exposing identity categories themselves as constructs. Here, therefore, transvestism appears to be truly transformative.

Ferly's thoroughly positive assessment of the creative potentialities of cross-dressing is almost diametrically opposed to cautionary views such as the one expressed by Zabus in her study of Cliff's *No Telephone to Heaven,* and those identified by Mardorossian in Condé's *Who Slashed Célanire's Throat?* and by Paravisini in José Alcántara Almanzar's "Lulú or the Metamorphosis" (1995). In *Célanire,* paradoxically, through the crossing and crisscrossing of identities, normative identities get reinscribed over and over again; in "Lulú," the cross-dressed body becomes an emblem of defiance and criminality and emerges from the text as dangerous, degenerate, and expendable, while in Cliff's *No Telephone to Heaven,* as Zabus concludes, camouflage has no intrinsic transformative powers but only manages to gesture toward a queer nation. Carefully probing and questioning the symptomatic status of cross-dressing practices as signifiers of "category crisis,"[53] Isabel Hoving also proposes that in certain contexts these practices might ultimately reinforce rather than undermine given definitions of gender. Hoving's exploration of contemporary Dutch-Caribbean writing begins with a consideration of how, in Surinam, there are different discourses to frame the transvestite, which are not necessarily subversive or postmodern. Hoving goes on to discuss the cultural critique accomplished by narratives (by Henna Goudzand-Nahar, John Jansen van Galen, Karin Amatmoekrim, Annette de Vries, and others) that represent pedophiles, transvestites, gay people, and incestuous relationships. These stories, in which different discourses of sexual transgression collide, are often organized according to the logic of abjection: the transgressive markers of social crisis disappear once they have served their goal—that is, the reconstruction of the main protagonist's normative identity. In contrast, Cándani's 2002 novel *Huis van as* (House of ashes) suggests that sexual border-crossers signify a more permanent alienation that is shared by all citizens of the postcolonial nation and its diaspora. Cándani's novel sees alienation as the main problem of the transnational Surinamese community, not its binary sexual and racial organization; the transvestite does not therefore emerge as the subversive border-crosser. Nevertheless, the discourse of transvestism is used to create a model of endlessly transformative desire. By juxtaposing these discourses of sexual transgression, the novel refuses closure; instead, it invites us to reconsider the main predicaments of Caribbean postcoloniality.

The Cross-Dressed Caribbean: Writing, Politics, Sexualities is informed by a refusal to distinguish between "critical" and "creative" pieces or to segregate linguistic areas and is organized according to a fourfold division that emphasizes as forcefully as possible how specific issues are "repeated," but always with a "difference." The aim is not to be comprehensive (clearly an impossibility) but to insist on the necessity of a debalkanization of Caribbean literature that goes beyond the limits represented by national and/or linguistic borders. The essays by Sato, del Valle Alcalá, Zabus, and Niblett in "Revolutions in Drag," the first section of this volume, focus on the clash between institutional centralist power and more or less effective forms of resistance enacted by antibinarism. The interventions of Oloff, Easton and Hewson, Smith, and Knepper in "'Passing' through Time," our second section, probe the temporal complexities of anti-binary resistance, showing how "past" and "future" projections of culture variously index and reflect "present" contexts of struggle. In "Theories in the Flesh," the third part of the book,

Santos Febres, Mootoo, Scott, and Mardorossian open up biopolitical and subjective production to a multiplicity of corporeal modes and to a post-binary ontology of gender rendered here, through performance, memory, and experience, as a constant flow of individual and collective "becoming." Importantly, this section evokes different cultural sources and contexts of queerness, cross-dressing, and gender transgressions: while Santos Febres refers to music and the voice of her iconic transvestite, Scott records the influence of Hollywood and Mootoo engages with the singing, dancing, and gentle-hearted starboys of her adolescence. "Symptoms and Detours," our last section, includes four comparative contributions by Strongman, Paravisini, Ferly, and Hoving. These essays subvert the logic of identity as difference reappropriated by sameness, contest the possibility of dialectical reconciliation in the post-binary "paradigm" and reiterate how cross-dressing is not necessarily a revolutionary or radical practice in all situations. By showing how transvestism can, sometimes, contribute to reinstating and reinforcing oppressive and repressive templates, Hoving in particular underlines, once again, the major role played by context in "repetition with a difference" and invites us to consider how reactionary reinscriptions can question and, at times, even annihilate the subversive possibilities of transvestism highlighted in other parts of the collection.

Notes

1. See Walker and Matthews, "Cops Tailed 'Dudus,'" and Hussey-Whyte, "Pink Wig."
2. Esquemeling, *Bucaniers of America.*
3. Bayley, "Donna Hope." See also Archer, "Accessories/Accessaries," and Ellis, "Out and Bad."
4. See Hulme, "Expanding the Caribbean."
5. Brathwaite, *Contradictory Omens,* 64; Glissant, *Caribbean Discourse,* 139; Walcott, *Omeros,* 320, "I sang our wide country,/the Caribbean Sea"; Benítez-Rojo, *Repeating Island,* 3.
6. O'Callaghan, "Naipaul's Legacy," 115.
7. "Marking World Day."
8. See Hulme, *Colonial Encounters.*
9. For more on this, see de Certeau, *Writing of History;* Hulme, *Colonial Encounters* and "Polytropic Man"; and McClintock, *Imperial Leather.*
10. Malefant, *Des colonies,* 232, qtd. in Fouchard, *Haitian Maroons,* 41.
11. Fouchard, *Haitian Maroons,* 41–42.
12. Cooper, "Enslaved in Stereotype."
13. Franco, "Invention of Traditional Mas," 18.
14. Saint-Méry, *Description topographique,* 1: 59.

15. Ibid., 1: 59–60.

16. Fouchard, *Haitian Maroons,* 43–44.

17. For more on Romaine the Prophetess, see Fick, *Making of Haiti,* 127–29, 307–08.

18. Rey, "Virgin Mary," 354, 350, 343.

19. Bhabha, *Location of Culture,* 86.

20. A. Trotz, "This Case Is About and For All of Us."

21. Chamoiseau, *Biblique,* 808.

22. Barringer and Forrester, introduction, *Art and Emancipation,* 1. The cover of this volume reproduces one of Belisario's sketches, namely the one captioned "Koo, Koo, or Actor Boy."

23. Belisario, *Sketches.*

24. Ibid., letterpress accompanying the lithograph for "Red Set-Girls and Jack-in-the-Green," facsimile reproduction in Barringer et al., *Art and Emancipation* (emphasis in the text).

25. Belisario, *Sketches,* letterpress accompanying the lithograph for "Queen, or Maam of the Set-Girls," facsimile reproduction in Barringer et al., *Art and Emancipation* (emphasis in the text).

26. Barringer and Forrester, introduction, *Art and Emancipation,* 1.

27. Martinez-Ruiz, Item 183, in Barringer et al., *Art and Emancipation,* 479.

28. Forrester, Item 38, in Barringer et al., *Art and Emancipation,* 432.

29. Lokaisingh-Meighoo, "'Jahaji Bhai.'"

30. Frydman, "Jamaican Nationalism."

31. Prater, "Transgender, Memory, and Colonial History," 22.

32. See, for example, Salkey, "Anancy and Jeffrey Amherst."

33. Belisario, *Sketches,* letterpress accompanying the lithograph for "Queen, or Maam of the Set-Girls," facsimile reproduction in Barringer et al., *Art and Emancipation,* (emphasis in the text).

34. See Aching, *Masking and Power.*

35. Barringer and Forrester, introduction, *Art and Emancipation,* 1.

36. Scher, "Copyright Heritage."

37. Ibid., 471, 472.

38. Gordon, *Kanaval,* 16.

39. Hardt and Negri, *Commonwealth,* 57.

40. Qtd. in Hulme, *Colonial Encounters,* 22.

41. For a fuller account of the Levantinization of the Caribbean, see Sheller, *Consuming the Caribbean.* Sheller suggests that "Europe's relation to the Caribbean can most profitably be understood if we return to its original entanglement with Asia" (108). Europeans, Sheller insists, "produced the idea of the Caribbean via a hybrid Orientalist and Africanist discourse characterised by an unstable logic of East vs. West, tradition vs. modernity, barbarism vs. civilisation" (109).

42. Bhabha, *Location of Culture,* chapter 4.

43. Garber, *Vested Interests,* 16.

44. Butler, *Gender Trouble.*

45. Walcott, "Caribbean: Culture or Mimicry?," 9.

46. Glissant, *Caribbean Discourse* and *Poetics of Relation.*

47. Benítez-Rojo, *Repeating Island,* 3.

48. Academic studies on sexuality in Caribbean culture have been on the increase in the past ten years. Most of these studies, however, focus on homosexuality and homophobia, on manifestations of normative and non-normative sexualities in particular islands or other equally specific locations in the Caribbean, but they do not tackle cross-dressing and transvestism, particularly not in the literary field. One possible exception to this is Sifuentes-Jáuregui's *Transvestism, Masculinity and Latin American Literature*, which brilliantly engages with the figure of the transvestite in the works of Alejo Carpentier, José Donoso, Severo Sarduy, and Manuel Puig. Sifuentes-Jáuregui's discussion of contemporary theories about gender in the context of Latin America usefully maps a geographical and cultural territory that is adjacent but not identical to the one explored in this volume. One should also mention Curdella Forbes's interesting study of gender and performance in the works of George Lamming and Samuel Selvon, entitled *From Nation to Diaspora*, which appeared in 2005, but mostly concentrates on hermaphrodism as a trope that can help to conceptualize West Indian gender. Worth listing is also a collection edited by Parker et al. and published in 2002, *Nationalisms and Sexualities*, a cross-cultural discussion of the ways in which national identities can inform and be informed by sexual, gendered, racial, and/or class identities. It does not have the Caribbean as its focal point, but both the collection as a whole and, in particular, the section entitled "Tailoring the Nation"—which foregrounds the "miscegenation of clothes" (Norman S. Holland), the ambivalent politics of clothing (Ann Rosalind Jones and Peter Stallybrass), and the ways in which the figure of the cross-dresser stands at the crossroads of sexism, racism, and imperialist/colonialist desire and fantasies (Marjorie Garber)—can perhaps be seen as an important precursor to our collection. Though there *have* been hardly any book-length studies of Caribbean cross-dressing, a few articles have started to appear on the subject, notably by Archer and Ellis.

49. Janice Raymond has controversially argued that male-to-female transsexuals are rapists who appropriate female bodies for themselves, concomitantly reducing them to being mere artifacts (*Transsexual Empire*, 104).

50. We are here following Leslie Feinberg's self-definition: "I am transgendered. I was born female, but my masculine gender expression is seen as male. It's not my sex that defines me, and it's not my gender expression. It's the fact that my gender expression appears to be at odds with my sex. . . . It's the social contradiction between the two that defines me" (*Transgender Warriors*, 101).

51. Sedgwick, *Tendencies*, 8.

52. Garber, *Vested Interests*, 17, 4.

53. Ibid., 17.

Revolutions in Drag

The Transvestite and Cubanness in Severo Sarduy's *De donde son los cantantes*

Paula K. Sato

THREE AVATARS of Cubanness took shape in the nineteenth and twentieth centuries, three embodiments of resistance to a U.S. imperialism that I suggest sought to Orientalize the Cuban. The third, the transvestite in Severo Sarduy's 1967 experimental novel *De donde son los cantantes*, the intended focus of this essay, cannot be understood without discussion of the first, made tangible in the person of José Martí, and the second, corporealized in Fidel Castro. Regarding the United States' Orientalization of Cuba, as nineteenth- and twentieth-century U.S. politicians entertained dreams of annexing the island, they fed those aspirations with images of their Caribbean neighbor as primitive, as racially other, and as femininely incapable of autonomy. Cuba was a damsel anxiously awaiting U.S. governance, much as the Orient awaited "the shelter of European occupation."[1] Statesmen such as Thomas Jefferson envisioned Cuba as part of the union from as early as the beginning of the nineteenth century. Throughout the nineteenth and the first half of the twentieth century, they justified that ambition through their construction of the United States as implicitly "masculine" (capable of governing) and of Cuba as explicitly "effeminate" (incapable of self-government). Whether consciously or not, in 1823 John Quincy Adams, then secretary of state, characterized Cuba using the terminology of an Orientalism whose advance from 1815 to 1914 coincided with the expansion of "European direct colonial dominion . . . from about 35 percent of the earth's surface to about 85 percent of it."[2] He surmised in a message to the U.S. minister in Spain that a Cuba severed from the European fatherland would be "incapable of self-support" and would naturally gravitate toward the United States, who, "by the same law of nature, cannot cast her off from its bosom."[3] Theodore Roosevelt, who, we know, saw a direct parallel between Europe's colonization of the Orient and U.S. aspirations to manage Cuba, wrote in a 1904 message to Cecil Spring-Rice of the British Foreign Office, "It is a good thing for India that England should control it. And so it is a good thing, a very good thing, for Cuba . . . that the United States has acted as it has actually done during the last six years."[4] As we recall, the United States had occupied Cuba militarily from 1899 to 1902. It would go on to set up a government of occupation from 1906 to 1909 and would continue to hold considerable sway over Cuban affairs until 1959—to the extent that Eric Williams maintained that by the 1920s, Cuba had become "in every sense of the term an American colony."[5] Williams argued that the United States intended to transform the Caribbean into an "American Mediterranean."[6] I suggest that it sought to make the Caribbean its Orient, and that Martí's and Castro's construction of Cuban Man must be understood within the context of Cuban resistance to a U.S. imperialism that Orientalized and feminized Cuba.

Offering a more nuanced view of gender than that put forth in Orientalist discourse, Martí argued that although the Cuban male was feminine in appearance, demeanor, and sensibility, he possessed a hidden but distinctly masculine, military disposition. Martí's resistance to U.S. imperialism was a celebration of Cuba's queerness, its ability to reconcile incongruent elements of race and gender by joining "black" with "white" and "feminine" with "masculine." His dream of racial inclusiveness had enduring value. Alejandro de la Fuente convincingly argues that political parties and cultural movements throughout the twentieth century, including that of the Cuban Revolution, based their claims to legitimacy on their adherence to Martí's racial ideals, often in direct defiance of the United States. However, revolutionary Cuba ignored Martí's queering of Cuban masculinity in its construction of the New Man, its symbol of the nation embodied in the person of Fidel Castro. And the new hypermasculine national identity, intended to send the message to Washington that Cuba would no longer allow itself to be the feminine object of U.S. power fantasies, was accompanied by an oppressive domestic policy against gays, who had come to be seen as effeminate and counterrevolutionary.

In this essay I will examine Sarduy's use of the Sino-Cuban transvestite in relationship to three constructions of Cubanness: Martí's late nineteenth-century queering of Cuban identity; the revolutionary government's mid-twentieth-century hypermasculine, and obligatorily heterosexual, New Cuban Man; Orientalization of Cuba that constructed her as effeminate and in need of the United States' masculine guidance and protection (read control and intervention). I will situate Sarduy's transvestite both as a return to the effeminate and queer origins of Cuban identity in Martí and as an extension of the Cuban leader who in his bid for racial inclusiveness overlooked the thousands of Chinese who came to Cuba as contract laborers from 1847 to 1874 and who fought in the Cuban wars of independence.[7] I will also situate Sarduy's transvestite as a subversion of the revolutionary government's hypermasculine, heteronormative construction of Cubanness, which transformed the Cuban homosexual into a social pariah and thus an internal exile.

Martí's Queering of Cuban Identity in Response to U.S. Imperialism

When campaigning for the second Cuban war of independence (1895–98) in the late nineteenth century, Martí concluded that defeat in the first (the Ten Years' War of 1868–78) was due to Cuba's failure to unite across color lines. In consequence, his dream of an autonomous Cuba became inseparable from his desire for racial fraternity.[8] In a well-known passage from "Mi raza" (My race)—an article published in *Patria* (1883), the newspaper founded by Martí in New York in 1882 and generally recognized as the Cuban independence movement's official organ—Martí proclaimed that Cuban whites and blacks were united by their jointly shed blood in the independence struggle: "To be Cuban is more than to be white, mulatto or black. On the field of battle, the souls of the whites and blacks dying for Cuba have ascended, united with one another in the air."[9]

Martí's dream of racial unity became consolidated with his resistance to U.S. imperialism as he awakened to the threat of racial violence during his fourteen-year exile in the United States (1881–95). In his article titled "A Terrible Drama: The Funeral of the Haymarket Martyrs," he wrote that the land that had promised to be a beacon of liberty and equality had become a monster of intolerance and greed that wanted to spread its tentacles to the entirety of North and South America. The violent massacre and lynching of Chinese immigrants, blacks, Amerindians and Italian Americans on U.S. soil became the topic of articles that Martí penned from September 1885 through March 1891.[10] He dedicated his final years to unifying a nation that would be self-governing and that, unlike its North American neighbor, would ensure the inclusion of all its citizens. Martí, who admired the French statesman who had served as major-general in the American Revolution, took Lafayette's failed dream of America as "a cherished and safe asylum" of "tolerance," "equality," and "peaceful liberty" and made it his dream for Cuba.[11]

In addition to defining Cuba as taking up the United States' dropped mantle of tolerance, Martí appropriated North America's construction of the Cuban as the United States' inassimilable racial, effeminate Other. In an article titled "Do We Want Cuba?" appearing in Philadelphia's *Manufacturer* on 16 March 1889, prominent Republican congressmen contended that Cuba was made up of three classes of people—Spaniards, "Negroes," and native Cubans of Spanish descent—all with varying degrees of inassimilability.[12] Moreover, the congressmen's language, uncannily similar to that of European Orientalism, painted Cuba as the United States' depraved racial, feminine Other incapable of self-rule and civic responsibility.[13] According to the *Manufacturer,* the Spanish race was the most inferior of all the white races. Cuban Negroes were more barbaric than the most degraded Negro in Georgia. And native Cubans of Spanish descent had not only the moral deficiency of the Spanish race but also an "effeminacy" and "lack of virile strength" that made them incompetent in matters of self-governance and incapable "of fulfilling the obligations of citizenship in a great and free republic." The U.S. congressmen concluded that if Cuba were to become a state in the United States, she would have to be populated with people of Anglo-Saxon ethnicity: "Our only hope of qualifying Cuba for the dignity of statehood would be to Americanize her completely, populating her with people of our own race." Rather than repopulating Cuba with "better" racial stock so that it could grant her the rights and privileges of statehood, the United States endeavored to impose its own racist structure on the island through discriminatory policies during its first military occupation and during Cuba's first (1902–33) and second republic (1933–59).[14] The same terminology that Edward Said uses to describe Europe's vision of the Orient at the time can be used to describe the United States' vision of Cuba. The United States saw Cuba as a space of "feminine penetrability," as "a locale requiring Western attention, reconstruction, even redemption," to borrow Said's terminology.[15] And the United States' construction of Cuba as its racial and effeminate other, functioning in a similar manner to Orientalist discourse, was used to promote interference in the island's affairs.

In *Orientalism*, Said demonstrates the ways in which an implicitly masculine imperialist discourse justifies the invasion of sovereign states through simultaneously feminizing the colonized and conflating the category "woman" with the need of masculine Western protection. Ironically, as it does so, it also constructs the Oriental woman as sexually willing, available for sexual exploitation, even rape.[16] The Orientalization of

Cuba has arguably been a component of Western conceptualizations of the island since Columbus first took possession of her, mistaking her for the Far East. The United States continued to Orientalize Cuba by inscribing her as a feminized social and geographical space in need of the United States' tutelage, protection, and occupation.

It is interesting to note that Martí did not counter U.S. claims with a categorical denial of Cuban effeminacy. Instead, he published the piece titled "A Vindication of Cuba" in the *New York Evening Post* on 25 March 1889. In the article he maintained that Cubans should not be "considered as the *Manufacturer* does consider us, an 'effeminate' people" simply because Cuba's "half-breeds and city-bred young men are generally"—and one could say the same of Martí himself—"of delicate physique, of suave courtesy and ready words, hiding under the glove that polishes the poem the hand that fells the foe." Cubans were fighting men who knew how to pawn their "trinkets" in a day in order "to pay their passages to the seat of war."[17] Thus, even though Cubans might seem "effeminate" because of their feminine appearance (delicate physique), courtly manners (suave courtesy), feminine gestures (polishing), feminine apparel (glove), feminine possessions (trinkets), and poetic sensibility, they "fought like men." This is because the Cuban, according to Martí, has the "happy faculty" of allying incongruities—of uniting not only "moderation with exuberance" and black with white, but also, it seems, the delicate appearance and poetic temperament of a woman with the fighting nature of a man.[18]

Sarduy's Transvestite as Parody of Martí's Queer Cuban

The central characters of Sarduy's novel, transvestites Auxilio Chong and Socorro Si-Yuen, reenact in parodic form Martí's construction of the Cuban as both artist of effeminate appearance and combative military man. In the opening lines, Auxilio, statuesque, but not in the classical sense, has sculpted herself in neon colors and camp. "Striped," she calls to mind the geometric shapes of Victor Vasarely (1908).[19] In Socorro's words, "You look like graph paper. Vasarelic" (92). Auxilio's speech is as much an imitation of art as is her appearance. As Roberto González Echevarría, the editor of Sarduy's novel, notes, her existentialist statement "I will be ashes, but I will have meaning./Dust will I be, but dust in love" is a paraphrase of the seventeenth-century Spanish sonnet by Quevedo y Villegas titled "Amor constante más allá de la muerte" (Steadfast love beyond death; 91, n. 2). Socorro is no less a reiteration of art than Auxilio. She labels herself Velázquez's "infanta" and "plateresque"

(175), thus as self-consciously baroque and as belonging to the style of fifteenth- and sixteenth-century Spanish architecture that mixed Gothic elements with Renaissance and intricate ornamentation with extravagant decoration (175, n. 2). Auxilio and Socorro also embody the masculine side of Martí's construction, becoming hypermilitary as they wield "Thompson machine guns, two-pronged knives, javelins, flamethrowers, pum-pum guns, hand grenades and tear-gas bombs" (117). Thus, as concomitant effeminate-appearing artists and military men, they possess the felicitous faculty of allying incongruous signs of gender that Martí both embodied and saw as distinctively Cuban. Queerly feminine *and* masculine, they are *"bearded ladies* in a Mongol circus," singing in soprano *and* bass, wearing a fragrance identified as both Fleur de "Racaille" de Caron *and* Shoulton Old Spice (125, 151–52, 204, emphasis added).[20]

However, Sarduy surpasses Martí in his vision of racial inclusiveness by creating a space in the island's landscape for Cubans of Chinese descent. Incidentally, if the Oriental is already a feminized male in Orientalist discourse, then Sarduy's Chinese transvestites are hyperfeminized. However, their femininity packs a punch. We have seen how Martí subverted the *Manufacturer*'s feminization of Cubans by revealing that their seeming "femininity" housed hidden agency and empowerment (hiding under the glove that polishes is the hand that fells the foe). Similarly, Sarduy reveals that the effeminate Oriental, far from being the silent, supine, passive figure that Orientalist discourse makes her out to be, is not anxiously awaiting Western man to define, conquer, or shelter her. Sarduy's transvestites wield an arsenal of weapons that are not just technological. While we see a temporary liaison in *De donde* between an older white male (the General) and the feminized Oriental (Auxilio and Socorro), the hierarchical relationship of white dominance and Asian subordination that we generally associate with a racialized Orientalist "Asian boy" fetish fails to materialize.[21] Auxilio and Socorro occupy the dominant position intellectually as they attempt to educate the General using a cryptic idiom that the latter does not comprehend. Thus, he fails to understand that their description of Flor de Loto, the diva of Havana's Shanghai Opera, as "a mirage" and "a pure absence," and their conclusion that "there is no water for [the General's] thirst" (121), is their way of saying that, similar to Balzac's Zambinella, Flor de Loto is not a "real" woman.[22] Sarduy further upsets traditional notions of sexual domination and subordination by representing Auxilio and Socorro as playing the "passive" role in a sadomasochistic tryst with the General and yet as exploiting him economically, as physically outnumbering the General two to one, as possessing an arsenal of military hardware that renders them technologically capable of domination, and as making the General their tool as they pillage his curio store. In addition, as transvestites, they "wield control of their queer representation," to borrow Eng-Beng Lim's phrasing,[23] simultaneously constructing themselves as effeminate and defying Orientalist stereotypes of the dominated, effeminate Asiatic gay who gazes with adulation at the white male from a subaltern position. Thus, both Martí and Sarduy destabilize the Orientalist tendency to collapse the term "feminine" with "passive," "subordinate," "exploitable." As we shall see, Sarduy will use similar counter-Orientalist strategies to undermine Castro's heteronormative, homophobic construction of the Cuban. As he does so, he will open up the possibility of imagining a Cuban manhood resistant to Western imperialism otherwise than through the narrative of the New Man.

Castro's New Man versus Sino-Cuban Gay or Models of Empowerment

Martí died on the battlefield in 1895, but his vision of a cross-racially unified Cuba lived on as the inviolable ideal in the national imaginary. Over the course of the twentieth century, Cubans wed themselves to Martí's dream of racial fraternity, and they did so against the grain of U.S. imperialism. Although his desire to create a country that was racially inclusive endured as the ideal of Cuban identity (if not necessarily as the reality that obtained materially, politically, or socially),[24] only half of Martí's vision of Cuban masculinity survived the Revolution. On the one hand, the masculine military side of Martí's construction became the very definition of the Revolution's New Man. On the other, the appearance of effeminacy in males, a sign of homosexuality in Latin America, became the signifier in Castro's Cuba of counterrevolutionary delinquency and, as such, grounds for incarceration.[25] Castro explicitly positioned the homosexual as not revolutionary and not Communist in an interview with Lee Lockwood first published in 1967: "We would never come to believe that a homosexual could embody the conditions and requirements of conduct that would enable us to consider him a true Revolutionary, a true Communist militant. A deviation of that nature clashes with the concept we have of what a militant Communist must be."[26] Thus, in Castro's mind, the New Man could not be gay. Moreover, the gay man could not be Cuban. As González Echevarría wrote in 1987:

The Cuban Revolution, following the declarations of Ernesto "Che" Guevara, proposed the creation of what he called—with shocking machismo—"the new man"; moreover, it proposed a redefinition of Cuban as well as Spanish-American identity. As the Revolution became radicalized and later institution-alized, its interrogation of national identity became an affirmation; its critique became an assertion. [Today] Cuban nationality is defined in relation to the political militancy of the individual. . . . [And] the national identity is taken on as a point of faith and is practiced as a doctrine.[27]

Thus, because Cuban nationality was "defined in relation to the political militancy of the individual," and the gay man, by nature, could not be a "true" militant, the homosexual could not participate in the Nation.

The particular brand of heteronormativity that obtained in revolu-tionary Cuba can only be understood in terms of Latin American con-structions of "heterosexual" and "homosexual." Oscar Montero notes that "the abject sign of deviance" in the gay Latino man is "effeminacy." Thus, the biological male who appears effeminate in dress or mannerisms is often assumed to be gay. And therefore, the transvestite is marked as gay, regardless of her sexual orientation. In addition, in Latin Ameri-can cultures, it is the biological male who penetrates the bodily orifice of another person, whether that other person is male or female, who is considered to be heterosexual. Only the biological male who receives the penis of another into one or more of his bodily orifices is considered to be homosexual.[28] With that in mind, a self-identified masculine Cuba can express the desire to screw a masculinized United States and remain consistent within the norms of Cuban heterosexuality, metaphorically speaking. A masculine Cuba cannot, however, be screwed and remain consistently heterosexual.[29] Whether the revolutionary government was conscious of the fact or not, the issue of sexuality became central to its strategy for making Cuba impermeable to further U.S. invasion (penetra-tion) and intervention.

The sexual identity expressed in Cuba's new international policy, the construction of Cuban Man as "he who screws but cannot be screwed," also became part of its new national policy, clearly sending the message to its citizens that one could not be Cuban and gay. Peter Marshall describes the state-driven homophobia in the 1960s that led to the surveillance of male ballet dancers, musicians, and writers, whose "dangerous" artistic professions were associated with homosexuality, and to the disbanding of the cultural magazine *Lunes de Revolución* (Revolutionary Mondays, the literary supplement to the pro-Castro newspaper *Revolución*), largely run by homosexual writers, artists, and intellectuals. The government also organized "night raids" and "a public campaign against homosexuals, who were rounded up without charge or trial and sent to work in . . . labour camps."[30] It is reported in the documentary *Conducta impropia* that over 60,000 homosexuals had been incarcerated in those camps by 1967. In the film, Cubans also attest to the labeling of gays as "social plague-bearers," "non-persons," and "vermin" and to a number of public moral purges of homosexuals carried out at the University of Havana and other schools. We generally think of the monster as the dangerous aggressor. Ironically, in revolutionary Cuba, the gay man became Cuba's monster because of his perceived vulnerability rather than aggressiveness. He had to be eradicated because he symbolized a feminine Cuba vulnerable to penetration, invasion, and occupation. He thus represented a threat to Cuban autonomy.[31]

In *De donde,* Sarduy also imagines a Cuban identity that is resistant to U.S. imperialism. However, he restores queerness to that identity by emphasizing Cuba's gender as well as racial versatility. Moreover, it is important to note that he does so in a manner that could be termed counter-realist, frequently obstructing the reader's willing suspension of disbelief by writing a story that vacillates between different versions of itself, by accentuating the noncorrespondence of his tale to a material reality existing beyond its pages, and thus by undermining the "truth" status of his text. Therefore, as his transvestite protagonists produce new versions of their own identities, versions that continually scream fiction, they become an allegory of the text itself. When joined with Flor de Loto, they also become an allegory of two opposing narrative strategies. In both the novel and his theoretical writings, Sarduy evokes two types of transvestism. In the first type, the transvestite is a trompe l'oeil, a fake that passes for reality. She is metaphoric of the realist text that pretends there is a reality outside of the text to which it refers and that recounts a fictional story while concealing its status as make-believe. In Sarduy's words, the realist text is a "mask" that "simulates dissimulation in order to dissimulate that it is only simulation," a mask that pretends there is a face hidden behind it when in fact there is only the mask pretending.[32] In the second, the transvestite constructs herself as an obvious counterfeit of gender. She simulates simulation: "What is simulated? Simulation."[33] If Flor de Loto constructs her identity according to the tenets of realism, Auxilio and Socorro subvert those tenets. In both instances, the final creation is a fiction of biological gender; however, the one passes for real, the other does not. The presence of these two opposing conceptions of transvestism in Sarduy's novel is emblematic of what Gustavo Pellón terms his "paradigmatic indecision."[34] Pellón demonstrates how Sarduy carries that indecision to the level of the sentence through his use of irony in the novels *Cobra* and *Maitreya*. In *De donde,* he also carries that indecision to the level of culture, geography, and climate: when Havana's Chinese theater transforms itself into a Catholic mass and a mambo-dancing Christ seeks the approval of the Yoruba gods; when the forest of Havana becomes the forest of the Summer Palace and the waters of the Almendares those of the Yangtze; and when Cuba's sweltering heat turns to snow. Pellón sees the rejection of "any ultimate assignation of meaning" as a general narrative approach in Sarduy's works, observing that since, as a writer, Sarduy cannot "escape the privileged position of authority, he opts for a strategy which will permit him to constantly dethrone himself."[35] It is as if to guard against the use of his own texts in the sort of exclusionary constructions that his writing opposes. One such construction is that of the New Man, which, in the words of González Echevarría cited above, was "accepted as an article of faith" and "practiced as a doctrine."[36] We have seen how its adoption led to the exclusion of homosexuals from participation in the Nation.

Sarduy does not, however, completely eliminate the New Man from his construction of the Cuban. Nor does he posit the Cuban gay as needing to be rescued from the New Man by a progressive, humanitarian, freedom-protecting Western power. In the penultimate chapter of *De donde,* "the invading, noisy, predatory helicopter," "the symbol of U.S. military might,"[37] serves as a reminder that the threat of U.S. invasion is real—hence the need for figures such as General Mortal Pérez.[38] However, Sarduy reminds us that the General is as much a construction of gender as is Flor de Loto—and not any less of a mirage. The decorated officer of the Cuban fleet, who conforms to the Revolution's ideal of the New Man, wears his bellicose air, his military march, and the uniform in which he invariably is clad as a performance of his identity (*De donde,* 108, 121, 123). As the novel's fictional author maintains when asked why the General, whose medals are entangled in Auxilio's hair, does not simply remove his coat: "My daughter, can't you see that if the General took off his medals, he would be like Lacan's painter bird without his feathers?" (101). The reference is to Jacques Lacan's 11 March 1964 seminar "What Is a Picture?" in which the French theorist states that if a bird were to paint, it would do so by dropping its feathers. Although the seminar was not published until 1973, Sarduy, a student at the Sorbonne and a member of the *Tel Quel* group, was apparently familiar with it when he wrote *De donde*. The implication is that just as the painter bird paints with its feathers, the General paints with his medals. The canvass on which the General paints, however, is himself; and because he, like Flor de Loto, is all appearance rather than essence, if he removes the medals that give him the appearance of being a general, he will cease to be the General.[39]

In addition, in a description of Cuban cosmology, Sarduy reminds us that the macho military man is just one among many elements composing Cuban identity, despite the revolutionary government's claims to the contrary. The blossoming cosmogony, "cosmogonía en ciernes," or what Sarduy names "Auxilio Conception of the Universe" (102), is a nascent story of Cuba's origins and evolution. The first characters appearing in the tale are the effeminate artist (Auxilio) and the masculine soldier (General Pérez). Their construction as "Siamese twins," thus conjoined at birth, recalls the simultaneous origin of the two faces—one effeminate and artistic, the other masculine and military—of Martí's foundational representation of the Cuban. The "binomial Auxilio-General" then sucks in two other characters, Dolores Rondón and Flor de Loto, to form a constellation in which the couples touch and look at each other. Stuck to the General, no doubt through his name of Mortal, is the ever-present "Unnamable Bald Lady" (101), a popular expression for "death," which recalls Martí's repeated references to the Cubans who died on the battlefield for Cuban independence. As Sarduy's nickname for the penis as well,[40] the Unnamable Bald Lady also resonates with Xavier Villaurrutia's 1936 homoerotic poem about the origins of a heavenly body of desire, "Nocturno de los ángeles" (Nocturne of the angels). In the poem, the constellation is "like a burning sexual organ" or "like the Gemini who for the first time in their lives / see each other face to face, look each other in the eyes," forming "unexpected couples."[41]

Similar to Villaurrutia's poem, Sarduy's "Auxilio Conception of the Universe" is about the origins of a constellation of couples and desire. Its principal players are Auxilio, the Chinese Cuban gay transvestite who desires Mortal Pérez; Mortal, the Hispanic heterosexual man of machismo who has a sexual encounter with Auxilio, who desires Flor de Loto (whom he mistakes for a woman) and who marries Dolores Rondón; Dolores, the Chinese mulatto heterosexual woman who desires Mortal for the power and social status that marriage to him will afford her; and Flor de Loto, the cross-dressing Chinese castrato who apparently desires to be left alone. In addition, as in Villaurrutia's poem, in Sarduy's blossoming cosmogony we see a constellation of couples that form and disengage; and its resistance to stasis opens it up to the possibility of endless numbers of new formations and combinations as well as to the possibility of its own dissolution.

As he treats the dynamic subjects of birth and change, Sarduy links the Sino-Cuban transvestite to the generative forces of Cubanness. This is evident in his construction of Auxilio as the womb in which Cuban culture is conceived ("Auxilio Conception of the Universe"). By implication, her absence from the Cuban constellation would be equivalent to cultural hysterectomy. The model of the universe with which Auxilio becomes pregnant could be likened to the big bang, to an explosion in perpetual motion either toward an ever-larger network of relations, and thus toward ever-increasing comprehensiveness, or toward its own eventual extinction.

However, we should mention that despite his ostentatious defiance of binary oppositions and his playful celebration of new combinations of sexual encounters, Sarduy does distinguish between sexual practices that are expressions of reciprocal desire and those that are expressions of unilateral desire. He distinguishes, for example, between consensual sadomasochism and stalking and rape. By frustrating rape narratives of the Oriental woman and the hyperfeminized Oriental castrato, Sarduy both evokes the Orientalist stereotypes that have made the rape of the Oriental seem socially acceptable and disrupts those stereotypes by scenes of empowerment in which the feminized Oriental either outmaneuvers and outsmarts her aggressor in order to evade victimization or is afforded the patriarchal protection that the West concomitantly offers her and deems her unworthy of. Sarduy further subverts Orientalist stereotypes by making her rescuer not white Western man, as is typical in Orientalist narratives, but a Chinese Cuban man resembling Sax Rohmer's notorious Oriental, Fu Manchu (*De donde*, 127–29).

I have suggested that in reaction to the United States' Orientalization of Cuba and the threat of U.S. invasion, Martí, Castro, and Sarduy each made room in their construction of Cuban identity for the combative military man. However, whereas revolutionary Cuba repudiated the effeminate male, and more particularly the homosexual, seen as penetrable, invadable, occupiable—precisely what Cuba did not want to be—Martí and Sarduy embraced the feminine in their constructions of Cubanness. Sarduy burst the West's image of an Orientalized Cuba as easily conquered and controllable by showing Sino-Cuban transvestites to be agents of their own identities and capable of military self-defense. As he did so, he drew on Martí, who had already problematized Orientalist stereotypes by showing a feminine appearance to embody masculine powers of agency and autonomy. Thus, even though Sarduy "Orientalized" his protagonists as he wrote from a place of exile in the West (Paris), he "disidentified" with Orientalism and Western imperialism, to borrow José Muñoz's terminology,[42] creating Sino-Cuban characters that celebrate their effeminacy while retaining their powers of self-determination. Instead of identifying with the Orientalist or Western gaze, he spoke from the nuanced perspective of a gay Sino-Cuban gaze, one of the many gazes essentially missing from a Western liberalism that prides itself in freethinking broad-mindedness while refusing to acknowledge that the person of color, or the Caribbean gay, gazes back.[43] Although I do not recommend the imitation of all their actions—for example, the wielding of military weapons while riding Vespas through the streets of Havana—I do propose that we consider Sarduy's Sino-Cuban transvestites as models of empowerment in the construction of femininity, Asianness, and Caribbeanness.

Notes

1. Said, *Orientalism*, 33, 179, 240–42.
2. Said, *Orientalism*, 41.
3. Qtd. in Williams, *From Columbus to Castro*, 410.
4. Ibid., 422.
5. Ibid., 464. As for the implication of Cuba's uncivilized nature, it is palpable in Roosevelt's 1904 Corollary to the 1903 Platt Amendment. In the Corollary, Roosevelt wrote that Cuba may "require intervention by some *civilized* nation" and "force" the United States "to the exercise of an international police power" (qtd. in Williams, *From Columbus to Castro*, 422, emphasis added). I will discuss the United States' racialization of Cuba later in the essay.
6. Ibid., 422.
7. See Helly, *Idéologie et ethnicité*, 221–29. See also Waters, *Our History*, 59–64, and *Cuba Commission Report*.
8. De la Fuente, *Nation for All*, 26–27.
9. Martí, "Mi Raza," *Obras Completas*, 299. My thanks to Gustavo Pellón for his helpful comments and for his aid in many of the translations from Spanish that appear in this essay. All translations are my own (as are any inadvertent errors) except where indicated.
10. Martí writes about the exploitation of American workers in "A Terrible Drama." In addition, in his article "The Chinese in the United States," he refers to the massacre of Chinese laborers in Rock Springs, Wyoming, on 2 September 1885, in Martí, *Inside the Monster*, 231–34. In "The Negro Race in the United States," Martí writes about the lynching of Negroes in Tennessee (ibid., 212–14). Martí deplores in his article "The Negro Problem" the demonization and attempted genocide of blacks in America, writing not only of racism but also of the continual rise in the hunting down of Negroes in the U.S. South (ibid., 209–11).

In "Indians and Negroes," Martí writes of the robbing and murder of both Amerindians and blacks (ibid., 226–30). In "Mob Violence in New Orleans," he recounts the lynching of eleven Italian Americans under suspicion of having murdered the Irish American Chief of Police Hennessy (ibid., 235–42).

11. "Dedication of the Statue of Liberty," in Martí, ibid., 133–57.

12. Bejel, *Gay Cuban Nation*, 11, and "Cuban CondemNation," 160.

13. Said, *Orientalism*, 32–33, 40.

14. De la Fuente notes that during the first U.S. occupation of Cuba, American troops "introduced segregationist practices in the army and public services"; and when they departed they left behind "a growing number of investors who" implemented "their racist ideas through discriminatory practices in the labor market and social activities" (*Nation for All*, 53).

15. Said, *Orientalism*, 206.

16. Ibid., 207.

17. Martí, "Vindication of Cuba," 236.

18. Ibid., 236, 238. Bejel demonstrates that although there is a tendency in Cuba to associate effeminacy with being gay, Martí's tolerance toward men of unmanly appearance does not equate to a tolerance of homosexuality (see Bejel's *Gay Cuban Nation*, 15–27, and "Cuban CondemNation," 162–63).

19. Sarduy, *De donde son los cantantes*, 92, n. 4. Further references to this novel will be given in parentheses in the text.

20. Fleur de "Racaille" de Caron is a play on words. The French perfume is called Fleur de Rocaille. "Racaille," meaning scum, is the term that Nicolas Sarkozy used in 2005 in reference to rioters in Parisian suburbs.

21. Lim, "Glocalqueering," 389.

22. Sarduy, whose Mortal Pérez stalks Havana's Chinese opera diva, seems to draw on the plot of Balzac's *Sarrasine,* in which the eponymous subject pursues the diva of Rome's Italian opera. Both Flor de Loto and la Zambinella are taboo beings, castratos—a word their texts evoke but never explicitly utter in reference to them. As castratos, they represent but can never be the ideal woman: their beauty is the promise of the fulfillment of masculine heterosexual desire, but they can never make good on that promise.

23. Lim, "Glocalqueering," 401.

24. See de la Fuente, *Nation for All,* for a detailed description of Cuba's celebration of miscegenation as the very essence of the nation in defiance of U.S. imperialism (especially 15, 178, 278). Note also that the Castro regime, which did the most to eradicate racism in Cuba, ironically, "also did the most to silence discussion about its persistence" (338). Moreover, de la Fuente notes that at the publication date of his book, the state-sponsored television continued to relegate blacks to stereotypical roles as marginalized individuals and thus "contributed to the persistence of . . . racist images" (323–25). Similarly, Juana María Rodríguez maintains in *Queer Latinidad* that "media depictions [in Cuba] continue to present light-skinned Cubans as the 'generic' representative of the nation and Afro-Cubans as something apart" (19–20).

25. Montero, "Signifying Queen," 163, and Smith, "Cuban Homosexualities," 258.

26. Lockwood, *Castro's Cuba,* 107.

27. González Echevarría, *La Ruta,* 50–51.

28. Montero, "Signifying Queen," 163, and Smith, "Cuban Homosexualities," 264.

29. This is not to say that the act of being screwed is a passive endeavor, although grammatically it is formulated as such in the English language. It is to say that revolutionary Cuba perceived the act of being screwed as deviantly passive and feminine.

30. Marshall, *Cuba Libre,* 170.

31. In "'Nobody Ent Billing Me,'" Gillespie observes a similar heteronormative "nationalist masculinized political resistance" to U.S. imperialism in Barbardos and a similar perception of the homosexual as a threat to the nation's efforts "to establish self-determination" (44, 50).

32. Sarduy, "Writing/Transvestism," 36–37.

33. Sarduy, "Copy/Simulacrum," 2.

34. Pellón, "Sarduy's Strategy of Irony," 7–13.

35. Ibid., 8, 12.

36. González Echevarría, *La Ruta,* 51.

37. Gillepsie, "'Nobody Ent Billing Me,'" 49–50.

38. Note that Sarduy evokes Cuba's vulnerability to U.S. invasion in the one section of the novel from which the General is inexplicably absent; and the General's absence is made all the more conspicuous by his longed-for presence on the part of Auxilio and Socorro.

39. Sarduy goes further than Balzac in his deconstruction of gender, revealing that the gender identities of all of his main characters are auto-constructions as equally artificial and stylized as that of his diva. Moreover, all gender in the novel is constructed through a process similar to transvestism. Although Dolores Rondón is biologically female, she constructs her feminine identity with the aid of bleach, elaborate coifs, makeup, wig, tight corset, glitter, and flowers ("Signifying Queen," 156, 159, 161). As Montero remarks, "By the time Dolores sets out for Havana's Presidential Palace, she is a tropical chimera, a construction of 'woman'" (168).

40. As Echevarría maintains, "la pelona" (the bald lady) is a popular expression for "death," but in Sarduy's novel it also refers to the penis (Sarduy, *De donde,* 93, n. 7).

41. Villaurrutia, *Obras,* 55–57.

42. Muñoz, *Disidentifications,* ix–xiv.

43. See Alexander, *Pedagogies of Crossing,* 171; Agard-Jones, "Le jeu de qui?," 188–89 and 193–94.

A Revolution in Drag

Reinaldo Arenas, or the Insurrection of Excess

Roberto del Valle Alcalá

A FRAGMENT from Virgilio Piñera's poem "La Isla en peso" presents water as the basic milieu of Caribbean corporeality and, by extension, of Caribbean identity:

> Los cuerpos en la misteriosa llovizna tropical,
> en la llovizna diurna, en la llovizna nocturna, siempre en la llovizna,
> los cuerpos abriendo sus millones de ojos,
> los cuerpos, dominados por la luz, se repliegan
> ante el asesinato de la piel,
> los cuerpos, devorando oleadas de luz, revientan como girasoles de fuego
> encima de las aguas estáticas,
> los cuerpos, en las aguas, como carbones apagados derivan hacia el mar.[1]

The peculiar materiality of water—forever shifting and unfixed—blurs the "solid" contours of extraneous definitions, including binary oppositions of colonial provenance. The Eurocentric semantics of "light"—so firmly rooted in rationalistic and "en-light-ened" contexts—are ill-adjusted to the specificities of Caribbean culture, as the essays in this volume show. The body drifts among a wealth of tensions and affects, permanently subverting or compromising the strict discursive shafts imposed by this imported "light of reason," which is also, typically, the light of binarism. As in Piñera's poem, the broad expanse of the Caribbean waters may sometimes conceal the remnants of defeat—a vast array of smoldering fragments—but it may also disguise a rebellious act of counter-definition. The "devouring" of "streams of light" might result in an alternative formulation of rationality, in an immanent logic of existence.

The present essay makes a case for such immanent resistance—for such "revolutionary" agitation—as captured by Cuban author Reinaldo Arenas in his autobiographical work *Antes que Anochezca*. A certain distance—a certain dissidence—from discourse-dependent notions of binarism (and anti-binarism) will therefore be claimed. The route of access, though, following the "spirit" of Arenas's intellectual and vital trajectory, will not be literal: we shall not scout for transvestite characters or motifs, but for transvestite writing. Cross-dressing permeates, I suggest, this author's autobiographical prose in a way that repudiates the illimitable efficiency with which some postmodern critics have tended to credit discourse.

The historical context of the Cuban Revolution offers a positive reference-point for the complex definition of "subversion" attempted by Arenas. The institutional rigidities paradoxically generated by the collective unleashing of emancipatory forces contrast with an internal limit of affective alliances and libidinal destabilizations. In other words, desire thrives against the grain of emergent—and, finally, hegemonic—binaries: in order to escape the crushing charge of "counterrevolution," Arenas's dissidents must often don symbolic "costumes" of conformity while internally subverting the regime's claims of normativity.

Arenas's text is a cross-dresser, a defier of binary logic that suspends the rational urgency of identification, of fixation, of labeling—in a way that reminds one of the performing transvestite. His subversive gesture originates in an understanding of personal history as marked by an original irreducibility of sexual life to discursive or juridical normalization. Libidinal circulation therefore becomes opaque, impenetrable in its immanence, and thus always already heterogeneous.

The very idea of opacity, which has gained great currency in Caribbean studies, denotes a mode of singularity that no rule of equivalence can contain: intelligibility, for the opaque, resides in its strategies of alliance, the composites it draws, and the textures it weaves. Taxonomies are inimical to opacity because they are concerned with first principles, with roots and essences. They may survive in the discourse of difference, in the identity-obsessed search for an origin, but they cannot resist the recognition of a space beyond discourse, beyond language, beyond logocentrism.[2]

Even if this space then lends itself to linguistic expression, to discursive framing in book form, there is a mode of writing that gestures away from normalization, an underlying opacity—predicated on libidinal circulation—that suspends, at least momentarily, the symbolic or juridical structuring of experience.

Homoeroticism in Arenas's memoir operates a radical decentering of sexuality qua symbolic/discursive category, favoring instead its immanent affiliation with the primordial rhythms of instinct and pre-linguistic materiality. In other words, Arenas's conceptualization of socio-symbolic space—the space of "identity" and discursive agency—is traversed by an internal moment of rupture or inconsistency; it is haunted, as it were, by the very exception on which language is predicated. The effect this has on a sexual politics marked by dissidence and ostracism is a productive renunciation of definition, an immanent coloring of agency and its subjective foundations with the rhythms of pre-discursive life. This elemental inflection of psychic existence stands in opposition to the representational forms (binary or otherwise) that discourse produces. Julia Kristeva, in her seminal 1974 book *Revolution in Poetic Language,* designated this mode of pre-discursive being with the term *chora:* "We borrow the term *chora* from Plato's *Timaeus* to denote an essentially mobile and extremely provisional articulation constituted by movements and their ephemeral stases. We differentiate this uncertain and indeterminate *articulation* from a *disposition* that already depends on representation, lends itself to phenomenological, spatial intuition, and gives rise to a geometry."[3] According to Kristeva's definition, this *chora* remains essentially immune to the referential logic of linguistic signification: its logic is one of pure immanence; it "precedes evidence, verisimilitude, spatiality, and temporality,"[4] and is therefore extraneous to the workings of discourse. No textual validation can be afforded, no temporalization, no referential sanction, no re-presentation. Choric immanence is the substance of a libidinal mass of undifferentiated drives and undialectized rhythms. The advent of the social (shorthand for discourse and its normalizing injunction to embrace definition) compels a certain distancing from the basal substance of primordial existence; it brings about a "fall" from the organic ties that had hitherto secured the libidinal integrity of the child in a dreamlike realm of compact sense.

Arenas's autobiography seems to follow this trajectory. Just as the Kristevan *chora* "is not yet a position that represents something for someone . . . nor . . . a *position* that represents someone for another position,"[5] that is, neither sign nor signifier, the first seventeen chapters of the book (little more than paragraphs in some cases) similarly consolidate a block of sense impermeable to the logical structuring of conceptual forms. The unrestrained rhythms of "nature" lay a supremacist claim on being and existence for a pre-adolescent Arenas, in what transacts as an impressionistic journey of discovery along the paths of burgeoning desire, mythical ken, and voluptuous excess. A cursory look at some of the titles heading the early chapters or sections may well shed light on this primordial unity of sense and sensation Arenas seems willing to establish: "The stones,"

"The grove," "The river," "The harvest," "The downpour," "Eroticism," "Violence," "The night, my grandmother," "The earth," "The sea." This mapping of the childhood universe is predicated on a cadenced weaving of the native milieu with its raw affects: the earth and its concessions to human sustenance—nourishment, everlasting shelter; the maternal body and its erstwhile attachments; the world of nature and "creativity"; the unruly powers of a sweeping and undiscriminating sexuality as yet unsignified or pre-discursive; and finally, far ahead, commanding in a sense the entire narrative, both proleptic and protracted, the perpetual promise of water.

The liminal structure of this progress to maturity, ever delayed by the stumbling encounter with discourse, with "the political" in its terrible bureaucratic inflection, betrays a fundamental precariousness of the visceral and esoteric quality sustaining literary creation. "My world was still that of the grove, of the house roofs, which I too climbed at the risk of falling; further afield was the river, but it wasn't easy to reach it; you had to go over the mountain and venture through places so far unknown to me. I was always frightened, not of wild beasts or those real dangers which could actually harm me, but of those ghosts which constantly appeared to me."[6] The magical nature of little Reinaldo's world grows out of a lack of rational conviction, the threatening proximity of death (as a series of vertiginously narrow escapes from lethal illness, accident, and so on, attest to), and the vague promise of a liquid beyond. It is this embodiment of water that will subtend the autobiography with a physical crystallization of utopian dissolution: first, as the river of blooming vigor and sexual offering, the Río Lirio—the "Lily River"—which, despite harboring "no lilies on its banks," blossoms in this primal scene of pre-adolescent desire with "more than thirty naked men swimming" in its waters. Next, and from that moment onward, as a permanent reference of inexhaustible liberatory power, the sea: "'The sea swallows up a man every day,' my grandmother would say. And I then felt an irresistible urge to reach the sea" (50). Poised at the limit of experience, this first evocation of the sea meets an opening—which will then become paramount in the course of the book—unto annihilation. Arenas describes in similar terms the temptations suggested by the tropical storm:

I wanted—not just to roll in the grass—but to soar upward, to rise like those birds, alone with the rainfall. I would get to the river, which roared as if it were uncontrollably possessed by violence. The strength of that overflowing stream swept almost everything, trees, rocks, animals, houses; it was the mysterious law of destruction, and also of life. I didn't know very well then where the river flowed to, where that frenzied race would stop, but something told me that I too had to go with the uproar, that I had to jump into those waters and get lost. . . . I had nothing more than those waters, that river, that nature which had welcomed, and was now calling upon, me at the precise moment of its apotheosis. (35–36)

Thus eroticizing the cataclysmic impetus of the natural element, a fundamental continuity between primordial affect and natural environment is established as pure self-referentiality, pure immanence beyond the parameters of discourse. The almost inarticulate textualization of his encounter with the sea—whereupon he falters, "What can be said of the first time I saw myself by the sea! It would be impossible to describe that instant; there's only one word: the sea" (50)—is here supplemented with an ecstatic marveling at the wild eruptions of unleashed nature. The sheer violence of the imagery sets a standard for the relational modality at work in this universe. The section entitled "Eroticism," for example, composes a carnivalesque fresco of sexual frenzies, where the rural milieu transpires as a great symphony of merry copulations, where animals and humans intermingle in a great ironic medley of explosive—albeit seemingly chance—encounters: a fable-like orgy where a hen is as good a sexual partner as a tree, and where "rural life" grows to a larger-than-life and mythically resonant dimension.

Arenas insistently invokes an ancestral *imago* of the peasant world of his childhood where "the real"[7] of material deprivation, plus nascent sexuality plus primordial attachments (and all of the other initial stakes of young Reinaldo's life), coalesces into a fantasized nucleus of loss—of visceral remembrance and pre-discursive being, as such irreducible to the life of agonistic politics the book soon launches into. Violence and eroticism merge in a turmoil of undifferentiated energy whence a totemic, indeed esoteric-sounding, profile of "the rural" emerges: "That theory maintained by some about the sexual naiveté of peasants is false; in rural milieus there is an erotic force which, generally, surpasses all prejudices, repressions, and punishments. That force, the force of nature, imposes itself. I think few must be the men in the countryside who have not had sexual intercourse with other men; in them, the desires of the body are above all the macho feelings our parents made an effort to induce in us" (40).

This visceral immanence of pre-symbolic affect operates a kind of optical magnification of life forms, libidinal trajectories, and even what seems to build up as ancestral knowledge about nature. Sexed anatomies grow in Arenas's eyes out of proportion—the grandfather's testicles, for example, become an occasion for regaled admiration, first ("My grandfather turned around suddenly and then it dawned on me that he had immense balls; I had never seen anything like that" [31]), and then of diffuse envy. The gigantic motif repeats itself across a number of characters/male genitalia. Characterization itself is often subjected to the magnifying lens of excessive, and in that sense, anti-mimetic, representation. The figure of the grandmother commands perhaps some of the primary moves in this direction. Bestowed with the attributes of a prescient visionary, illiterate yet wise, ancestrally strong and resilient, this Mother Earth figure combines a metaphysical vocation for superstition, belief and tragic pathos with the menial pains of poverty-stricken survival. The character is introduced hyperbolically on page 4, as the cosmic fulcrum of this phantasmal universe, endowed with the profound anti-positivism of instinctual immanence: "The center of the house was my grandmother, who peed from a standing position [que orinaba de pie] and spoke with God; she was always reproaching [le pedía cuentas a] God and the Virgin for all the mishaps threatening or befalling us" (20).

Reinaldo's mother offers a stark counterpoint to the under-rationalized figure of the grandmother, who, despite numerous attempts at logical explanation (her reportedly being at the helm of the household, for example), remains in the order of a primordial undifferentiatedness, a telluric potency uncontaminated by the symbolic logic of loss/separation/irrecoverability. The mother, on the other hand, is loss at its symbolic worst. In point of fact, Arenas can't resist the interpretative gesture—which becomes something of a leitmotif over the pages—of pinning down his mother's frustrations to her having been abandoned by his father. This acute sense of mis/displacement in a world characterized by a mass redistribution of affect, opens up a gap, a psychic rift whereupon the larval universe of the grandmother, of pansexual encounters and watery fadings, will phantasmatically recede to a pre-liminal position, crystallizing in the "real" of an unsymbolizable presence.

We can now discern the radical immanence I have referred to when dealing with the realm of experience that the first fifty-odd pages of the memoir acquaint us with: a realm where the binary logic peculiar to discursive/symbolic discriminations is exorbitant and fundamentally unavailing. This pre- or anti-binary space is what I have associated with Kristeva's notion of the *chora:* "a modality of significance in which the linguistic sign is not yet articulated as the absence of an object and as the distinction between real and symbolic."[8] A basal kernel of *jouissance* or, in other words, unsymbolized and unsymbolizable experience, is thereby secured; one which Arenas's entry into discourse will then sediment/conceal as an inexhaustible root of selfhood, and which the tragic matter of ostracism and persecution will then make incessant—yet inflected—reference to. It seems that, having secured a primordial kernel of affect, the subsequent fall into discourse will remain forever incomplete, inauthentic even, and, for that very reason (however terrible the ordeal), substantially ineffectual.

I would now like to concentrate on a number of passages from the memoir, where the alterity implied in this clash of orders (this fundamental incommensurability of sexuality with the Revolution, of primordial affect with institutional control) is brought to light, and to question the very status of homosexuality in the book as part of the hegemonic block of discriminations it seeks to revoke. I would like to begin with the excuse of literary influence—or at least what passes as influence, inspiration, and affinity, in the book. Arenas's evocations of Virgilio Piñera and José Lezama Lima serve the double purpose of establishing an aesthetic standard for his own poetics, and postulating a radical continuity between creation and affect. The critical distancing this seeks to achieve takes the bureaucratization of Cuban literature as its target—a castrating process implying the relocation of the writer as an instrument within the State machinery. Notably, the supreme manifestation, according to Arenas, of this process lies in the UNEAC (the Unión Nacional de Escritores y Artistas de Cuba), and the prominent figures associated with it (Nicolás Guillén, Roberto Fernández Retamar, and so on). Piñera and Lezama Lima constitute, at the opposite end of the bureaucratic spectrum, an inspirational bedrock of honesty, mired in the agonistic efforts of life, poetry, and subversion (terms that end up establishing an obvious ratio of synonymy in the lives of both authors).

The portrait of Piñera composed by Arenas suggests a visceral disregard for convention, propriety, and orthodoxy (whether strictly aesthetic or political); a permanent slippage beyond the margins of discursive fixation (in a particular stance, ideology, or creed) befitting the eccentricity of this "homosexual, atheist and anti-communist" (105): "Virgilio broke away from the journal *Orígenes* towards 1957 and created, along with José Rodríguez Feo, another, much more irreverent, practically homosexual, journal, under a dictatorship like Batista's, [which was] reactionary and bourgeois. The first thing Virgilio did in the journal *Ciclón* was to publish *The 120 Days of Sodom* by the Marquis de Sade" (106).

Homosexuality (or sexuality, *tout court*), for Piñera, is a further occasion for controversy, liminal exertion, and oppositionality, rather than for the normalized/normalizing adoption of an identity. Virgilio Piñera was a *loca de argolla* (a "shackle gay"), according to Arenas's ironic taxonomy of Cuban homosexuals. This was the "scandalous homosexual type, incessantly arrested at some bathroom or beach," and consequently paying a high price for being so. And yet—or rather, precisely because of that frontal nature—"as a *loca de argolla,* he was an extremely authentic character, and knew how to face the cost of that authenticity" (105). Authenticity is exactly what the Revolution had stolen from many—the supreme quality lacking in a world of corruption and prudishness, authoritarian imposition and bad theatrical make-believe. What Virgilio Piñera represents is the diametrical opposite: suffering incarnate without the—forever spurious—promise of transcendence/expiation/redemption. Piñera is the rightful inheritor to that ancestral world of the narrator's grandmother, peopled by shadows and mysteries, superstitions and tragedies cloaked in the balm of a rainstorm, a river—or that purely immanent, that genuinely anti-discursive, promise of the sea.

The theoretical kernel of the book, so to speak, is precisely this disavowal of contemporary political reality in Cuba: a radical gesture of refusal based on the charge of inauthenticity. A nurturing antidote to this cultural and moral wasteland is what Piñera and Lezama Lima have to offer in their different ways. Literature in them flows from the source (which the Revolution, with its lethal profusion of bureaucratic discipline, had emaciated) of undifferentiated affect sustaining the early evocations. The contrast between two totems of culture like Lezama Lima and Alejo Carpentier is unambiguous:

> I had met Alejo Carpentier and suffered a devastating experience before that person who handled data, dates, styles and figures like a computer, refined indeed, but obviously dehumanized. My meeting with Lezama was completely different; I was before a man who had made of literature his own life; before one of the most cultured persons I've ever met, and yet, one who didn't turn culture into a means of ostentation, but, simply, into something to which to hold on in order to avoid dying. . . . He also had that creole gift of laughter, of gossip; Lezama's laughter was something unforgettable, contagious, which never let one feel completely desolate. (109)

What Carpentier (and his pro-Revolution affiliates, at that) lacks is not a certain stylistic virtuosity or general literary merit, but the material, antibureaucratic truth of laughter and conversation: "laughter," as

Mayra Santos Febres has pointed out, "minimizes power, criticizes it."[9] Lezama's creole "gift" defies the binary distribution, in discourse, in power, of rational and logocentric utilities. Carpentier's devotion to discursive certainties—to "data, dates, styles and figures"—betrays, on the contrary, a logic of categories and essences that erases the opacity, that is, the "irreducible singularity" of unregulated life.[10] Lezama's literature does not seek ontological certainty; it does not aspire to fixity, to authority, to identity—his literature is the writerly dissolve of his laughter, an excuse for survival. In naming his laughter "creole," Arenas frees Lezama from the weight of genealogy, of discursive purity, and elevates it, in the words of Édouard Glissant, to the fluid recesses of "Relation"; that is, in the direction of interweaving lines of descent, of being without identity, with futures and without origins. Creole laughter extends the realm of being beyond stasis,[11] putting up resistance in terms that discourse cannot control. The wound from which it flows (the wound of exile, of ostracism, of physical torture or censorship) is equal to the wound upon which the transvestite thrives: "Transvestism means protecting oneself by multiplying the body, making it irreducible to a single line."[12] Laughter, humor, parody are the proliferations the sexual-and-political dissident can avail himself of; the multiplicities, irreducible to a single line, he can extend beyond the misery of socio-symbolic existence.

A strictly terminological, or rather lexical, aside may help us resituate this narrative in the broad problematic of compulsory gender ascriptions. The word *loca*, which is the feminine for "mad," and which Arenas ironically uses (drawing on homosexual jargon) to designate passive homosexuals, undergoes a permanent process of redistribution across his gallery of types. Despite the basic dichotomous opposition between the "effeminate," passive homosexual upon whom the grammatical mark is bestowed, and the active "man," Arenas constantly subverts this provisional order he, at first sight, endorses. As a result, we end up confronting a universe of overt, festive, and disorderly sexuality, beyond the confines of categorization and normativity. "In Cuba, when you went to a club or to a beach, there wasn't a specific area for homosexuals; everybody shared together, without there being a division which placed the homosexual in a militant position. This has been lost in the more civilized societies, where the homosexual has had to become some kind of monk of sexual activity, and to segregate himself from that part of society, supposedly not homosexual which, unquestionably, excludes him too" (133). The homosexual of his youth is characteristically ambivalent toward the univocal determinations of gender: *loca* or otherwise, his ambiguity derives from a blind spot in discourse where the naturalizing traces of identification, meaning, and referentiality are shown to be inadequate, incommensurable with the pool of bodily affects desire arises from. In a later moment in the book, when narrating his self-expulsion from the country through the port of El Mariel, Arenas remarks on this dual aspect of official discourses on homosexuality: active homosexuality would not be considered actual homosexuality (301). The mark of degeneracy and antisocial/counterrevolutionary disposition would therefore fall exclusively upon the *loca*. Arenas's own ambiguous—even protean—self-fashioning as homosexual exploits the crudeness of such epistemologies, displacing their logocentrism and binary anchoring. His homosexual parody (parody *of* homosexuality *from* homosexuality) is, in that sense, a carnival of name tagging and category mocking, whereby gay identities are fluidly enacted, estranged, and destabilized. According to Arenas, clandestine sexual encounters in Cuba involved a degree of transvestism—a measure of "passing," as Santos Febres has put it, "the black cat as a white hare"[13]: homosexuality was a dynamic and fluid disguise of being, rather than a unilateral assertion thereof.

The central position accorded to the sea, in what is an emblematic display of key allusions, increases the fluid quality of Arenas's eroticism, and the distorting disavowal of clear sexual profiles. Thus, the Caribbean gains specific prominence as a privileged site of personal reinvention. Its contagious fluidity disintegrates symbolic boundaries and discriminations, opening up the space of opaque—that is, in Glissant's idiom, non-determinate, rootless, and for that very reason, irreducibly singular—articulations and proliferations. Caribbean self-fashioning (that is, self-fashioning in the Caribbean Sea, in and through its waters) can only be synonymous with perpetual transformation and movement—indeed, something the institutional apparatus, with its categories and identitarian loyalties, cannot possibly tolerate. Coming to the sea, hiding in the sea, or simply recalling the sea constitute vantage points in the memoir, singular moments with an autonomous and intractable temporality of their own, loaded with affective/libidinal content and creative associations. "Because the sea was really what eroticized us; that tropical sea full of extraordinary adolescents, of men who swam sometimes naked, or with light trunks on. Going to the sea, beholding the sea, was an enormous party, where one always knew that some anonymous lover awaited among the waves" (126–27). Once again, the liquid element—which so clearly permeated the work and lives of Piñera and Lezama—blossoms with adolescent bodies. Again, the promise of a primordial dissolution in the night of raw, unmediated, unsignified physicality contests the dry dehumanizations of official literature, sexual definitions, and bureaucratic power. Those bodily waves truncate the brutal aspirations of the regimental signifier, of the pure limits of State reason. Rather than strictly supplementing its legislation with more—albeit allegedly subversive—discourse, that is, with more signifier, those waves expose the rift inhabiting discourse, the moment of failure, the no-go space internal to language and its normalizing compulsion. The outcome is a genuine carnival of indeterminate crossing—more radical and traumatic (in the sense that its ontology is not that of symbolic expression, but rather that of its unsymbolizable exception) than mere counter-signification. "Sometimes we made love underwater. I became an expert; I got hold of a mask and a pair of flippers. The undersea world was wonderful; seeing those bodies underwater. A couple of times I made love to somebody who also had a mask" (127). Identities collapse in the sea rhythms of fluidity, while bodies undergo their emancipation from power. Underwater sexual encounters stage a carnival of illicit freedoms and impossible meanings[14]: they violate taxonomy and discrimination in a submarine alliance that disregards discursive regulation and political regimentation. It is significant that this utopian suspension of sociopolitical reality—this defection from positive dystopia—should take place in the sea, among the waves, and that its mode of expression be that of physical association. After all, as Edward Kamau Brathwaite has said of the Caribbean Sea itself, "the unity is submarine."[15]

The uncompromising, vitalist theatricality of the sexual encounter contrasts with the poor masquerades of the UNEAC and its supposedly fair literary contests, and with the insufferable inauthenticity of its official upholders. Even the terribly violent mise-en-scène of the inmate *locas* at the Morro prison, their often bloody quarrels and acts of humiliation, is preferable to the murderous "productivity" of the State apparatuses. The problem, or rather, the institutional fear, of antisociality (that is, the enigma of pre-symbolic affectivities and primordial attachments connecting with the magical world of the author's childhood) lies simultaneously at the root of concrete sexual oppression and, what we could perhaps call, the regime's epistemological totalitarianism: its refusal/inability to allow existence beyond the juridical or discursive matrix it produces. Thus, in the name of a collective quest, of a certain notion of positive—"revolutionary"—transcendence, the radical heterogeneity of life and creation is forced into discursive fixation, territorialized—in the language of Deleuze and Guattari—as a finite set of either/ors: *locas* and *hombres verdaderos* ("real men"[16]), communists and anticommunists, revolutionaries and antirevolutionaries, patriots and traitors. What cannot be hemmed in on this regulative basis is precisely what Arenas's homosexuals—both frenzied and unprincipled—disrupt with their indocile bodily rhythms. The space of poetry is thus ontologically indistinct from the space of sex: the orgiastic cannot be extricated from the literary, if both are to retain their authenticity.

The ambivalence of what Reinaldo Arenas variously terms "creative work," "the complete image," and "beauty" (113), and which finds expression in both art and sexuality, serves as a mode of extension beyond the margins of reality and, in no simplistically escapist manner, into the realm of the possible. This flight into the possible elaborates upon the formal precondition of sublimation—namely, loss. However, such a primary move of separation, brought on by the advent of linguistic/symbolic signification, cannot conceal the multiple synchronicity experienced at the heart of subjective life. In other words, loss is never truly—thoroughly, or otherwise securely—lost. A measure of "undeadness" inhabits the subject even after her/his apparently successful entry into discourse. This is the precise sense of what Lacan calls *jouissance,* and which suggests a certain aberrant pleasure-in-pain, a certain psychic scar accounting for the traces of primordial life still alive in the linguistic/discursive subject. It is this excessive life which poses problems to the logic of discourse,[17] since it cannot contain it within its productive framework. And yet, unaccountability is the basis of opacity, the foundation of that mode of resistance that preserves the body and its affects from the enslaving light of normalization.

Beauty, whether strictly poetical or furiously erotic, draws its energies from a privileged view on that uncanny underbelly of psychic history. In Kristeva's words, "The imaginary universe . . . as signifying jubilation, nostalgic of a fundamental or nurturing non-sense, is nevertheless the very universe of the *possible.*"[18] The concept of literary creation attributed to Piñera and Lezama Lima, and ardently embraced by Arenas himself, cannot dispense with this melancholic reparation, which, by the very pre-discursive nature of the mourned object, remains inaccessible and exorbitant to the normative logic of a Revolution with a capital "R":

> Beauty is in itself dangerous, conflictual, for every dictatorship, because it engages a domain beyond the bounds within which that dictatorship subjects human beings; it's a territory that escapes the control of the political police and where, therefore, they cannot reign. That's why it irritates dictators, and

why they try to destroy it at any cost. Beauty under a dictatorial system is always dissident, because every dictatorship is in itself anti-aesthetic, grotesque; to practice it [beauty] is for the dictator and his agents an escapist or reactionary attitude. (113)

Notwithstanding this compulsion that drives him to write on, before night falls,[19] Arenas is all along addressing a certain night that has already fallen, and which the figures suggested by terminal AIDS place at the forefront of self-fashioning.[20] The principal inadequacy of a discursive reading of Arenas's sexuality/poetics is already contained in this notion of immanent otherness. I am tempted to use Eric Santner's idea of "creaturely life" as a precise gloss on Arenas's visceral resistance and opacity to definition: "The opacity and recalcitrance that we associate with the materiality of nature—the mute 'thingness' of nature—is, paradoxically, most palpable where we encounter it as a piece of human history that has become an enigmatic ruin beyond our capacity to endow it with meaning, to integrate it into our symbolic universe . . . What I am calling creaturely life is a dimension of human existence called into being at such natural historical fissures or caesuras in the space of meaning."[21]

Antes que Anochezca is densely populated with such "enigmatic ruin[s]," forming an erstwhile—I would call it "traumatic" in the strong Freudian sense—core of basal meaning whereupon classificatory/discriminatory/dichotomizing efforts invariably founder. This is not to say that Arenas's writing itself does not partake of a discursive structure and normalizing presuppositions, but rather, that the subjective profile it offers is always already incomplete, riven by the larval haunting of a certain "thingness" in selfhood, of a certain prehistory without discursive securities.

This immanent (or internal) disparity of self is the ontological buttress Arenas has recourse to, thereby invalidating accusations of depravity, treason, or counterrevolutionary ideology, regardless of their discursive efficacy. This radical incommensurability of self (in other words, this *jouissance* we have already alluded to), which Santner further describes as "the unimaginable enjoyment of self-being in otherness,"[22] is also what disables, in Lacanian-inspired terms, Judith Butler's classic deconstruction of gendered binaries.[23] Her critique is predicated on the radical co-extensiveness of sexuality with its discursive matrix. No space is allowed for being outside of linguistic determination; no life is acknowledged, in that sense, in symbolic suspension. To view Arenas's resistance in terms of discursive subversion (that is, of subversion within discourse: the "gender trouble" Butler calls for) would be to overlook the anti-symbolic, or indeed "real," core of the book—that fundamental/subterranean cluster of sources underlying the properly discursive maneuverings of the Cuban Revolution. *Antes que Anochezca* exposes the radical incommensurability of discourse with its cracks or structural moments of failure, the propaganda of state socialism and patriotic polemic with the raw materiality of multiple sexual encounters and corporeal display. It puts forth a notion of subjectivity that implies an internal(ized) fissure, a fundamental incapacity of the discursive order to effectuate its control.

This very notion of symbolic suspension is what Arenas's trope of "the night" embodies: a polysemous and genuinely opaque—in the inflection we have been following—inscription of external and internal otherness, pervading the psychic scenes of terminal illness (death) and original attachment (birth). Along with the sea—the sea of transformation, indeterminacy, and identity-suspension—night, whether literal or figural, marks a definitive departure from the constricting symbolic economies of the Cuban State and its institutional politics. And every departure in this book explores the possibility of new life, or more life, beyond the present one—life which is nevertheless based on an immanent condition of excess.

The strategic positioning of AIDS at the thematic center of the book's introduction (whose title, "The end," is in turn paradoxical and ironic) places radical alterity—the absolute otherness connoted by the sense of incurability—at the root of symbolic articulation. Identification is thus indelibly branded with an immanent gap, always already traversed by a moment of inconsistency or discontinuity, which, far from rendering the socio-symbolic matrix efficient in spite of its rifts, is revealed as the proper stuff of selfhood.

Images of otherness are legion in the book. However, it is perhaps the opening scene in the first chapter (entitled "The stones"), where an infant Arenas is confronted with literal self-estrangement in the figure of an intestinal worm, that commands the greatest power of association. Excess becomes incarnate in this figure of unsymbolizable "thingness," this fundamental residue emerging from within. Being opens upon the abyss of a strange invasion, which diachronic fissures in discourse will retroactively confirm as a central moment of self-fashioning:

> I was two. I was naked, standing; I bent down and brushed my tongue against the earth. The first taste I recall is the taste of the earth. . . . We ate that earth in the house *rancho;* the *rancho* was the place where the livestock slept; that

is, the horses, the cows, the pigs, the chickens, the sheep. . . . One day I felt a
terrible pain in my belly; I couldn't make it to the toilet, which was outside the
house, and used the pot which lay under the bed where I slept with my mother.
The first thing I released was an enormous worm; it was a red animal with lots
of legs, like a centipede, and it kept jumping inside the pot; it was no doubt
furious at having been expelled from its element in such a rough way. I grew
very frightened of that worm, which now appeared to me every night trying to
get back into my belly, while I clenched to my mother. (17)

This figuration of otherness as literal immanence is significantly resonant
with Slavoj Žižek's account of post-Enlightenment subjectivity, where the
"other" scene of discursive truth, the fundamental resistance to rational
transparency put up by life itself, is not exiled from the realm of the
subject, but acknowledged as its impossible or traumatic foundation: "In
the pre-Kantian universe, humans were simply humans, beings of reason,
fighting the excesses of animal lusts and divine madness, but since Kant
and German Idealism, the excess to be fought is absolutely immanent, the
very core of subjectivity itself (which is why, with German Idealism, the
metaphor for the core of subjectivity is Night, 'Night of the World,' in
contrast to the Enlightenment notion of the Light of Reason fighting the
surrounding darkness)."[24]

The roots of subjectivity are rediscovered in this opacity the Caribbean
is so aware of. In its relational mode, in its avoidance of roots, of fixity,
of univocal essences, life has its source. Logos is no longer sufficient. The
positive textures of discourse are too constrictive. Arenas's own "Night
of the World" ushers the reader into the cavernous inside of his self and
its literary avatar. The chilling propinquity of death and birth confirms
the opening of life beyond discourse, the radical inaccessibility, the impenetrable "thingness," against which symbolic meaning is constructed.
Transgression's transports—those of selfhood as monstrosity, as first and
last Other—are the mark of an abyssal residue that no State apparatus,
no positivized "Light of Reason," can harness. The night is indomitable
life, excess beyond symbolic measure, typification, and taxonomy.

Where rebellious discursivity isolated an excess of meaning, the *real*
body of excess, of pre-discursivity and multiple possibilities, offers its
resistance. On a Caribbean beach, crowded with dissidence and desire,
the lights of definition, redefinition, articulation, and identification
slowly flicker out. Night begins to fall. To say it with Hegel, "The human
being is this night, this empty nothing, that contains everything in its

simplicity. . . . One catches sight of this night when one looks human beings in the eye."[25]

The downpour's on. And the body, still spinning its dark regions.

Notes

The author wishes to acknowledge the support of Instituto Franklin–UAH and its project "E Pluribus Non Unum: Alternative Lineages of American Modernity."

1. "The bodies in the mysterious tropical drizzle/in the day-time drizzle, in the night-time drizzle, always in the drizzle,/the bodies opening their millions of eyes/the bodies, dominated by the light, retreat/before the murder of the skin,/the bodies, devouring streams of light, explode like fire sunflowers/above the static waters,/the bodies, in the waters, like suffocated coals drift towards the sea" (Piñera, *La vida entera*, 27–28).

2. See, for example, Édouard Glissant: "Agree not merely to the right to difference but, carrying this further, agree also to the right to opacity that is not enclosure within an impenetrable autarchy but subsistence within an irreducible singularity. Opacities can coexist and converge, weaving fabrics" (*Poetics of Relation*, 190). For more on the question of opacity, see, for example, Santos Febres in this collection.

3. Kristeva, *Revolution*, 25–26.

4. Ibid., 26.

5. Ibid.

6. Arenas, *Antes que Anochezca*, 24. Further references will be given in parentheses in the text; all translations of Arenas are mine.

7. It is one of the tasks of this essay to relate Lacan's notion of "the real" (*le réel*), which designates that order of psychic life that cannot be symbolized, that escapes the regulations of discourse, to Arenas's postulation of a primordial realm of anti-discursive and anti-categorical—read anti-binary—sexuality.

8. Kristeva, *Revolution*, 26.

9. See Mayra Santos Febres, "The Caribbean and Transvestism," 162, in this volume.

10. Glissant, *Poetics of Relation*, 190.

11. "Relation is movement," says Glissant (ibid., 171).

12. See Santos Febres, 165, this volume.

13. Ibid., 163.

14. The centrality of "masks" in the passage is paramount, as it emphasizes the theatrical dimension of those encounters.

15. Qtd. in Glissant, *Poetics of Relation*, vi.

16. Again, this opposition between so-called *locas*, or passive homosexuals, and "real men" occurs in the book without aspiring to taxonomical fixation. In that sense, his own playful appropriation of macho stereotypes destabilizes categories and displaces sexual reference from discursive fixity. See Arenas, *Antes que Anochezca*, 103.

17. In a similarly Lacanian vein, Eric L. Santner calls this form of resistance to discourse, as manifested in the pre-linguistic or pre-symbolic traces of psychic existence, "creaturely life." See Santner, *On Creaturely Life*.

18. Kristeva, *Revolution,* 113.

19. The title, it is explained in the book, originates in a draft the author began while hiding from the Cuban police in the 1970s. The pages he wrote then were conceived and composed under the literal constraint of natural light—writing "before night falls" (11).

20. "Now nightfall advanced again in a more imminent way. It was the night of death" (11).

21. Santner, *On Creaturely Life,* xv.

22. Ibid., 2.

23. See, for example, her analysis of Foucault's introduction to nineteenth-century French hermaphrodite Herculine Barbin's diaries, in Butler, *Gender Trouble.*

24. Žižek, Santner, and Reinhard, *Neighbor,* 160.

25. Qtd. in Žižek, *Ticklish Subject,* 29–30.

"Cyaan Live Split"

Under-Dressing, Over-Performing, Transgendering, and the Uses of Camouflage in Michelle Cliff's *No Telephone to Heaven*

Chantal Zabus

To Ingrid

THE INSTABILITY of gender, complicated by the vagaries of nationalism, has been at the heart of Jamaican fiction. Michelle Cliff's *No Telephone to Heaven* (1987), like Patricia Powell's *A Small Gathering of Bones* (1994), documents the growth of the Jamaican nation under Michael Manley (in his first term, from 1969–80) up to the disillusionment with his "politics of participation," while addressing the plight of gender-variant people. The novelty in Cliff's novel is that nationalism, construed as a resistance to American imperialism, is performed by a "queer" faction, whose bathetic attempts to engender a new nation fail yet augur multiple transfigurations.

As the lesbian Chicana writer Cherríe Moraga has said in an interview, "nationalism" is a "bad," "dangerous" word, which is difficult to rehabilitate because it evokes "KKK, and Bosnia, and 'ethnic cleansing.'"[1] But in Cliff's novel, nationalism is revisited—however eccentrically—from the perspective of Clare Savage, Cliff's light-skinned *tragic mulatta,* and by Harry/Harriet (or H/H), a nonoperative transgendered cross-dresser, raised as a male, but gender-transposed to varying degrees. H/H's queerness acts as a foil to Clare's repressed lesbian identity, which is part of Cliff's autobiographical vestment in her character, as an avowed lesbian, who left Jamaica, lived in England, and now resides in the United States.

While being in dialogue with such canonical texts as Shakespeare's *The Tempest,* Charlotte Brontë's *Jane Eyre,* and the historical figure of Pocahontas,[2] the novel attempts to question history and subtly blends the military uses of camouflage in attempting to overthrow American imperialism (and thereby "over-performing," as I will call it) with the *passing* condition in terms of race and sexuality.

Before addressing over-performing, I would like to discuss H/H's initial refusal to be a transgender passing subject. It manifests itself not so much in his cross-dressing as in his under-dressing, which entails wearing underwear appropriate to the opposite sex.[3] There are at least two instances of H/H's under-dressing and cross-dressing in the text: the first one occurs when H/H is seen wearing "a bikini-bra stretched across his hairy, delicately mounded chest."[4] The second takes place in a bar where H/H plays the role of a polygamous prince to bemused American tourists. Interestingly, both episodes take place when Clare and H/H are in their early twenties, that is, about sixteen years before they join the militia and become freedom fighters for the nationalist, anti-imperialist cause. The novel dangerously shuttles between these two time periods while "under-dressing" acts as a prelude to "over-performing" in H/H's later years.

In the first episode, the twenty-year-old Harry/Harriet is attending a Christmas party that a young, wealthy Jamaican—Buster Said—has organized while his parents were away. H/H is introduced to the reader as a "boy girl" and as Buster Said's relative—"Buster's brother-sister, half brother-sister actually," because H/H's mother was Said's maid. His neither/nor-yet-both condition is tolerated, "as if measuring [the other guests'] normalness against his strangeness." His bikini bra across his small yet hairy chest as well as the panties "cradling his cock and balls" (21) like a jockstrap are ridiculed. His pouting offer of "pussy," which he loudly shares with the amused crowd, is funny, yet not disturbing. His farcical dream of joining the Royal Ballet in England is playfully attuned to the popular compounding of choreography with queer male sexuality as well as colonial notions of mimicry and second-rate derivativeness. H/H could easily have joined efforts with Man-Man on V. S. Naipaul's *Miguel Street*.[5]

That same campy scene is revisited in the novel's fourth chapter, where the reader is informed retrospectively that "some girl throwing up into the deep end of the pool" (21) at Buster Said's Christmas party is the twenty-year-old Clare Savage, who has just made love to the wealthy Paul H., while, unbeknown to both of them, Christopher, the orphan from the dungle—the Jamaican "jungle"—has brutally murdered all the members of Paul H.'s family. In the truck scene with H/H and the other guerilla fighters, which opens the novel but takes place more than a decade later, Clare reminisces and is brought back to the Christmas party where she vomited after perfunctorily exchanging fluids with Paul H. and drowning his semen in champagne. H/H's lighthearted, compassionate comment to Clare—"'Cock-juice don't mix with champagne, sweetheart'" (88)—should not deter from its innate seriousness, for it sheds light on H/H's hands-on experience of male-male desire and his traumatic sodomy-rape while a boy.

On the day after the Christmas party, while on the beach with Clare, H/H sports "his/her Pucci bikini" across "his/her furry chest getting the odd stare" (89). As in the previous excerpt, the emphasis is on the juxtaposition of hair, which is gendered male, with a bikini bra. Even though at a later point, H/H claims that he wants to be a woman, it is clear from these two scenes—the pool scene and this (first) beach scene—that H/H does not wish to appear to the outside world as a woman and he is not trying to *pass* as one. His demeanor at this early stage, however, has a compulsive, fetishistic aspect, which H/H shares with some heterosexual cross-dressers. H/H *flaunts*—a quintessentially camp verb, which has also been applied to butch-femme relational displays and to drag queens or drag kings—his adorned body. He is thus campy "in gesture, performance, and public display,"[6] in his constant laughter and frivolity, and in his fascination with quintessentially feminine trappings.

A short theoretical detour through camp is therefore necessary to pinpoint H/H in his early twenties in Manley's Jamaica. In her 1964 seminal essay, Susan Sontag described camp as a "certain mode of aestheticism[,] . . . one way of seeing the world . . . not in terms of beauty, but in terms of the degree of artifice."[7] In that sense, H/H's camp is rooted in style and artifice, the way camp became so in the 1970s in the United States and England, when Euro-American sexual politics started to trickle down through the media to the Caribbean and before camp became politicized—putting camp into campaigning—in the 1990s.

In a very apt "disguise that fails,"[8] H/H deliberately sabotages his female impersonation. His privileging of form over content, his love for the excessive and the artificial, which are characteristics of gay culture in the 1970s, allow "exploration of feelings (and laughter) in the shared recognition of socially oppressive codes and structures."[9] The queer camp displayed by H/H here offers precisely that exploration and recognition. Cliff could have more effectively deployed H/H's camp, especially in its transvestitic capacity to assimilate dominant culture while undermining authority. But H/H's temporary lapse into an excess of femininity is ultimately ridiculed and engenders easy laughter because the cross-dressing is purportedly approximate; it is only under-dressing, casually flirting with drag. H/H is also, in a very subtle way that augurs his future transgendered status, cultivating a "male femininity," to reverse Judith Jack Halberstam's "female masculinity."

If one accepts Judith Butler's definition of drag as "an effort to negotiate cross-gendered identification" and, taking her cue from Freud's 1917 essay "Mourning and Melancholia" on melancholia as the effect of an ungrieved loss, to "allegorize heterosexual melancholy," H/H-almost-in-drag points to the interstitial, the sexually unperformable, which is performed instead as gender-identification, thereby comforting rather than eroding heterosexuality. For Butler, "sex" and "gender" are fictions, produced by stylized acts of bodily performance; sex is embodied gender. Yet she prefers the term first introduced by Eve Kosofsky Sedgwick, "performativity," which she distinguishes from "performance" as a "bounded 'act'" with theatrical overtones, in the sense in which performativity consists in "a reiteration of norms which precede, constrain, and exceed the performer and in that sense cannot be taken as the fabrication of the performer's 'will' or 'choice.'" In that histrionic sense, H/H's "performance" in the pool scene is more akin to theater—sex is life, gender theater—than it is to the arbitrary compulsiveness of performativity. But as Harry gradually transitions to *become* Harriet and the slash between H1 and H2 fades away to make room for H3, his initial "performances" will subtly collapse into his/her (*hir*) compulsive "performativity." By the same token, that which was drag, as the province of straight drag performers, becomes drag as cross-gendered identification, which, Butler cautiously asserts, "is not the exemplary paradigm for thinking about homosexuality," although, she hastens to say, "it may be one."[10]

According to Butler in *Gender Trouble,* drag as cross-dressing that draws attention to itself illustrates such performativity: "In imitating gender, drag implicitly reveals the imitative structure of gender itself—as well as its contingency."[11] Nicholas Hammond has taken Butler to task for failing to examine "the important role of body as spectacle."[12] Likewise, Joseph Harris in *Hidden Agendas* rightly ratiocinates that if, according to Butler, gender is "performative," "then perhaps we could ask how it is that the performance of drag can itself implicitly 'misfire' in its capacity to reveal itself as performance."[13]

Notwithstanding such terminological prowess, it remains that H/H's camp, as it is substantiated in the language of drag as in gay male theater and its venues, is "a means of signaling through the flames."[14] Cliff mentions that, at the pool party, H/H is "*only* one, after all, one that nature did not claim" (21; italics in the original). H/H's flaunting of a bikini bra is thus not only tokenistic but singular. And it is on account of that singularity that the crowd is not hostile, as if more of such individuals would test the crowd's tolerance threshold. Another reason why such public flaunting is tolerated is that it is not aimed at seduction, for, as Anne Bolin has noted, "the male is still inside, beneath the outside sartorial system of female."[15] Richard C. Cante builds on Esther Newton's early stance, whereby "camp often stands in as a substitute for the 'real' enactment of gay sexuality," by reading camp "as a representation of the inherent 'failure' of all human sexuality. A man as drag queen restages the frustration or impossibility of 'straight' homosexual desire (to be desired by a man as a man) by dressing as a woman. Also, he distances himself ironically from *all* forms of representation, including the codes of gender and sexuality, through his campiness."[16]

In other words, H/H is not "the novel's lesbian," as Cliff claimed in an interview[17]; he is the embodiment at this early stage in his life of the very blockage or failure of his queer desire. Alternatively, Cante admits that one could view this scenario of foredoomed failure through the lens of Slavoj Žižek's Lacanian claim that "desire is that very thing—embodied in language, or the symbolic order (the Big Other)—that, through fantasy, continually re-creates itself by repeatedly restaging the frustration of that lack of fulfillment for the sake of which we supposedly act."[18] If I follow Žižek, then, the failure of the drag queen's desire is his desire.

Even if H/H is not exactly a drag queen in full attire in the pool scene and in the (first) beach scene, s/he is surfing on the crest of a wave, exulting in that very failure, which is *hir* desire. Not surprisingly, H/H's later transformation into a guerilla fighter against the one-party government, like his move from under-dressing to over-performing and like transitioning from male to female, reeks of camp. This camp inflection in turn augurs, somewhat ironically, "Queer nation," the queer activist movement initiated in the United States in the early 1990s, which endeavored to juxtapose nationalism with camp.[19]

Cliff further fans the fire of camp in another episode at the Pegasus bar where Clare and H/H are having a drink. The Pegasus is actually an upmarket Kingston hotel for businessmen, but that the bar is named after the winged horse born from the blood spurting from Medusa, as Perseus cuts off her head, serves Cliff's purpose in emphasizing the Medusa dimension of Clare, as we will see later.

In this second episode, H/H's lips are smeared with lipstick and his eyelids covered with sparkly red, gold, and green Rasta colors. The Pegasus bar is made to suggest "a galleon on the Spanish Main" (121), which H/H renames "Triangle Trade" (120), for it is indeed shaped like a transatlantic slave ship carrying on board conspicuously queer creatures ready to be thrown off, like vile cargo, into the deep sea. H/H evokes the

Middle Passage but revisits it from a campy perspective, suggesting that the Pegasus management should "hang some whips and chains on the walls, dress the waiters in loincloths, have the barmaid bare her breasts" (121). His carnivalesque suggestion in turn conjures up both Jamaica's commodification of its Spanish and English colonial past for tourists' consumption and the steamy S/M atmosphere of gay bathhouses-cum-bars' subculture.

H/H's further allegation that "our homeland is turned to stage set too much" (121) follows appropriately on Jamaica's flashy performance for the tourist industry and the private body's staging of its own queerness. What is more, H/H can thus cleverly shift the conversation to the Renaissance, which Clare studies in London. The Renaissance is indeed both the historical era of overseas expansion through voyaging and colonizing non-Western territory and a period that allowed boy actors to perform female roles on stage. These performers, H/H intuits, were "on the queerish side" (121). This in turn sets the stage for the question that H/H asks Clare about whether she has ever been tempted by "pussy, sweetness . . . loving your own kind" (122), which meets with Clare's uncomfortable dismissal. This timid allusion to same-sex desire possibly reflects on Clare's unexpressed lesbianism (and possibly young Cliff's), which H/H is attempting to draw out, and on H/H's own desire to be loved as a woman by a man and, as we shall see, by a woman, as in lesbian mtf Kate Bornstein's sense of "gender outlaw."

Despite the fact that H/H is wearing a proper jacket but refrained from wearing an earring so as not to embarrass Clare in public, his "man/woman's painted visage" (125) causes the wide-eyed American tourist who approaches them a shock that he can barely disguise. He had indeed assumed "respectability" in Clare's whiteness and in H/H's dignified dinner jacket that the tourist could only see from the back.[20] This scene is one of the most hilarious and theatrical in the novel, as Clare catches on to the American's dismay and, faking an Oxbridge accent, has the tourist believe that she and her husband are also visitors to the island, whereupon Clare introduces H/H as "the crown prince of Benin, in Africa" and adds that she is "his first wife" (125). Swiftly, H/H picks up the joke and, extending his hand, introduces himself as "'Prince Badnigga, and this is my consort, Princess Cunnilinga; we are here for the International festival of Practitioners of Obeah'" (125). The American tourist's bewilderment is at its highest when H/H further blends nationalism with drag by presenting his colorful Rasta-style eyelids as "'the colors of our national flag. . . . At the first sign of manhood each young warrior in our country must do the same. . . . Like most ancient customs it has a practical basis . . . going back to the days when we devoured our enemies'" (125). This heady concoction, mockingly mixing African exotica such as rites of passage, polygamy, witchcraft, and cannibalism, with exacerbated nationalism and sexuality, in the implicit coupling of "bad nigger" and cunnilingus, that is, the oral stimulation of female genitals by a man or a woman, is as explosive and intoxicating in shock value as the very rummy cocktail that Clare and H/H are sipping. This "over-performance" reeks of excess and caricature, as well as despair. Despite its slapstick comic effect, this scene of disorderly conduct sets H/H to thinking about unrevealed aspects of a guilt-ridden past.

H/H reminisces about his training as a twelve-year-old boy at Calabar School, where, upon reading Plato's dialogues, he questioned the teacher's authoritative reading of Greece's golden age, arguing that it was not so golden after all, since slavery existed and women were living in confinement. The teacher retorted that since H/H was a "battyman-in-training, [he] should cleave to Plato" (123). "Battyman," being a derogatory Jamaican term for a male homosexual, further indicates that, even as a pubescent boy, Harry came across as homosexual, if not a Greek ephebe. Moreover, "batties" were also icons of nonblackness, since the affirmation of black identity in Jamaica is often attached to unrelenting animosity toward homosexuality.[21] Distressingly, the young H/H's "homosexuality," or at any rate his effeminacy, is mediated by childhood sexual abuse in the form of a sodomy-rape by a bemedaled authority in the garrison of Her Majesty:

> My asshole was *split* when I was a bwai by an officer at Up Park Camp. . . . I was waiting for the bus to come. The man came over. Said something about what a sweet lickle t'ing I was . . . except he said "monkey," sweet lickle monkey. Afterwards I worried about the books. For I had lost them. . . . I have been tempted in my life to think *symbol*—that what he did to me is but a symbol for what they did to all of us, always bearing in mind that some of us, many of us, also do it to each other. But that's not right. . . . Not symbol, not allegory, not something in a story or a dialogue by Plato. No, man, I am merely a person who felt the overgrown cock of a big whiteman pierce the asshole of a lickle Black bwai—there it is. That is all there is to it. (128–30)

Yet that is not all there is to it, since, besides setting the stage for his later Butlerian allegorization through drag, the harrowing story of H/H's rape (even though there is no trace of dissent through struggle) is mirrored in the forcible penetration of Jamaica by colonizers and in both the island's and H/H's passive status in the receptor role, as an insertee. Despite the resulting feeling of "guilt . . . or shame" that H/H experienced as a child and then as a grown man, he is eager to dismiss the thought that he is a transgendered cross-dresser as a result of his being raped. He recounts that, as a boy, he borrowed lipstick from the maid, perfumed his wrists, and adorned his ears with "delicate hoops" (128). As the recipient of his confession, Clare dismisses this possible causality, and Cliff seems likewise eager to disimbricate H/H's cross-dressing from his past sexual abuse. However, what looks like sexual abuse and, in some cases, statutory rape can, paradoxically, be the genesis for the affective states of an individual's future sexual encounters.

In this scene of traumatic recall and possibly delayed understanding, that the white officer's clothing is "a khaki uniform" (128) sheds light on H/H's later joining the Jamaican anti-imperialist revolutionary struggle, where s/he dons a khaki uniform. The specter of the militia and of the nationalistic response to Jamaica's sodomy-rape by American imperialism lingers in the next scene, where both H/H and Clare drive in a Rover to a secluded beach, owned by an absentee American landlord. Even though H/H's armaments—a cutlass, a rifle, and a box of shells—are to shoot down coconuts from the trees, in a possible symbolic castration, his self-description as "a 'fairy guerilla'" (130) augurs his later fate as a freedom fighter and "over-performer." Their subsequent lovemaking—"Touching gently, kissing, tongues entwined, coming to, laughing" (130)—seals the mutual recognition of their in-between condition, yet through the sweet eroticism of an insider transgression.

Indeed, such a caring and loving relationship does not mean that H/H is not gay and that Clare is not lesbian since, in opposite-sex-same-sexuality, a gay man can have sex with a lesbian without the two of them calling themselves "bisexual" or by any other term.[22] "For we are neither one thing nor the other," declares Clare, to which H/H replies that they will someday have to make a choice: "Cyaan live split. Not in this world" (131). "Split," which, one recalls, referred to his anal penetration as a child and connotes a psychoanalytical *Spaltung*, is here shifted to his refusal to meander in his sexual and political choices. Over-performing might then be H/H's excessive response to being "split." When Nadia Elia claims that "s/he is more than lesbian,"[23] she is right, but she fails to specify in what way. Even though Cliff has said that H/H is "a man who wants to be a woman and loves women,"[24] s/he does not desire women exclusively. S/he is more akin to a "male lesbian," similar to the *'yan kifi* in Hausa (Northern Nigerian) society, where *'yan daudu,* that is, male transvestites who "act like women," have sex with each other and call it *kifi* (lesbianism), as well as have sex with women.[25] In that respect, the possible cultural continuities with regards to sexuality between West Africa and diasporic communities in the Americas certainly deserve to be further investigated.

When we meet H/H later in the novel, in chapter 8, she is a registered nurse who is, rather coincidentally, taking care of Clare. This reunion takes place in a Kingston hospital, after an indeterminate number of years during which Clare, after dropping out of the London Institute, got involved with Bobby, a maimed, shell-shocked Black deserter. Bobby, it turns out, has been contaminated by Agent Orange, the defoliant chemical used by the United States in the Vietnam War at a time when "masculinity really meant the military; it meant Agent Orange and burning foreign people with chemicals."[26] Bobby incarnates an eroded masculinity, beleaguered by sexual humiliations in the U.S. military (he was asked to penetrate a dead woman) and subsequent painful, psychoanalytical sessions in Germany in 1969. After he slips out of Clare's life, she futilely searches for "the slender Black man *in camouflage*" (167, my emphasis) through the streets of Paris, whereupon she decides to return to Jamaica by boat.

When Clare wakes up to H/H's smiling face in a Kingston hospital ward, she learns that she has contracted an "infection in her womb" that will make her "probably sterile" (169). Cliff artfully juxtaposes Clare's uterine infection with H/H's proud announcement that "Harriet live and Harry be no more" (168). In other words, H/H acts on her decision "to be[come] a woman" at the very moment that Clare sadly muses on "her future as a woman" (170), thereby somewhat conventionally aligning womanhood with reproductive motherhood. This device makes Clare and H/H therefore function as communicating vessels of sorts, whereby gender roles get in turn confirmed and infirmed.

H/H has indeed moved from being a "battyman-in-training" as a young boy to a pseudo-drag-queen under-dressing in his twenties. In a later shift, he then moves from this "under-dressing," draggish phase, which is conventionally considered as one aspect of the 1970s gay sensibility (along with the "leather man" and the gay "macho"), to cross-dressing as a nurse, complete with uniform and red, beribboned cap. More clinically speaking, our Little Red Riding Hood has moved from the initial gender confusion in his childhood, and the corollary self-concept that he was more like girls than boys, to assuming a primary identity as a woman and a transgender subidentity, which entails successfully passing as a woman.

Yet s/he has not rejected the transsexual identity, because H/H has not considered at this point hir phenotypic transition from m to f. She has indeed not envisaged what she calls a "castration" (168) because she considers it too expensive and hir family has ostracized her.

By using the rather crude and clinical term "castration," Harriet is showing her awareness of the availability of technology, however imperfect, but also her approximate understanding of sex reassignment surgery (SRS), since the process of "transition" should ideally involve hormonal treatment and psychotherapy. Hir understanding of transsexualism in the 1970s is possibly based on hearsay, since gender dysphoria clinics (such as those set up by the sexologists John Money and Harry Benjamin in the United States or Dr. Burou's Clinique du Parc in Casablanca, Morocco) only flourished in the late 1970s before closing down in the late 1980s.[27] Instead of undergoing surgery, Harriet takes up gender roles traditionally assigned to women, such as that of the nurturing nurse and grassroots worker, thereby reinforcing stereotypical gender roles for women. While awaiting the completion of the m-to-f transitioning process, which does not take place in the scope of the narrative, s/he therefore appears as a spectral transbody before SRS and before a possible future as a transgendered or transsexual passing subject.

Within the scope of Cliff's narrative, H/H remains a woman-identified cross-dresser with a penis and testicles dangling between her legs. In other words, Harriet is a social woman with male genitals, as is found, for instance, in the American Indian *berdache* or Zuni (now relabeled Two-Spirit) culture.[28] She is also a nonsurgical m-to-f transsexual or "being-with-a-penis," like mtf Beth Elliott, the "infiltrator" at the first lesbian-feminist conference at UCLA in 1973,[29] who intends to live as a woman without undergoing the sex change surgery. It is intimated that if Harriet's condition were known in the Kingston area where she works as a nurse, she would presumably be "harried" (a hint at her former identity) and "ston[ed]" (171).

Were Harriet to envisage a full-fledged m-to-f transition, she would have to rely on Jamaican human rights organizations for free hormonal therapy and surgery. Such a trans-positive aid to sex reassignment, with the appropriate funding and guidance from the Jamaican government, might, however, be slow in coming. Jamaica is no "transsexual empire," which, with its association with Janice Raymond's trans-negative 1979 book,[30] might be a good thing, but it is not a posttranssexual country either,[31] let alone a post-posttranssexual country that would effortlessly host Harriett's transfeminism.[32] Likewise, despite laudable queering impulses to revisit Caribbean literature and history, Jamaica, as well as the Caribbean generally, has not yet articulated a culture-specific transgender theory that would give the lie to Euro-American transgender theory and activism. In other words, Caribbean theoretical practices still need to wrestle with the ever-increasing LGBTQI2 (Lesbian-Gay-Bisexual-Transgender-Queer-Intersex-Two-Spirit) spectrum, and the Caribbean still needs to provide its own post-queer or polygenderal theories.

Within the confines of *No Telephone to Heaven,* H/H's full-fledged cross-dressing may be construed as a move away from "straight" homosexuality, that is, desiring a man as a man (H/H refers playfully, in one of her letters to Clare, to falling in love with Jean-Jacques Dessalines while reading C. L. R. James's *The Black Jacobins* [146]), to desiring a man as a nonoperative transgender woman. Beyond the confines of the novel, the reader can even imagine H/H after surgery, desiring women, as in the earlier (second) beach scene with Clare, as well as desiring men. The move beyond sexual binarisms that queer theory initiated in Western academic circles as of the 1990s is here aborted, for the next step into new multiple sexualities never truly takes place.

H/H as a non- or pre-operative transgender is, of course, through her "choice,"[33] affirming her desire to *pass* as a woman, which reflects on Clare's desire to pass as white, Cliff having distributed race and sexuality over Harry's and Clare's bodies in uneven degrees. Cliff's novel (as well as her poem "Passing"[34]) is intertextually aware of *Passing* (1929) by Nella Larsen, an author of Danish-Caribbean descent, and of Larsen's character, Clare, whom Butler convincingly cast as a specter of racial and sexual ambiguity.[35] In the second part of the novel, as in her dealings with Bobby, Clare tries to be accepted as black, in a reverse "lactification complex,"[36] which is her father Boy Savage's perplex, as seen in his successful "blending in" tactics and in his lessons in "self-effacement" and the "uses of camouflage" (100). Her light skin, however, erases any identification with any black person or movement.

Clare's metamorphosis is slow and induced by her readings. In a scene set in London where Clare is studying, she is reading *Jane Eyre,* and after identifying for a while with Rochester's bride, she opts for "wild-maned Bertha" (116), the legendary "mad woman in the attic." At some other point, Clare remembers her father, Boy Savage, once coming home with a hair gel called Tame to master her curlicues. After she refused it, he called her Medusa: "Do you intend to turn men to stone, daughter?" (116). Clare's cosmetic concern with keeping her curlicues untamed signals her ideological will to "become" black, which is enacted in the (second) beach scene with H/H, where melanin rises to the occasion and she becomes darker under the contact of H/H's lips (131). Clare does want to turn into Medusa. The mythological Gorgon often acts as the primary trope for the dark, vital power of female sexuality and her blood from decapitation by Perseus, who embodies a most trenchant aspect of masculinity, engenders the hybrid Pegasus, who is conjured up in the name of the Kingston hotel. Clare's metamorphosis into wild-maned Bertha and Medusa, both tentacular, threatening figures to male conceptions of a stable female sexuality, also signals Clare's rupture with her father and with the corollary condition of *passing* as white.

In her famed essay "The Laugh of the Medusa," Hélène Cixous uses, in her repartee to Freud, the Medusa figure to introduce what she calls the "other bisexuality," which is multiple, variable, and ever-changing, and "doesn't annul differences but stirs them up, pursues them, increases them."[37] Admittedly, Cixous is being more poetic and rhapsodic than theoretical, but "this other bisexuality" is to be seen as women's retort to what Cixous perceives as men's glorious phallic lighthouse of monosexuality. It is more about the recognition and acceptance of both sexes in one person than a true bisexuality. In the context of the novel, Clare has sex with two men—Paul H and Bobby—and never with a woman. However, because she has sex with H/H, who is a female-identified man at the time of intercourse, Clare is "the novel's lesbian," a role that Cliff had assigned to H/H. Cliff has "split" the true biracial lesbian of the novel, her own autobiographical ego, into Clare and H/H. Cliff has, in a way, mastered the art of narrative camouflage.

Cliff certainly has previously displayed contradictions in representing the "indigenous" gay/lesbian subject. In the prequel to *No Telephone to Heaven, Abeng* (1984), Cliff is keen on affirming an intrinsically indigenous Jamaican culture through its oral traditions, its folk practices, and its long history of anticolonial resistance, yet she also critiques the oppressiveness of the indigenous postcolonial nation-state that entrenched homophobia and sexism. *Abeng*'s Mma Alli is a lesbian mythical character who has the reputation for "touch[ing] a woman in her deep-inside and make her womb move within her."[38] As such, in Timothy Chin's words, she "represents the possibility of an 'indigenous' or even 'Afrocentric' precedent for a non-heterosexual orientation."[39] Like the early eighteenth-century leader of the Windward Maroons, Coromantee warrior Nanny, Mma Alli, the proto-lesbian, Amazon-like warrior figure is a slave-leader. She has this idiosyncratic capacity to render an enemy bullet harmless through catching it between her massive buttocks, which tells a lot about the power of women's lower regions.

Such matronly heritage is at odds with the nation that Manley and his successors wanted Jamaica to be, despite notable reforms introduced by the Manley administration such as the enactment of a minimum wage for houseworkers and amendments to the bastardy law, which originally prevented illegitimate children from inheriting from their fathers. Cliff's agenda for a non-heteronormative nation is reflected in H/H, who, as a university-trained nurse who also tapped into the obeah and myal-women's knowledge, is called "Mawu-Lisa, moon and sun, female-male deity of some of their ancestors" (171). During her European stay, Clare also finds this dual quality in such ambivalent figures as the "manly girl" (156), Joan of Arc in Notre Dame Cathedral in Paris, and Pocahontas, the Powhatan girl cross-dressed in virile feathery costume, whose statue Clare admires at Gravesend, Kent, and whose story turns Clare into a guerilla fighter against American imperialism. Clare takes up Pocahontas's story where she left it off, by arriving back home with a high fever, the way Pocahontas would have done, had she not died of smallpox on the ship bound to New England but close enough to the British shore for the English to claim her body.

The uses of camouflage are given a further twist when H/H doubles as a nationalist and Clare chooses to join the band of guerilla fighters, which for a moment dispel the discomfort of in-betweenness, of Clare's confused racial allegiance, and of H/H's status as gender outlaw. Camouflaging as in armed resistance sheds light retrospectively on the "second skins"[40] both Clare and H/H have ragged themselves in. Yet both their ambiguities reflect on Cliff's own lesbianism and the uses of camouflage inherent in being homosexual in a heterosexist society, which John Rechy has called "enemy territory." He argues, "We [homosexuals] become strangers in a strange land, sinners in the eyes of religionists, criminals in the eyes of some lawmakers—that is, outlaws. That early separation forces the homosexual into roles and *camouflage* in order to survive a hostile environment. . . . We might even call it gay theater."[41]

Cliff's uses of camouflage and theatrical performance have to be assessed in their military guise and in terms of cross-dressing and cross-gendering, for the en-gendering of the new Jamaican nation is performed by Clare and Harry/Harriet who both, significantly, cannot reproduce and thus conjure up "the adamantine refusal of slave-women to reproduce" (93) but can engender, even transgender, a new, feisty nation-in-drag.

Not only does their engagement with the Jamaican nationalist struggle provide a narrative platform from which Clare can remember her past aboard the truck leading her into the Jamaican heart of darkness, but it also opens and crowns the novel. In the opening chapter, an older Clare, presented as the "daughter of landowners, native-born, slaves, émigrés, Carib, Ashanti, English" (5), is aboard a rattling, rickety, open-backed truck making its slow ascent through the Cockpit Country in the company of twenty people, who seemingly differ from Clare on account of their blackness, poor social origins, and the use of a register like Jamaican "dub."[42]

Despite such intra-cultural differences, they are all dressed in khaki military *uniforms* which, as the word indicates, make them look alike but also help them "blend with the country around them—this dripping brown and green terrain" (5). This terrain is "ruinate," a distinctive Jamaican term "used to describe lands which were once cleared for agricultural purposes and have now lapsed back into . . . 'bush'" (1). The notion of "lapsing back" signals a prelapsarian bush, which over the years may transform into a "high ruinate," that is, a primordial forest before population settlement and whose transformation hints at ongoing metamorphoses and the retrieval of Jamaican *herstory*, or rather, *hirstory*, before Columbus's first visit in 1494, the British crown in 1655, self-government in 1944, and Jamaica's independence as a Commonwealth state in 1962.

Another difference between Clare and her fellow soldiers is in the use of *khaki*. The mid-nineteenth-century Urdu and Persian origins of the word meaning "dust-colored," which came to designate the dull brownish-yellow fabric used in military clothing, point to the art of camouflage. Whereas Clare previously experienced camouflage as racial passing, for most of the truck-dwellers, "khaki was not new" (5). Ironically, these khaki uniforms are discarded American army fatigues, which were stolen from white American youths high on dope, come to dance at reggae festivals and Jamfests, or inherited from another place, another period "under the crown and among the vestiges following independence" (5). This sartorial history further contributes to the ultimate irony, which is that history cannot be rewritten by such small-scale guerilla fighters whose "survival dress" (5) is borrowed and ineffectual. Also, their camouflage is invalidated by the bright gold shining in their Rasta knitted caps, which recalls H/H's colorful makeup at the Pegasus bar, and is sure to give them away in the bush, the way the bright head-gears in part contributed to the Aztecs' defeat in their resistance to the Spaniards.

In that pseudo-military, stagy context, the reader is introduced to Harry/Harriet as a nurse at a Kingston hospital, who owns a camouflage jacket all to hirself. "Her name was Harriet; in the jacket she became Thorpe" (7), after the guerillas' habit of calling each other by the name of the former, presumably dead soldiers who had worn the jackets, possibly the Jap-stalking GIs whom Jamaicans would see in Kingston's open-air movie-theaters. The Naipaulesque derivativeness of their disguise is hinted at in the borrowed names but also in the delusion such a pathetic clique has in mimicking "real freedom-fighters, like their comrades in the ANC" (7). But Cliff/Clare saves them from mimicry by this heartfelt omniscient commentary: "but that *is* what they were, what they *felt* they were, what they *were* in fact" (7). Significantly, Harriet has put on a third skin.

Khaki is also the nondescript color of Kingston's poor, of the "old men squatted in stained khaki" and of mad Christopher, "de watchman," whose clothes have "turned from khaki to crocus sack" (178). Christopher is a pitiful scavenger wading his way through the ghostly shanties, disfigured by the food shortages occasioned by the one-party government. In the last chapter, entitled "Film noir," Christopher plays the role of a native monster howling in a tree and attacking an elegant, silk-clad actress playing Nanny the Coromantee warrior, whom Cliff elsewhere envisioned as "an old Black woman naked except for a necklace made from the teeth of white men."[43] In this scene she is rescued by Cudjoe, who allegedly held the British to a standstill, in a romanticized film of Nanny and Cudjoe by a white American film crew. As the monster's bellows are suddenly silenced by helicopters and lights flood the valley, the reader is made aware of the fact that the camouflaged guerillas including Clare and Harriet are hidden in the bitterbush above the stage set and, as a result of having been betrayed, are sprayed by the "real" military in a surprise attack. It is intimated that Christopher is killed and so is Clare (208).

H/H, the preoperative transgenderist, survives, so that Clare and H/H are now "split" and Harriet can live as what Cliff termed, referring to herself, "a double agent."[44] As the very embodiment of not only "a third sex" but of the possibility of numerous genders, s/he unsettles the boundaries of bipolarity and opposition in the gender schema. The plea for a "third gender" finds its political equivalent in Clare and H/H's attempt to overthrow Manley's People's National Party (PNP) despite its proffered socialism, which was toppled in 1980 by Edward Seaga, with his Jamaican Labor Party (JLP)'s democratic capitalism. This led, however, to a weaker economy, which favored Michael Manley's return to power in 1989. In 2008 the prime minister of Jamaica, Bruce Golding of the JLP, caused quite a stir in Britain when he said in a BBC interview that he would never knowingly have a gay minister in his cabinet. This pronouncement reaffirmed the idea of the nation as a conventionally masculine entity. Portia Simpson-Miller and the PNP's victory in the Jamaican general election of January 2012 might temporarily interrupt the masculinization of Jamaica: she has declared, in fact, that she would not have a problem with gays serving in her administration.

Harriet's survival and, we assume, her continued fighting emblematize the necessity to stop, at that particular historical point, the perpetual en-gendering of Jamaica as an alpha-male nation, with its unremitting homophobic and transphobic violence. Yet Jamaica is no "queer nation," and, as we have seen, no "post-posttranssexual empire" either. Cliff's gesturing, through her character's under-dressing, cross-dressing, and over-performing, ultimately belongs with costumed actors, second-rate disguise, and other uses of camouflage. But the very fact that writers such as Cliff initiate such gesturing is proof that the Caribbean stage-set can hold because of its intricate scaffolding and the capacity for make-believe of its performers.

Notes

1. Weatherston, "Interview with Cherríe Moraga," 72.

2. See Zabus, *Tempests after Shakespeare,* esp. 132–40.

3. See Carlisle, *Human Sex Change,* 57–128.

4. Cliff, *No Telephone to Heaven,* 21. Further references will be given in parentheses in the text.

5. Naipaul, *Miguel Street,* 3–18.

6. Dynes, "Camp," 189.

7. Sontag, "Notes on 'Camp,'" (1964), 275. See also Pellegrini, "After Sontag," 168–93.

8. Core, *Camp,* 9.

9. Glass, "Queer," 38.

10. Butler, *Bodies That Matter,* 235–36.

11. Butler, *Gender Trouble,* 187.

12. Hammond, "'All dressed up . . . ,'" 168.

13. Harris, *Hidden Agendas,* 25.

14. Davy, "Fe/male Impersonation," 245.

15. Bolin, "Transcending and Transgendering," 447.

16. Newton, *Mother Camp,* 338–39; Cante, "Pouring on the Past," 149.

17. Qtd. in Raiskin, *Snow on the Cane Fields,* 191.

18. Cante, "Pouring on the Past," 149, is drawing on Slavoj Žižek, *Looking Awry,* 6.

19. Berlant and Freeman, "Queer Nationality," 196.

20. An American tourist is unlikely to have been a guest of the Pegasus hotel in Kingston, as his presence would have been more appropriate in hotels for tourists on Jamaica's northern coast, such as Montego Bay, Negril, and Port Antonio. Warm thanks go to John Gilmore for pointing that out to me when I was giving a version of this paper at the University of Warwick, UK, in March 2009.

21. This is certainly the case with the controversial Jamaican "raga" lyrics by Buju Banton and Brand Nubian.

22. On "opposite-sex-same-sexuality," see Garber, *Vice Versa*, 46–47.

23. Elia, "'A Man Who Wants to Be a Woman.'"

24. Qtd. in ibid., 352.

25. See, for instance, Gaudio, "Male Lesbians."

26. Case, "Final Frontier," 330.

27. See Hausman, *Changing Sex*.

28. See Roscoe, *Zuni Man-Woman*.

29. Forfreedom, "Lesbos Arise!," 4.

30. See Raymond, *Transsexual Empire*.

31. Stone, "'Empire' Strikes Back."

32. The adjective "post-posttranssexual" refers to the title of a conference that took place at the University of Indiana, Bloomington, in 2011.

33. H/H's choice does not necessarily preclude bisexuality. See Garber, *Vice Versa*, 39.

34. Cliff, *Claiming an Identity*, 3–7.

35. Butler, *Bodies That Matter*, 167–85. The work of Caribbean-born author Audre Lorde, replete with women warriors and amazons, also had an impact on Cliff's fiction.

36. The phrase is from Fanon, *Black Skin, White Masks*.

37. Cixous, "The Laugh of the Medusa," 254.

38. Cliff, *Abeng,* 35.

39. Chin, "'Bullers' and 'Battymen,'" 137.

40. Prosser, *Second Skins*. In his book, Prosser used Didier Anzieu's concept of "second skin" from the latter's *L'épiderme nomade et la peau psychique*.

41. Rechy, "Outlaw Sensibility," 124 (my emphasis).

42. An analysis of "dub," Jamaican Patwah, Pidgin, and Coromantee as interstitial registers lies beyond the scope of this paper.

43. Cliff, *If I Could Write This in Fire*, viii.

44. Ibid., 79.

"Not Woman Enough Everywhere"

Gender, Nation, and Narration in the Work of
Patrick Chamoiseau

Michael Niblett

TOWARD THE end of Patrick Chamoiseau's novel *Biblique des derniers gestes* (2002), the protagonist Balthazar Bodule-Jules reflects on his participation in various struggles against oppression around the globe. The success of his involvement was compromised, he feels, by his not being "Palestinian enough in Israel. Not Jewish enough in Germany. Not Zapatista enough in Mexico. Not Black enough in South Africa. . . . Not Dominican enough in Guadeloupe. Not gay enough in San Francisco. . . . Not woman enough everywhere."[1] If Balthazar's litany points to the need not only for solidarity among resistance movements but also for greater identification with their participants, his final assertion (from which this article takes its title) underscores the importance of gender politics to strategies of opposition. Indeed, the imbrication of patriarchal discourse in colonial frameworks has made challenging conventional gender roles a key part of attempts to overturn such frameworks. But this questioning is integral also to the rethinking of the politics of rebellion and national liberation, which have often perpetuated oppressive gender relations. Not only is this a case of highlighting the central role women have played in liberation struggles; it involves too an interrogation of the masculinist paradigms that define identity, with the reorientation toward a feminist perspective potentially able to open up an alternative understanding of subject relations more generally. The putting into question of the male/female and masculine/feminine binary oppositions destabilizes their "natural" status, while simultaneously pointing beyond models of selfhood predicated on the objectification and subjugation of the term marked as "Other" in the dyad.

To be more woman in Balthazar's sense, then, is in part to pursue this radical critique (rather than simple reversal) of gender and identity models. Interestingly, Chamoiseau himself has been accused of being, as it were, "not woman enough everywhere" in his earlier fiction and theoretical writings. Critics such as Richard and Sally Price and A. James Arnold have charged that the way he and his fellow créoliste Raphaël Confiant "theorize gender and deploy masculinist strategies in the practice of their profession erases and silences women."[2] Nevertheless, when reiterating his more general reservations about the créolistes' output in a later article—*"Créolité:* Power, Mimicry, and Dependence" from 2004—Arnold stresses that he "would like to make an exception for the recent work of Chamoiseau," which aligns itself "with the more open and dialectical position of [Édouard] Glissant."[3] Although Arnold does not refer specifically here to either gender politics or *Biblique,* both the latter novel and the 1997 novella *L'esclave vieil homme et le molosse* (The old slave and the dog) approach issues of sexuality and gender in a more interrogative and self-conscious fashion than Chamoiseau's previous fiction. Lorna Milne has suggested that the experiences of the titular slave in *L'esclave vieil homme* point to a revision of the opposition Arnold considers to operate in the earlier works between the hyper-virile masculinity of the maroon and the feminized (but always male) *conteur,* or storyteller.[4] It is not the intention of this article to analyze in detail the extent to which these criticisms of Chamoiseau's earlier work are valid. Instead, I want to focus on how *Biblique* reconfigures the gendered tropes of rebellion, particularly in light of the transvestism and sexual dimorphism of a number of its characters. The novel attempts to move beyond the image (found in Césaire's poetry, for instance) of the sacrificial male hero whose death en/genders a national consciousness. In so doing, it necessarily registers a concern with rethinking epic discourse and the politics of individual and collective identity.

In the encounter between the "New World" and Europe, the colonizer's initial codification of the land as feminine—a passive "virgin wilderness" in need of penetration by the rational, sovereign male colonist to ensure its productivity—aimed at naturalizing the conquest by equating it with the patriarchal model of gender relations: as Doris Sommer glosses it, "What could be more legitimate than courting and winning a virgin?"[5] But this strategy, like that of the accompanying feminization of the colonized to justify their subjugation, required in turn the careful policing of gender boundaries, for its legitimacy depended on the maintenance of the stereotypes of men as "masculine" (and hence active, rational, and dominant) and women as "feminine" (and hence passive, emotional, and submissive).[6] In tandem with this discourse ran an infantilizing strategy, one that deployed the imagery of the patriarchal family unit to mystify domination as parental protection on the part of the colonizer. While common to various expressions of colonial authority, the familial paradigm, as Richard D. E. Burton points out, has had a particularly marked impact on Martinican society, where it has "for over one hundred and fifty years, and especially between 1870 and 1950, served to govern and inform the relations linking France with its Antillean colonies."[7] At the heart of this discourse is the idea of France as the Mère-Patrie, as both the mother and father of the adopted overseas "infants," orphaned by the loss of "mother Africa."[8] Again, traditional categorizations of gender are crucial here, with the Mère-Patrie frequently embodied as a symbolic maternal presence—a soothing, nourishing projection—behind which stands the real, active, and regulatory power of the patriarchal father (the masculinist reality of Napoleonic domination behind the image of the soft, feminine Empress Joséphine, for example).[9]

This familial ideology has been complemented by the historical imposition of the model of the nuclear family. In *Le discours antillais* (*Caribbean Discourse*), Glissant describes how the colonial authorities in Martinique, especially following emancipation in 1848, sought to enforce this model so as to maintain social stability, compartmentalizing people within rigid productive units (168).[10] Although there was massive deviation between reality and the prescribed structure, nevertheless its constant official promotion has had psychological repercussions. "The triangular organization father-mother-child," notes Glissant, "imposed by the structuring will of the system, manifestly contradicts the cultural tendencies inherited from Africa. These tendencies have not been strong enough to come to the fore in an 'autonomous' process of structuration" (168). The result of this shoehorning of lived experience into a disjunctive model is an emotional instability around the family. But it also provokes an unconscious refusal of the imposed structure, which culminates in what Glissant calls an "anti-family." The latter is not "the simple reverse of an 'ideal' family, for which the model would have been occidental. Instead, it exhibits the principles of a true and original social organization, of which the Martinican is lacking a collective consciousness" (170).

I will return to the specific issue of the family later. At present I want to focus on the more general theme of resistance to, but also imbrication in, the dominant modes of identity relations. As the above examples attest, the gendered schemas that underpin these relations must be challenged if their ability to naturalize oppressive ideological and material frameworks is to be undermined. This in turn would contribute to the emergence of the kinds of autonomous structures Glissant highlights in relation to the family, and so ultimately to the refashioning of the social whole. These connections are imaged explicitly in *Biblique* through the figure of Polo Carcel, a hermaphrodite *danmyé* warrior who lives in the forest. Looking back on his friendship with Polo, Balthazar reflects that he met similar intersexed figures in many of the countries in which he fought for anticolonial causes: "Often, in these places of men with balls [that is, resistance fighters], he received the unexpected support of one like Polo Carcel, as if these places of brutal force were favorable to the apparition of a conjunction of sexes" (745). The emergence of political resistance is thus matched by the emergence of a resistant body, one that defies the binary logic of the dominant order. This is complemented by a rebelliousness of gender. For not only is Polo anatomically intersexed; he also combines "two persons in one body": Balthazar can see in him "the *madame* fully, and the *monsieur* fully. . . . The two voices did not express the same opinion. It seemed to [Balthazar] that he talked with a couple of different people" (743).[11] The appearance in the combat zone of those like Polo thus indicates how the destabilization of fixed sex and gender categories must be incorporated into the general assault upon colonial/imperial structures.

However, Polo's physical condition causes him to be shunned by the other *danmyé* warriors. His fate would seem to be emblematic of the way the resistance to gender norms he represents has been suppressed in the wider struggle for liberation. Indeed, Balthazar's definition of areas of rebellion as "places of men with balls" underscores the prevailing masculinist logic. As Arnold has shown, this gendering of the political field has been reinforced by the literary representations of a number of male writers from the Francophone Caribbean, with the "phallogocentric discourse of Césaire's vision of Negritude" one of the key reference points.[12] Arnold cites in particular Césaire's play *Et les chiens se taisaient* (And the dogs were silent), which features an agonic male protagonist—the Rebel—whose tragic, sacrificial death unites the community and raises collective consciousness. The Rebel displays a kind of supermasculinity, one that resists the discursive feminization of the colonized male yet still remains locked in the colonial erotic framework, its features defined against a sexual norm occupied by the male colonizer, the liberation it promises inseparable from a masculinist heterosexual paradigm. This latter point is emphasized by the play's representation of the Mother and the Lover, symbolic female figures confined to stereotyped roles. As Arnold observes, "The suffering male hero of Negritude must transcend these representations of feminine weakness in order to realize his salvatory maleness in the radiant future beckoning beyond his present sacrifice of self."[13] The renewal of the community and the shaping of national consciousness are thus marked out as male prerogatives.

Though a new sense of nationhood is engendered, therefore, the reduction of the female presence to a symbol while real power is located in male activity perpetuates the familial discourse that has couched Martinique's relationship to the metropole. Moreover, the theme of sacrifice—of "salvatory maleness"—continues another trope used to mystify this colonial history, that of the heroic white male whose sacrificial work helps liberate the oppressed (a figure best encapsulated by the abolitionist Victor Schoelcher).[14] More generally, the connection in *Et les chiens* between a founding tragic sacrifice and the suppression of an Other (here, the feminine) indicates the formal affinity between Césaire's discourse and traditional European tragedy. According to Glissant, the latter is bound to "root" identity, an exclusive mode of Being that affirms its legitimacy by tracing an origin back through the linear time-span of filiation to a "founding episode."[15] It is this "retelling (certifying) of a 'creation of the world' in a filiation" that allows a community to "proclaim its entitlement to the possession of a land, which thus becomes a territory."[16] Rooted in a single origin, filiation requires either the assimilation or the annihilation of the other; it hence strives for a homogeneous order inaugurated by an individualizing act, that is, by the agency of a sovereign individual (Christ, for example, or, in this instance, the Rebel). Tragedy plays out the rupture and ultimate restoration of a filiation through the sacrifice of the hero, whose violent death purges and redeems the community; it is an individualizing act that awakens a people to its history, inaugurating a new Genesis and line of filiation. However, this affirmation is achieved via the exclusion and objectification of those whose "otherness" becomes the guarantee of sovereign selfhood. Indeed, the sacrificial victim's death and the atonement it provides is what enables the repudiation of those not thereby redeemed. "The fact is that all Tragedy, in the Western sense, is discriminatory," writes Glissant. "It reconstructs the legitimacy of a filiation; it does not give on to the scattered infinity of Relation" (*Le discours,* 266).

Such tragic narratives thus frame a conception of collective or national identity based on principles of exclusion and sovereign self-sufficiency. Though Césaire's discourse is aimed at establishing such self-sufficiency for an oppressed community in the form of a radical alterity—a necessary undertaking in the context of the decolonization struggles of the mid-twentieth century—nevertheless its replication of these underlying principles prevents the full expression of a Caribbean history defined by disjunction and the entanglement of cultural legacies. The turn to more relational concepts of identity on the part of Glissant and the créolistes, responding to the need for a form capable of articulating this specificity, initiated a concomitant revising of the epic framework in which the emergence of collective consciousness had been communicated.[17] Thus does Chamoiseau's *Texaco* seek to move beyond the binary oppositions that characterized Negritude, evoking instead a diversity of histories the creolization of which thwarts any attempt to reconstruct a pure line of filiation for Martinique. But while the subsequent epic narrative succeeds in unfolding a relational vision of the Martinican community, concretized in the squatter settlement of Texaco, it perhaps fails to free itself from the masculinist paradigm. Although it is Marie-Sophie who founds Texaco, her characterization as a *femme à deux graines* (woman with balls) indicates that the business of nation building continues to be encoded as a masculine activity. The way she gives birth to the community in place of having children again suggests that the physical body of the woman is being absented, turning the female into a symbol while real power is invested in traits demarcated as masculine.

It could be argued, however, that Marie-Sophie's adoption of such traits hints at a destabilizing of the conventional boundaries of sex and gender. Her ability to be a woman and act in the fashion associated with those "with balls" might be read as undermining the "natural" pairings of female/feminine and male/masculine. But this theme is not one that is developed explicitly in *Texaco;* hence, it remains unclear how far masculinist discourses are being interrogated here. *Biblique,* on the other hand, makes a leitmotif of gender instability, while self-consciously foregrounding the sexed and gendered constitution of discourses of rebellion. Indeed, it replays the Césairean tropes of the agonic male rebel and the female lover, enabling them to be rethought and revised. The novel opens with Balthazar's announcement of his forthcoming demise, the victim of his failure to prevent the successful colonization of Martinique; and yet at "the beginning of his death pangs [*agonie*]" his thoughts turn first not to his anticolonial struggles but to the seven hundred and twenty-seven lovers he has had (33). But if this seems to presage a return of the rebel as virile supermale, it will soon become apparent that Balthazar's *agonie* is of a very different kind than that of Césaire's suffering hero. As he looks back on his past, Balthazar begins to reassess his experiences and self-image as a rebel. His last years at home are spent coming to terms with his shortcomings in a painful process of self-recognition, an unraveling of the skein of his life that—narrated with an elegiac air—contrasts sharply with the sense of conflagration and transcendence through sacrifice that defines the Rebel in *Et les chiens*. Moreover, whereas this transcendence is associated with an excision of feminine influences, Balthazar's central epiphany stems from his realization of the integrity of women to his development. He comes to understand that far from being the self-sufficient masculine rebel he believed himself to be, his character has been shaped by the instruction he has received from various female figures.

The most significant early influence on Balthazar is Man L'Oubliée, the female *mentô*[18] who adopts him after the death of his parents, victims of the machinations of the evil Yvonnette Cléoste. Man L'Oubliée lives in the forest, where her understanding of the flora and fauna enables her to lead a self-sufficient existence. She imparts this knowledge to Balthazar not through verbal instruction but by way of bodily practice; her young pupil learns to begin "modeling himself on her, imitating her gestures" (159). The techniques he acquires in the forest will be vital to Balthazar's later survival in various war zones. However, it is only in his dying days that he recognizes Man L'Oubliée's importance to his anticolonial activities: "He went over again in his mind those incredible moments next to Man L'Oubliée, and began to become conscious that she had initiated him into all that he would become. He reviewed her gestures and ways, and discerned the imperceptible teaching that this admirable woman had offered to him" (805). In addition to the role played by the *mentô*, the novel emphasizes the involvement of women in all the struggles Balthazar attaches himself to, where they often educate him in the ways of combat. The narrative thereby challenges the portrayal of national liberation as a male prerogative.

What makes Man L'Oubliée so interesting with regards to this challenge is the wider allegorical resonance of events in the forest, the most explicitly mythical narrative strand in the text. Having established the folktale-like scenario of the struggle between the protective, quasi-magical powers of Man L'Oubliée and the evil supernatural force of Yvonnette Cléoste, the novel invests these characters with allegorical weight. Yvonnette, whose obsession with adopting Balthazar has morphed into a destructive hatred or "morbid desire" for him (151), stands in some part for the French assimilation of Martinique—the asphyxiation of the island via the Mère-Patrie's supposedly nourishing (and maternal) policy of subsidization. Man L'Oubliée in contrast becomes the allegorical figure for Martinican independence, the symbolism of her self-sufficient existence clear: "[She] had no need of anything or anyone, her life nourished itself from itself in the sober magnificence of a full autonomy; that which was vital to her did not come from the outside but from the depths of herself" (168). The opposition between these two surrogate mothers thus functions also as a critique of the colonial familial discourse, with Yvonnette representing its pernicious influence and Man L'Oubliée suggestive of an alternative model that draws on its own resources to structure itself.

The use of Man L'Oubliée as a figurehead for the prospective independent community might appear to replicate the disempowering symbolization of the female body noted earlier. However, there is a crucial difference here: far from absenting the physical body of the woman in order to make her a symbol, the symbolic power of Man L'Oubliée depends precisely on her corporeality. Not only is this corporeality the repository of the cultural memory that will provide Balthazar with his education, but also—and in contrast to the depiction of Marie-Sophie as a *femme à deux graines*—the bodily gestures through which this memory is preserved are demarcated as specifically feminine. Hence, it is this femininity that Balthazar carries inside himself: as he performs in his old age the gestures Man L'Oubliée taught him, there is about his movement "something joyous, smooth and powerful, an impeccable display that suggested omnipotence and, more unexpectedly, a wisdom consonant [*consubstantielle*] with a total femininity" (167). Such total femininity, then, is not only inseparable from his constitution as a figure of resistance, but also (as Man L'Oubliée's allegorical figuration shows) from the full liberation of the community. Those traits encoded as "feminine" cannot be transcended in the articulation of freedom (as they are for Césaire's Rebel); rather, they remain vital to its success.

Why this might be so is revealed more clearly in the account of the next phase of young Balthazar's life, which also elucidates what "femininity" should be taken to mean here—for its integrity to the full articulation of community is not to be seen in terms of the incorporation of an essentialist category, but rather relies upon the unraveling of such categories. Balthazar begins to spend less time in the forest, moving to the town of Saint-Joseph so that he can be educated by the Communist intellectual Nicol Timoléon. What he learns in the home of his new tutor would at first seem very different from the knowledge imparted to him by Man L'Oubliée. His time in the forest was defined by the transmission of a nonwritten cultural memory connected to an understanding of the land, the narrative framed by mythic and folkloric tropes (the tested hero, the magical helper).[19] His time in Saint-Joseph is one of instruction in politics, history, and literature, the narrative adopting elements of the bildungsroman novel to chart his development, which culminates in the apparent consolidation of a sovereign identity (that of the masculinized rebel). Indeed, Balthazar's introduction to Nicol Timoléon's family at first looks to be the start of socialization into the bourgeois nuclear household; it seems to signal a move from the imaginary (the forest as the realm of the maternal and sense perception) to the symbolic, or the site of paternal law, with Nicol Timoléon's book-lined study and the (masculine) public sphere of political meetings inducting Balthazar into new social networks and categories of identity. However, appearances prove deceptive. Nicol Timoléon's family trio does not form a father-mother-daughter unit, as Balthazar initially supposes. Sarah Timoléon is sister, not wife, to Nicol, and her daughter, Anaïs-Alicia, is the result of a liaison with a "person not truly of this world" (393). Most significantly, Nicol is in fact a woman, Déborah, sister of Sarah, with whom s/he is incestuously in love.

Thus both the model of the nuclear household and the gender distinctions upon which it is predicated are subverted here. Moreover, Déborah-Nicol's transvestism disrupts not only the categorization of bodies but also the gendered partitioning of the public (masculine) and private (feminine) spheres. Her activism within the local Communist party undermines the encoding of political resistance as a task for men, a fact her fellow party members recognize when they decide, on discovering her secret, to keep it quiet: "In a country where women remained at home busying themselves with the children, to reveal that the most ardent of militants in Saint-Joseph was a woman did not seem like a very good idea" (380). The fact that Balthazar's explicitly anticolonial education derives from Déborah-Nicol again underlines his indebtedness to women for his rebel selfhood; but something more is going on here too, a de-essentializing of masculinity and femininity that enables what they represent to be understood and deployed in a new way.

Initially, Déborah-Nicol's adoption of a masculine persona is connected to her positioning of herself as a revolutionary: "Déborah at a stroke had cut her hair. Her ardour and revolutionary force were such that her body no longer had the ethereal womanly curves that make a woman. She had narrow hips, broad shoulders, a physique vibrating with rage and energy that could pass without problem for one of a man. She called herself Nicol instead of Déborah, and became a man" (378). Here then masculinity appears as the mode of identity best suited to the expression of resistance; and yet the fact it is at the same time shown explicitly to be a role that one performs—the fact we see masculinity constituted through the act of transvestism—emphasizes that such gendered characteristics are not essential traits, and cannot be aligned with a particular sex. With gender norms thus put into question, the text then draws attention to the fluidity of Déborah-Nicol's identity in order to stress that those features conventionally associated with masculinity are not the only qualities through which resistance can be articulated. Speaking to Balthazar both as a woman and as a man, Déborah-Nicol

> passed between these two states with such ease that the young man no longer knew at what moment *Nicol* was there, and at what moment *Déborah* expressed herself. [Balthazar] preferred Déborah; this feminine personality was more rounded but energetic, total, violent. . . . When the protestations rose up in an apocalyptic tidal-wave ready to sweep everything away, it was a case of Déborah. With Nicol, all became formal, teacher's words, flowery French, manners and proprieties. . . . In that condition she effected the gestures that she thought to be those of a man. (432)

Despite his preference for Déborah, however, Balthazar realizes that these "two personalities were inseparable: Déborah nourished Nicol, and Nicol was a source of moderation for Déborah; one was not worse off than the other for it was not one or the other, . . . *it was always both at the same time*" (433). Not only are feminine-encoded traits shown to be as capable of conveying active resistance as masculine ones, therefore, but also "masculine" and "feminine" emerge as the markers of particular qualities that, while they may have been attached to one sex on account of social conventions, do not have to remain the exclusive property of that sex. The feminist critic Nelly Richard suggests that central to the rethinking of gender should be the question of how to specify "what is 'particular' to the feminine without remitting in an essentialist way to the metaphysics of being (in this case, of 'being a woman') as a natural referent of an identity *signed by and consigned to* the fixity of an origin."[20] Déborah-Nicol's transvestism, in making explicit the adoptability of gender roles across the sexes, points to how the specificity of "femininity" as the result of a certain lived experience can be retained, while simultaneously keeping it open as a set of values able to inform the behavior of all.

However, it becomes clear that Déborah-Nicol's rebellious identity is not as free from traditional gender politics as it at first appears. Moreover, it is in danger of ossifying into a one-sided posture that cannot fulfill its potential. The reasons for this stem in part from the implicit assumption Déborah-Nicol continues to make regarding the effectiveness of "masculine" values to resistance. Although in her articulation of the latter she shifts between genders, her understanding of the overall direction such resistance should take continues to uphold an approach structured by concepts whose traditional masculinist codification has yet to be transformed by the inclusion of a feminist perspective. Commenting on the way in which particular forms of thought—rationality, logic, scientific abstraction—were institutionalized as masculine, Richard stresses that the "fact that knowledge has a (masculine) master does not impede women from taking it over by storm and extorting those formulas that best prepare them to critique the masculinity of those knowledge systems."[21] This critique (which is thus not a rejection of, for example, rationality as such) entails the incorporation as an interrogative tool of those values that have been marginalized as "feminine," such as sensibility, corporeality, and affectivity. Though Déborah-Nicol conquers "masculine" knowledge systems for her own ends, she does not question—indeed, she implicitly affirms—the implications of their past gendered encoding (just as her anticolonial intellectual position draws upon Western paradigms without her having reflected on this relationship: when Balthazar points out to her that her library is "purely Western in orientation and that she reasoned and fought with concepts and ideas derived from Western thought," she can only fall silent [427]). Further, she is initially dismissive of those "feminine" traits, like affectivity, that do not appear to her to have any role in the liberation struggle, and so misses their re-visionary potential.

The one-sidedness of Déborah-Nicol's character in this respect is most clearly illustrated through the contrast that is established with her sister's daughter Anaïs-Alicia. The latter is the binary opposite—but also complementary other half—of her aunt. An ethereal creature defined by her affectivity and "sweetness," she seems able always to uncover another side to the brutalities Déborah-Nicol rails against, to empathize with the human element in each catastrophe:

> When Déborah-Nicol recounted to her the landing of colonialist sailors, the sweet child saw there the pathetic beauty of men lost at sea who found finally the sanctuary of a landscape. If Déborah-Nicol described to her the horror of an Amerindian charge against the fires of bombardment, she forgot the blood to magnify the defiant heroism that haloed the massacre. . . . For any situation, she effortlessly unearthed the unexpected charm of a very human detail, the axis of a positive vision that Déborah-Nicol did not see and that Anaïs-Alicia presented to her with such sweetness that the combative teacher suspected her of being simple-minded. (400)

Though Anaïs-Alicia's affectivity and empathy are of course not female traits (a point emphasized by Déborah-Nicol's contrasting worldview), as noted above they have conventionally been designated as "feminine" values; and increasingly *Biblique* will stress that such values, albeit understood unconventionally as not belonging naturally to a particular sex, must be integrated into concepts of resistance and freedom. The problems that arise from a failure to do so are highlighted by Déborah-Nicol's own limitations. Her concern strictly for the mechanics of exploitation prevents her from sensing the ways in which a community can bind itself together in the face of its deprivations. So, for example, when she takes the young Balthazar on a visit to the workers on the plantations, he realizes that "despite everything" Sunday remains a joyful time in the popular quarters, a day of "staggering fetes" (537). But to Déborah-Nicol such joy appears "indecent": "*The world is preyed upon by ogres and these people dance! There is blood in the air and these people sing!* She held herself stiffly, refused to wiggle her hips, affected to understand nothing of the music and to not know how to dance" (537–38, emphasis in the text). The inability to grasp how these activities, through their affirmation of community, are vital to the struggle against oppression is an indication of Déborah-Nicol's wider failure to consider fully the reconstructive—and not only reactive—side of liberation.

Such shortcomings underline the need for that redemptive, human sensibility embodied in Anaïs-Alicia. Though on their own the qualities of affectivity and empathy, which underpin the alternative vision she articulates, are as limited as Déborah-Nicol's narrowly denunciatory attitude, when combined with resistance and efforts at structural reorganization they point the way to the thoroughgoing transformation of social relations. Gradually, both Déborah-Nicol and Balthazar come to recognize this, but its implications are only fully grasped by the latter towards the end of his life. It is then that he connects his earlier abandoning of Anaïs-Alicia—he left Saint-Joseph for the forest and found her vanished on his return, an event that precipitates his consolidation of a sovereign rebel selfhood—to the realization that "none of the freedoms he had given birth to [*engendrées*] with his weapons had truly flourished; there remained in his wake only death, pain, and oppression organized now by those who had been his brothers in combat" (838). The image of Balthazar parenting the liberty of various communities returns us to the motif of the male who engenders national consciousness, and so to Césaire's masculinist Rebel. But his failure here—the perpetuation of relations of domination in the "postcolonial" world—emphasizes the need for the incorporation of the "feminine"—of the legacy of Anaïs-Alicia—as part of a more general reformulation of notions of identity, itself integral to the attempt to effect a political change able to bring true freedom from past ideologies and social structures.

What this incorporation of the "feminine" might mean for the transformation of models of selfhood and community can be approached through Nelly Richard's arguments regarding the subversive effect of "feminine" values on discourse. Taking as her starting point the marginalized position of these values, she contends that to feminize the dominant cultural framework is to submit it to a resistant rereading, one that undoes the "normalizing control of masculine/hegemonic discursivity" by exposing it to the "rebellious surpluses (body, libido, pleasure, heterogeneity, multiplicity, etc.)" of the "feminine."[22] Thus, summarizes Richard, "this theoretical aperture which extends the contestatory valence of the feminine to a range of anti-hegemonic practices—in order to weave solidarity-based alliances transversal to the categorizations of sex and gender linearly defined—holds, for me, the advantage of breaking down a biological determinism in which anatomical functions (being a woman/being a man) and symbolic roles (the feminine/the masculine) correspond naturalistically, based on the myth of an original body's Singular Identity."[23] This passage emphasizes how the "feminine" can become a basis for political resistance as a marker for a set of social values to which opponents of the dominant order can adhere, thus uniting both sexes on the grounds of common sociopolitical desires. Indeed, Richard's remarks return us to the rebellious genders of the hermaphrodite *danmyé* warrior, Polo Carcel, who might now be viewed as a utopian figure for the call to break with the "myth of the original body's Singular Identity." His bursting of the shell of sovereign subjectivity makes Polo the literal embodiment not only of the idea of "femininity" as a contestatory category through which to "weave solidarity-based alliances," but also of the revised form of subject relations required to help fulfill the political drive for liberation.

As noted earlier, people like Polo constantly appear to Balthazar in war zones, their mix of sexes and genders signaling resistance to those binary categorizations imposed by the ruling order. Such resistance is "feminine" in Richard's sense of the term since it is different from—and, as Polo's exclusion by the other *danmyé* warriors emphasized, is further marginalized by—the masculinism of the traditional rebel posture, while also representing social values around which oppositional elements can rally. It is "feminine" too in terms of the values that define Polo's selfhood: here, two identities relate to each other in one body; and while one self might occasionally be "dominated by the other" (744), the rapport remains a dynamic, interactive one between specificities. Making this possible are the "feminine" traits of affectivity and empathy that characterize Polo's selfhood, and which revise the male and female sides within him in such a way as to render the claim to identity no longer the assertion of a sovereign self over and against an objectified other. Instead, it is based upon an empathetic identification made *in relation to* the other, something Glissant defines in terms of a shift in understanding from *"comprendre"* to *"donner-avec."* Both are ways of knowing, but the first ("to understand"), via its etymological link with *prendre* ("to take"), suggests an appropriative comprehension that reduces the other "to the model of my own transparency"; in contrast, the second ("to give-with") conveys a form of knowledge predicated on an acceptance of and a "giving" to the other in the sense of recognizing oneself through mutuality.[24] It is thus by way of this concept of "giving to" that the connection can be made to the "feminine" values of affect and empathy.

Accordingly, Polo's effacement of the "partition" between the sexes signals the effacement of a reified boundary between subject and object. He points toward a more relational form of identity, one that, when pursued alongside the fight to ensure that material conditions permit equality between those placed in relation, would help secure true freedom from ingrained patterns of domination.[25] He thereby also underlines to Balthazar how the latter's not being "woman enough everywhere" brought his liberation politics up short. Indeed, Balthazar's failure to achieve fully the kind of relational identification outlined above is emphasized by the shortcomings in his dealings with women. Even as he fought against the *chosification* of oppressed peoples, moving outside of himself and his homeland to relate to—to "give" himself to—their cause, he continued to conceive of women as objects to be conquered. He realizes in his old age that he "had possessed [women] but . . . had not loved them" (315), that "he had not regarded them enough, . . . not esteemed them enough, he had always considered the prize of their cunt as the whole prize, and it was most often at this stage that he had stopped" (435). This failure to do more than objectify and consume women in "cannibal-loves" is, he sees now, the failure to free himself from conquistadorial structures (505). He goes on to make a further connection with his disposition to "play the martyr" (506). By locking himself into such a posture, shouldering the sacrificial burden of all in a self-affirming manner that closes him off to others, he forfeits reciprocity with, and hence cannot fully relate to, those around him.

From Balthazar's groping toward a revised model of gender and subject relations we can move finally to Chamoiseau's own attempt to transform traditional epic narrative form. *Biblique* continues the interrogation of how communal or national consciousness is to be expressed. In its critique of the figure of the martyr, it builds on *Texaco*'s search for a structure able to articulate the cultural entanglements and disjunctions of Caribbean history, moving beyond the tragic discourse that underpins *Et les chiens*, with its problematic connection to root identity, filiation, and an exclusive sacrificial founding act. Where *Biblique* goes further is in its attention to the excision of women in this discourse. Its incorporation of a revised notion of femininity, as part of an explicit deconstruction of conventional gender categories, unravels previous narrative tropes. Indeed, the expanded sweep of the novel as compared to *Texaco*—the move from a Martinican epic to a global one referencing liberation struggles worldwide—can be understood in terms of the incorporation of the "feminine" insofar as the latter is linked to the formulation of a relational model of identity able to mediate between specificity and contingency. In this way, the model provides also for a form of mediation between the national and the global; and it is this that we see reflected in *Biblique*'s expansive, accretive form, its accumulation of histories and epic stories. In the political conflicts surrounding the attempts of oppressed communities to claim equality in a global framework, the "feminine" can come to stand for a series of resistant social values decoupled from strict biological correspondences. Integral to these values is the potential they have for reconstructing subject relations on different axes from those that structure reifying or conquistadorial identifications; hence must Balthazar be "woman enough everywhere" to bring the promise of his rebellion to fruition.

Notes

1. Chamoiseau, *Biblique des derniers gestes*, 808. Further references to this novel will be given in parentheses in the text. Unless otherwise stated, all translations from the French are mine.
2. Richard Price and Sally Price, "Shadowboxing in the Mangrove," 19.
3. Arnold, "*Créolité*," 24.
4. See Milne, "The *marron* and the *marqueur*," 72–73.
5. Sommer, *Foundational Fictions*, 56.
6. Ibid., 57.
7. Burton, *Famille Coloniale*, 19.
8. Ibid., 41.
9. Ibid., 81.

10. Glissant, *Discours antillais,* 168. Further references to this book will be given in parentheses in the text.

11. For convenience, I refer to Polo only as "he" here, just as the novel does initially; interestingly, once Balthazar discovers Polo's secret, the text begins using the plural definite article (les/des/aux Polo Carcel) to describe him/her.

12. Arnold, "Erotics of Colonialism," 169.

13. Ibid., 170.

14. Burton, *Famille Coloniale,* 67.

15. Glissant, *Poetics of Relation,* 143.

16. Ibid., 47, 143.

17. On the need to revise and rearticulate epic discourse, see Glissant, *Poetics of Relation,* 47–62.

18. A healer with great power and an expansive knowledge of local history, the landscape, sacred customs, and cultural rituals.

19. On the conventions of the folktale, see Propp, *Morphology of the Folk Tale.*

20. Richard, *Masculine/Feminine,* 27.

21. Ibid., 14.

22. Ibid., 22.

23. Ibid., 22.

24. Glissant, *Introduction,* 71.

25. Chamoiseau has stressed the importance of pursuing this material transformation if the revised form of subject relations he postulates is to be fulfilled. See *Écrire en Pays Dominé,* 300–301.

"Passing" through Time

El hábito hace al monje

Nineteenth-Century Cross-Dressing and (Bi-)Sexuality in Benítez-Rojo's *Mujer en traje de batalla*

Kerstin Oloff

In 1823 Enrique Faber, a doctor of European origin working in Cuba, was accused by his estranged wife of being a woman. Over the course of the ensuing trial, s/he was exposed as such through a humiliating physical examination and condemned to ten years' imprisonment for *her* "horrible crimes," which included having lived as a man "being really and perfectly a woman," having married another woman, and having made use of an instrument for the sexual act.[1] For the "insult and scandal that she ha[d] caused the Republic," she was sentenced to ten years in a correctional institute (later lowered to four years).[2] As documented by James J. Pancrazio, her case continued to evoke public interest in the years to come: the court proceedings of her trial were published in 1860 in the Cuban juridical journal *La Administración*, she was dedicated an entry in Francisco Calcagno's *Diccionario biográfico cubano* (1878), and her life was the subject of the novels *Enriqueta Faber, ensayo de novela histórica* (1894) by Andrés Clemente Vázquez and *Don Enriquito* (1895) by Francisco Calcagno.[3] This fascination with Enriqueta may at least partly be explained in light of Jacqui Alexander and Mimi Sheller's observations on female sexual autonomy. As Alexander states, "Women's sexual agency, [their] sexual and erotic autonomy have always been troublesome for the state. . . . Erotic autonomy signals danger to the heterosexual family and to the nation." The cross-dressed woman takes center stage in these texts, since she disturbs and disrupts the patriarchal colonial artifice and "the processes of heterosexualisation."[4]

Reimagining this historical figure provides an opportunity for Antonio Benítez-Rojo to explore issues surrounding female erotic agency that lie at the juncture of processes of racialization and heterosexualization. In this novel, "inter-bodily relations" become a site for the negotiation of "human dignity and thus for freedom in its widest sense," as Sheller puts it in a different context.[5] Benítez-Rojo paints a bleak picture of nineteenth-century Cuba, one of an emergent disciplinary society in which racial, patriarchal, and class oppression converge in the (white) conjugal family. It is through part 2—unfolding in Europe and Haiti and based on the life of the fictional character Maryse who lives through the Haitian Revolution—that Benítez-Rojo provides a Foucauldian lens through which to read his protagonist. Dismantling patriarchal conceptions of the family, Benítez-Rojo insists on the rejection of heteronormativity and on the queering of narratives of the past as a crucial step toward the full decolonization of contemporary Caribbean discourse and society. Further, through the protagonist's queer self-understanding, the novel puts in dialogue the nineteenth and twentieth centuries, redirecting its critique toward Cuban discourse on the nation and the post-revolutionary institutionalization of homophobia in the sixties and seventies.

Part 2 of the novel, named after Maryse, features a character called Achille Despaigne, a slave owner in pre-Revolutionary eighteenth-century Haiti through whom Benítez-Rojo inserts Enriqueta's case into the larger context.[6] Despaigne is a profit-driven, self-proclaimed expert on slaves and their value on the market who gradually develops methods to dispose of corporal punishment in order to maximize the "efficiency" of his "workers." Despaigne utilizes mechanisms that ensure the slaves' increasing individualization: he notes down the name, price, sex, skin color, height, and weight of each slave, as well as nation of origin (163); he traces behavioral patterns, records behavior, quality and quantity of the work accomplished, beliefs, sexual conduct, illnesses, and so forth (163–64) and distributes work accordingly. Further, he attempts to "improve the race" (165) by pairing tall men with wide-hipped women. Benítez-Rojo represents modern biopower in the colonial context as working both on the level of the individual and on the level of populations, which it seeks to control through discourses revolving around morality or, in the nineteenth century, through pseudoscientific discourses such as eugenics and positivism.[7] As Foucault has argued, the modern capitalist disciplinary modality of power reverses the relations of audibility and visibility of the system of sovereign power. Power is exercised through inconspicuous but detailed direction and organization of activity and "imposes on those whom it subjects a principle of compulsory visibility."[8] For Despaigne, the disciplinary modality of power proves more cost-effective than brutality; he even considers building a panoptic tower—"a round tower, something like a lighthouse"—to follow every movement of his slaves with a telescope (164). According to Foucault, Bentham's panopticon is not qualitatively different from other modern institutions but "merely reproduces, with a little more emphasis, all the mechanisms that are found in the social body."[9]

Pre-revolutionary Haiti provides a lens through which to read Enriqueta's life in colonial Cuba. When Enriqueta first arrives in Cuba as Enrique, her mentor Maryse complains that Havana is the "city of paperwork," and Enrique's application to become a doctor requires other people's testimonies regarding his morality and conduct (442). Through his characters' extensive travels, Benítez-Rojo's novel brings out the global interconnectedness of eighteenth- and nineteenth-century political and economic developments, and it is in this context that he examines the emergence of modern understandings of sexuality and gender. It is in colonial Cuba that the effects of an emergent panoptic society are most strongly felt in the novel and that global capitalism shows its ugly racist and patriarchal face.

Slavery in Cuba was not abolished until 1886 and was central to the island's economic and social organization, as Cuba had emerged as the leading producer of sugar at the end of the eighteenth century. It was a highly hierarchical and racialized society with few possibilities for social mobility. Maryse bitterly complains, "Slavery reigns over the island. No one can avoid this sad reality" (432). Slavery also partially determined the gender roles available to white middle- and upper-class women, who were "subjected to seclusion, discrimination, limited options, and gross double standards of acceptable social behaviour,"[10] even more so than in other Western—metropolitan and colonial—societies. As Martínez-Alier explains, "By controlling the access to female sexuality, control was exercised over the acquisition of undesirable members by the group."[11] In colonial Cuban society marked by machismo, white women had to be virtuous, chaste, pure, passive, and the guardians of the family's honor. Given the highly racialized context in early nineteenth-century Cuba, the dominant discourse on morality and honor did also extend to race, as all those considered "nonwhite" were—not unlike "fallen" women—constructed as "impure."[12] An interracial marriage—and, more specifically, a union between a white woman and a black/mixed-race man—would thus become a "moral" problem for the rest of the family, whose social position and reputation would be threatened by such an alliance. The discourse on "morality" was thus a thinly veiled attempt to preserve the political and social status quo, which was threatened from all sides. In this context, interracial marriages became a matter of political concern, so much so that colonial authorities deemed it necessary to introduce legislation to regulate and restrict such unions.[13] In nineteenth-century Cuba, patriarchal, race, and class oppression converged in the family, and here, more specifically, in the white woman's body and her sexuality. As Alexander explains, "Attempts to manage sexuality . . . are inextricably bound to colonial rule. In fact the very identity and authority of the colonial project rested upon the racialization and sexualization of morality."[14]

The problematic status of interracial relationships surfaces in an exchange that takes place before Enrique's wedding to Juanita and is voiced by her aunt, Doña Asunción. After finding out about the bad state of her health due in part to malnourishment, Enrique asked the aunt to allow Juanita to move in with him, but the offer is rejected. Doña Asunción emphasizes her niece's honor, reputation, education, and "purity" of blood (476) and indirectly suggests that Juanita is not a bad match in marriage for Enrique. Without relatives, Enrique has no proof of his family honor and "pure blood." According to Martínez-Alier, those who had no family "were frequently forced to marry down" (21). To fit into Cuban society, Enrique has to play by the local rules regulating family life. It is against this racialized moral background, in which a white woman's conduct is invested with the honor of an entire class, that Enriqueta's "crime" is judged.

The colonial *machista* concept of the family—based on the naturalization of gender divisions, racial and female oppression, and compulsory heterosexuality—played a structuring role in the development of national discourse and often continued to structure social life. By emphasizing the centrality of gendering and compulsory heterosexuality to colonial society, Benítez-Rojo makes it clear that a critique of homophobic and sexist ideologies is vital to a full decolonization of Caribbean discourse and, more specifically, of the concept of the Cuban nation. As Bejel explains, from the beginning of modern Cuban history, Cuban nationalist leaders "ha[d] often defined the homosexual body, implicitly or explicitly, as a threat to the health of the body of the nation," thus ironically making it a constitutive element of it.[15] In his analysis of José Martí's novel *Amistad funesta* (1885; Fatal friendship), for instance, Bejel shows how the "manly woman" is constructed as a threat to the "national family" (27). However, as he argues, it was after the Revolution and the institutionalization of the repression of homosexuals in the sixties and seventies—most notably through the UMAPs (forced labor camps for "antisocial" members of society that existed from about 1965 to 1968), the "Yellow Brigades" (aimed at reeducating "effeminate" schoolboys), the First National Congress of Education and Culture in 1971 (which passed a number of homophobic resolutions)—that, by opposition, "the category of homosexuality became a more obviously constitutive part of the very concept of the Cuban nation."[16]

This provides the context for Benítez-Rojo's celebratory exploration of Enriqueta's cross-dressing and her sexuality, both of which have contributed to making her a figure of considerable public interest in Cuba. In the court proceedings of her trial in *La Administración,* Enriqueta is described as having an "an exceedingly mannish" character, as possessing the "spirit of a man imprisoned in the body of a woman."[17] In other words, she is described as a cross-gendered "invert." In her own declaration before the court, she similarly states that "her temper not being, since childhood, suited to women's habits," her uncle arranged her marriage to Renaud in order for her to adopt "the true behaviour of a woman"; heterosexual marriage is viewed by her uncle as the potential "cure" for a perceived "gender deviance."[18]

With regard to her second, same-sex marriage, her former wife Juana and Enriqueta's statements disagreed on the timing of Juana's realization that the latter was a woman. While Enriqueta stated that Juana had known her sex prior to marriage (a statement she later revoked), her former wife claimed not to have known until later, and to have been deceived through the use of an "instrument" for the sexual act.[19] Enriqueta's claim is clearly unthinkable within the official discourse, in which Juana is described as "innocent" and "naïve," the opposite of the gender deviant who upsets social norms.[20]

It is similarly unthinkable within the two above-mentioned novelistic treatments of her, *Enriqueta Faber* (1894) by Andrés Clemente Vázquez (for whom Faber was "a precursor of feminism and the equality between the sexes" as Pancrazio puts it)[21] and *Don Enriquito* (1895), republished as *El casamiento misterioso* (1897; The mysterious marriage), by Francisco Calcagno. As Powell demonstrates, both novels use Enriqueta as a symbol (for Cuba or the threat of foreign corruption, respectively).[22] Despite the respective authors' opposing attitudes toward social change, the possibility of a sexual relationship between two women is repressed in both texts. Vázquez's novel (which traces Enriqueta's life from the Napoleonic battlefields to Cuba and beyond) seeks to redeem Enriqueta by denouncing women's inequality and hence demonstrating how her actions were merely a response to social inequality. As Vazquez's Enriqueta puts it, "Woman had always been a slave, considered a piece of furniture, a thing, an object destined simply for the pleasures of the male sex."[23] Throughout, the fight against gendered oppression is linked to racial and class struggle (Enriqueta even befriends the children of Toussaint L'Ouverture). Yet the "threat" of female same-sex eroticism remains always close to the surface; for instance, when Carlota (Enriqueta's dead husband's sister) declares her love for Enriqueta, the sentiment is immediately sublimated as sisterly and any future "threat" is prevented by (the fictional) Carlota's death (96); later on in the plot, Enriqueta's declaration to her wife-to-be, Juana, also works as a rebuttal of the charge of same-sex eroticism: "My temperament being cold as marble, it is not in need of the strong impressions of material love" (174). Ultimately, Vazquez's novel seeks to erase the "queer" Enriqueta from history and render her sexuality invisible, despite his overall sympathetic representation of the female struggle for equality.[24]

In Calcagno's much less sympathetic portrayal focused on her life in Cuba, Enriqueta serves to provide a negative example of moral depravity that, in the words of Powell, evokes "the need for strict moral control, for women to embrace stabilizing roles . . . as wives, mothers, and defenders of the home and, by extension, the nation."[25] Enriqueta is derided throughout and functions as the potential obstacle to the heterosexual romance (between Catibo and Juana) that allegorizes the ideal national family (from which she needs to be ousted). While same-sex desire is denied through Enriqueta's proposition that she would serve as the father for any children Juana might have as a result of extramarital affairs, it nevertheless disturbs, as becomes clear in a mocking exchange between the governor general and the bishop: "But, what objective, father, could this same-sex marriage have? To this I find no solution.—Nor I."[26]

In contrast to these two novels, Benítez-Rojo's twenty-first-century version follows Enriqueta's original claim that Juana was in fact aware of marrying a woman. In *Mujer,* they thus live for a very brief time in a fully fledged relationship, despite the fact that Juanita enters it merely for financial security. Further, Enriqueta's relationship with Juanita is not the first physical and emotional relationship she has had with a woman. The six parts are in chronological order and are named after Enriqueta's lovers/partners except for part 2 ("Maryse"). Narrated in parts 3 and 4, both of her two previous relationships with women take place before her time in Cuba, but after the formative time spent with Maryse's wandering circus, where she gradually adopts a nonjudgmental attitude toward same-sex and nonconjugal heterosexual relationships. In the remaining two parts, 1 and 4, Enriqueta engages in two heterosexual relationships.

The structure of the novel, then, emphasizes her bisexuality; or rather, one might say, it demonstrates her "queer" anti-identitarian refusal to define her sexuality. Unlike the version of Enriqueta that emerges from the court proceedings, this Enriqueta is no invert: she is conscious of her performance of gendered roles, whether masculine or feminine; furthermore, instead of claiming a "male" sexual desire, she insists that she loves other women as a woman (482), a possibility that has been erased from the legal documents. This is of course significant also in another context, since gender inversion was still commonly associated with homosexuality during the time of the UMAPs, when sexual orientation was inferred from "inverted" mannerisms.

Throughout the novel, Benítez-Rojo engages with contemporary issues surrounding sexuality and gender, most obviously articulated in his portrayal of Enriqueta as "queer" and a conscious performer of gender. Following the second-wave feminist distinction between gender and sex, Benítez-Rojo consistently de-links gender from sex, revealing gender as a cultural product rather than a natural effect of the sexed body. Enriqueta learns to imitate masculine behavior, including movements, gestures, and the right way of sitting (220), but this does not change her personality or "nature." Being a "man" initially costs her some effort since, unlike her destitute double Fauriel, who was from birth raised as a boy, she has been socialized as a woman. In *Mujer*, it is particularly through the character of Maryse that Benítez-Rojo clearly alludes to an understanding of gender as performance. Maryse—who has worked for many years performing in opera and theater—compares Enriqueta's "becoming" a man to taking on a role in a play (190); she claims that "el hábito hace al monje" (69, 192—literally translated, "the clothes make the monk"). Powell has therefore emphasized *Mujer*'s theoretical closeness to Judith Butler's claim that gender "is performatively constituted by the very expressions that are said to be its results."[27]

In certain respects the perspective offered in *Mujer* also differs from the one popularized in the field of Queer Studies. While second-stage feminists in the seventies saw "womanhood" as a basis for political solidarity, Black feminists critiqued the fact that "woman" was based on its White middle-class version and emphasized the interrelatedness of class, racial, and gendered oppression. Postmodernist constructivist feminists further challenged and deconstructed gender categories. As Caroline New summarizes, "As strong social constructivism became increasingly fashionable, many scholars, including feminists, came to identify the social world with the cultural realm, with discourse or 'text.'"[28] For

Butler, even sex and sexual difference do not preexist socialization, but are socially constructed, and she claims that there is no subject behind the performance of gender. There is a difference, then, between showing that gender is a performance (rather than a natural correlative to sex), and Butler's theories regarding the performativity of gender, in which the focus shifts from material forms of oppression to the discursive level.

While for Butler there is no "sex" as such, since it is always already "gender,"[29] in *Mujer* there is a continued emphasis on the sexed body as outside of the cultural realm of the performance of gender. Enriqueta's female body constitutes a continuous obstacle to her performance of masculinity. Unlike the categories of gender and sex that belong to the transitive dimension, the characteristics of the body (including sexual difference) belong to the intransitive realm, something unaltered by the fact that the human knowledge of it is always mediated.[30] This emphasis on the extra-cultural reality of the body provides the lens through which to read Enriqueta's trial, in the process of which Enriqueta has to undress in front of the judge, two doctors, and a scribe and is forced to undergo a humiliating bodily exam to "fix" once and for all her social identity. It is ironically the necessity of the physical exam to determine the possession (or lack) of a phallus as well as the emphatic assertion that she is "really and perfectly a woman" that severs the supposedly natural link between her sex and the social identity that it implies. Yet it also painfully reminds the reader of the inescapable of her sexed body (inescapable in the nineteenth century, that is), as well as of the fact that the power of oppressive gender orders derives precisely from their referring to an actual, extra-cultural sexual difference.

Further, Enriqueta's time with the traveling circus and her relationship with Fauriel emphasize that class affects all aspects of one's life, including one's gender performance and sexuality. Benítez-Rojo engages here in a dialogue with Angela Carter's *Nights at the Circus*. Carter's protagonist Fevvers provides a positive example of how a highly self-conscious performance of gendered identity can be empowering, but *Nights at the Circus* also explores the limitations of "gender as performance" as a form of resistance. In particular, the male clowns in the circus represent constructionist theory devoid of any idealist capacity of reconstructing new models. They engage in parodic castration, but the clowns' castration does not result in change, as the phallus simply grows back. The clowns therefore mimic and deconstruct, but these practices are not equated to opposing patriarchal narratives. In Benítez-Rojo's rewriting of the clown scene, a cross-eyed clown develops an unhealthy obsession with Enriqueta (who, at that point, dresses in women's clothes). As a co-owner of the circus, Enriqueta occupies a special place, not having to work for her living and enjoying sexual relations with two different men. One evening, Enriqueta finds the clown Vincenzo on her bed with a fake phallus that he pretends to masturbate. Vincenzo flees before she can identify him, and a deeply disturbed Enriqueta seeks comfort with Maryse and her rich white Cuban lover Robledo. After Vincenzo's irruption in her room, Enriqueta understandably feels threatened by the gender violence implied in this culturally charged symbol, but the phallus in this scene is also a mark and mask of Vincenzo's disempowerment. As Maryse reminds Enriqueta, there is a significant economic difference between her (a wealthy widow) and the circus performers, who see her as out of their reach. Through a conversation that involves the wealthy, somewhat dim-witted, plantation owner Robledo, Benítez-Rojo reflects on the relation between social status and "beauty": "Think of the unsatisfied desire of those who are at a disadvantage compared to us, the beautiful people. . . . Think of how terrible it must be to feel unappreciated because one is cross-eyed or hunchbacked or lame or simply ugly.—Or a slave, added Maryse" (140). "Beauty" and "ugliness" do not, of course, refer straightforwardly to physical attributes, but acquire their relative value in a cultural context overdetermined by race, age, and social status. In the (ex-)slave-holding Caribbean societies, "whiteness" was often seen as more desirable than "blackness," as a direct result of racial social stratification. Through Maryse's comment, Benítez-Rojo offers an understanding of racism as a specific kind of classism, one that Robledo exhibits in his discourse on beauty. Of course, Robledo includes himself in his own definition of "beautiful" people. His "beauty," which makes him nearly irresistible to Maryse despite the fact that he is a slave owner, is connected to his wealth: "He dressed in black and from his left ear hung a majestic grey pearl in form of a pear; his greying hair, gathered at the back by a ribbon of red silk, was almost as long as mine" (117). Of course, the pearl in his ear—which he nonchalantly loses in a roulette game—was paid for by slave labor. His long hair and the hair band that blur the gender boundaries between him and the narrator become markers of Robledo's superior class position.

This emphasis on class is sustained throughout the novel. Enriqueta's ability to cross-dress, to inhabit a dual social identity, and to enjoy sexual relations with both men and women depends on her inherited wealth. Her inheritance sustains her adventures: she is able to pay for her medical school; she can support herself, owns various houses, and is able to have two servants; she has money and property to fall back on; she can even buy a French identity for her invented male alter ego (a Cuban national), and she has enough money to wipe her suspected desertion from the official archives. Furthermore, her cultural capital (her upper-class education and upbringing) and her social connections with people in positions of influence (such as her uncle who is an army doctor) clearly facilitate her role changes. In Cuba, where she lacks social and familial connections, her position is much more fragile, a fragility accentuated by the fact that her family fortune is rapidly dwindling.

Enriqueta's position of privilege becomes most obvious through Benítez-Rojo's insertion of her destitute double named Fauriel, a cross-dressing woman with whom Enriqueta has a relationship in France until the latter is recruited into the army, deserts, and disappears from the novel. Prior to her recruitment, Fauriel was among the poorest students at medical school and was only able to attend thanks to a state fellowship (245). Since her parents were poor, they had chosen to register and raise her as a man in order to avoid the double oppression of gender and class and to ensure that she would be able to practice a profession rather than needing a dowry. Fauriel moves and acts like a man (252) but, unlike Enriqueta/Enrique, she is unable to buy herself several identities and cannot escape being a man socially, except for the few occasions when Enriqueta takes her to dances dressed as a woman. Like Enriqueta/Enrique, she has also had sexual encounters with men, consummated in public bathrooms. One night, after confessing her love for one of her university professors to Enriqueta and describing their failed attempt at sex in a public toilet, she emphasizes the difference there is between them: "I am tired [estoy cansada] of being a man. . . You don't have any idea what it means to me to speak to you from woman to woman, even if only for two or three hours. It means being myself [yo misma], speaking with my own voice, being able to tell you that I love a man. . . . If I hadn't been born poor, I could be married [casada] to someone!" (260). Fauriel consistently uses the female form of adjectives in Spanish, a heavily gendered language. Unlike Enriqueta, who will eventually choose to live permanently as a man in Cuba, Fauriel feels imprisoned by the masculine identity that was imposed on her. Fauriel's fate is decided by the fact that rural nineteenth-century France was profoundly patriarchal, and "families consistently demonstrated a preference for male offspring" for economic reasons.[31] Fauriel's cross-dressing is not subversive, but a function of patriarchal oppression. While Benítez-Rojo clearly does not see masculinity or femininity as "essential" qualities, he does acknowledge that gendered social roles have a strong structural and material reality that is not easily overcome. In Enriqueta's heterosexual relationships with Robert and Christopher and her lesbian relationships with Nadezda and Fauriel, it is her cross-dressing and the secrecy that surrounds her sex that makes up part of her attraction to them. Fauriel's sexuality instead is severely restrained by her cross-dressing, and she longs for a more conformist relationship of which she never had any experience and therefore does not perceive as potentially oppressive.

Fauriel's desertion and disappearance starkly contrast with Enriqueta/ Enrique's flamboyant life and ability to choose between destinies. Enrique serves as an army doctor in Russia and in Spain, where she gets captured. As a war prisoner, she has a brief relationship with a Scottish doctor named Christopher and becomes pregnant with his child (whereas the historical Enriqueta had a child with her first husband, a French army officer). Benítez-Rojo's Enriqueta chooses not to inform the father, to have this child by herself and out of wedlock. Her wealth is what makes it possible for her to withdraw to a private cottage and have a child as a single mother without having to conceal her pregnancy from any employers, without having to fear poverty, and without fearing the dishonor attached to illegitimate pregnancy—clearly not an option readily available to most women in nineteenth-century rural France. The notion of a "pure" maternal instinct is thus thrown into question and revealed as partially influenced by social, cultural, and material circumstances. While Vazquez's novel evokes motherhood as a way to emphasize Enriqueta's "natural" femininity, Benítez-Rojo's Enriqueta's claims never to have felt "more woman" (409) than after her son's birth are qualified—denaturalized—by this emphasis on other factors.

Benítez-Rojo's vision presents gendered oppression as part of capitalism's perpetuation of an unequal division of labor and therefore echoes the views of contemporary socialist feminists such as Chandra Talpade Mohanty, who argues for an antiracist feminism that would entail decolonization, anticapitalist critique and solidarity among the oppressed.[32] Enriqueta's individual(ist) struggle for the right to study and to exercise a profession is contrasted with the struggle for Black civil rights and the decolonization of Haiti represented by the character of Portelance, who is an aide to Toussaint L'Ouverture (a variation on Vazquez's plot line). The novel clearly portrays their respective actions as part of the same struggle. *Mujer* is attentive to the interrelatedness between class, race, and gender oppression and further adds an emphasis on female sexuality (both heterosexual and same-sex) to Vazquez's concerns. Enriqueta comes to display a "queer" self-understanding and refuses to normalize sexuality; as she phrases it, "Even supposing that such amorous overflow was the consequence of an abnormal psyche, I never perceived it as a disgrace, a limitation, illness or chronic aberration, not even as a worry. My desire took shape in a natural way, as if it was a physiological function" (481).[33] In addition to these explicit statements refusing to label her sexual desires, the naming of the chapters gives central importance to the objects of her desire in structuring the narrative of her life. Perhaps her two most striking title choices are "Nadezda" and "Christopher," since brief encounters are given preference over going to war and the birth and death of a son. It is here useful to turn to Rosemary Hennessy who seeks to historicize sexuality, arguing that until a paradigm shift occurred at the turn of the nineteenth century, gendered behavior was seen as more important than who was the object of one's sexual desires. While in the Cuban context gender continued to function as an assumed indicator of sexuality,[34] gender, in Hennessy's argument, was "gradually and unevenly" replaced by defining identity through sexual object choice.[35] The reification of "human potential for sensation and affect into sexual identities" (105)—of gay and straight identities—emerged with the recruitment of women into the workforce and structural changes in capitalist production that, among other things, produced newly desiring consumers (99). Pursuing this line of argument to trace the eventual emergence of Queer Studies toward the end of the twentieth century, Hennessy argues that "queer identity"—undefinable, mobile, anti-identitarian, free-floating, cultivating "ambivalence as a structure of feeling" (108)—is the expression of the middle-class service worker under late capitalism. According to Hennessy, the potential danger of theories and identities based on sexuality—whether straight, gay, or queer—is that they separate sex from class, disavowing the centrality of class struggle. *Mujer,* however, explores the complex interconnections of racial, sexual, and gendered exploitation. Enriqueta's in many ways postmodernist and queer self-understanding offers us a view of the past through a recognizably contemporary lens and thus calls our attention to the lessons that *Mujer* may hold for the second half of the twentieth century.

Do the clothes, then, make the monk? Gender, for Benítez-Rojo, is clearly a construction, and he de-links it from sex and sexuality in a consistent way, something that post-revolutionary Cuban ideologues were unable to do. Benítez-Rojo's engagement with feminism and issues surrounding gender and sexuality is conducted from a perspective that emphasizes the interrelatedness of racial, gendered, and class oppression and that situates the Caribbean as paradigmatic within an international perspective of global capitalism. As he writes in *The Repeating Island*, "The history of the Caribbean is one of the main strands in the history of capitalism, and vice versa" (5). While the novel invests utopian hope in Enriqueta's individualist resistance based on sexuality, subversion of gender roles, and a performative identity, Benítez-Rojo also introduces two subplots that double Enriqueta's fate and offer divergent perspectives. Fauriel is a poor Enriqueta; Portelance is, one might say, a political Enriqueta, since his involvement in the Revolution of Haiti contrasts with Enriqueta's more individualist fight against gendered and sexual oppression. *Mujer* cannot, and does not attempt to, provide a commentary on lesbian and gay experiences in Cuba today, but it seeks to redress the discursive construction of the Cuban nation, which has, as Bejel has pointed out, historically relied on a negative representation of homosexuality. Revisiting the life of a female cross-dresser, whose sexuality has been "tamed" or ridiculed in nineteenth-century literary treatments, his novel seeks to restore Enriqueta's sexual agency. Benítez-Rojo's critique, then, is two-pronged: it exposes the colonial origins of heteronormativity and invites us to reflect on the constituent homophobia of national discourse; it also invites us to apply Enriqueta's vision to revolutionary Cuba, denounces its homophobia, and exposes/highlights the re-entrenchment of traditional concepts of femininity and "natural" sexuality.

Notes

1. "La Administración, periódico jurídico, administrativo y rentístico," in Pancrazio, *Enriqueta Faber,* 86. This useful recent edition offers a compilation of texts on Enriqueta, including extracts from chronicles, novels, and the summary of the legal proceedings.

2. "La Administración," 87.

3. Pancrazio lists further texts published through the nineteenth and twentieth centuries (11–12). Another novel that may have been inspired by this case but that does not name Enriqueta is *Póstumo el envirginado* (1892; Posthumous, the en-virgined) by Puerto Rican Alejandro Tapia y Rivera, who lived in Cuba from 1857 to 1862 (Lizabeth Paravisini-Gebert drew my attention to this possible interconnection). The novel imagines the life of a soul that had previously inhabited a male body, is reincarnated as a woman, but still remembers *his* previous life. The soul with masculine habits becomes "en-virgined" but transgresses social boundaries in many ways, entertaining the possibility of relationships with both men and women, possessing masculine and feminine qualities,

cross-dressing, and turning into an advocate for female rights. In its transgressive approach to sexuality and gender, his novel contrasts strongly with the two Cuban novels mentioned here. Benítez-Rojo wrote an introduction to this novel for the 1998 edition published by Galaxia Gutenberg.

4. Alexander, "Erotic Autonomy," 64, 65. See also Sheller, *Citizenship from Below*.

5. Sheller, *Citizenship from Below*, 22.

6. Sklodowska suggests that this character is inspired by Juan D'Espagne, mentioned by Bacardí Moreau at the beginning of the nineteenth century (*Espectros y Espejismos*, 211).

7. On nineteenth-century positivism in Cuba and the discourse on the "degradations of human nature" (Benjamín Céspedes, qtd. in Bejel [29])—including homosexuality—see part 1, chapter 2, in Bejel, *Gay Cuban Nation*.

8. Foucault, *Discipline and Punish*, 187.

9. Ibid., 233.

10. Martínez-Fernández, "'Male City' of Havana," 105.

11. Martínez-Alier, *Marriage, Class and Colour*, 109.

12. Ibid. Eric Williams famously stated that "slavery was not born of racism: rather racism was the consequence of slavery" (*Capitalism and Slavery*, 7).

13. For more on this, see Martínez-Alier, *Marriage, Class and Colour*, 13, 27.

14. Alexander, "Redrafting Morality," 133.

15. Bejel, *Gay Cuban Nation*, xiii.

16. Ibid., 103. Several critics have pointed out that *Mujer* makes indirect references to post-revolutionary Cuban homophobia (see, for instance, Collard and Powell).

17. Pancrazio, *Enriqueta Faber*, 55.

18. Ibid., 59.

19. Ibid., 82.

20. Ibid., 56.

21. Ibid., 29.

22. Powell, *Fabricating Faber*, 21.

23. Vázquez, *Enriqueta Faber*, 59.

24. As Powell reports, Vázquez goes "to great lengths to mitigate Faber's transgressiveness, her attempt to 'be' a man, by way of emphasizing her femininity, and by repeatedly highlighting her role as mother" (*Fabricating Faber*, 100). The elision of her sexuality and of her transgressiveness is repeated in later texts (that often are based on Vazquez's novel), including, for instance, Emilio Roig de Leuchsenring's account from 1946, also reprinted in Pancrazio's edition (143–56).

25. Powell, *Fabricating Faber*, 29. See also Cuadra, "Entre la historia y la ficción."

26. Calcagno, *Don Enriquito*, 165.

27. Butler, *Gender Trouble*, 33. Powell, *Fabricating Faber*, 190.

28. New, "Sex and Gender," 55.

29. Butler, *Gender Trouble*, 43–44. See also New, "Sex and Gender," 57.

30. New, "Sex and Gender," 56, 66.

31. Dalby, "Women and Infanticide," 346.

32. See Mohanty, *Feminism without Borders*.

33. Benítez-Rojo's twenty-first-century understanding of key issues such as sexuality, history, and the unconscious comes to the fore when the supposedly nineteenth-century narrative voice of Enriqueta speaks of "rhizomatic stories," "stories of the mangrove" (460), and justifies her lack of interest in psychology by reminding us that she is pre-Freudian (481).

34. Lumsden, *Machos, Maricones, and Gays*.

35. Hennessy, *Profit and Pleasure*, 99–100. Further references to this book will be given in parentheses in the text.

"Love the Drag . . . but Your Purse Is on Fire!"

Cross-Dressings in the Religious Imaginary of *Aelred's Sin*

Lee Easton and Kelly Hewson

WE WOULD like to begin our essay with three seemingly disparate but related fragmentary moments.

> The story goes that on some unnamed festival day, Tallulah Bankhead, drunk as usual, attended Mass at St. Patrick's Cathedral. A thurifer, a robed acolyte swinging a smoking gold pot of incense on a gold chain, preceded the procession of priests down the aisle, and when Bankhead spotted him, she yelled, "Love the drag, darling, but your purse is on fire!"[1]

> In the 1940s it was illegal for a [Canadian] male to be dressed as a woman in public, a violation called, "Disguised by Night." Herbert's feminine physical appearance made him look like a high-class fashion model when dressed as a woman . . . . He was sentenced to four months' imprisonment in the Guelph Reformatory, spending his 21st birthday in prison in October of 1947.[2]

> The two photographs arrived today. Krishna brought them up in the post. I've propped them up on my desk on the verandah where I do the estate work. J.M. and Edward.[3]

The first is an anecdote featuring a famous American bisexual actress in a Catholic church who drunkenly calls a priest's robes "drag," inadvertently yet critically drawing attention to the instability of the gendered meanings of ecclesiastical garments. The next provides the historical context for the Canadian John Herbert's *Fortune and Men's Eyes* (1967), a play that demonstrates the state has long had vested interests in policing the bodies of citizens along hetero-patriarchal lines as well as reminding us that the roots of Canada's and the Anglo-Caribbean's various national laws—specifically those which govern gender, sexuality, and dress—reach back into early colonial times, when the practice of cross-dressing was a source of much royal concern and admonishment.[4] From the legacy of these hetero-patriarchal ideologies sprout new laws: there is not much distance, after all, between the Canadian Conservative government's legislation criminalizing anal sex under the age of eighteen and the legislation in Trinidad and Tobago and Barbados designating gay and lesbian sex as criminal.[5] Lastly, we offer a gesture that functions in Lawrence Scott's *Aelred's Sin* as the culmination of a voyage of excavation, self-reflection, and repair: a creole man sets a picture of his deceased gay brother, who had once been a monk, in a place of pride in the family's West Indian estate home. From New York to Toronto to England and the Caribbean: all coordinates within the Black Atlantic, all limning out a space where racial, sexual, and gender identities converge and overlap.

The creole man to whom our last fragment refers is Scott's narrator, Robert de la Borde. Structured as his memoir, *Aelred's Sin* charts Robert's journey to England from Les Deux Isles, precipitated by his desire to re-member and understand aspects of his brother's life in all its dimensions: as monk, as roving scholar, and, most significantly, as a homosexual. We have argued elsewhere that Scott's text embodies a process of narrative repair and have suggested it is fruitfully viewed through Gilroy's still controversial nomination of the Black Atlantic.[6] But we recognize the literary exploration of homosexual identity that Scott undertakes, and his text's foregrounding of the devastating costs of homophobia, racism, and colonialism demands a fuller investigation, given the particular way heteronormative masculinities in the Caribbean silence and exclude same-sex-desiring identities.[7]

Our investigation begins with Scott's decision to set his novel in a Catholic monastery as the plinth upon which to establish Robert's construction of Jean Marc de la Borde's story. Certainly, the setting functions to underscore the Church's intimate connection with the colonizing process—in fact, by housing most of the novel's action in a English monastery, Scott demonstrates Christianity's underwriting of "the fatal triangle" of slaves, sugar, and ships (434). That the "heart" of Christianity is powered by colonizing energy is evident not only in the Church's conversion initiatives but in the accompanying project of education, two points Scott makes in the novel's prologue (18). Further, though, such a setting provides him with the opportunity to explore what initially appears to be a purely homosocial space, devoid of women and, at first glance, femininity. While structured as a celibate (and presumably heterosexual) space, the Ashton Park monastery, rather, is better conceived as a hom(m)osocial space[8] which, concomitant with its circulation of a full range of same-sex desires, Scott's novel opens for examination. Moreover, the novel's setting within what is a transnational structure whose global reach makes it a significant and oft-underestimated purveyor of homophobic ideology reminds us that social space not only is representational but also encompasses specific lived spatial practices that cross national boundaries. Since the Church remains one of the central supporters of codes of respectability within the Caribbean, Scott defies many of the foundational binaries that structure social space along hetero-patriarchal lines, not only in the Caribbean but elsewhere in the Black Atlantic.

To explore this point, we take up the trope of cross-dressing, which has a vexed position in discussions of race, gender, and sexuality in both North America and the Caribbean.[9] It is to Fanon's construction of homosexuality as un-Caribbean that we refer and his weighty opinion that even if men from Martinique cross-dress, they remain, despite their gender-bending same-sex-desiring ways, real men who can "take a punch like any he-man."[10] To counter Fanon's assertion, we turn to the work of Marjorie Garber, who argues in her classic text *Vested Interests* that cross-dressing "offers a challenge to easy notions of binarity,"[11] calling into question categories such as female/male, and, especially germane to our inquiry, black/white, hetero-/homosexual, Caribbean/non-Caribbean. This destabilizing power is our departure point for our analysis of the relationships in *Aelred's Sin* structured around two cross-dressed figures: Jean Marc de la Borde and the enslaved boy Jordan. Both these figures embody the challenges to binarity that, Scott suggests, have structured hegemonic forms of masculinity in the Caribbean such as that which Fanon articulates. According to Garber, however, cross-dressing has a generative function too: the transvestite creates "what looks like a third term," but which she emphasizes is actually "a mode of articulation" and of central interest to our analysis, "a way of describing a *space* of possibility."[12] The transvestite, one can say, is a way of thinking through binarity *otherwise*. It is in this "otherwise thinking" that we locate not only the novel's sometimes submerged critical voice but also its dominant reparative voice.

At first glance, a novel set in a Catholic monastery would not appear to be the vehicle for what we propose to explore. However, as Tallulah Bankhead intuited and Marjorie Garber has shown, the "queerness" of ecclesiastic vestments in modern times has long signified cultural anxiety. Indeed, there is within Western culture a long tradition of using ecclesiastic costume to question and play with gender conventions.[13] In Scott's novel, set within a homosocial space where homosexual desire always threatens to erupt, when J.M. dons the ambiguously gendered robes of the monk, his racial identity—his brown skin—comes to the fore. Identified as the repressed feminine, J.M.'s suddenly transvestite body disrupts the all-too-fragile imaginary line separating homosocial and homosexual desire within the monastery that is so central to maintaining forms of hegemonic masculinity centered on heterosexuality. That this disruption is tied to race is not surprising. As Gayatri Gopinath argues, when queer desire encounters race, "the queer racialized body becomes a historical archive for both individuals and communities, one that is excavated through the very act of desiring the racial Other."[14] This excavation reveals the less-discussed historical roots of cross-dressing within the coercion of the enslavement, reminding us that far from always being a critical, transgressive, and liberatory practice, cross-dressing too is complicit in the colonial legacies of the Black Atlantic.

What follows then is a close reading of Scott's text that begins by exploring the concept of a religious imaginary, the one Scott represents largely within the confines of a Catholic monastery in England, which for all intents and purposes is a transnational space that constructs and positions its members as white, desireless men. We move to explore how this religious imaginary works to discipline J.M./Aelred into a sexless, homosocial subject in a white world. Here the instability of ecclesiastical vestments emerges full force: placed on Aelred's racialized body, the monks' frocks (re)introduce both femininity and homosexuality into this supposedly ideal, de-sexed space. Next we turn to the novel's portrait. Inspired by David Dabydeen's *Hogarth's Blacks* (1987), this fictional portrait forms a crucial counterpoint to the naturalized and naturalizing cross-dressing of the monks at Ashton Park: the cross-dressed boy in the portrait operates as a critique of the uses of clothing to enforce the white master's ideas about race and gender in the Black Atlantic's founding moment. Scott's novel, however, allows for cross-dressing to be viewed also as a means for repair and redemption, which might counterbalance the forms of hegemonic masculinities that dominate the hetero-patriarchal space of the Caribbean.

A Place Untouched by Time: Conceiving the Social Space of the Religious Imaginary

Kenneth Routon concludes in his review of work in the field of transnational studies, referring specifically to an ethnography of Yoruba-based religious practices in the Caribbean, that there is a "need to consider forces other than capitalism . . . as the mediums through which transnational identifications are forged."[15] Routon's observation is especially applicable to Scott's *Aelred's Sin,* which outlines a sometimes neglected force in creating transnational identities—the Catholic Church, an entity that routinely moves individuals, money, and images across national boundaries. As Povenilli and Chauncey note, transnational and globalization studies have tended to produce analyses focused on how increased speed and density of communication exchanges, linkages, and movements change the local, the regional, and the global in capitalism.[16] Noting the impact of Puerto Rican migration to New York, Povenilli and Chauncey emphasize that queer scholars must also come to terms with how transnational movement between these regions shapes sexual identities.[17] Scott, too, is interested in exploring transnational migrations and their effects on sexual identity in the Black Atlantic, but he chooses to focus also on movements in *time* which, far from compressed, extend over nearly a millennium: from the story of Aelred, the twelfth-century homosexual monk who wrote about how to live chastely within a homosocial space, to the critical moment of the Black Atlantic's emergence, to the moments of Caribbean nations' independence in the 1960s, to Black Power and Gay Liberation in the 1970s, and ending in 1984 at the time of another great crisis, AIDS. Rather than focus on the speed with which communication occurs, Scott emphasizes the measured, repeating rhythms of centuries-old Christian monastic life, whose social space exists alongside and intersects with that of capitalism but cannot be reduced to it. Scott's blurring of temporality fits into the patterns identified by Judith Halberstam's observation that queer cultures disrupt and rework heteronormative patterns of time and development to produce alternative temporalities.[18] Scott's reworking—re-membering—of time and history disrupts the Church's claims to eternal and ahistorical existence. In *Aelred's Sin,* the Church is a third space—a queer space, if you will—in which Scott explores the race/sexuality/gender triumvirate.[19]

The writer explores this space of possibility in the novel's prologue, where he deftly sketches out the social space of a "religious imaginary." This space, we suggest, can be usefully separated by examining three intersecting components: image, practice, and affect—with a focus on how they function to colonize J.M.'s desires. Scott's initial images foster the notion that there is an ideal space of unitary identity. For J.M. in particular, the social space of the Church is imaged forth as orderly, de-sexed, and therefore safe masculinity, best captured by the figure of Dom Maurus, whose denatured body has "armpits [that] smelt of incense" (19). Although devoid of desire, this paradise is not devoid of color. This is a world of whiteness with "white marble" altars (18), "white wafers of communion" (19), "white pages" (18), and monks with "white hands" (18). Jean Marc de la Borde's imagined community has been inspired by his education in a Catholic-run school, where all colors of boys were equally embraced in the "white cotton habit" of the priest's dress (19),[20] where there is, it would appear, no difference that makes a difference, a space, too, where men can kiss and still be friends. These powerful spatial representations suggest that the Church will offer an inclusive space for all.

J.M. is attracted not only to the rich images of the Catholic Church but, more specifically, to the lived practices of the monastery and the potential of agency that adherence to its rituals promises. Faced with the death/suicide of his lover Ted, J.M. has nowhere to find himself in what Charles Taylor calls the "social imaginary"—the techniques whereby a narrative or discourse makes sense of the practices of a society[21]—so he relocates himself, imaginatively then actually, into a space deeply affecting to his younger schoolboy self: the "measured order" of the Benedictine monks' day, "controlled by the tolling of bells" (33). In this apparently timeless social space, there are no "bullers," only brothers, recruits from Catholic schools across the globe, "fully clothed and named, baptised anew" (34).[22]

The many stories of saints and martyrs that J.M. reads and hears have strong affective appeal, but none so strong as Dom Placid's retelling of the original Aelred's tale. In the tale's representational space, J.M. learns of "a band of men living and working together for love" (22). In the new wooden building on the River Rye, Aelred of Rievaulx found a space where "he could confess his love without fear, as in the *Song of Songs*" (23). J.M. is seduced by this loving hom(m)osocial space: "The boy went back to school with his heart full of passion and his head filled with ideals" (24). He holds fast to the notion promised by Aelred, the monk after whom J.M. will be renamed, that through adherence to the rituals of a holy communal life, one can experience power, the power of the transcendental; control, through the practice of celibacy; and, ultimately, love.

Scott, then, figures forth a religious Christian imaginary whose contours are those of overwhelming whiteness and repressed same-sex desire—or at least sublimated homosexual love—and largely absent of women and representations of femininity but for the white replica of "Michelangelo's *Pietà*: the limp, naked, dead Christ in Mary's his mother's lap" (18). As Margaret Gibson explains, the figure of Mary in Christian myth is symptomatic of a hom(m)osexual salvation economy that posits women as the feminine-maternal, who mediate the primary father-son bond and other same-gender ties.[23] It is J.M.'s transvestite status that will disturb this collapsing. As creole he is neither white nor black, and as a buller, he fits neither within the heterosexual economy of Les Deux Isles nor within the monastery's deliberately contained, carefully prescribed homosocial space.

Puttin' on "the Aelred": Lived Space and the Pedagogy of the Postulant

Andreas Gruschka outlines how the impulses governing Theodor Adorno's famously inspiring pedagogical imperative that education must ensure there never be another Auschwitz were, unfortunately, reduced, through the domination of practical pedagogy in postwar Germany, to a series of tasks to be learned. Gruschka identifies this as "the pedagogy of postulates."[24] What resulted, he concludes, was the defining of tasks for democratic education without considering the conditions under which they may be realized.[25] We see a productive parallel between such criticisms and what we call here the pedagogy of the *postulant*. At the same time, the monastery and its religious imaginary are governed by an inspiring pedagogical imperative: love thy brother. As with Adorno's imperative, love thy brother—which one would assume to encompass the spectrum of male desire—gets reduced within the religious imaginary through a set of tasks and ceremonies to what is ultimately white hom(m)osociality. This reduction, similarly, fails to take into account the conditions under which its imperative may be realized.

In *Aelred's Sin,* the pedagogy of the postulant is the teaching that novitiates undergo to ascertain their vocation and learn how to engage it in the communally sanctioned fashion. Consisting of lessons in proper appearance, comportment, and attitude, this education, much like the colonial education of J.M.'s childhood, is about learning how to assume a white persona and, in J.M.'s case, to redirect his same-sex desires toward socially sanctioned homoerotic acts. Like the cross-dressing man or woman who must learn the ways of the opposite gender to successfully pass as the other, J.M. must learn the ways of whiteness and what is passable homoeroticism within the monastery. No small part of the pedagogy of the postulant is captured in the homoerotic ritual where the novices are stripped and clothed following "the rubrics according to the ancient traditions of monasticism" (31). His own clothing taken away, J.M. is clothed in a cassock, a girdle, a knee-length scapular and cloak, and then, following Catholic ritual, his feet are washed and kissed by the other monks. Finally, he is embraced and offered the monastic kiss of peace on each cheek. By the end of the ceremony of clothing, the old J.M. has been replaced by the "new" Aelred whose position is securely enmeshed with the space of hetero-patriarchy.

Or is it? On closer scrutiny, this "new" Aelred is a rather precarious creation, its instability highlighted by the ritualistic and carefully prescribed actions and statements of the clothing ritual. These ceremonies serve to anchor the performative meanings of the new habit in which J.M. finds himself garbed. The utterances and gestures are intended to secure the original signification of these "frocks," as a term, along with "gown," which denotes a male monk's attire. However, in the twentieth century, the ecclesiastical gown is not easily contained within its formerly masculine signification. As Bankhead's quip shows and Garber affirms, the monk's gown is loaded with gendered meanings, which are often used by contemporary performers to highlight and critique the gendered roles we inhabit.[26] Within the monastery and through its ancient chants, the feminized meanings presently ascribed to frocks, girdles, and gowns are renounced and repressed so that it seems natural for a group of men wearing dresses to live together, to kiss and hug each other without questions of homosexuality—indeed any sexuality—being raised.

Simultaneously, "the new man" is "put on" with a new name: "Aelred," the white monk of a millennium earlier. The performative nature of this "new" white identity is underscored by the novel's complicated use of color. J.M., brown himself, arrives in a brown suit that is carefully folded and put away in order to don, appropriately, the black frock, appropriate because "black" is the absence of color—ironically suggesting the way whiteness itself goes unmarked. Designed as a uniform to promote equality among brothers, the black frock attempts to cover up all traces of race, gender, and desire, but in so doing simply reinscribes whiteness. This inscription is not the same as the whiteness in Scott's prologue. Unlike the religious imaginary where all are encompassed within the priest's white habit—white combines *all* colors—this inscription of whiteness obliterates all difference. It is only the black boots of Ted, which J.M. wears into the monastery, that remain a grounded signifier, a reminder to the "old man" [J.M.] of Ted's dark skin and his and Ted's illicit love.

Crucially, the pedagogy of the postulant is not simply occurring on the level of representation, but also in lived spatial practices to which the postulants and initiated adhere. After the clothing ceremony, the monastic kisses given to Aelred are delivered by the monks "with their hands firmly placed on his shoulders" (36). Fraternizing among the monks is strictly regulated, hence the oft–repeated "never in twos, always in threes" (136). In the monastery, this triad is a disciplinary tactic that encourages the monks to police each other, to prevent the formation of more than the allowed-for spiritual friendships. In theory, while this ancient postulate may have once sufficed—as the example of the threesome of the original Aelred, Simon, and Waldef would attest—in conditions of cross-dressing, which we maintain are the conditions of the monastery, this postulate comes undone. Primarily, this unraveling occurs because the attitudinal requirements of this white space are resisted by the key players in the triad: Benedict, Aelred, and Edward.[27]

Among the attitudes expected in the monastery are obedience and deference. The eyes are to be lowered, suggestive of a lack of contact—indeed, when permitted to look, they are to look only *at* the performance for its proper enactment. However, some eschew this attitude: they have the vision to *look through* the various performances each engages in and are unable or unwilling to follow the house rules. Were Benedict, Aelred's appointed "guardian angel," capable of seeing Aelred only as a novice, the postulate would be observed. However, incited by a glimpse of Aelred's naked calf, Benedict finds himself caught in his own desires and sees in Aelred his former lover, Claire. Likewise, if Edward could perceive Aelred only as his brother monk, all would be contained, the line between the homosocial and homosexual secure. But he too sees through "Aelred" and his white performance to J.M.'s blackness, which he desires and, critically, upon which he acts.[28] These (mis)recognitions position Aelred as the transvestite, a category crisis, as Garber reminds us, that activates the repressed desires—hetero, homo, racial—that Ashton Park's inhabitants have assiduously denied. All these excessive desires disrupt the white hom(m)osocial economy of the monastery and its regulatory practices just as Benedict, Aelred, and Edward keep breaking the rules—meeting in twos and making more than eye contact.

When put into practice, the pedagogy of the postulants falls short of its desired goal if only because the pedagogy fails to consider its contexts—specifically the disruptive possibilities of difference and desire—so fixed is it on their containment and flattening. While it may have been possible in the time of post-Conquest England to contain same-sex desire through specific homoerotic acts, in the twentieth century these rituals are less efficacious. J.M.'s performance of "Aelred" is flawed: while he is able to dress the part, he cannot achieve the endpoint comportment and attitude of his white persona. J.M. refuses the choices on offer in this unitary world where all desires, genders, and races are subsumed into a hom(m)osexual salvation economy. In part, rejection is possible because of J.M.'s sudden sense of himself as a racialized subject who desires to know more about his history, the specific instances of his emergent subjectivity as a black man. If the Caribbean has no place for bullers, neither does the monastery: it seeks to either deny or displace same-sex desire. Central to this realization is the portrait that hangs in the stairway at Ashton Park.

The Portrait—Representational Space and the Pedagogy of Repostulation

Brother Aelred is dusting when he notices a portrait of a "gentleman of wealth" whom he speculates to be the previous owner of Ashton Park. He discerns from a barely legible title plate that the man is a Duke. But it is "the wide open face of the black boy" (77) kneeling at the man's feet that affects Aelred, initially provoking a memory of his childhood playmates, friends he was not allowed to invite to the house. Following this recognition of his family's privilege and prejudice, he gets drawn into the portrait's representational space—the world of which the picture speaks. The details of its background—towers and spires, and a port from which a tall ship was setting sail—along with the white Duke and the black boy in the foreground—draw us as well into what is a portrait figuring that disastrous emblem of modernity, the displacement and enslavement of black people by white people for white profit.

Transfixed by the portrait's representational space, Aelred finds himself caught up in a process of identification that is also linked to crossdressing. He notices the silks, satins, and taffetas in which the boy is dressed. "He mirrored and mimicked his master. He was a diminutive, his master's doll" (78), an observation followed by Aelred's face being "superimposed upon that of the boy whose face shone from beneath, so the black face seemed to be his own" (78–79). A memory floats up—one of his friends has been left out of the cricket game and was "jabbing at [J.M.'s] face pointing to the color of his skin. 'And you, de la Borde, all you French creole!'" (79). He remembers the story his nurse used to tell him of the captive boy Mungo. At this moment, "taking his eyes off the black boy, he saw Benedict standing in the open door staring at him . . . at his naked legs" (81). In this double moment, Aelred occupies a queer position: he is both viewed and viewer, at once the scopophilic object of another man's desire—occasioned by the revelation of his body beneath his ambiguously gendered clothes—and a (male) speaking subject who identifies for the first time with his racialized past.

Pivotal to our interpretation is Benedict's desiring gaze. He associates Aelred with Claire, to whom he was engaged to marry. Scott makes clear that J.M.'s "youth and his androgynous looks allowed [Benedict] to imagine Claire and have fantasies" (395), which "had stopped him on the staircase to look at [Aelred's] legs and [lift] his *habit* in the Lady Chapel" (395–96). By identifying J.M.'s "habit" here and elsewhere, his "smock," terms that generally denote female garb, Benedict positions Aelred as the feminine object of his male gaze: the transvestite in the monastery. This moment of queer desire—which Aelred's cross-dressed body activates—reinforces Gopinath's claim that "barely submerged histories of colonialism and racism erupt into the present at the very moment when queer sexuality is being articulated."[29] For Aelred, trying to understand the links between his viewing "the black boy's face, Benedict's disappearance, and then the distinct sense that Benedict had been staring at his naked legs" (81) becomes the central impetus to the story's unfolding. As Gopinath argues in relation to Stephen Frears's *My Beautiful Launderette,* "Queer desire does not transcend or remain peripheral to these histories but instead becomes central to their telling and remembering: there is no queer desire without these histories, nor can these histories be told or remembered without simultaneously revealing an erotics of power."[30] The black boy, dressed to mirror his master, points to the racial and imperial roots of cross-dressing. Presumably bought by the Duke, the boy is forced to dress in garb that mimics his owner—precisely as J.M. has been "dolled up" in the white monk's clothes to become Benedict's and the monastery's "Aelred." The spatial relations conceived within this portrait, however, are not restricted to Ashton Park and the imperial center. Elsewhere, in the northern corner of the Triangle, white painters were busily portraying indigenous people there in white garb—the "civilizing" garb of the white man and woman.

This is cross-dressing by coercion. Far from being resistant, empowering, and transgressive, which is often how cross-dressing is theorized, this form of cross-dressing is emasculating and debasing. For this is an instance of the body, in this case a black body, being disciplined through the forced donning of white man's apparel. Like Aelred, the black body is being "dolled up" into a white man's idea of what a black boy should be replete with its appropriate attitudes: in this case one of adoration, the attitude the Abbot promotes Aelred to adopt toward the Church when Aelred has confessed his homosexual transgressions. Significantly, the attitude portrayed in the boy is linked to the dog at the foot of the other side of the Duke; both are "plaintive" as they look up at their master—while the Duke himself is looking at neither the boy nor the dog, but "beyond the frame of the painting" (78). His narcissism—his "riches" surround him, not only in the form of jewels but also in his pets, both the boy and the dog, both domesticated and subordinated—and his ill-got power, evidenced by the context of the background, are what we see. What Aelred's seeing provokes is a crystallizing moment of identification—his connection with the boy in the painting opens him to a fuller understanding of his own racialized past—facilitated through the remembered stories of Mungo, who "[came] from Africa" to Malgretoute (79), channeled through the voice of Aelred's black nurse.[31]

The portrait articulates the hom(m)osocial space of the religious imaginary with the spaces of capitalism and modernity. Although the monastery may have existed prior to capitalism, it is nonetheless complicit in its operations—slave trade—and shares its hetero-patriarchal structure. The chants and rituals that contain the feminine and regulating homoerotic desire are shown to be deficient in the face of colonialism, which introduces another variable into the equation: race. This powerful signifier attracts and releases other forms of difference—those of gender and sexuality. The absence of women in the portrait is recapitulated in the novel: where women are present, they appear as memories of nurses and nurturers. The boy figures as the feminine collapsing into the masculine, implying that capitalism shares the hom(m)osexual orientation of the monastery. What is present in the picture is time and history, and now that these are in the monastery, Ashton Park cannot be J.M.'s home—it could be "Aelred's," but not J.M.'s.

Cross-Dressing and the Boy: Creating Spaces of Possibility

While the portrait of the Duke and the boy offers a powerful critique of the racial, sexual, and gender relations that structure the religious imaginary of the Church, we want to also emphasize the generative, productive capacity of cross-dressing that Scott presents in the novel. Here again the focus is on the youthful Aelred and the boy in the painting. Like the cross-dresser, "the boy" is viewed as offering a space of possibility partly because he is a category crisis. An embodiment of either female masculinity or masculine feminization, the boy occupies the space "precisely where this instance of masculine feminization overlaps with female masculinity."[32] The product of meticulous cross-dressing, the boy is seen as potentially liberating subject position because he presents the possibility of rejecting the imperatives of hegemonic masculinity.[33]

In the novel's religious imaginary, the boy offers the hope of safely combining same-sex desire within a heteronormative space that maintains the homo/hetero binary. The original Aelred's story, which serves as such an inspiration for J.M. the boy, distinguishes between the monk's boyhood desires and those of the more mature man. When contained within the boy, homoerotic and homosocial desires are marginally tolerable but are totally unacceptable within a man—especially when masculinity is de facto heterosexual.[34] Therefore, it is J.M.'s boyishness that initially characterizes him in Ashton Park, and it is this quality which enables Benedict to love him "not as a woman, not as Claire, but as Aelred, [my] bonnie lad" (396). Later, when our Aelred has transgressed the line between the homosocial and permissible homoerotic (chaste kisses and careful hugs), Benedict can locate the resources to love him unconditionally only if Benedict remembers Aelred *as* a boy. It is the novice's attire that makes it possible for Benedict to position him as the boy, as the feminine masculine, a position that generates reparative, redemptive power.

In *Aelred's Sin,* the trope of the boy is also represented in Jordan—the name Aelred gives to the unnamed boy in the painting after he sees a gravestone in the monastery's cemetery. This gravestone is distinguished by what looks to Aelred like the head of a young African male, whom he imagines to be Jordan. Aelred's unearthing of Jordan's history illustrates how "the queer racialized body becomes a historical archive for both individuals and communities, one that is excavated through the very act of desiring the racial Other."[35] Through imagining Jordan's narrative—which he constructs as a story about a boy living and dying in the confines of Ash Wood, the house pre-monastery—Aelred feels back through *time* to an understanding of another's suffering and recognizes his complicity. There is a transvestite moment here as well. Aelred identifies with Jordan as a boyish object of the white gaze, but he also sees him as his subject. As a boy, Jordan functions in Aelred's education as the catalyst for repair when he merges with the *boy*hood lover, Ted, a coming together which re-presents and reinforces J.M.'s homosexual identity. Significantly, the boy allows for J.M. to emerge from Aelred's feminine robes of whiteness and contained homoeroticism: contra Fanon, however, he comes out as a man who, despite everything, really is homosexual.

Through his identification with Jordan and his feminized position within the portrait, J.M. understands his own position within the monastery, which is that of the boy whose desires are being shaped to ensure his destiny as the unraced, unsexed transvestite. In this sense, the cross-dressed Jordan, the black boy, opens up to J.M. a space of possibility, a questioning of binaries. Through his identification with Jordan, J.M. also refutes Fanon's suggestion that homosexuality is a Western export—that homosexuals in the Caribbean and Africa don't exist. When Ashton Park, unable to countenance sexuality in any of its members, asks Aelred to be "fixed," he submits to analysis with a Dr. Graveson—the Grave's son—who attempts to help Aelred normalize his feelings for Edward and Benedict. In one of the sessions, Aelred begins to recall a dream of a "small black boy . . . climbing in through [his] bedroom window," which Graveson reads off as Aelred's "dark self, which [Aelred is] fearful of confronting" (434). Aelred rejects Graveson's reading, asking whether he had not heard of the "slave trade, the plantation society," which, for Aelred, comprises a "tropical collective unconscious" (434). Graveson rejects this Black Atlantic psychoanalytic reading, just as Aelred ultimately rejects psychoanalysis partly because he demands that his black identity and its history be acknowledged and partly because he understands that the form of spiritual friendship offered by Ashton Park, and underwritten by psychoanalysis, is "not my ideal, but . . . one given to me, which masked my true [homosexual] nature" (433). Through his affective merging with Jordan, and Jordan's merging with Ted, through stories from a racialized collective unconscious, J.M. now insists on the legitimacy of his desire and the subjectivities it produces. This self-enlightened outcome would make Adorno proud, for J.M. is now equipped "to be different without fear" (114). Psychoanalytic stories like those told about Aelred of Rievaulx pose as timeless, eternal, like the Church itself, but become another form of masquerade—of cross-dressing—that must be refused in order to achieve a fuller identity as a black gay man.

The Reparative Power of the Transvestite

One of the surprises that Scott's novel provides is how Aelred's cross-dressed state makes him more open to the feminine, especially as it enables him to re-member his past. As Scott writes, "Another boy's face grows in Aelred's mind and as it does, he hears the voice of his nurse, and begins to speak to himself *as if he were her*" (79). In this instance of imaginative gender crossing, he occupies momentarily the feminine voice, which provides him with a new level of receptivity to the old story of Mungo, who came from Africa to the de la Borde estate. This receptive position is an anodyne to his earlier humiliation as the receptive bottom in the rape, staged at the supposedly safe space of the Catholic school. Gender crossing here is not about resistance, although it will lead to that; it is about opening, revelation, and a (counter) Enlightenment.[36] Not so much an appropriation of the feminine as it is a possession by the feminine who, while other, is also himself.[37] This possession does not result in paranoid mimicry or serve as a critique of gender restrictions as such; rather, it is, as Sedgwick argues, a form of repair.[38] Aelred's sudden possession by the feminine allows him to engage in what will become a transformation of the pain-producing, lost object into an object capable of providing sustenance—what Melanie Klein calls love.[39] As Aelred states, "There are these disjunctions in my life which I must yoke together if I am to survive" (434). His encounter as Aelred with both Mungo/Jordan and Edward provides him with the resources to make a new object—a new J.M who carries an agglomeration of affects that will sustain and nourish him.

Through the series of cross-identifications that his time in monk's frocks engendered, J.M. is able to recast the original Aelred's sin—which he identifies as the forgetting of Jordan and Mungo within the white homosocial space of Aelred's monastery—in racial terms. While living with Edward, J.M. is overwhelmed with guilt about Jordan. According to J.M., his rejection of the monastery means, "I feel I have betrayed [Jordan], by leaving his grave untended, by leaving his portrait unvisited, and I may never walk again in Ashton Park where he was killed" (434). He also casts as sin the original Aelred's practice of spiritual friendship, and in so doing, he affirms gay desire: "I do want to express my love physically and sexually in a full way. . . . It was never possible for me as a young boy to conceive of my love for Ted as really legitimate. It was a sin. I call it Aelred's sin" (435).

In the final fragment in our opening, the pictures of J.M. and Edward, a gay couple, are placed side by side in Robert de la Borde's estate home. J.M. is not cross-dressed: he appears as himself—a gay black man. His photo and the photograph of Edward, his white lover, become a reworking of the portrait we described earlier, and posit other images to counter those we have identified in the religious imaginary. The representational space of these other portraits composes a more capacious and flexible imaginary where same-sex desire is accepted into the heart of the home. Unlike the Malgretoute of J.M. and Robert's youth, the estate house reinscribes a male triangle now healed. Instead of the homophobia that structured the initial homosocial triad, which led to Ted's death, possibly at Robert's hand, and then to J.M.'s exile, a new triangle is constructed: J.M.; Edward, his white lover; and the newly queered heterosexual Creole brother, Robert. Robert's (and by extension Scott's) writing of J.M. and Ted's story and placing the picture of J.M. and Edward at his desk in the center of Malgretoute is a visible rebuke to the Caribbean "discourses of anti-colonial nationalism, masculinity and heteronormativity [which] work together in constructing homosexuality as a category outside of the Caribbean even as it legislated within national boundaries."[40]

"Cross"-Dressings: Reconciliation and Repair

We have shown how the trope of cross-dressing activates queer desire, destabilizing hom(m)osocial space while at the same time revealing the role of history and race. Just as Bankhead's quip "drags" the medieval dress of the Catholic Church into the twentieth century, Scott's *Aelred's Sin* drags the Church—the eternal Catholic Church—back into time and history. As Robert notes, "J.M., my brother. . . . So, so Ted, so those spirits from the past. So Aelred of Rievaulx, so Jordan, the letter J as clear as light carved in the moss on the Christian cross. . . . Time and memory. Memory and time" (417). Scott's deliberate focus on space and time shows first how things fall apart but then shows that the resources for reassembling these parts—differently—are already at hand in the concept of love.

This critique, therefore, is not dressed in the camp colors of drag or in paranoid readings of discipline and desire. Rather, written from the depressive or reparative position, it is more indirect and embedded. This is not to say that the pain of enforced exile, homophobia, and racism is not present. Scott argues that the pain of histories cannot be forgotten for "himself, Benedict and Edward, who sought a new beginning without a past. But it was their pasts which had returned: their personal pasts, their collective past, the past, all here, to make this particular present" (392). Cross-dressing in this novel can be viewed in the productive sense of positing a new space of possibility. In Scott's novel, "cross"-dressing becomes a form of reconciliation and repair.

But how to move this close reading back to the question of masculinities in the Caribbean? We contend that the fictional social space Scott's novel describes functions allegorically. J.M. is forced to England partly because there is no place for same-sex-desiring men on Les Deux Isles. A quick survey of work by Thomas Glave and Linden Lewis on Caribbean masculinities suggests that conditions for same-sex-desiring Caribbean men remain problematic, with tolerance, never mind acceptance, slow to come.[41] J.M.'s flight from home is not to be read simply as a trip across the ocean, but as emblematic of the flight from the symbolic, structural, and direct violence that marks the lived lives of many homosexual men. The argument that "optional exile or relocation . . . does not escape the gender-sexual [we would add racial] complexes of Caribbean identity but magnifies them" is what *Aelred's Sin* takes up.[42] Positioned within a Black Atlantic space, the literary monastery can be understood as a stand-in for the larger social spaces generated by heterosexuality and patriarchy and the forms of hegemonic masculinity they produce, and not only in the Caribbean. Scott's novel has us bear witness to how destructive the inability to accept the full range of male desires is to buller men (Ted) and gay men (Edward) while simultaneously truncating the emotional life of those who fall outside the parameters of "normative" desire—Benedict and Robert. In this regard, it is important to note that Robert—initially self-identified as heterosexual—comes to recognize his desires as less rigidly so. As he absorbs more of his brother's story, he finds J.M. is to him about sexuality as Jordan is to J.M. about race. Affected, Robert, in one of his final meditations, is able to imagine himself as "other": "Would I have kissed Benedict on the mouth? Funny how I keep considering this now. . . . Then I wonder. I mean, I could do some of these things. Why am I not impelled in this way?" (416). Whatever the answer, Robert acknowledges that becoming his brother's scribe, putting on his brother's identity, has left him "changed" (417).

Notes

1. "Tallulah Bankhead."

2. "John Herbert."

3. Scott, *Aelred's Sin,* 445. Further references to this novel will be given in parentheses in the text. Robert's brother is named Jean Marc, referred to throughout the novel as J.M., except when he is in the monastery, where he is referred to by his bestowed name, Aelred. When Aelred leaves the monastery, he leaves "Aelred" behind and is hence referred to again as J.M.

4. The meaning of cross-dressing and the extent to which it signifies disruptions, contestations, and/or realignment of gender/sexuality in Elizabethan and seventeenth-century literature is under discussion, but numerous sermons of the time frowned on the practice of cross-dressing.

5. Alexander, *Pedagogies of Crossing.*

6. Easton and Hewson, "Returning to Repair."

7. Glave, "Between Jamaica(n) and (North) America(n)," 120. See also Alexander, "'Not Just (Any) Body.'"

8. We here are playing on Irigaray's concept of the "hom(m)osexual" economy, which Margaret Gibson argues also structures the Christian salvation economy, which Scott represents in *Aelred's Sin.* In denominating a space hom(m)osocial, we are emphasizing both its masculine and its same-sex-desiring characteristics.

9. See, for example, the issues raised around *Paris Is Burning* in North America and the polarizing responses toward cross-dressing in carnival spaces in the Caribbean and Canada.

10. Fanon, *Black Skin, White Masks,* 100.

11. Garber, *Vested Interests,* 10.

12. Ibid., 11, our emphasis.

13. Ibid., 210–15.

14. Gopinath, *Impossible Desires,* 1.

15. Routon, "Trance-Nationalisms," 500.

16. Povinelli and Chauncey, "Thinking Sexuality Transnationally."

17. Ibid., 440.

18. Halberstam, *Queer Time and Place,* 2.

19. Since Scott positions the Church as part of the Black Atlantic and the two brothers are both sons of plantation owners, a muted class analysis is present.

20. The white robes suggest the Cistercian Orders. J.M. joins the Benedictine Order, whose robes are black. Interestingly, the Cistercians opposed Aelred of Rievaulx's attempts to build a monastery at St. Mary's in York. Scott complicates easy black-white binaries and suggests that such polarities have roots in earlier English history.

21. Taylor, *Modern Social Imaginaries.*

22. When the same-sex practices of J.M. and his boyhood friend Ted are discovered, both are labeled "bullers." The term is a linguistic and political act, which emerges out of specific Caribbean contexts and is not equivalent to the Anglo–North American denominators "fag" or "queer" (Crichlow, *Buller Men,* 37). "Buller" is a label that invokes shame, filth, and disease. Its deployment lends its users in this novel the "entitlement" to punish the so-called "buller" boys: J.M. and Ted are "fucked in the arse" (245) by their offended schoolmates.

23. Gibson, "Guiltless Credit and the Moral Economy." Gibson draws on Irigaray to argue that a salvation economy is "a hom(m)osexual economy because it is structured through the couple of father and son; this couple relies on the exchange and mediation of women to secure the same sex-gender tie or bond. The father and son need the bodies of women, principally the mother figures of Eve and Mary, to open up and later secure the path and redemptive turn of the sinner back to God-the-father through the son" (http://www.yorku.ca/jspot/3/mgibson.htm [accessed 13 May 2012]).

24. Gruschka, "Critical Pedagogy after Adorno," 243–44.

25. The shadow of the Holocaust lies in the novel in Miriam's invocation of the Shoah with respect to homosexuals' deaths in the camps. Scott implies an analogous relationship between the holocaust, AIDS, and the slave trade.

26. Garber, *Vested Interests,* 211.

27. Edward, a white Welsh boy, joins Ashton Park shortly after J.M. becomes Aelred. He and Aelred cross the line of spiritual friendship and are asked to leave the monastery. They both eventually leave Ashton Park to live together as lovers. Edward subsequently dies of AIDS.

28. Edward's X-ray vision clearly appears limited to seeing J.M.'s blackness. He has a touristic fascination for J.M.'s "exotic otherness." Their relationship ends, the reasons unspoken. But through J.M.'s ministrations to Edward as he dies of AIDS, they achieve the spiritual friendship that eluded them early on.

29. Gopinath, *Impossible Desires,* 2.

30. Ibid., 2.

31. An idea worth exploring elsewhere is that articulated in Fuss, "Interior Colonies"—that the psychoanalytic theory of identification was also a by-product of modernity.

32. Noble, "Zoom, Zoom."

33. Ibid.

34. This equating of mature masculinity with heterosexuality not only draws on Freud but also underscores how Ted's murder/suicide is the product of his betrayal of this equation. As the perfect man, he was to be hetero not homosexual.

35. Gopinath, *Impossible Desires*, 1.

36. By this we mean the sense of enlightenment as "illumination," but we are also gesturing toward the historical period of the "Enlightenment," which eventually saw the construction of the subject category of the "homosexual," as Foucault has famously argued. By using this term, we tentatively suggest an oppositional epistemology that stems from individual meanings.

37. See Hewson, "Interview with Earl Lovelace," in which Lovelace explains the shifting of voices in his novel *Salt*, operating as a kind of possession by the other found in Shango religious practices. We see Aelred's talking to himself in Toinette's voice as a similar kind of possession.

38. Kosofsky Sedgwick, "Paranoid Reading," 4.

39. See ibid.

40. Sharpe and Pinto, "Sweetest Taboo," 262.

41. Lewis, "Caribbean Masculinity."

42. Sharpe and Pinto, "Sweetest Taboo," 271.

Little Miss Muffet Meets Spider Anancy

The Use of Drag in Sistren's *Muffet Inna All a Wi*

Karina Smith

Little Miss Muffet sat on a tuffet
Eating her curds and whey
Down came a spider
Who sat down beside her
And frightened Miss Muffet away.

IN *Vested Interests,* Marjorie Garber argues that the purposes of cross-dressing and the meanings it generates are multiple: among other things, cross-dressing "can be a trickster strategy for outsmarting white oppression, a declaration of difference, a gay affirmative or a homophobic representation."[1] In this essay I will focus on *Muffet Inna All a Wi* (1986) by the Jamaican Sistren Theatre Collective to investigate how, drawing on the tradition of cross-dressing found in the Anancy folktales to outsmart "white" and/or patriarchal oppression, this 1986 play, performed at the height of the Seaga era, challenged neoliberal discourses and the social construction of gender roles that kept and still keep women oppressed.

Sistren was formed in 1977 by thirteen working-class Jamaican women who were employed in the Manley government's Impact program. The women were invited to work with the Jamaican theater practitioner Honor Ford-Smith on a skit for the annual Workers' Week festival in Kingston, Jamaica. Following the success of the skit, the women continued taking drama classes at the Jamaica School of Drama with Ford-Smith, eventually forming Sistren Theatre Collective in 1980. Between 1977 and 1980, Sistren members developed an innovative theatrical methodology that drew on Jamaica's oral tradition and combined it with popular and avant-garde theater techniques, most notably those of Ngũgĩ wa Thiong'o, the Filipino Educational Theatre Movement, and Enrique Buenaventura.[2] While Sistren's popular approach to creating theater has some parallels with Jamaica's roots plays—what Deborah Thomas describes as "popular plays performed in patois" that "draw from a variety of stock characters to humorously present situations familiar to their largely lower-class audiences"[3]—its major difference was in the company's commitment to presenting feminist issues onstage.

In the 1980s, Jamaican Prime Minister Edward Seaga fostered very close ties with the Reagan administration and the International Monetary Fund, both of which imposed their respective policies on Jamaica, such as the Caribbean Basin Initiative (CBI) and the Structural Adjustment program.[4] In addition, politically aligned criminal gangs became increasingly violent during this period, largely with the influx of hard drugs such as cocaine into Kingston and the partial replacement of the politician with the drug don as patron in downtown communities. Prior to this, these communities were dependent on political MPs for their material needs, such as housing and utilities. Amanda Sives argues that the transition from politician to don was due to the lack of material resources that could be distributed following the "implementation of neoliberal structural adjustment and stabilization policies."[5] As we will see, in Sistren's *Muffet Inna All A Wi*, the Seaga government's neoliberal policies are held up as forms of violence against women. Sistren theatricalizes the impact of neoliberalism by showing how working-class women are affected by political tribalism, gunmen in their communities, work in the Free Trade Zones (set up to satisfy aspects of Reagan's CBI), and the promotion of consumerism in the face of the grinding poverty of many working-class Jamaicans.

From its inception, Sistren has been committed to performing plays that bring the social construction of gender to public attention. In all of Sistren's plays, the male characters counterbalance the traditional stereotyping of women in mainstream Jamaican theatrical productions and ridicule the construction and cultivation of "masculine" identities within certain Jamaican subcultures, such as the male-dominated music scene. In the group's debut production, *Bellywoman Bangarang* (1978), a play that addresses the issue of sexual violence against women, Sistren parody Jamaican male stereotypes, such as Rude Boys and quasi-Rastas, and comment on the performance of sexually aggressive heterosexual masculinities. The male characters in *Bellywoman* are represented in two ways: as comic caricatures and as nameless, faceless rapists. In *Bellywoman*, the female actors transform themselves into males through the adoption of subcultural markers of masculinity associated with the 1970s reg-gae music scene: Dread talk, "skanking" gestures, and the use of wash-cloths to wipe away sweat.[6] Sistren's impersonations, which attempt to deflate the enormity of the Jamaican male ego, trigger much hilar-ity among audience members because they ridicule the seriousness with which many young Jamaican men regard their membership in particular social groups, such as the Rude Boys. Equally, they can be frightening and disturbing. Reflecting on Sistren's *Bellywoman Bangarang*, Cobham and Ford-Smith suggest that the onstage presence of the cross-dressed female actor "creates a sense of shared vulnerability"[7] with women in the audience, particularly when male sexual violence is represented. Sistren's technique of covering the sexual predators' faces with stockings is a per-formative strategy that heightens the threat of aggressive male sexuality in the society.[8]

Cross-dressing has long been practiced on the Jamaican stage, par-ticularly in the annual Christmas pantomime[9] and in the West African–derived folk tradition Jonkonnu.[10] Cobham and Ford-Smith point out, though, that in the Jamaican pantomime male to female cross-dressing is the norm, and "female figures are usually caricatured as shrewish, clumsy, overbearing, and vain by exaggerating their breasts, hairstyles, or the shrillness of their voices."[11] From the very beginning, Sistren's plays reversed the gender parody found in the pantomime by utilizing female-to-male cross-dressing not only to caricature Jamaican men but to make an explicit political statement about the treatment of Jamaican women in the machinery of the State. In reviews of Sistren's productions, theater critics praised Sistren's skillful use of cross-dressing on the stage but never resorted to the term "drag" to describe it.[12] Moreover, the group's former artistic director, Honor Ford-Smith, describes Sistren's male characters as "male impersonations," and with reference to *Bellywoman Bangarang,* she writes, "From the point of view of the director, the use of male imper-sonations offered a wonderful opportunity to satirize gendered gesture and movement in a way which explored the mannered fragility of mas-culine beauty."[13] This essay is concerned with exploring Sistren's use of "male impersonation" in a particular play, *Muffet Inna All a Wi.* As we have seen, Cobham and Ford-Smith use the term "male impersonation" to describe Sistren's female-to-male transformations, but I would argue that their use of the term is imprecise. The reason for my concern is that the term "male impersonation" implies that the performer is pretend-ing to be male, masquerading as the opposite sex, "living difference," to use Judith Butler's expression in *Undoing Gender.* I prefer to use the term drag for the following reasons: drag suggests that the performance is a parody, it shows very clearly that gender is socially constructed and performed, it is self-conscious, and it operates as a continuum from the obvious markers of gender difference at one end to complete disguise at the other. I would also restrain from defining Sistren's members as drag kings: as Judith (now Jack) Halberstam suggests in *Female Masculinity*, "Whereas the male impersonator attempts to produce a plausible performance of maleness as the whole of her act, the drag king performs masculinity (often parodically) and makes the exposure of the theatricality of masculinity the mainstay of her act." Further, Halberstam points out that "the male impersonator and the drag king are not necessarily lesbian roles."[14] Arguably, Sistren members do not qualify as "drag kings," in that parodying men is not the main purpose of their performances nor do they "become" men or try to pass as "male," and they do not identify as lesbians, nor do they explore homosexual desire in their plays.

Tapping into the English and Jamaican pantomime traditions, which are usually based on nursery rhymes and fairytales, *Muffet Inna All a Wi* fractures the English nursery rhyme "Little Miss Muffet" in which a garden spider, descending from its web, frightens a dainty young girl so much that she runs away, leaving behind her curds and whey. By replacing the common, garden-variety spider with the West African Spider Anancy, the folk hero and trickster of the *Anansesem*, this Miss Muffet is, in an ironic twist, empowered rather than frightened away, mainly because the Spider trickster forces her to fight for her rights. By retelling the nursery rhyme, Sistren expose the gender binary as a fraudulent construction. While Sistren do not generally use drag to defy binarism per se, I will argue that in *Muffet Inna All a Wi* the gender binary is destabilized through the presence of the gender-ambiguous Spider Anancy, which, through further cross-dressing, transforms itself into the following male roles: a Jamaican DJ, an auctioneer, a politician, an executive, and a factory boss. In each transformation, the shape-shifting and cross-species spider/(wo)man creates chaos in order to prompt the timid, downtrodden Miss Muffet to take action against her oppressors, creating a liminal space—through its function as a subversive trickster—in which gender rules are turned upside down.

Sistren's Anancy is also referred to as Pitchi Patchi from the Jonkonnu tradition. Like the Spider trickster, Pitchi Patchi shape-shifts "becoming all things to all people—ever changing, ever constant—wearing multi coloured attire yet changing his headdress on different occasions."[15] Both the Jonkonnu and the Anancy traditions have West African origins and were used during slavery as covert forms of cultural resistance. Sylvia Wynter, in her article "Jonkonnu in Jamaica," suggests that Jamaican folklore, particularly the Jonkonnu, was a form of "guerilla cultural resistance" to the market economy: the colonial authorities could not decode the African-derived "masks," a term she uses to describe the entire costume, and were frightened by some of the Jonkonnu charac-ters, the ox-head mask being one example.[16] The double meaning in the attire of the Spider Anancy character in *Muffet Inna All A Wi* continues the tradition of using folklore to resist the brutality of capitalism, this time manifested in the Seaga regime's neoliberal policies.

As we have seen with *Bellywoman Bangarang,* Sistren's techniques for theatricalizing Jamaican masculinities are largely based on what Butler describes as "the signifying gestures through which gender it-self is established."[17] The male characters in *Muffet Inna All a Wi* are also either stock types, such as the factory boss and the policeman, or Jamaican male stereotypes, such as the Rude Boys and the DJ. Most of the male characters are performed by Spider Anancy, disguising itself in male attire while the Rude Boys are performed by the other women in the company who simply don hats and sunglasses, deepen their voices, and adopt swaggering gaits to portray their male alter egos. In addition, they mimic the linguistic patterns Jamaican men use, largely to create a distinction between the male and female characters but also to temper the more sinister moments in the play, particularly those in which sexual violence is threatened. One example is the language used by the Rude Boys to communicate with their boss:

Rude Boy 1: Ease boss, ease.
Rude Boy 2: Just cool Boss, cool . . .
Rude Boy 1: Boss, after I and I deh pon de corner yah, a reason wid I and I bredrin de gal yah a come listen to wha I bredrin a she to I man.[18]

In this passage Muffet is being identified as a police informer, putting her at enormous risk of violence and possibly even death, as according to Rude Boy 1 she was deliberately eavesdropping on his conversation with his male counterpart. Yet another example is the DJ who draws on ex-pressions made popular in the dancehall, such as "Yardie Massive" and "London posse," and used to describe criminal gangs involved in gun and drug crimes in disadvantaged communities in Kingston and parts of the Jamaican diaspora.

Cross-dressing can still be a dangerous practice in the Caribbean, but within the realm of the theatrical space it is considered acceptable because of the elements of play and make-believe in character creation—of course, the extent of the audience's acceptance often rests on the proviso that the gender binary will be restored once the play has ended.[19] In her introduction to *Crossing the Stage,* Lesley Ferris suggests that "theatrical cross-dressing has provided one way of playing with liminality and its multiple possibilities and extending that sense of the possible to the spectator/reader; a way of play, that while often reinforcing the social mores and status quo, carries with it the possibility for exposing that liminal moment, that threshold of questioning, that slippery sense of a mutable self."[20] It is very hard to measure the audience's response to Sistren's use of cross-dressing, but Sistren's parody of Jamaican "masculinity" has led at least one Jamaican male theater practitioner to complain that the company's male characters are all "bad men." Owen "Blacka" Ellis, who wrote Sistren's 1993 production *Kulchafusan,* suggests that Sistren's use of drag alienates men: "The Sistren women always play male roles in their productions, why can't a man play the part? The characters that are created for men are very often the villian [*sic*], the negative, the bad man. . . . If you recognize that there are good men, then you contribute to a trend that men would want to be a part of."[21] Ironically, the male-to-female drag performances in *Kulchafusan* were singled out for high praise in a review of the production for the *Jamaica Gleaner* by Michael Reckord, titled "Sistren Play Brethren Superbly." In the review, Reckord notes the impressive performances of Sistren actors Becky Knowles and Maxine Osbourne, who were able to "sustain" the male roles to a degree never before achieved by Sistren.[22] As Helene Keyssar points out, the absence of men in feminist plays and/or the roles created for them "are rarely simple matters of revenge or rectification. . . . More frequently, feminist plays attempt to pay attention to the lives of women—as individuals, in relation to each other, and in relation to men."[23] In order to resist political forces hostile to its existence, during the 1980s Sistren constructed a militant feminist image, which, as we will see, is exemplified in the theme of *Muffet Inna All a Wi.* Sistren's representation of men can be read as misandrist but, in fact, the one-dimensionality of the male characters is designed to keep the focus on women's issues. Moreover, when women dress up as men, they alter the social power dynamic by "introduc[ing] the possibility that there is no authentic gender, and tap[ping] a male fear of being replaced, a fear that someone other than men can be better than men."[24] Ellis's criticism can be better understood in the context of his involvement with Fathers Incorporated, a group established by Barry Chevannes in the 1980s to discuss the representation of Jamaican men in the media and to instill the responsibilities of fatherhood.[25] Ellis's views were echoed by Keith Noel, who accused the group of "preaching" about women's issues.[26] What both Noel and Ellis are missing is that given the political conservatism in Jamaica during the 1980s, Sistren provided an alternative representation of women from that of the mainstream media. Parodying "masculinity" through the use of cross-dressing is a deliberate feminist strategy the group employed to display the way in which female roles in Caribbean performance traditions are usually one-dimensional.

In *Muffet Inna All a Wi*, Sistren deploy Spider Anancy as the main character to create a liminal space in which gender fluidity is paramount: by exposing gender to be a performance that can be changed as easily as putting on a new set of clothes, the Spider demonstrates the importance of disguise in exposing and reconfiguring "naturalized" hierarchies of power.[27] In *Muffet Inna All a Wi*, though, there is another layer of complexity: a woman is disguised as the Spider trickster, giving her access to Anancy's magical ability to manipulate the social order. In their discussion of the trickster figure in postcolonial performance, Gilbert and Tompkins posit that the African-Caribbean Anancy "usually *enacts* his/her subversiveness through language," while "the Amerindian trickster tends to *embody* subversive (and regenerative) power—at least in theatrical contexts."[28] While Spider Anancy in *Muffet Inna All a Wi* does use wordplay and riddle to weave its magic, the transformation of the female actor into the male-impersonating spider, and then into the male characters such as the factory boss, locates Sistren's trickster closer to its Amerindian equivalent.

In the plays of the First Nations Canadian playwright Tomson Highway, for example, the Ojibway trickster figure, Nanabush, is used as a source of cultural pride and as a comic device. Cross-dressing as both men and women, Nanabush intervenes in the lives of the characters to bring about the regeneration to which Gilbert and Tompkins refer. In the play *The Rez Sisters,* for example, Nanabush transforms into a seagull, a nighthawk, and a male Bingo Master in order to transform and heal the female characters in the play. At the same time, Nanabush's activities are comical—in one scene, Nanabush follows behind the female characters mimicking their gestures and ways of speaking. In *Muffet Inna All a Wi*, the sequences involving Spider Anancy, acting as the Spider rather than in male disguise, are represented as sinister: the music changes tone, the lights are dimmed, and the female characters behave like puppets manipulated by a string. In the theatrical context, the similarities between Highway's trickster and Sistren's lie in their direct involvement in bringing about social change through intervention in the lives of the characters; both trickster characters, Anancy and Nanabush, are noted for their magical powers. The main difference is that Nanabush rarely speaks in *The Rez Sisters* whereas Anancy chants riddles throughout *Muffet Inna All a Wi.*

Although Anancy's gender in West African folktales is often ambiguous, as for its Amerindian counterpart, in the Jamaican tradition the trickster is usually regarded as male, hence the reference to the Spiderman hero that appears in most writing about the Jamaican oral tradition. In Jamaican Anancy stories, the Spiderman trickster is an immoral being, servant of the Sky-god Nyame, who weaves a web of trickery in order to feather his own nest. At the same time, he is the crafty underdog who finds ways to outsmart the authorities. He plays "betwixt and between" the gender binary, transforming himself into male and female characters to carry out his plans, or remaining androgynous if it suits him better. In this sense, he represents a powerful tradition of resistance to slavery and other forms of subordination as well as the realm of possibilities for creating alternatives in one's everyday life. According to Ruth Minott Egglestone, "Anancy is a paradox. . . . [He] is a hero and yet he is a thief, a schemer, a conman, a manipulator, a womaniser, a mocker, a treacherous friend."[29] In *Muffet Inna All a Wi*, Spider Anancy is responsible for the oppression that Jamaican working-class women experience on a daily basis, a situation the trickster creates to challenge the prevailing gender order.

In *Crossing the Stage*, Alisa Solomon makes the important point that "a woman's disruption of her own oppression can be as powerful and destabilizing as tweaking the binary."[30] Sistren's *Muffet Inna All a Wi* addresses the issue of Jamaican working-class women's oppression, particularly violence against working-class women, in 1980s Jamaica. Focusing on the issue of gendered violence, *Muffet Inna All a Wi* presents an overt political commentary on the abuse of women within an entrenched patriarchal system that exploits them as sexual objects and cheap labor. In *Muffet Inna All a Wi*, the oppression of Jamaican women is blamed on Spider Anancy's trickery. As Anancy chants:

Poor lickle Muffet
All tru life she a ruff it.
Just a stab and rape everywhere she go.
Lord is just life she a look
But every turn she get a juck.
Do nuh do it again it hot please no. (4)

Muffet, the name of the everywoman character in the play, suffers at the hands of gunmen, politicians, and factory bosses who use her as a sexual, political, and economic pawn. Violence in downtown Kingston permeates all aspects of Muffet's life: Muffet 1 is raped and her belongings stolen as she struggles to protect her teenage daughter Cassandra from "Rudeboy" sexual predators in the community; Muffet 2 is caught in the cross fire between rival political gangs and is later implicated in her local MP's corruption; Muffet 3's dreams of marrying an executive soon turn to nightmares when her husband abuses her; and Muffet 4 goes to work in Jamaica's Free Trade Zone (FTZ), where she is forced to sew hundreds of garments per day—and is fired for protesting against the low pay and poor working conditions. By naming the four main female characters in the play Muffet, Sistren deliberately subvert the image of the dainty Miss Muffet by portraying the strength and resilience of Jamaican women who, when dealing with violence and exploitation on a daily basis, fight back in a manner akin to their male counterparts. Using a hoop to signify his web, Anancy traps Muffet in precarious situations in which she has to fight for her freedom. By channeling Anancy's trickery, the female characters are successful in unsettling the gender order and, by extension, imagining alternative possibilities for their lives. As we will see, in the final moments of the play, Muffet attacks the factory boss, tying him up in the skeins of Anancy's web.

Muffet Inna All A Wi also engages dialectically with Jamaican society in the 1980s through its appropriation of the male-dominated world of the Jamaican music scene. Although Gilbert and Tompkins and Sharon Green describe *Muffet Inna All A Wi* as a reggae musical, it is my argument that Sistren's choice of the DJ narrator to introduce key events in the play is a reference to the shifts in reggae that occurred during the 1980s, particularly the depoliticization of the lyrics in favor of slackness and violence.[31] Further, the presence of a woman impersonating a male DJ subverts both the misogyny and the homophobia explicitly expressed in much Jamaican music of the time: while male DJs make jokes about cross-dressing and "battymen,"[32] in *Muffet Inna All a Wi* they are the butt of the joke: not only are their rhythms, moves, and styles being copied, their "masculinity" is parodied by a woman in drag. In *Muffet Inna All a Wi,* Spider Anancy is costumed in a black pantsuit, from which hang strips of white cloth; s/he also wears a gold Spiderman mask. In Spider Anancy's first transformation as the DJ, s/he merely exchanges the mask for a black hat around which is a band of red, gold, and green Rasta colors. While female Jamaican DJs, such as Tanya Stephens, Lady

Saw, and Ce'Cile, who came to prominence in the 1990s, are contesting the "ideological framework that positions masculinity as transcendentally powerful"[33] through their celebration of female empowerment, Sistren go one step further by blurring the gender binary that keeps the ideological framework intact.

In *Muffet Inna All a Wi*, part of Spider Anancy's trickery is in making the four Muffets think that gender inequalities in Jamaican society are based on the "natural" differences between men and women. Spider Anancy does everything he can to keep Muffet downtrodden; his riddles perpetuate the patriarchal ideology that women should be subservient to their male counterparts. At the beginning of the play, Anancy chants:

> Now you see me, now you don't
> Try to know me but you won't
> Bite you tongue and tek yuh lot,
> Meekly wait and Murmur not.
> Murmur not, Murmur not.
> Flash it. (4)

Naana Jane Opoku-Agyemang argues that although the Anancy tales often "create balance between the genders," they also have "the potential to obstruct pathways to change and transformation, more specifically for the female gender."[34] In *Muffet Inna All a Wi*, Sistren expose the way in which Anancy tales transmit the gender ideologies that keep women oppressed. While the harm caused to women is usually a source of humor in written Anancy tales, in Sistren's play the theatricalization of violence against women, and Anancy's role in conjuring it, are not seen as laughing matters.

In the same way that Lady Saw and other female Jamaican DJs subvert women's objectification in the male-dominated dancehall by reclaiming the space for the promotion of female sexuality, Sistren use the arena of the dancehall to bring the audience's attention to the objectification and commodification of women in beauty pageants and the feminized labor force of domestic work and the FTZ. In *Muffet Inna All a Wi*, Anancy transforms into an auctioneer, selling the Muffets to the highest bidder:

> *Trickster: (Enters as auctioneer)* Step right up, step right up, who will start de bidding. (Chants)
> Dem tings here nice like sugar and spice
> Sexy like de best dress chicken and rice.
> Come up, come up and pick your choice . . .

Now who will have si young black beautiful wench,
Well bred, thorough bred (Woman steps out of circle takes sash from auction-
  eer parades like beauty queen contestant) . . .
Auctioneer: 32, 34, 50 going, going, going gone.
Auctioneer: Now who will have dis prize of a woman to be a shef [*sic*] in the
  kitchen, a lady in the living room, and a whore in the bedroom. (4)

The exploitation of women as domestic and sexual labor is exemplified
through the staging of the auction/beauty pageant—an event in which
women are valued for their domestic skills, beauty, and sex appeal rather
than for their intelligence. Not only does this sequence parallel slave auc-
tions in which the physically fit body of the slave was dissected anatomically, it theatricalizes the objectification and commodification of women
in the capitalist economy; women are constructed as property and their
bodies are sold as chattel to the highest male bidder. In this sequence,
Sistren is denaturalizing the dominant gender ideology by using food,
animal, and sexual imagery to portray the construction of women as
objects of desire.

It is the commodification of women in the capitalist modes of production that finally drives Muffet to take action against her oppressors.
Anancy, disguised as a factory boss by donning a suit and tie, presides
over all the Muffets, who mime repetitive actions as though working in a
garment factory:

Trickster: Paradise production in association with . . .
Presents the C.B.I. . . . starring President Boops
The fastest gun slinger in the West side of the White House.
Ladies and Gentlemen, welcome to Jamaica's Freezone—
Truly a gateway to the world's market place.
Where women work very hard
The wages are low, trade unions they don't know.
The sun is shining bright and everything is alright. (4)

When the female workers start to complain about their low wages and
poor working conditions, Anancy, turning his hoop into a mirror, distracts
the women temporarily with consumer culture and romance narratives.
For example, an advertisement for deodorant is performed in which a
model, holding an oversized bottle of roll-on, tells of losing her virginity
when wearing "Senola." The sequence, used for comic effect, makes stark
the ways in which the media often draws attention away from the unjust
realities of daily life, particularly the uneven power dynamic between

men and women in Jamaican society. The play ends as the Muffets, sick of being treated badly by the male management of the factory, start dancing and chanting to the sound of African drums. They circle the factory boss, tie him up in a web, and finally overcome exploitation. The four Muffets chant, "I muffet nuh frighten, I muffet nah run, I Muffet gwine stand up and do what must be done" (3). The Muffets display Jamaican women's "cunning," which Carolyn Cooper claims "is one manifestation of the morally ambiguous craftiness of Anansi"[35] and their difference from the Little Miss Muffet of English nursery rhyme fame.

Sistren's *Muffet Inna All a Wi,* therefore, creates a liminal space in which the gender order is challenged, if not reversed. Through the use of cross-dressing, Sistren poke fun at constructions of Jamaican "masculinity," and through the use of drag represent male characters in the same way that female characters have long been represented on the Jamaican stage. Having a woman play Spider Anancy adds new meaning to Garber's notion of transvestism as a trickster strategy. Sistren's Anancy manifests itself as male characters in order to infiltrate male-dominated domains, such as the Jamaican music scene and factory management. Although Anancy generally plays tricks to reinforce the gender order, Sistren use the trickster figure to open up the possibilities for women's lives in Jamaica, and the wider Caribbean.

Notes

1. Garber, *Vested Interests,* 303.
2. Cobham and Ford-Smith, introduction, xxii–xxiii.
3. Thomas, *Modern Blackness,* 235.
4. Henke, "Jamaica's Decision," and Sives, "Changing Patrons."
5. Sives, "Changing Patrons," 80.
6. Cobham and Ford-Smith, introduction, xxxi.
7. Ibid.
8. Smith, "Demystifying 'Reality.'"
9. The Jamaican pantomime, with its roots in the English pantomime tradition, includes a male-to-female drag queen among its stock characters.
10. The Jonkonnu, which draws on both the West African Egun-gun masquerade and the English mumming tradition, includes the character of Bellywoman, which is traditionally performed by a man in drag.
11. Cobham and Ford-Smith, introduction, xxxi.
12. Morris, "Important Production," 5.
13. Cobham and Ford-Smith, introduction, xxx.
14. Halberstam, *Female Masculinity,* 232.
15. Jamaican Cultural Development, *Jonkonnu.*
16. Wynter, "Jonkonnu in Jamaica," 37.

17. Butler, *Gender Trouble* (1990), viii.

18. Sistren, *Muffet Inna All a Wi*, 1. Further references to this play will be given in parentheses in the text.

19. Garber, *Vested Interests*, 70.

20. Ferris, "Introduction: Current Crossings," 8.

21. Qtd. in Sistren, "Can I Call You Sister?," 34.

22. Reckord, "Sistren Play Brethren Superbly," 3D.

23. Keyssar, *Feminist Theatre*, 2–3.

24. Rosenfeld, "Drag King Magic," 214.

25. Reddock, "Interrogating Caribbean Masculinities," xiv.

26. Qtd. in Wilson, "Sistren Theatre Collective (Jamaica)," 44.

27. It is noteworthy that the spider/man Anansi also exposes and explodes another "naturalized" hierarchy of power, the one that positions humans above other animals. In this volume, the connection between cross-dressing and transcending or challenging the boundary between humans and nonhuman animals, albeit in different contexts, is also investigated and foregrounded by Wendy Knepper, Carine M. Mardorossian, and Roberto Strongman.

28. Gilbert and Tompkins, *Post-colonial Drama*, 235.

29. Egglestone, "Philosophy of Survival," paragraph 23.

30. Solomon, "It's Never Too Late to Switch," 158.

31. Ross, *Real Love*.

32. Cooper, *Noises in the Blood*, 150.

33. Thomas, *Modern Blackness*, 255.

34. Opoku-Agyemang, "Gender-Role Perceptions," 120.

35. Cooper, *Noises in the Blood*, 47.

Cross-Dressing and the Caribbean Imaginary in Nalo Hopkinson's *Midnight Robber*

Wendy Knepper

WHILE SEXUAL violence and homophobia remain rife in the Caribbean, many twentieth-century and contemporary Caribbean writers take a richly experimental and dissident approach to inscribing gender and sexuality, contesting patriarchal heteronormativity in the process.[1] In this context, I want to consider how Nalo Hopkinson's queer fictions not only challenge hegemonic constructions of gender and sexuality but also explore new frontiers for identity formation, citizenship, and community. Through creolized works of speculative fiction, which depict the sexual lives of marginalized subjects, Hopkinson "blurs the line between the erotic and the fantastical."[2] She explores the queer or what Eve Kosofsky Sedgwick refers to as "the open mesh of possibilities . . . when the constituent elements of anyone's gender, of anyone's sexuality aren't made (or can't be made) to signify monolithically."[3] Her novels—*Brown Girl in the Ring* (1998), *Midnight Robber* (2000), *The Salt Roads* (2003), and *The New Moon's Arms* (2007)—and short stories, including the collection entitled *Skin Folk* (2001), destabilize conventional constructs of gender and genre through techniques of transposition, recoding, and intermixture. Through the virtual, a new kind of erotic imaginary emerges, fluid and mobile yet responsive to history.

This chapter contributes to an understanding of Hopkinson's oeuvre and its place in the Caribbean queering of culture by considering the motif of cross-dressing in *Midnight Robber*.[4] This coming-of-age story focuses on the life of Tan-Tan, a young girl who works through the trauma of sexual violence by taking on the guise of the Midnight Robber, a figure traditionally associated with the carnivalesque expression of Trinidadian masculinities.[5] Masquerading as the Midnight Robber, Tan-Tan travels through communities and worlds, reconfiguring her identity through performance and performativity. Following on from the work of Rosi Braidotti, who argues that transposition "stresses the experience of creative insight in engendering other, alternative ways of knowing,"[6] I propose that Tan-Tan, the nomadic, cross-dressing hero(ine), serves as a kind of avatar for the narrative discourse itself, which moves through space and time as well as across disciplines of knowledge in order to reincarnate identity in a more pluralistic, experimental fashion. As will be demonstrated, Hopkinson's narrative employs the motif of nomadic cross-dressing to express alternative constructions of identity and community through a virtualized Caribbean queer imaginary.

Cross-Dressing and the Transgender Warrior

Cross-dressing and the carnivalesque as well as encounters with non-human subjects serve as experiences through which Tan-Tan articulates her identity as a "transgender warrior," a term used by Leslie Feinberg to refer to all those who blur or bridge the boundary of the sex or gender expression.[7] Marjorie Garber argues that "one of the most important aspects of cross-dressing is the way in which it offers a challenge to easy notions of binarity, putting into question the notions of 'female' and 'male,' whether they are considered essential or constructed, biological or cultural."[8] The thirdness of cross-dressing is "a mode of articulation, a way of describing a space of possibility."[9] Before turning to an in-depth analysis of how this thirdness operates in *Midnight Robber*, it is important to consider how Hopkinson virtualizes Caribbean places and identities in the context of science fiction, inviting the reader to consider Caribbean gender and sexuality in virtual terms as both real and unreal, linked to history and running counter to it.

Set on the planet of Toussaint and its dub version called New Half-Way Tree, Hopkinson's *Midnight Robber* takes place in a queer place and time, which does not exactly correspond to the Caribbean as we know it. Tan-Tan lives on Toussaint with her father, Antonio, and mother, Ione, until violence erupts when Antonio murders Ione's lover. When Antonio is exiled to New Half-Way Tree, Tan-Tan accompanies her father to this lawless New World setting where Antonio asserts patriarchal power by raping his daughter Tan-Tan on numerous occasions, resulting in unwanted and aborted pregnancies. Eventually Tan-Tan fights back, committing patricide in the process. Her father's lover, Janisette, seeks revenge. Forced to flee the community, Tan-Tan (once more pregnant) cross-dresses as the Midnight Robber and enters into exile, living with a community of douen[10] and then undertaking a peripatetic lifestyle, accompanied by companions of other species. Finally, she confronts the past in a carnivalesque showdown with Janisette where, in the guise of the Midnight Robber, she recounts her experiences of sexual violence, heroic deeds of resistance, and discovery of new identity politics. Through the queer art of Robber Speech, she reclaims her position in the community, but her identity and that of her unborn child have been significantly transformed, as will be seen, through various travels and transpositions. She engages with displaced histories and stories from the region not as an origin or a genesis but as a series of crossings and recrossings. This a-chronological exploration of Caribbean nodal points might be said to form a new kind of network, something akin to Édouard Glissant's concept of the rhizome as a relational system of identity formation.[11] As a result, Hopkinson links the motif of cross-gender masquerade through time and space to a more radical, decentered reworking of Caribbean communal identity and the cultural imaginary.

Through science fiction, Hopkinson reconfigures known relations to peoples, histories, and places, offering alternative configurations of personal and collective identity in a virtualized Caribbean setting. Judith Misrahi-Barak observes that Hopkinson creates "a future in which part of the Caribbean tradition is contained and yet which is a world apart."[12] For instance, the references to Tan-Tan and the planets—Toussaint and New-Half Way Tree—may seem fantastical to a reader unfamiliar with the Caribbean, but they allude to actual aspects of Caribbean culture. "Tan Tan" is a well-known carnival character. In 1990 the carnival artist Peter Minshall created a dancing mobile of Tan Tan as Queen of the Carnival, accompanied by Saga Boy (a term that refers to a well-dressed, pleasure-seeking man, often a playboy type) in the role of King of the Carnival. Thus, in *Midnight Robber,* the name Tan-Tan serves as a metafictional allusion to the role of masquerade and the carnivalesque as well as highlights the theme of gender performativity in the novel.

Similarly, the names of the planets call attention to gendered identities and spaces: the planet Toussaint refers to Toussaint L'Ouverture, a masculine hero of the Haitian Revolution, and New Half-Way Tree alludes to an actual place where market women rest on the way from market to downtown Kingston, Jamaica. By linking these two planets, one associated with Haitian masculinity and the other with Jamaican femininity, Hopkinson remaps Caribbean spatial, temporal, and gender relations. Moreover, Hopkinson's alien worlds draw on Jamaican, Trinidadian, Haitian, Grenadian, and Guyanese cultural, historic, and linguistic references. Displaced through the genre of science fiction, these worlds do not represent a particular Caribbean island or diasporic community, but a freely blended, trans-Caribbean space of fantasy. This reconfiguration serves to remap the Caribbean archipelago as a virtual space: offering a "vision of plurality where irreducible rocks of identity enter constantly into relational forcefields across the Caribbean Sea."[13] This virtual Caribbean provides an alternative space through which to explore the legacies of empire and discover alternative New World approaches to gender and sexuality.

Likewise, when Hopkinson transposes Caribbean cultural and sacred figures to the realm of science fiction, she gives them new, virtual meanings that are associated with the Caribbean queer. The figure of the Midnight Robber plays an important role in Tan-Tan's early childhood as a figure of terror. As a baby, when Tan-Tan cries, Ione warns her daughter to shush lest the Midnight Robber come and take her away (48). In contrast to this traditional interpretation of the Midnight Robber's role, Tan-Tan's eshu, a cybernetic mentor, teaches her to confront and overcome terror by appropriating and transforming the identity of the Midnight Robber: "In years to come, the little girl Tan-Tan would ask the eshu to show her images of the Midnight Robber. Fascinated and frightened at the same time, she would view image after image of the Midnight Robber with his black cape, death-cross X of bandoliers slashed across his chest, his hat with its hatband of skulls. The Midnight Robber, the downpressor, the stealer-away of small children, who make too much mischief. The man with the golden wooing tongue. She would show him. She would be scarier than him. She would be Robber Queen" (48). By introducing the Midnight Robber as a figure from the archive—retrieved by the cybernetic eshu—Hopkinson transposes the realm of Caribbean culture to the domain of sci-fi technologies.[14]

Moreover, the eshu's interventions as a mediator, protector, and narrator serve to underscore the ways in which gender is socially constructed and therefore open to reconstruction. The eshu of Midnight Robber is an AI (artificial intelligence) system used for communications and information, but this mediating technology takes inspiration from the sacred figure of Eshu[15] in Yoruba and New World spiritual traditions. In Caribbean culture, Eshu is an Orisha who plays an important role in Santería, Candomblé, and other sacred traditions. This trickster figure is the protector of travelers and frequently plays games that enable individuals to gain a new understanding of the world. For instance, one story about Eshu represents him as walking down the road wearing a hat that is red on one side and black on the other. After he walks through a certain town, the villagers argue as to whether or not the stranger's hat was black or red. While the villagers on one side of the road had only seen the black side, the villagers on the other side of the road had only seen the red half. Just as they are about to come to blows, Eshu reappears to clear up the mystery. The moral of the story is that a limited perspective deceives the individual and prevents one from perceiving the multifariousness of identities in the world. The eshu in Hopkinson's narrative performs a similar role by encouraging Tan-Tan to adopt a multi-perspectival, transformative view of identity.

Specifically, the eshu encourages Tan-Tan to adopt a cross-gender role by dressing up as the Midnight Robber. In telling the story of women who engaged in transgender acts and cross-dressing as a means of self-emancipation, the eshu establishes a counter-history that challenges patriarchy and heteronormativity: "Earth was like that for a long time. Men could only do some things, and women could only do others. In the beginning of Carnival, the early centuries, Midnight Robbers was always men. Except for the woman who take the name Belle Starr, the same name as a cowgirl performer from America. The Trini Belle Starr made she own costume and she uses to play Midnight Robber" (29). This ludic approach to gender corresponds to Kate Bornstein's notion of gender play as a way of changing constructs and rewriting the rules that structure the performance of gender.[16]

But the Robber identity holds quite a different meaning for Tan-Tan's father. When Antonio comes home to confront his wife about her infidelities, he sees that Tan-Tan is playing her "favourite game" as "Carnival Robber King" (14). He plays the game of "Robber King and Queen" with her, tickling her, rubbing her tummy, and telling her that she is pretty like her mother (17). Thus, the role play as Robber becomes a kind of incest game. In encouraging his daughter to play the role of consort to him, the father can be seen as affiliated with the socially repressive function of carnival, which can serve the interests of the powerful rather than the oppressed.[17] Thus, Hopkinson's use of the Caribbean carnival motif is nuanced: cross-dressing is shown to serve hegemonic, patriarchal interests as well as enable new modes of identification that challenge gender norms. As will be seen, the transformative power of carnivalesque cross-dressing emerges when it fosters equality and social transformation rather than serves as a vehicle for patriarchal violence.

Through the virtual Caribbean experience, Hopkinson interrogates the legacies of colonialism, particularly the links between the history of slavery and sexual violence. Merle Hodge has pointed out that "Caribbean society was born out of brutality, destructiveness, rape; the destruction of the Amerindian peoples, the assault on Africa, the forced uprooting and slavery of the African; the gun, the whip, the authority of force."[18] As a result, the private sphere became politicized: the history of violence made its presence felt in lived relations "between adult and child, between black and white, between man and woman."[19] In an analysis that looks forward to the work of R. W. Connell and Barry Chevannes on masculinities, Hodge sees the "black man in the role of dispenser of violence" as a "descendant of the white slave-overseer asserting an almost bottomless authority over the whipped."[20] In *Midnight Robber*, Antonio takes on the role of dispensing violence as he kills his wife's lover and rapes his daughter. Antonio and Tan-Tan experience a traumatic dislocation of time, space, and corporeality as they undertake the dimensional shift (journey) between planets. The feeling of confinement is likened to the Middle Passage, and Tan-Tan experiences this shift as a nightmare come to life (74–75). During this space and time of transposition, the incest theme comes to the fore as Antonio refers to Tan-Tan as his "doux-doux darling" and "little Ione" (75). When they land in the new world, Antonio addresses his daughter, "You dear to me like daughter, like sister, like wife self" (76). In associating this psychological shift in the father-daughter relationship with the somatic effects of a torturous and disembodying migratory experience, Hopkinson creates an interwoven language for trauma that draws together personal fantasies and collective culture memories. This voyage into exile highlights the alienating consequences and effects of the Middle Passage, which severed family relations and served as a prelude to sexual violence.

At the same time, various facets of Caribbean space, time, and identity are scrambled through the transposition between worlds, signaling the possibility of New World transformation. Tan-Tan feels as though she grows a manicou rat's tail, while her father looks like a mongoose (74). Hopkinson evokes a cross-species Caribbean imaginary, which brings together the manicou (a native of the Caribbean) and the mongoose (brought to the region through empire), suggesting the intermixture of all kinds of species through the global Caribbean experience. Tan-Tan and Antonio's travels through space are associated with a calypso song about wanting to disembark while traversing the turbulent Itanami river rapids (74). This traditional sailor song about travels through Guyana, sung in creolized English, evokes New World mobility and trade. Thus, the dimensional shift between the worlds of Toussaint and New Half-Way Tree highlights the ongoing reconfiguration of subjectivity, community, and cultures throughout the Caribbean's long history of mobilities.

On New Half-Way Tree, the masque as Robber Queen proves a means to recode gender relations and transform social relations. Soon after landing on the planet, Tan-Tan discovers that she has a half-sister (Quamina) and a stepmother. For her ninth birthday, Quamina gives Tan-Tan a Carnival Robber Queen doll, which has "two bubbies" so that Tan-Tan will know it is female (138). Antonio gives Tan-Tan her mother's wedding ring, a symbolic way of commemorating his new relation to his daughter as a spousal figure. That night, Antonio rapes Tan-Tan for the first time. Rape is associated with the repression of memory as Antonio disidentifies with the present and returns to the time of his youth. In this alienated space-time continuum, he misidentifies his daughter as his desired lover, Ione. When he physically possesses Tan-Tan, aside from the physical violence, he disturbs her perception of time. This results in a severe psychic schism for the binary split of good/bad Tan-Tan. Seeing the Robber Queen doll nearby, in the midst of the rape, she fixates on a new concept of self as "Tan-Tan the Robber Queen, the terror of all Junjuh, the one who born on a far-away planet, who travel to this place to rob the rich in their idleness and help the poor in their humility" (140). Thus, just as she did in Toussaint, Tan-Tan takes on the role of Robber Queen as a means of resistance.

For Tan-Tan, cross-dressing offers a way to reconfigure her identity in space and time, especially in the face of traumatic temporalities. Drawing on Judith Butler's theory of performativity, Elizabeth Freeman suggests that what makes drag show iconic and drag-like is the remediation of time through "the performer's play with anachronism, ungainly or exaggerated gesture, off-beat timing, and peek-a-boo suspense."[21] She observes: "Thinking of drag in terms of time, that is, might allow for a more dynamic sense of performance and performativity that encompasses reception as well as address, and might capture the gestural, sensory call-and-response by which gender is built or dismantled within a given space or across time."[22] Such an approach to gender performativity can help to explain how Tan-Tan gains access to a new sense of time and history that helps her to work through the traumatic past. For instance, in the town of Chigger Bite, Tan-Tan confronts a man who makes sexual advances, which trigger flashbacks of her earlier rape. But when the man's mother enters the scene and starts whipping her son, Tan-Tan transfers her rage from the son to his mother. Identifying herself as Tan-Tan, the Robber Queen (246), she exhorts the mother not to hurt her son. This incident is one among many that enable Tan-Tan to confront her traumatic past, trauma in the various communities through which she passes, and the historical trauma of the colonial past. To offer another example, in Begorrat Town, she encounters an indentured servant (284–86) and undergoes flashbacks. Thus, the motif of cross-dressing is affiliated with a cathartic process of working through colonial trauma, both individually and collectively.

Moreover, Hopkinson extends the transformative potential of cross-dressing by introducing cross-species communities and relationships, which further challenge notions of gender, family, and community. Tan-Tan's first encounter in New Half-Way Tree with a douen, named Chichibud, marks the beginning of an ongoing dialogue about the categorization of species, sexual development, and gender that challenges prevailing communal discourses of identity. Both human and douen species are unable to decipher the gendered and sexual identities of the other. The douen thinks that Tan-Tan is a boy, and when Antonio corrects him, the douen responds that human "he" and "she" are all the same (94). At the same time, when Tan-Tan refers to the douen as a compère or equal, she is told that the creature is nonhuman and therefore not to be considered as equal (121). Chichibud and other douen are infantilized by the human community (128); eventually, Tan-Tan learns to do the same (139). However, her perspective changes after Chichibud takes her to the douen community for protection and she learns more about the species through cohabitation. While most of the douen community remains hostile to her presence and some members engage in species discrimination, Tan-Tan is confronted with new constructs of sex and gender that challenge notions of species. The "cow-sized packbird Benta," who initially appears to be a species of bird, turns out to be a female of the douen species. One such hinte (the name for a female of the douen species) turns out to be the wife of Chichibud (152, 181–82). Instead of difference, Tan-Tan begins to find points of resemblance and understand that Benta has been speaking all along: socially constructed prejudices deafened and blinded her, preventing her from recognizing the hinte's actual identity and abilities (181–82).

Encounters with nonhuman species also play an important role as Tan-Tan embraces a transhuman concept of self and community. During the raids, she feels as if somebody is speaking through "the way the Carnival Robber Kings wove their tales, talking as much nonsense as sense, fancy words spinning out from their mouths like thread from a spider's behind: silken shit as strong as story" (245). Not only does Tan-Tan associate herself with the spider who weaves tales, but others also start to tell stories that conflate her life history with episodes from stories told

about Anansi the spider. Traveling with a hinte companion and a rolling calf,[23] she embraces an alternative form of communal life. Reponses
to this identity and community vary considerably. In some settlements,
girls play at being Robber Queen (288). In other instances, Tan-Tan is
described as a nonhuman being with eyes like fire and ratbat wings like
"'Shaitan out of Hell heself, and two heads, one in front and one in
back'" (258) who spits green poison and flies (258). Tan-Tan comes to
accumulate a wealth of meanings and interpretations. Thus, the transformative power of cross-dressing as the Midnight Robber is affiliated with
a nomadic, wide-ranging exploration of identity and community.

Stephen Whittle argues that the ability to be "fluid in one's gender
challenges the oppressive process of gender and the power processes
which use gender to maintain power structures."[24] Potentially, even if
not always, carnival represents this unpredictable, disruptive potential
for social transformation. Antonio Benítez-Rojo describes carnival as a
"system full of noise and opacity, a nonlinear system, an unpredictable
system, in short a chaotic system beyond the total reach of any specific
kind of knowledge or interpretation of the world."[25] For Tan-Tan, the
transgressive potential of carnivalesque cross-dressing is finally fulfilled
toward the end of the narrative when the act of cross-dressing becomes
a means to confront the terrors of the past and embrace the fluidity of
identity. Melonhead (a man who loves Tan-Tan) makes her a new Robber
costume. Unlike Antonio, who engages in selfish sexual fantasies of coupling with his daughter as Midnight Robber, Melonhead embodies a new
masculinity, desiring to help Tan-Tan to express her transgender identity
and come to terms with her sexual history.

At Carnival, Tan-Tan confronts multiple versions of self: she is surrounded by many Midnight Robbers, including those masquerading as
Tan-Tan, New Half-way Tree's Robber Queen. Here the ritual of the
Robber performance becomes a means to confront the terrors of her own
personal sexual history, particularly when she runs into a figure of the
past who threatens to destroy her: her father's jealous lover, Janisette, who
blames Tan-Tan for the sexual abuse she suffered as well as the murder
of her father. Facing Janisette, Tan-Tan gives a Robber speech that bears
witness to the terrors of her sexual past. Improvising a dub poem (a form
initially gendered as masculine),[26] she tells the story concerning the events
that led to the killing of her father. The tropes of Robber speech (a fantastical account of deeds and migrations throughout epic time) provide a fitting
structure for a story of gender violence born of the legacies of colonialism.
When she finishes her poem with the traditional words "sans humanité"

(meaning "no mercy"), the crowd cheers Tan-Tan's winning performance. This "transgender warrior" successfully defends her life and that of her unborn child by unleashing the carnivalesque potential of *J'Ouvert* as the day when the hidden and silenced is brought out into the open.

It's All in the Remix: Dubbed Worlds and Gender Dubbing

Elleke Boehmer's suggestion that a "form of exegesis" emerges from "within the postcolonial text or context"[27] might be applied to the use of "dub" as an interpretive practice and performance at work in *Midnight Robber.* The narrator describes the relation between the planets as comparable to the original song and its dub version: "You know how a thing and the shadow of that thing could be in almost the same place together? You know the way a shadow is a dark version of the real thing, the dub side? Well, New Half-Way Tree is a dub version of Toussaint, hanging like a ripe maami apple in one fold of a dimension veil" (2). Rather than presenting the worlds in a binary of civilized/uncivilized, Hopkinson calls attention to the commonalities or the touch points of the shadow and the real. Hopkinson visualizes the overlapping of light and darkness and points to the similarities and points of convergence between worlds.

The relations between worlds can be interpreted as a form comparable to a "dub" album, which consists of an A side and a B side with the latter being a remix or alternative version of the song on the A side. This repetition with a difference became the basis for extrapolation and multiple remixings of the multiple source materials, creating a third space of abstraction and possibility. Philip Maysles traces dub music to the proliferation of sounds and musicality heard in the slave hold of the Middle Passage,[28] while Michael E. Veal observes that dub operates through a musical language of "fragmented song forms and reverberating soundscapes."[29] Dub is the art of memory and forgetfulness, resonant and imperfect, hearkening back and looking forward to the new. This "sonic metaphor for transatlantic culture" extends the lyrics of a song into an instrumental or "pure sound" territory.[30] Like a dub artist, Hopkinson embraces the transatlantic aesthetics of repetition, distortion, and transformation, but she does so in order to imagine alternative worlds and other ways of describing the transgender experience.

The practice of dubbing is applicable to the performance of gender in *Midnight Robber.* Tan-Tan's Midnight Robber replays the original masculine model for this Caribbean masque through the female body and operates in a way that serves to fracture, fragment, and restructure the language and rhythms of the original to create something new. New possibilities for gender performativity and sexual identity emerge through the iterative process of cross-dressing. In Toussaint, Tan-Tan's role-play is linked to a Freudian fixation on the father figure as well as a mode of resistance to terror. In New Half-Way Tree, the Robber Queen doll serves as a double for Tan-Tan's developing adolescent body. While being raped, Tan-Tan fixates on the doll, and the lifeless, masquerading form serves as a symbolic double for her in that moment. Following the incidents of serial rape as well as the murder of her father, Tan-Tan goes into exile and adopts the role and rhetoric of the Robber. Performances as the Robber are often fragmented and interrupted by flashbacks to the rape scene. This crisscrossing of cultural and personal memories as well as the transgendering of the original Robber figure serves as a medium through which Tan-Tan learns to enact her own identity, using repetitions with difference and improvisational acts in order to discover her own rhythmic expression of gender and sexuality.

Similarly, history and knowledge are recoded through this dub-like performance that fosters slippages and disrupts binary oppositions between the original/copy, rational/irrational, past/future, technological/magical, and here/there. In Hopkinson's *Midnight Robber*, the Caribbean is deconstructed, fragmented, and reordered as a strange new space and place of exploration. While Caribbean storytelling and other vernacular forms introduce the motif of "signifying" upon the region's culture and history, science fiction brings the free-flying fragments of the past into a possible future. Told by Tan-Tan's eshu, the narrative is enabled by the presence of a developing fetus whose technology allows it to function as a receptor and tracking device in the Toussaintian web of the Grande Anansi Nanotech Interface.[31] Through this high-tech act of storytelling, Hopkinson foregrounds the queer space-time continuum of the birth experience as the child leaves the space of the womb via the passage of the birth canal and enters the world: the child departs from a watery home of amniotic fluid and heads for the world of oxygen and exile from the mother's body. This otherworldly experience of migration frames the story of Tan-Tan's transgender migrations in *Midnight Robber*, providing a porous and embodied form of narrative rather than a rigid, rational framework. This reproductive story of origins provides the child with its prehistory, which began with transhuman, transgendered relations. The analysis of masculinities, the postcolonial Caribbean family unit, incest, sexual development, and the role of cross-dressing, all take place within a queer natal space-time continuum.

Tan-Tan names her child Tubman, an act of transgender dubbing that recalls, repeats, and opens up its historical source in unexpected but highly resonant ways. Harriet Tubman (circa 1820–1913) was a leading abolitionist and "conductor" in the Underground Railroad who made nineteen trips to the South and led more than three hundred slaves to freedom. Nicknamed "Moses," Tubman can be seen as a transgender hero/ine who took whatever steps and strategies necessary to attain freedom for herself and others. Reportedly, Tubman cross-dressed as a man when she went South to help her husband to freedom, and thus she represents the figure of the crosser and cross-dresser where the activity of transgender disguise enables the crossing over from slavery to freedom. Tubman also partakes in the history of cross-dressing as part of black history and fiction. In *Vested Interests*, Garber notes the transgender influence of William and Ellen Craft's *Running a Thousand Miles for Freedom*, a text that featured "the runaway slave woman disguised as a man,"[32] on Harriet Beecher Stowe and Mark Twain. Introducing the name Tubman speaks to this motif in African American history as well as African Canadian history, for many of the escaped slaves fled to Canada. The figure of Tubman evokes multiple border crossings between the South and North. Hopkinson can be seen as creating her own dubbed version of Harriet Tubman when her transgender border-crosser, Tan-Tan, chose the name of a transgender hero/ine, Tubman, for her son.

Tubman's transgender identity traverses, bridges, and blurs fixed categories of identity by replaying and repeating the known associations with Harriet Tubman in new contexts. Tubman's transition from slave to freed person and transgender masking represent multiple categorical displacements in the understanding of the body, gender, and identity, which resonate through Tubman's distinctly new disruption of multiple binary categorizations in *Midnight Robber*. Harriet Tubman's history and identity link challenges to gender and the construction of human identity through slavery and post-slavery: where the slave confounds the status of human/nonhuman because the body is understood as a human commodity, the emancipated slave represents a supplement to the understanding of the human because identity has already been configured as other than human. Consequently, the name "Tubman" invokes the categorical disruption of binaries such as enslaved/free, man/woman, and nonhuman/human.

This disruptive potential is amplified by Hopkinson's hybrid configuration of Tubman as transgender cyborg who incorporates sacred technologies for communication across the universe with nonhuman entities, such as eshu and Granny Nanny.[33] The eshu narrator explains that Tubman is plugged into the universe because Nanny instructed the nanomites[34] in the child's "mamee blood to migrate into" the growing tissue and alter the child so that it can feel nannysong and correctly calibrate the self in connection with the Grande Anansi Nanotech Interface (328). The child's living tissue is altered, and this posthuman body[35] is actually a "bodystring" that sings to Nanny tune (328) or a kind of instrument that is comparable to a radio capable of transmission and a musical instrument. Just as Harriet Tubman confounds categorical interpretation, Hopkinson's Tubman disrupts the human/nonhuman division because the infant combines both human and cybernetic parts. Tubman forges links between (post)colonial history and an alternative future through a hybrid embodiment of the transformative potential associated with processes of emancipation, cross-dressing, transgender naming, and cybernetic incorporation.

The novel is construed as a posthuman tale transmitted to the reader via Tubman as a receptor and transmission device. Likewise, through the motif of cross-gender identity, the narrative discourse brings the reader into contact with various discourses that call "human" identity into question. The new "Tubman" brings together multiple discourses that trouble a conventional understanding of human identity in terms of race, technology, and gender: the post-slavery body, the cyborg, and the transgendered body. The technologies of Caribbean culture are transmitted via the infant as a new kind of storytelling technology embodied in the queer space and time of the womb. Through the virtual space of narrative, both reader and child are auditors and initiates into a posthuman world; they come into this world through entangled prehistories consisting of displaced, fragmented, and symbolic colonial and postcolonial stories of the queer Caribbean. As a reproductive technology, the narrative of Tan-Tan and Tubman engenders new ways of thinking about the technologies of the self[36] and opens up alternative possibilities for self-identification and society.

This tale of postcolonial legacies, cross-dressing, transhuman communities (Tan-Tan's relations to the douen and rolling calf), posthuman bodies, and New World exiles creolizes science fiction to explore existing and alternative possibilities for Caribbean gender and sexuality. Significantly, Hopkinson describes New Half-Way Tree as "the dub version of Toussaint, hanging like a ripe maami apple in one fold of a dimension veil" (2). This virtual identity, both self and other, offers a pluralistic approach to identity. The maami apple hangs between worlds: it is neither a fruit on the Tree of Knowledge nor a New World symbol of paradise regained. Rather, we might envision a hybrid tree, standing in-and-between Half-Way Tree in Jamaica and Toussaint's symbolic tree of selfhood and liberty with its multiple regenerative roots.[37] The free radicals (or radicles) of the New World come together in the resistant fold of translocated meaning that links diverse references to (post)colonial history and Caribbean places with strenuous efforts to attain freedom in past, present, and alternative world configurations. Hopkinson's opaque poetics, like those of Glissant, disclose hidden relations and rhizomatic upcroppings in the Caribbean imaginary. The translocated maami apple symbolizes the slippages between worlds: the fractures and relations that underpin Caribbean history and identity. This symbol of the dubbed relations among worlds defies binary oppositions of good/evil, knowledge/innocence, and here/there. The "mammee apple" (*mammea americana*), which is actually not an apple but another species of fruit, with a bitter rind that encloses a sweet, aromatic flesh, defies easy categorization. Situated in the fold, the maami apple represents an interstitial perspective, a virtuality born of mobility, mixing, and experimentation.

Similarly, cross-dressing, transhuman relations, the carnivalesque, and the birth of the posthuman are facets of this kind of alternative worldview where the queer potential of multiple perspectives, overlaps, excesses, and resonances develop their own resonant rhythms and unfurl new perspectives. Of course, individuals may continue to replay the roles passed down and reproduced through family and community, but *Midnight Robber* places emphasis on social transformation. Hopkinson draws on the tools of Caribbean culture—masquerade, carnival, call-and-response techniques of storytelling, and dub—to explore the contexts, conventions, and legacies that shape Caribbean gender and sexuality. Through dubbing, she replays fragments and reconstructs the tools of vernacular culture as a means to foster a fully emancipated Caribbean imaginary. Far from a retreat into the past, this queering of Caribbean culture achieves its critical edge and radical potential through the lives of individuals who renegotiate and reconstitute the uneven, phantasmagoric spaces of memory, migration, and desire.

Notes

1. Lorde, "Age, Race, Class, and Sex," 245; Hodge, "Shadow of the Whip," 189; Jarrett, "Song to Pass On," 1234; Chancy, *Searching for Safe Spaces,* 28–29; Glave, "Whose Caribbean?," 679–80. Two important book-length studies include Boyce Davies's *Black Women, Writing and Identity* and Conner and Hatfield Sparks's *Queering Creole Spiritual Traditions.*

2. Hopkinson and Nelson, "Making the Impossible Possible," 110. See also Hopkinson, "Profession of Science Fiction, 60," 5–10.

3. Sedgwick, *Tendencies*, 8.

4. Hopkinson, *Midnight Robber*. All references to the novels will be given in parentheses in the text. My reading responds especially to Collier's "Spaceship Creole," where he argues that the vitality of Hopkinson's novels "derives from a clever syncretization of the generic features of science fiction and dystopia with the operational fabric of Caribbean folk culture" (455). In "Vanishing Bodies," Boyle argues that Hopkinson articulates a more fluid model of racial and gendered identity through her manipulation of generic conventions (177–91). Recent discussions of Hopkinson's manipulation of the genre include Ramraj, "Nalo Hopkinson: Transcending Genre Boundaries," 135–53; Ramsdell, "Nalo Hopkinson and the Reinvention of Science Fiction," 155–72; Ramraj, "Nalo Hopkinson's Colonial and Dystopic Worlds in *Midnight Robber*," 131–38; and Dubey, "Becoming an Animal in Black Women's Science Fiction," 31–51.

5. The Midnight Robber approaches carnival-goers and holds them up with tales of his wanderings and dreadful deeds. His Robber speech or personal narrative often includes an account of events that took place over centuries, beginning with the Middle Passage and throughout the long history of empire in the Caribbean. Threatening carnival-goers, his dreadful performance mixes the language of the Bible, the terrible boasting of a pirate, and the theatricality of the showdown elements in Western cowboy stories. In exchange for this performance, the carnival-goer pays the Robber and is allowed to pass. Often, there are showdowns among multiple Robbers. For an account of the identity of the Midnight Robber and an assessment of this figure's potential for social critique, see Honoré, "Midnight Robber," 124–31.

6. Braidotti, *Transpositions*, 6.

7. Feinberg, *Transgender Warriors*, x.

8. Garber, *Vested Interests*, 10.

9. Ibid., 11.

10. In Caribbean folklore, particularly from Trinidad and Tobago, the term "douen" refers to the "lost soul" of a child who was not baptized or christened before death. Neither male nor female, the douen is destined to roam the land, searching for children who have not yet been baptized or christened in order to lure them away from home. Hopkinson's douen are actually another species, but she also plays with this coded meaning in her narrative.

11. In *Poetics of Relation*, Édouard Glissant observes, "Rhizomatic thought is the principle behind what I call the Poetics of Relation, in which each and every identity is extended through a relationship with the Other" (11).

12. Misrahi-Barak, "Beginner's Luck," 96.

13. Dash, "Postcolonial Caribbean Identities," 794.

14. Hopkinson argues that the sacred and folkloric traditions of the Caribbean can be seen as "fantasy/science fiction/magic realism." See Watson, "Conversation with Nalo Hopkinson," 167.

15. The proper name Eshu refers to the Orisha, as opposed to the eshu in Hopkinson's fiction.

16. Bornstein, *My Gender Workbook*, 191.

17. Some critics view carnival as a safety valve that serves the interests of the hegemonic order, because it allows for the release and evacuation of potentially transformative sociopolitical energies. However, other critics argue for the transformative potential of carnival. Puri summarizes these debates in *Caribbean Postcolonial*, referring to the work of Roberto da Matta, Robert Stam, and James Scott (244).

18. Hodge, "Shadow of the Whip," 189.

19. Ibid., 189.

20. Ibid., 191.

21. Freeman, "Introduction," 161.

22. Ibid.

23. A rolling calf is a particular kind of duppy with fiery eyes and flames issuing from its nostrils.

24. Whittle, "Gender Fucking or Fucking Gender?," 210.

25. Benítez-Rojo, *Repeating Island*, 295.

26. Sharpe, "Dub and Difference," 611. Jean "Binta" Breeze initiated a form she called domestic dub as a way to counter the masculinist orientation of dub poetry.

27. Boehmer, *Colonial and Postcolonial Literature*, 243.

28. Maysles, "Dubbing the Nation," 92.

29. Veal, *Soundscapes and Shattered Sounds*, 2.

30. Ibid., 219, 197.

31. The "Grande Anansi Interface" or "Grande Nanotech Sentient Interface" is Granny Nansi's Web for communication on Toussaint planet. The name of this Web-like interface is intriguing because it evokes the name of Anancy the spider, who inhabits the web of Caribbean folklore. The concept of the "World Wide Web" (the Internet) is also implicit in this idea of a worldwide interface that connects people in a futuristic universe.

32. Garber, *Vested Interests*, 285.

33. The name "Granny Nanny" (or Nanny as she is sometimes known) calls to mind Nanny Maroon, a leader of resistance to slavery in Jamaica.

34. The world "nanomite" is related to the play of words on "nanotechnology" and "Nanny technology." Nanny seeds the tools, machines, building, and earth with nanomites, which are described as her hands and body (10). In the case of Tubman, the nanomite is similar to a high-tech (nano) bug (mite) that enters the bloodstream and enables the baby to interface with the technologies of the universe.

35. Hayles and Haraway refer to the posthuman body as one that is reconfigured through new technologies and cyberspace. My postcolonial reading of posthumanism is indebted to the work of Eshun, Weheliye, Carr, and the Afrofuturists. Hopkinson has been an active participant in debates about Afrofuturism (see Hopkinson and Nelson, "Making the Impossible Possible").

36. Foucault, "Technologies of the Self," 223–51.

37. When Toussaint was captured in 1802, he is reported to have said, "En me renversant, on n'a abattu à Saint-Domingue que le tronc de l'arbre de la liberté des nègres; il repoussera par les racines, parce qu'elles sont profondes et

nombreuses" [In overthrowing me, you have cut down in Saint-Domingue only the trunk of the tree of liberty; it will spring up again by the roots for they are numerous and deep]. The French inscription appears below a bust of Toussaint, which is located in front of the dungeon at Fort de Joux, France, where he was imprisoned and died.

3

Theories in the Flesh

The Caribbean and Transvestism

Mayra Santos Febres

Translated by Roberto del Valle Alcalá

IN THE BEGINNING was a siren floating down the stairs of a Caribbean mansion. The mansion was cross-dressed. Its backyard furniture in Filipino wicker, its marble floors, the air-conditioning exhaling a fresh breeze, as if from some other latitude; even the calla lilies, doubly reflected on the built-in mirror, bore witness to the spell. Siren was another piece of jewellery. Her perfectly finished face, her curls, her arabesque-embroidered night dress were all bits of fantasy. Siren's voice was the only true thing. With that voice, she would bewitch the audience, she would transport them to regions of the unnamed, to a place where the sorrows flowing from primal violence have their origin. That foundational violence, the first sting of desire . . .

This was the first image unleashing the words of what five years later would become *Sirena Selena vestida de pena*. The novel as a germ-cell was born out of another image—the vision of a boy drugged out of his mind, singing boleros and picking up cans round the edges of a bar. This image, that of disaster, began to filter through the seams of the previous one. Both incarnate the cross-dressed Caribbean. Grief dressed up as spectacle; privation as glamour; screaming as seductive whisper. Through this adolescent transvestite I found my way of representing the Caribbean—that Caribbean which clothes its sorrow and poverty in fantasy and exoticism so as to name it, sing it in boleros, mourn it on stage. In order to reveal the complexity of Caribbean islands, I had to find a way of naming them from the double axis of seduction and sorrow, of fantasy and that onslaught which sharpens jaws for revenge and devouring. Upon that axis is founded their best survival strategy.

Caribbean transvestism is a survival ruse that has not been evoked much in the arts and literatures of these lands. I already knew about "Las tretas del débil" (The ruses of the weak), explored by the Argentinian critic Josefina Ludmer. Saying "no" and meaning "yes." A form of saying which keeps quiet in order to name silence; a way of inserting biography into the midst of other "official" discourses whose version is accepted, and which helps the voice of the excluded to make itself heard. Ludmer discovers these ruses in the rhetorical turns used by the Mexican nun Sor Juana Inés de la Cruz when she writes her *Carta atenagórica* (Atenagoric letter) to ward off attacks from the eighteenth-century patriarchal Church led by the Bishop of Puebla. The Mexican nun names the body, places it at the center of her discourse, and propounds it as another text where her passion for knowledge can be read (even if she is a woman and a nun, and, according to the Church, she must keep silent and obey). And yet Ludmer does not see such a ruse; or rather, she does not study it as another strategy of survival and attack against received violence. But it is one: making a spectacle out of the mute body is another ruse of the weak. This ruse plants the body at the center of discourse; it parades the marks that inscribe it as evidence of violence received by the body. It reveals its scar, its mutilation, as an offense to the eyes and "sensitivity" of the attacker. Thus, the body exposes the marks inscribed by power upon its skin. It turns the body into an offensive weapon. It proposes the body as spectacle and explains, for example, how it has been loaded with the indelible mark of History, and also how History has sold certain bodies, has wounded, silenced, disowned certain bodies to establish an official version of facts. The body is the text that remains outside of discourse but that, from its margin, names what the voice of the excluded cannot pronounce. Voice says one thing and the body another. Voice is the song of the Siren, which charms other bodies and takes them with its own to the place of shipwrecks.

But why doesn't the voice of the enforced body use the direct discourse of reason? Why does the body as spectacle reveal its scar so obliquely? Why does it embellish and make it up? Why, in hiding, does it highlight it? Why does the transvestite Caribbean sing and make itself up instead of shouting its grief in denunciation?

The Cuban writer Severo Sarduy speaks of transvestism while drawing inspiration from hunting and the survival strategies of those insects that change their appearance in order to secure their survival. He explains that the male transvestite does not imitate woman. For him there is no *woman*, because he knows (and his tragedy is that he never ceases to know) that he, that is, she, is an appearance, that her realm and the strength of her fetish cloak an insurmountable fault in a previously sage nature. Human transvestism is therefore an imaginary apparition and the convergence of three mimetic possibilities: metamorphosis, camouflage, and intimidation.

Through metamorphosis, the transvestite attempts to surpass his model, to become something better, to conquer at last that fault in his nature. Yet even metamorphosed, the transvestite manages to camouflage his nature,[1] to protect himself from the attacks of his predators, of those who have catalogued him as an inferior being, animal fodder, worthy of disdain and mockery. However, since the makeup and artifice are too obvious, the transvestite must admit the existence of his disguise and use it as a defensive weapon. He uses the excessiveness of its mask to paralyze and terrorize, as certain animals use their appearance to hunt or to defend themselves, to make up for natural defect or lacking skills. To cross-dress is then to be reinscribed and erased, as well as to intimidate. It is to know that at the center of one's own experience of self there is something wrong, a foundational error. That one should be something else, better oneself in another modality of being. Thence comes the thrust to become an other. But metamorphosis is never complete. Then, transvestism becomes camouflage or an intimidatory weapon. The transvestite is thereby placed under the spotlight. He is shown as an exotic animal, as a tender and weak prey to desire, in order to achieve one of two things: either to disappear from the earth along with other exotic things, or to brew his venom for the upcoming fight. The transvestite disguises himself because if he were to show his real face, he would only encounter annihilation. The transvestite uses song and stand-up humor because if he were to use official logical discourse, he would only have that discourse negate him. A being like him is impossible, improbable. He can be categorized neither as animal nor as human. That's why the transvestite I wanted to represent my Caribbean sings. In a melodious voice, he chants his grief among the rocks; leads the helmsman to the snare, makes him run aground, destroy himself. He survives, pursues his search. Longing for an impossible metamorphosis, he wants out of the blemish—being born in a poor island, where nobody is black or white, European or Asian or native or African; where identity is such a vertiginous mix it cannot even be named. Against a world of fixed categories, of demarcated identities, histories of liberation and nation-state foundation, we, Caribbean folk, perceive our "oddity." We posture as heirs to cultures which are not our own, we negate identities we never really got to know, we think ourselves citizens and natives of countries where we have never lived. This is our blemish, which now globalization and cultural hybridity have us share with other beings on this planet. That is to say, it becomes less of a blemish. And yet, for that reason, we relish discussing our anomaly, redefining it as a strategy for struggle and survival. Now there are many of us transvestites across the world, and we must hazard a name for the ruse. Disciplining and discussing the mise-en-scène of a defense strategy may prove a way of building up ever more powerful alliances against that power which alienates us from our own bodies. To attempt a "logical" contribution, that is, to theorize our duplicity and the knowledge pulsing inside, is yet another way of conceiving knowledge. To name such a knowledge means to render it soluble and protean, over against the fixed logical categories of traditional modern reason. What Caribbean experiences with the mask and cross-dressing reveal is the danger of categories. Categories name and segregate. Categories lie at the very root of that duplicity. We know this in body and voice. That is why we propose to know from a different place, from some alternative to categories. We propose to know from obliqueness, that is, from the opaque disguise that mocks the light of Reason.

In his postcolonial studies on nation and narration, the Indian theorist Homi Bhabha isolated a strategy germane to transvestism: parody as a ploy of confrontation with colonial power. By means of parody, the colonized mimics and mocks the colonizer. Laughter minimizes power, criticizes it. This strategy, also identified by Fanon in his seminal essay *Black Skin, White Masks,* explores the duplicity of colonized identities. This duplicity has been accorded several names: W. E. B. Dubois's "double consciousness," Chela Sandoval's "oppositional consciousness," "the carnivalesque" in Bakhtin, Derrida's *différance* at a discursive level, postmodern hybridity in global identities. But the logic of transvestism conceals other dilemmas. Parodic imitation and split consciousness are still mired in binary thinking. On one side stands the oppressed, and on the other, the oppressor. Parody reveals and denounces, from the margin, the locations of power. But it labors from the void of the oppressed. That is, the oppressed as unacknowledged. His/her discourse is unintelligible: it can only be named, staged, via the deferred and distorted discourse of the Other. S/he only acknowledges his/her difference when disguised as the Other, when s/he adopts the discourse of the Other to mock and criticize it.

But transvestism is much more than parody; it is the parody of parody. Transvestism cuts through the discourse of the powerful Other to mark another point of departure—a point which is no void; for it has already developed an identity. This identity is opaque, contradictory—and yet his/her own. It was born out of parody. The transvestite knows he is always already negated, and dresses up to erase, cancel out, and at the same time exaggerate, a disguise with another disguise.

In the Caribbean, transvestism rules supreme among the mise-en-scènes of popular culture. Carnivals are the preferred scenario for men to dress up as women. In Santiago Apóstol, in Puerto Rico, the character of the *loca* cannot be absent from the parade. In the Dominican Republic, the *gagá* black men wear ample red skirts with a huge white phallus hanging from them as they march through the streets of Baní, La Romana, Santiago. Thus they invoke good luck and fertility, at the same time that they dispel evil spirits. The secret shows of transvestite cabaret in Cuba, as well as the more commercial and tourist ones of Santo Domingo and Puerto Rico, are some of the privileged sites where the full vitality of the transvestite is deployed. They stage and embody that double hybridity, the concurrence of the impossible in a single body. An inversion of power is thereby named. Man dresses up as woman in order to feminize—that is, negate—that is, render laughable, his dubious masculinity, his problematical association with patriarchal power. For better or worse, colonialism has prevented a full display and development of patriarchy in the Caribbean. For better, because Caribbean women can more easily slip through the cracks of a weak native patriarchy—one that is heavily dependent on structures imported from the colonizing countries. For worse, because manliness is all too aware of its frailty, and sometimes chooses violence to prevail. For better, because on account of being so frail, many Caribbean masculinities can be reconfigured in different ways, growing porous and malleable, mocking themselves. For worse, because laughter may sometimes fail, and still preserve and magnify frustration.

Yet Caribbean transvestism is complex. It does not just revolve around the axis of gender. In most cases, two axes converge upon transvestite transformation—gender, but also race. It is often a man—black, mulatto, or *jabao*—who wants to dress up as a white woman. He just rehearses one of the most typical Caribbean performances, that of "passing"—passing the black cat as a white hare, in a racial masking which greatly determines the imaginary of pigmentocratized societies. Pigmentocracy installs a pyramid of power and privilege based on the skin tonalities of the inhabitants of ex-slave societies. Given that, in the Caribbean, purity is elusive and hybridity incommensurable, those of "light" complexion receive, claim, and defend class privileges that often intersect with race privileges. The "darker" ones seek to "better their race" by dint of unions likely to lighten skin color, or by means of diverse cosmetics (smoothing, nose surgery, liposuction, hair dye, contact lenses, lightening lotions) with which to cover over the *fault* of being black. The dark body cross-dresses as a white one, not in order to parody it, but rather to attempt a metamorphosis. Turn the caterpillar into a butterfly. Yet the metamorphosis is never achieved. Not even after generations of whitening does black become white. White appearance continues to show its cultural seam—that Caribbean condition which roots identity in mixture. Caribbean whites can never pass as Europeans. Many experience a daily yearning for what they never were and will never be. They long for the identitarian determination of their grandparents, who were Dutch, Spanish, German, French, Italian—or so they think. But they, they are and always will be minor whites, suspect whites, potential blacks. Ever since the beginning, colonization consigned a separate category for them—*indianos, latinos, creoles*. They are a being halfway through white and black, pining for a culture of which they know they are deprived. The Puerto Rican author Edgardo Rodríguez Juliá defines this state in his essay *Caribeños:* "It so happens that marginality renders tradition problematical, blurring it even when it is visible, placing it alongside other traditions which also demand the attention of the marginal (writer). . . . Marginality means shouldering the burden of many. It is the poor unhappy child rubbing his nose against the glass pane of a patisserie; such abundance on display is both neighbouring and distant; even appropriating it through the eyes and the imagination, it will never be altogether his."

This is the tragedy the Caribbean folk—whether black, mulatto, *jabao*, or white—seek to surpass: foundational violence, the sting of desire. The tragedy is nurtured by the sheer discourse that propelled Caribbean identity as a regional, national, or modern identity. In other words, it lies at the center of the same linear, logical thinking of Western reason and its way of conceiving History. Édouard Glissant points in the direction of conflict, contending from the logical standpoint of the illegitimate. Every History is the recount of filiations, of genealogical trees tending across time and space, a line of succession and legitimacy. Illegitimacy threatens to dissolve a community. If the line of legitimacy is broken, the chain of filiations ceases to signify and community rambles around the world without possibly claiming a primary need. Any tragic action would absorb this disequilibrium. Transvestism is a tragic action staging and embodying the logic of the illegitimate. It points toward what Glissant proposes as the counterweight to the logic of legitimacy—which is the logic of transversality or the poetics of Relation. Through the transversal, linearity is ramified. It abandons the violence of lines, of categories excluding the hybrid in favour of the pure. In heterogeneous Caribbean societies, the transversal and the relational propose a synthesis that is not achieved through reunion but through expansion. Linearity is totally replaced by the contingency of the diverse. And, says Glissant, that which protects diversity is *opacity*. Caribbean transvestism departs, neither from the parodic vacuum nor from that synthetic hybridity which restores the linearity of the legitimate, but from the opacity of that which proves mute but present in the body beneath the voice and its discourse. Opacity is not in the song, but in the tone of voice—which is the only true thing, even if it is a falsetto. Thus Caribbean transvestism does not point out the excess of specificities, but the free connections between those specificities, hoping to dissolve with this freedom the chaos of its confrontations, as well as the linear violence which founds them on the islands and the body.

This is the logic of Caribbean transvestism. That is why in his eerie poem "Vestido de Novia," the Cuban poet Norge Espinosa defines the transvestite as a being connecting purity with abjection, show with opacity, and parody with unveiling:

> De quién a quién habrá robado ese gesto esa veleidad
> Esos párpados amarillos esa voz que alguna vez fue de las sirenas.
> Quién
> Le va a apagar la luz bajo la cama y le pintará los senos con que sueña
> Quién le pintará las alas a este mal ángel hecho para las burlas
> Si a sus alas las condenó el viento y gimen
> Quién quién le va a desvestir sobre qué hierba o pañuelo
> Para abofetearle el vientre para escupirle las piernas
> A este muchacho de cabello crecido así vestido de novia.[2]

Thus is the untranslatability of the gesture, the untranslatability of the body presented as prey and show for the mockery, abjection, desire, and dream of becoming other. "Thus," this adverb, is a way of naming Caribbeanness. According to Benítez-Rojo's conclusion to his theoretical essay *La Isla que se repite,* Caribbeanness is walking "in a certain fashion," a manner of being, and of being *in* the body that resists logical categorization and preserves its opacity—and therefore its difference. Transvestism means protecting oneself by multiplying the body, making it irreducible to a single line. Thus, transvestism compels a suspension of the logic of the real, and replaces it with the logic of the probable. It bewitches the audience. It makes them accept multiplicity as an occasion for celebration, and as a defense and a threat. It infects with "abnormality" and "illegitimacy" all those witnessing the exploit. Underneath its veneer, the wound is opaquely revealed. The audience are enjoined, compelled to acknowledge their own—those wounds pulsing in dissimulation among disguises, so disowned and yet so real.

In the beginning was a small heap of matter, a body perhaps, slipping through the waters. Somebody shouted "Island!" and the Caribbean was born, somebody lusted for that flesh and turned it into a monster, a Siren. Siren accepted his fantasy, and made it over into her costume. Playful, seductive, and bitter, she educated her voice and sang the sorrows of all the shipwrecks blamed on her. She turned her own sorrow into a simulacrum, and the simulacrum of her voice into a snare for further havoc. The sea grew populous with shipwrecks and sirens—so many were there that now it's impossible to tell the monsters from the victims of so much crying.

Notes

This essay was first published as "Caribe y travestismo" in Maeseneer and Van Hecke, *El artista caribeño como guerrero de lo imaginario*. I would like to thank Mayra Santos Febres for having read the draft of this translation, and Massiel Hernández, happy encounter, for having brought her Caribbean next-door.

1. I have retained Santos Febres's original allusion to the "male transvestite" in Sarduy and throughout this piece as "el travestido." However, it should be noted that the rendition of Spanish null subjects, possessives, and reflexive pronouns into English results in a text that is far more marked for masculine gender than the original.

2. "From whom will he have stolen that gesture that whim/Those yellow eyelids that voice which once belonged to the sirens./Who/Will switch off the lights under the bed and paint him those breasts he dreams about/Who will paint the wings of this bad angel made for mockery/If the wind doomed his wings and they moan/Who who will undress him on which grass or kerchief/To slap the belly to spit on the legs/Of this long-haired boy thus dressed as a bride."

On Becoming an Indian Starboy

Shani Mootoo

FOR INDIANS crossing the Kala Pani to work as indentured laborers on the sugar cane estates of the Caribbean (from 1834 onward, just after slavery of African peoples had been abolished) an opportunity existed to reinvent themselves in lands where their histories were unknown, where even caste, for instance, for the enterprising and daring, could be changed. When prospective Indian laborers, just off the boats, were asked by the British officers at the port of entry in Port of Spain, what their name was, many didn't understand the question and answered with the name of the place in India from which they had come, and others, indeed understanding the question, decided, why not? In a new land they might as well become whatsoever and whomsoever they fancied, and in clever moves gave answers like Maharajah and Rajkumar, and these words became their surnames. On my father's side, one of the first ancestors to leave India (Calcutta) to work as a laborer on a sugar estate was a man named Bulaki. Not a month after his arrival, it was noted by the authorities that Bulaki was a Hindu pundit. He was immediately released from his obligations at the estate, and, rather, pressed into full-time service as a pundit for a wide area. Bulaki was often paid in kind for his services. From the sale of excess goods, his enterprising wife was able to amass a previously unimaginable fortune that would eventually include a roadside shop, a cattle farm, a taxi service, a bus commuter service, real estate, and an orange estate. I sometimes fantasize that Bulaki was really a man named something like Alibhai, that he boarded the ship to Trinidad as a Muslim, only to find himself surrounded by Hindus. This man Alibhai thought, "Ah! There is business to be had here," and his passage across the Black Waters was one, too, of Muslim laborer-recruit to Hindu priest. Of course—I quickly add—Hinduism and all its attending positive and negative ways is so bred in the marrow of this family I come from, that I only fantasize here. But I suspect that once an Indian from India stepped foot on one of those boats in the nineteenth century, bound for the islands of the British Empire, in leaving behind language, family ties, community, tradition in general and very specific religion rites in particular, he or she was transitioning into a queerness of no return. Many of us in more recent times have responded to a restlessness no doubt provoked by that earlier rupture, and migrated elsewhere yet again. And, now, far from Trinidad, I for one continue to don new clothes, and to invent entirely new ways of being. By dint of the original displacement, I am destined, sometimes to limp along, sometimes to jump up, in a continuously challenging carnival of queerness. It is the how, and the why, of the stories written.

THE VERY first cinema that I was ever exposed to was when I was a child in Trinidad. My mother's father used to take me regularly, every other week, to the Metro Cinema in San Fernando to see the latest Indian movie that had arrived on the island. The only language I knew at the time was my child's version of Trinidad-style English. The movies were likely in Hindi, and even if there had been subtitles they would have been useless, as I was not yet reading fluently. But, thanks to a continuum of themes and actors from one film to the next, I quickly picked up the story lines and recognized certain stars. I had been very enamored then of Shashi Kapoor and his Elvis-look-alike brother Shammi, and in no time they and the roles they played became my models.

One could say that to this date the model of masculinity I am most at home with in my own performance of a female masculinity is that of the Indian starboy, as we called him back then, the one who was wronged, fought for justice in the fairest but loneliest of ways, the one who, only when outnumbered by an impossibly large gang of heavy-metal chain-wielding thugs and subjected to a beating that left him with a bloody but neat gash on the side of his forehead, would finally be forced to clench his fists and resort to violence. Against all odds and those kinds of numbers, he would, somewhat reluctantly at first but then with dance-like agility and the studied precision of a ninja, deliver a series of blows that would result in his winning back his dignity, the family that had mistakenly shunned him, his and their reputation, and the girl who had danced, sung, and cried with him (in his attire of incredibly beautiful vests and rakishly worn scarves) through wheat fields, around lakes, and on the slopes of the Himalayas.

On returning home from those movies, I would stand in front of the mirror, an angled gash of red painted on my forehead, or a Band-Aid applied just above my eyebrow. I would slip my thumbs into the loops of my jeans, and in a flash draw my guns, or deliver a fistful at the face of my imagined enemy, or with a studied chivalry, lean my side against the dresser in my room as I applied an equally studied and contradictory softness of the gait of the starboy as he looked longingly, yet smugly, at the object of his desire. I imagined her looking back up at me, noting my bloodied forehead, admiring my cream-colored scarf, my tall cowboy boots, and accepting me fully for all that I was and was not.

In the days of the 1960s, the people in my country (not the country of my film-influenced imagination, but Trinidad) who held the balance of power, in more ways than one, were still the whites—recently arrived expatriate Scottish and English ones, as well as the local ones descended from British and French plantation owners whose families had been on the island many generations longer than mine. From seven years old until I was eleven, I attended an exclusive private primary school in Vista Bela, Trinidad, where my sister and I, and one other brown-skinned girl named Joy, were the only nonwhites. The remaining eighteen students were a mixture of Trinidadian white children of bank managers and business owners, and children of white foreigners who were stationed on the island, attached in some administrative way to oil companies or construction companies. At that school our sole teacher was a white English woman, named Mrs. Kelly. Although my father was a doctor, he was of South Asian descent, meaning he was an Indo-Trinidadian, further meaning he was dark-skinned. I watched him, forever polite to anyone regardless of class, or race, defer just that much more, however, to white managers, administrators, business owners. In turn we, his family, were let into those people's private lives, feted fully by them. In yet another twist in the rope of reciprocations, our house was always full of white children come to play with us and to swim in our pool, one of the only two private swimming pools in the town then. At the cocktail parties my parents frequently held, white couples were, by far, in the majority. Whiteness, the power it wielded for no other reason than itself, the style it seemed to own, was, naturally, as coveted as it was despised. White women, as evidenced by calypsos—for instance, The Mighty Sparrow's: "Two white women traveling through Africa / find themselves in the hands of a cannibal head hunter / I envy the Congo Man, I wish I could go and shake his hand / but me, you know how many trap I set? / And still, I never eat a white meat yet"—and by a good number of rumored affairs and broken hearts, were often objects of desire, and while there was a certain amount of social mixing allowed on the streets, in the sheets this was all but forbidden, by all sides, in general. None of this was lost on a hyperaware child.

When *The Sound of Music* played in the cinema, the Indian starboy in me came face-to-face with her—or perhaps I should say, *his*—first big love, Liesl, the eldest daughter of Captain Von Trapp. I so yearned throughout that movie, and the fourteen other times I saw it, to jump into the picture on the screen, transformed into my own version of Shammi Kapoor, to give Rolf, Liesl's Nazi love interest, a good thrashing, and to win the heart of Liesl, and the approval of her father, Captain Von Trapp. If the origins of that white object of desire have been laid bare, old learnings die hard. You make a promise not to ever look at a white woman again, but before the line of that promise has been drawn, one rounds the corner, and you are left shaking your head at yourself, saying, well, indeed, promises were made to be broken.

In my Trinidad days I did not come across women whom I could have pegged to be lesbian, the word even unheard of in my world then. But every fiber of my self seemed to act and react in different ways from all I saw of how the other females in my family, in our social world, and even on the public street operated. I scanned rooms, crowds, the streets, for others who might be like myself. I had the uncomfortable sense that my body (torso thick and waistless, eyes big wide open always staring, lips pouted in stern curiosity, slow to crack a smile, legs itching to run run run, arms wanting to swing a cricket bat, hands to snap at, stop a frog in mid-leap) was playing tricks on me. I offered myself the explanation that I was really a boy, a fact that would in time become clear to all—and I would win back my dignity, the family that had mistakenly shunned me, my and their reputation, and the girl who had danced, sung, and cried with me . . .

Time passed. No magic ever occurred, but tricks were still played: breasts grew, belly rounded, back and arms took on the proportions handed down by grandmothers, mother, and the daily profusion of Indo-Trinidadian-style sweets. From comments flung down like bits of dung that had accidentally dirtied the hands, I knew that certain kinds of female people and male people were laughed at, scorned, ridiculed, not accepted into "our" circles. I sensed that I was one of those nameless, community-less people.

It was clear that I would never be as pretty as girls who looked and performed the applauded version of what girls were supposed to be, and that I wouldn't be . . . and didn't want to be . . . as competent as they were in the ways of courting and being courted by boys, or be the object of potential mothers-in-law's interests and inquiries. To quietly underscore and ensure all of this, I adopted a dress code that all but made me invisible. Jeans with loops for a good wide belt, wide enough for a holster and gun (which I wouldn't have used, except to scare away bores and bigots), baggy shirts that hid my straight-sided torso, with a collar and buttons (that could be done up and a tie worn, just in case), and on my feet flat, casual sandals or slippers, or easy-to-make-the-quick-getaway-in sneakers. This became my uniform, and it was in studied opposition to that of "real" girls—my sisters and the other girls in my school, the women with whom my mother socialized—who all wore a uniform of their own: blouses without sleeves that exposed their upper arms, round open necks that gave a glimpse of their neck and upper chest area, skirts, or slacks—never pants—that had side-zippers sewn flat, and which reached above their ankles so that they didn't trail their shoes, and had little slits up the sides just above the ankle bone, and they mostly wore shiny open-toed shoes with slight heels that made them look as if they were tiptoeing about. While they dressed for the male-female, heterosexual schedule of time, where boyfriends, marriage, babies, and so on were points along their route that told them how well they were doing, I dressed not to be noticed at all. And it is in the big expansive magical unruly baffling world of whiteness, both coveted and despised, that from young I instinctively sought cover. I just kept hoping that one day I would awaken to find a black stallion with a thick blond mane and tail contained in the garage, saddled and, though restless, waiting—I would leap onto its back and ride it away—either to real oblivion, or to unforeseen, redeeming glory.

Thirty years later, in Canada, the body passed on by ancestry and culture remains, juggled still into the old uniform which is occasionally modified, at least to keep up with changing fashions in jeans, shirts with collars, these days to take advantage of the current trend in cowboy boots and two and three toned runners. The Indian starboy's demeanor, too, persists. But in a predominantly white, lesbian landscape, particularly the one where on Friday nights girls become boys—girl/boys surely cursed by not having been brought up on milky sweets, yet blessed at birth with the tendency for the smaller breasts, the concave bellies, the bony backs—I often find myself fitting a bit like a square peg in a round hole. On those same Friday nights the Indian part of the Trinidadian in this starboy lifts his head. He knows better than to kohl his eyes, even though he wants to. By comparison he is flamboyant: God knows I have tried but I can't help that the bright-colored scarf (silk, wool, embroidered cotton, pashmina, genuine pashmina, 100 percent handmade pashmina—pull it through a wedding ring, you'll see!)

and earrings, rings and neck chains—pukka silver all—confounds the femmes and confuses the white-T-shirt butches, and what feels tough on the inside gets called, strangely, soft by the object of desire. Soft butch.

It is said that the soft-hearted, slow-to-fight starboy of old has been replaced in Bollywood by a tougher man, whose dance style is aggressive, his hand heavy on the throat of his love—a move made necessary in part by the West's manhandling of Bollywood and naming of the old starboy's ways as fey. On a recent trip to Delhi, India, I studied men on the streets—the bicycle rickshaw and auto rickshaw drivers, roadside sellers, pedestrians, sons, fathers. Many still sported earrings, all wore the most stylish scarves, several wore kurtas down to their knees, and all wore slippers. They all looked, in Western terms, gay. I bet few were, though.

The Indian man on the street, soft-looking, stylish, is this butch's new starboy.

BUT THEN again, it is in my novels, in my love poems, and in my short videos, where, one might say, I, most successfully, transcend boundaries imposed, by family, society, and immigration, on me. It is in my writing and in my creative artwork that the Indian starboy rears up to fight injustice and to ask for tolerance and acceptance as a person in a country and in communities that are constantly transitioning. It is through my writing he shows his quiet forcefulness. It is in this work that I am at my fiercest, but on the street, I carry the trepidation, still, imposed generations ago. It is, I admit, on the page, and not so easily in my day-to-day living, that I dare attempt to purse my lips and blow at the borders of lesbian identity, create new spaces where, assuming that gender is a trillion-headed Venus, the inequalities and discrimination of genders within lesbianism itself get addressed, and where that multiplicity of genders is celebrated.

As I gain confidence as a writer in the public realm, the butch in me—soft, fey, faggish, Indian-identified, whatever—wants to take the access and success I am finding and capitalize on it. I have been using my work, one step at a time, to show readers in the broader public my queer world, to ask them to feel along with me. Every book and every work is a coming out, as, in my own strategy, my audience is both the like-minded, queer person, and the one who is appalled by my identity or existence.

To BE seen and listened to by at least one other person is a blessing. To be seen and heard by a community of like-minded people, friends and well-wishers, is healing. To be invited back by the mainstream gatekeepers is empowering.

Crisscrossing Identities in Maryse Condé's *Who Slashed Célanire's Throat?*

Carine M. Mardorossian

In "Order, Disorder, Freedom, and the West Indian Writer," Guadeloupean Maryse Condé emphasizes the importance of recognizing the ways in which Caribbean women writers subvert the orthodoxies that defined the previous generation of writers and critics. She argues that these female authors not only challenge the ideological dogmas established by male authors but also replace their predecessors' masculinist tenets and constraining "order" with "disorder" and "freedom."[1] In this essay, I examine how in *Who Slashed Célanire's Throat?*, Maryse Condé brings into relief the workings of identity-constitution in a way that echoes the "disorder" that her nonfictional but also fictional corpus as a whole brings to our conventional understandings of gendered identity. The choice of this particular fictional work to highlight Condé's *theoretical* intervention is not incidental. In *Célanire*, the process of normalization of gender is rendered even more dramatically visible thanks to the use of the fantastic as a genre. In this most unorthodox of tales, the fantastical functions as the literal and dramatic embodiment of the workings of hegemonic identity construction, and as the dramatization—through very physicalist and hence visible manifestations—of how norms of gender identity are given meaning via configurations of crossing. Indeed, as her polemical tale illustrates, gender gets paradoxically naturalized not through an essentialist rhetoric of biological fixity, but through its association with other identities such as race, nationality, and sexuality that stabilize gender *by default*, that is, through its implicit association with racial purity or heteronormativity, for instance. In other words, cross-gendered dynamics are consistently and inevitably shown to be imbricated with (and circumscribed by) transgressions of sexuality, nationality, or race in a process of associative rhetoric.[2] It is then, paradoxically, through the crossing and crisscrossing of identities that normative identities get reinscribed over and over again.

What is more, as in most of Condé's fiction, "disorder" in *Célanire* is embodied by the difficulty of reconciling the creolized and hybridizing ethos that animates the novel with the characters' disturbingly insistent reproduction of normative identities.[3] Indeed, on the one hand, the author's and her protagonist's association with the Caribbean evokes the racial and cultural intermixing, creolization, and hybridity that define the region by virtue of its history of social struggles and slavery, emancipation and migratory displacements.[4] On the other hand, the tripartite racial system of the Caribbean (black, mulatto, white) has not succeeded in challenging social boundaries, which are reproduced in surprisingly consistent ways. Rather, it has generated a hierarchical framework that keeps track of genealogies along class lines. The Caribbean is a world, in other words, where the crossing of racial and cultural barriers does not necessarily constitute a threat to the hierarchies of color and class that are perpetuated across social lines. Condé makes no excuses for this paradoxical coexistence of both endless racial/cultural crisscrossings *and* rigid social and ethnic boundaries: her fiction thrives on such incongruities.

Nevertheless, the theorization of the cross-gendered dynamics in Condé's world is complicated by the fact that her novels are full of characters who seem to unproblematically reproduce the most egregious stereotypes of femininity and masculinity. From female characters who shamelessly use their sexuality for social advancement (or freely subordinate it to men's will) to male characters whose excessive and prominently exhibited masculinity echoes dominant cultural norms of machismo, the representation of gender in Condé troubles our critical efforts at identifying sites of salutary subversion/crossing in matters having to do with gender or sexuality. This difficulty is compounded by the fact that such seemingly essentializing gestures occur in the context of the most ostentatious transgressions of identities of all kinds, thus producing the "disorder" that has long defined Condé's fiction and scholarship. In *Who Slashed Célanire's Throat?*, for instance, the young protagonist Célanire's controversial tenure as director of the Foyer of Half Castes, a home for interracial orphans in Adjame-Santey, Africa, is characterized by her unapologetic overhaul of the gendered conventions that constitute African society[5]: she not only uses the Foyer to shelter the royal concubines who are escaping abuse and the practice of female circumcision, but she also refuses to return the girls to King Koffi Ndizi when the latter writes her a letter demanding that she do so. Instead, she proceeds to give her female protégées jobs as monitors and teaches them how to read and become self-sufficient in a society that expects them to be subservient. Yet, despite the feminist tenor of her actions, she also paradoxically reproduces the most egregious female stereotypes to accomplish her goals, either posing as a virginal figure clad in white or using her sexuality to attract and manipulate men. The Foyer thrives under her direction, but it is partly because her female staff is busy fulfilling the wildest Orientalist fantasies of influential men in exchange for financial favors and the promise of a secure future. Yet at the same time, Célanire's embodiment of the most stereotypical gendered behaviors recasts the very concept of embodiment as enactment since her bewitching sexualized feminine essence is juxtaposed with her personification of the ingénue woman and followed by her aggressive and sexually predatory behavior vis-à-vis the gay Moslem character Hakim. It is not, then, that Célanire is not *really* what she appears to be but that she embodies feminine and masculine roles in such quick succession that her polyvalent being cannot help but expose the gender/sex binary as a construction that reductively separates the body from the cultural constructions that constitute it.

Condé's recasting of the notion of gender identity, in other words, distinguishes itself from other forms of post-essentialist or constructionist analyses in that it takes place, as it were, on top of a familiar essentialist scenario that anchors gender in what are presumed to be stable because natural bodily characteristics. In having Célanire personify normative femininity even as her heroine's deeds radically challenge gendered conventions, Condé exposes the limits of this constructionist scenario, which, in emphasizing gender as a cultural construction imposed on the ground of sexual difference, leaves sex intact in its pre-discursive essentiality. Instead, rather than expose the meanings attached to the body (which would reinscribe the body's putative essentiality), Condé attacks the hegemonic readings of the corporeal meanings we call sex by reconceptualizing the ground of sex itself or, rather, the notion of sex as ground for gender. When we first meet the protagonist, Célanire Pinceau, she appears as the literal personification of sexual difference, since she wears, as it were, her sex on her face. Célanire's throat was slashed when she was stolen from her mother as a baby to become a sacrificial offering, and the hideous scar that resulted from the botched decapitation (and which she perpetually hides behind a ribbon) functions as a physical marker of her threatening sexual difference: or, as a critic insightfully puts it, its "folded layers of cicatrix exert the attractive and repulsive powers of the female sexual organ."[6] Like the sexual difference it embodies, this hyperbolic representation becomes a site of both attraction and repulsion. And like the female sex, it is tellingly the site of both "veiling" and medical intervention/manipulation as Célanire's adoptive father, a doctor enthralled with the idea of creating his own Frankenstein's monster, saves her life through an infusion of chicken blood and much surgical prowess. It also mirrors how, as a seductive grown woman, Célanire both fascinates and repels in her efforts at redressing the wrongs of the past and overcoming gender oppression.

The scar signifies the impossibility of separating sex and gender in an economy where the two are constitutive of one another and where the body that matters (to echo Judith Butler) is as discursive as the meanings that constitute it through gender. Thus undermining the referential/metaphorical binary through which we typically approach gender identity, Condé reveals the arbitrariness of a process of identification whose meaningfulness is no longer inherent in the supposedly discrete category of gender but exposed as meaning-giving, a relational rather than ontological act. In this context, the assumption that gender acquires its meanings by accruing signification onto biological sex is exposed in favor of a postmodern model that undermines the sex/gender binary itself.

Sociological definitions of gender traditionally differentiate "sex" and "gender" in order to highlight the social and cultural interpretations that turn sexual difference into more than biological difference.[7] In fact, most introductory Women's Studies classes begin with such a sociological approach, thus establishing a gender ontology in which the duality of sex (male-female) forms the basis of gender identity (masculine-feminine). As Judith Butler claims in her influential *Gender Trouble*, this ontology relies on the "invocation of a nonhistorical 'before'"[8] that reinforces the duality of sex as well as the gendered characteristics that are said to mirror sex. According to Butler, this creates the illusion of the unity of sex and gender in a binary system (the male's masculinity and the female's femininity) that is seen to necessitate heterosexual desire. Male and female desire "therefore differentiates itself through an oppositional relation to that other gender it desires."[9] A causal relationship is established between sex, gender, and desire, and any alternative to normative gender configurations is seen as pathological, as "chimerical representations of originally heterosexual identities"[10] so that the original gender ontology can be reified and rationalized. As a result, figures such as the "assertive female," the "effeminate man," or the "lipstick lesbian" are immediately marginalized by the dominant discourse.[11]

Like Butler, Condé is interested in exposing the causal relationship that is assumed between sex, gender, and desire. Whereas others might define the concept of gender by presupposing that a set of phenotypical characteristics identifies "women" who are then oppressed on that basis, Condé explores the concept as a social construction that shifts as her characters interact with one another. So, for instance, in relation to the gay male character Hakim, Célanire crosses gendered boundaries by taking on the role of the aggressive sexual predator who comes closer to raping than to seducing. In relation to her soon-to-be husband Thomas de Brabant, however, she is the personification of a sexualized form of femininity that masculinizes him (when they are married, a gender role reversal occurs as he "softens" and she hardens). This reconfiguration challenges the view of gender as a stable identity circumscribed by a visible bodily taxonomy to which various traits and behaviors are attached *a posteriori*.

Rather than have her protagonist assume a marginalized but stable identity, Condé has her enact various renditions of the heterosexual contract in such quick succession that the naturalized association of gender normativity with heterosexuality is exploded. It is because Célanire's gender identification shifts according to the person she is interacting with as well as in relation to her crossing of other identity categories that gender and sex are exposed as ideological structures. The framing of "neutral" (because anatomical) sex versus "biased" (because socially constructed) gender is replaced by a model that reveals the cross-fertilization of identities that constitute the gender/sex system. Indeed, as Condé's novels repeatedly make explicit, gender only becomes meaningful through its relation to other identity categories insofar as it consistently functions as a figuration for other types of identity crossings. In other words, it is not because of a character's preexisting sexual identity that certain gendered traits/stereotypes come to be ascribed to him/her, but because of his or her transgression of categories (of class, sexuality, race, or nationality) that gender comes to matter (and be) at all (and vice versa: the crossing of gender is inseparable from the transgression of racial boundaries). Gender and transgender dynamics thus function as figurations for the crossing of boundaries of sexuality and race in an economy that redefines what was once perceived as discrete categories as sets of cross-fertilizing ones (gender, race, class, nationality, and so on).

In *Célanire*, for instance, the protagonist's crossing of gender boundaries is inseparable from her status as a Guadeloupean of mixed race and, more specifically, from the fluctuations that characterize the textual references to her skin color as well as sexuality throughout the novel. On the one hand, when we are first introduced to Célanire as a missionary worker landing in Africa in 1901, she stands out because of her lack of conformity to gender expectations, while, on the other, much is made of the shifting color of her skin. Unlike her fellow female missionaries, she is an "oblat" who cannot be called "sister" because she has not yet sworn allegiance to the order. She is neither gossipy nor talkative: "She had never shared their little enthusiasms, their exaltations, their frights, never listened to their confessions and gossips."[12] She tellingly and repeatedly elicits distrust among men who suspect her of duplicity because she lacks transparency. The leader of the missionary group, R. P. Huchard, "distrusted her and thought her capable of doing the worst," (15) while upon meeting her, the governor's second-in-command and her soon-to-be-lover Thomas de Brabant immediately wonders what might be hiding behind her words (32). She is difficult to pin down, as she is not disobedient but not docile either (15, 20). And what is more, her arrival coincides with the death of Mr. Desrussie, the director of the Foyer of Half Castes for whom she was supposed to work and whom she is now scandalously slated to replace: "A woman would be promoted to the rank of director. Come on! And a black woman into the bargain!" (25).

These serial gender transgressions occur in the context of a series of unnatural deaths and fantastical occurrences with which, in the popular imaginary, the young protagonist is soon suspiciously associated. Significantly, they also trigger a series of statements about Célanire's "blackness," since the heroine's dark complexion paradoxically leads to racial indeterminacy rather than racial identity. While, on the one hand, much is made of the darkness of her skin—which is described as "black-black" (116) and as something that "set her apart, that dark skin that clothed her like a garment of deep mourning" (1)—on the other, this focus on the taxonomy of skin ironically fails to lead to the stabilization of race as referent, since she is soon identified as mixed race and later even as white. The fluctuating and somewhat disorienting descriptions of her dark coloring enact a form of race crossing that functions as a figuration for gender crossing, since these discussions of her shifting racial difference only arise in the context of her lack of gender conformity. Thus no longer a stable, coherent, or pre-given identity, blackness—like gender—becomes a crucial aspect of the workings of narrative, since what matters is no longer whether, but *when*, characters are black or white. This representation shakes the dominant discourse's investment in "regimes of corporeal visibility,"[13] regimes that anchor race in signs of bodily difference (breast size, skin color, nose shape, and so on), and it exposes racial identity as a site of crossing that functions as a figuration for the characters' violation of gender or class boundaries.

Condé thus exposes the supposed incontrovertibility of the economies of visibility through which identities such as gender and race are produced and through which they are constantly reinforced culturally. It reveals that when we destabilize the stereotypical traits associated with gender rather than the gender/sex binary itself, we implicitly acquiesce with the notion of gender as an unassailable identity and collude with its hegemonic deployments. To demonstrate the shifting nature of the term and its necessary interdependence with other identities, Condé focuses, then, on the visible yet changing taxonomy of sex itself in a way that radically challenges our conventional understanding of gender. In her novels, the biological body is never just a backdrop of visible and invariable difference (the scar as a stand-in for the vagina) on which social meanings of gender or race are imposed but is itself a site of visible transformation (Célanire as prostitute, ingénue, feminist, wife, and, last but not least, mother). The transgressions of identities Célanire embodies are depicted not as what follows from but as what constitutes the supposedly discrete categories of social analysis that gender and race represent.

It is, Condé reveals, precisely because her assertive and feminist actions cross-gender expectations in a society that defines itself through a strict separation between men and women that the dominant discourse sees her as the embodiment of every possible social transgression. She crosses every conceivable boundary, between life and death, between races, genders, classes, sexualities, and even between species as she becomes associated with the wild dogs and horses that somehow magically appear to avenge her past. In fact, from the very outset of the narrative, Célanire is described in animalistic terms, as evidenced by references to her "dents carnassières" (20) [carnivorous teeth] or to "her long black braid, that looked like it had a life of its own as it snaked down her" (87). We know that she was brought back to life as a baby through the infusion of animal blood (162). Furthermore, she is consistently compared to predatory animals such as the "carnivorous spider entangled in her web" (80), "a cat about to devour a mouse" (60), or "a python about to swallow its prey before uncoiling itself to digest it in voluptuous pleasure" (60). "She is as agile as an eel" (61), while for the Africans whose customs she constantly challenges through her feminist ideals, she is the "horse" the bad spirits rode to find their way to Adjame-Santey (33).

These recurring references expose, I argue, the ideological process through which sexual and racial alterity is produced, not through its anchoring in natural difference, but through its association with various tropes such as animality, dirt, and disease. In keeping with dominant and stereotypical discourses of gender and race, the characters' attempts to fix Célanire's otherness repeatedly slip into references to her animalistic countenance. It is significant, in this respect, that the characterization of the protagonist is developed predominantly through the focalized perspectives of the people she encounters: Karamanlis le Grec; Hakim the converted Moslem; Thomas de Brabant, the newly appointed governor; his wife, Charlotte; Charlotte's daughter, Ludivine; Célanire's adoptive father, Pinceau; and so on. These are the characters through whose perspectives we come to know Célanire and who consistently fall back on various tropes of otherness when they cannot make sense of this "split sex" (130) whose threatening crossing of boundaries they thus seek to contain.

Furthermore, the narrator relates the most outrageous assumptions about Célanire with a detachment that obscures the existence of or the need for judgment. As a result, the reader may not even become aware of the way the narrative is a dramatization of how gender stereotypes get produced and reproduced. Because the distinction between who Célanire is and how she is seen is constantly blurred through the narrator's adoption of a free indirect style where irony is veiled, the fantastical associations through which the reader comes to know Célanire might be taken as the narrator's hyperbolic or metaphorical representation of the protagonist's reaction against constraining gender norms rather than as the narrative enactment and exposition of the workings of representation and identity itself. Thus, when male characters repeatedly comment on how "bewitching" Célanire is, her mesmerizing influence might be seen as a function of her behavior rather than of the manner her wayward ways will necessarily be inscribed by the dominant discourse. Instead, the narrative and the focalized perspectives it represents is a literal dramatization of the ways in which this "split sex" (130) is othered over and over again in ways that become indistinguishable from who she is. For instance, whether Célanire is having a lesbian relationship with Tanella, the concubine and acquitted murderer of the king's maternal uncle Mawourou, is less significant than the fact that her violation of gender norms can only be inscribed and understood through a transgression of heteronormativity.[14]

In other words, the discourses of sexual, racial, and even animalistic alterity in the narrative do not occur in isolation from one another but are generated through their inextricable interrelations. One form of transgression is given meaning through its articulation with another, which epitomizes how the dominant cultural gaze deploys discourses of otherness in its effort to establish an economy of differentiation and exclusion. This is precisely why hegemonic discourse sees any challenge to the heterosexual paradigm as incompatible with a stable gender identity: a threat to heteronormativity is necessarily perceived as a subversion of gender conventions (a "real" man cannot be gay, a lesbian cannot be a "real" woman, etc.). The transgression of the boundaries of sexuality is made sense of through the crossing of gender boundaries and vice versa. In *Célanire,* this figuration of crossing highlights the interdependence of the categories of sexuality and gender with tropes of animality that crisscross to generate and reaffirm socially acceptable differences. For instance, when Célanire openly engages in an intimate relationship with Tanella, one of the nurses at her Home for Half-Castes is "adamant that Célanire had the power to shed her body like a snake shedding its skin in the undergrowth. One night . . . , the young girl had entered Célanire's room unexpectedly and had seen a little heap of soft, shapeless flesh and skin in front of the wide-open window. Hiding behind a closet, she had watched as the young woman returned in the early hours of the morning. Her mouth smeared with blood, she had slipped back into her mortal coil and calmly returned to bed" (75). Célanire's crossing of gender and sexual boundaries is given meaning through tropes of animality that highlight the interdependence of categories such as sexuality, race, species, and class, which are generated through their interrelations rather than through "real" or "natural" differences. The crossing of one category of identity functions as a figuration for the transgression of another.

A similar logic of crossing defines the description of Hakim, another transgressor of normative social boundaries since he is a gay man and converted to Islam. When Hakim reminisces about his past and the marginalization he has experienced as "a half-caste mockingly nicknamed Toubadou, 'white boy,' growing up an outcast among other outcasts . . . ridiculed by the Africans, held in contempt by the French" (71), he tellingly says that Betti Bouah ("one of the richest merchants of the region, of royal blood" [28]), whom he had thought of as a friend, "had always despised him because he wasn't an Akan, he was merely a bastard, without a race" (71).[15] This equivalence established between racial and sexual illegitimacy exposes the entanglement of identities through which the dominant discourse produces normativity. Obviously (although ideology has done much to cloud the evident nature of the following claim), one can be an illegitimate child and still have a "race" just as one can be legitimate and not be an Akan, which highlights the inextricable and sometimes unexpected articulation of identities through which illegitimacy is established.[16]

Similarly, Célanire's fantastical and cannibalistic transmogrifications into wild dogs or horses throughout the narrative function as the literal embodiment of the process of racial interpellation through which the dominant symbolic order seeks to reinstate the binary structures of self and other, male and female, human and animal, gay and straight, black and white. At the same time, the vocabulary used to describe Célanire's racial difference is rendered unstable precisely because of its dependence on tropes such as animality or excess, which inevitably evoke stereotypes of class, sexual, or racial difference. The novel thus resists the very hegemonic inscription it stages, since it denaturalizes—through the fantastic—the process through which sexual and racial otherness is produced and fixed in discourse to guarantee the normative self. In so doing, it introduces again and again a gap between racial traits and the materiality of the body. We are told, for instance, that Célanire "had not liked Lyons, where her color signaled her presence like a beacon wherever she went" (5). Yet in Adjame-Santey, where we assume that her race will not single her out, people still "turned their heads and tried to figure out this odd creature, black of skin but speaking the language of white men, living among them, and dressed like them" (5). That her racial identity is configured through its association with the trope of linguistic competence highlights again the gap that exists between racial identity and corporeality. Similarly, as mentioned earlier, discussions of the degree of her racial difference significantly only arise in the context of her lack of gender normativity, thus revealing that, far from being sites of stable and essentialized difference, gender, sexuality, and race are complexes of social meanings that expose the symbolic nature of identity and challenge the concept's yoking to the body. Gender, like race, in other words, is exposed as a product of language rather than of visible biological otherness.

The reconceptualization of identity that such a postmodern intervention offers challenges, I contend, our post-Butlerian critical eagerness to celebrate "gender trouble" indiscriminately, that is, without recognizing how gender norms are paradoxically the product of configurations of crossings. Identificatory structures are thus revealed as complicated sets of crisscrossing categories that point to the structural interdefinition of racial, national, class, and gender identities (these are always already internally hybridized). Rather than see cross-gendering as the crossing of supposedly stable and preexisting gender boundaries, this reconceptualization thus teaches us to look at the mobile relationships between gender, race, sexuality, and class as these are worked out within narrative. It reveals how normative identity is naturalized through language and rhetorical association rather than through a visible or "natural" site of difference. It also helps us challenge the epistemology of visibility in which our conventional understanding of gender and race is moored. Indeed, if gender's meanings are dependent on its interrelationships with other identity categories, then its association with the body is exposed as a ruse of power rather than as a fact of nature.

Condé's intervention in *Célanire* is to gender what the Martinican philosopher Frantz Fanon's postcolonial analyses were to race. Just as Fanon revealed the "historical-racial schema" beneath race and racism's epidermal logic as a racial narrative that teaches us to see the so-called "fact of blackness,"[17] Condé's fantastical tale exposes the processes that undergird the normalization of gender and the so-called "fact of sexual difference." As such, it epitomizes the kind of "theorizing in the flesh" Deborah McDowell identified as defining black women's fiction in her influential 1995 essay "Transferences."[18]

Notes

1. Condé, "Order, Disorder, Freedom." Caribbean women writers, she argues, "displease, shock, or disturb. Their writings imply that before thinking of a political revolution, West Indian literature needs a psychological one. What they hope for and desire conflicts with men's ambitions and dreams. Why, they ask, fight against racism in the world when it exists at home among ourselves?" (131–32).

2. In fact, without such associations, the naturalized categories of gender and race would simply lose their bearings and meanings. I am singling out gender and race as sites of "naturalized" identity because of their automatic yoking to the body and corporeal signs in hegemonic discourse.

3. See Mardorossian, *Reclaiming Difference*, for an analysis of the ways in which Condé's and other Caribbean women's writings epitomize the "disorder" Condé celebrates insofar as they contest and radically "rewrite" some of the most foundational concepts in Caribbean and postcolonial studies (race and hybridity, resistance, and agency).

4. As Glissant puts it, although "hybridity" and creolization increasingly define the world as a whole, the Caribbean "may be held up as one of the places in the world where Relation presents itself most visibly" (*Poetics of Relation*, 33).

Indeed, in light of the region's size and history, the processes of cross-cultural interaction and exchange that occur there have happened in a condensed and accelerated manner. This also explains why its literature occupies such a representative status in postcolonial studies today.

5. Condé's selection of Africa as the setting of her tale at the beginning of the novel is significant insofar as she has consistently sought to evoke and challenge Afrocentric paradigms through her fiction's hybridizing ethos. The "return" to Africa in *Célanire* is, not surprisingly, revealed as no return at all.

6. Abramson, "Review of *Célanire Cou-Coupé*," 306.

7. For an overview, see Watkins and Chancer, *Gender, Race, and Class*.

8. Butler, *Gender Trouble*, 4.

9. Ibid., 30.

10. Ibid., 41.

11. Sawicki, "Foucault, Feminism and Questions of Identity," 301.

12. Condé, *Who Slashed Célanire's Throat?*, 18. Further references to this edition of the novel will be given in parentheses in the text.

13. Wiegman, *American Anatomies*, 4.

14. Condé powerfully summarizes the incommensurability of postcolonialism and feminism in the scene where Célanire comes to the rescue of the young concubine. Tanella is slated to die for her murderous act of self-defense. To the crowd that amasses in front of the Foyer where the young girl takes refuge, Célanire appears as a colonizing rather than liberating force. And this, despite the fact that the crowd is not sympathetic to Tanella's cause: "They did not necessarily want her to be put to death like customs demanded it, but they were demonstrating along with the others to signify that it was time for the French with their creatures, their governors, their priests, and oblats to leave them to their customs and go back home" (27). In other words, the woman-identified alternative is simply not an option, because it is conflated with the power of colonialism and the colonizing mission. The only choice available, Condé reveals, is between a misogynist option that supports African traditions and a pro-feminist stance that reinforces colonialist rule. Spivak ("Can the Subaltern Speak?") and Lata Mani have both written extensively about this double bind of gender in relation to the practice of sati in India. Demanding its abolition in the nineteenth-century amounted to supporting the white colonialists' civilizing mission, while challenging the colonizers' rule by upholding tradition necessarily resulted in the oppression of the women over whose body these colonial struggles were literally taking place. Similarly, Célanire's objection to female subjugation only reinforces the conviction among Africans that she is there to do the colonizers' bidding.

15. The Akan are an ethnic group from Ghana and the Ivory Coast that includes the Fante and the Twi.

16. My reading highlights the equivalence established between "bastard" and "without race" through apposition, a construction in which two terms are placed with one another as explanatory equivalents and have the same syntactic relation to the other elements of the sentence. In the English translation by Richard Philcox, however, the comma establishing this relation of equivalence between race and sexuality has been removed, thus obscuring the economy of meaning and figuration I am bringing to light in this paper.

17. Fanon, *Black Skin, White Masks*, 1968, 109.

18. According to McDowell, black women's imaginative works constitute a form of "theory in the flesh" that is obscured when theoretical investigation is too narrowly conceived. She argues that institutions of higher learning often define theory in ways that exclude women of color. While women of color have been steadily producing a more "narrowly conceived" version of theory, McDowell states, their fiction continues to be fodder for theoretical interventions in academia. Condé's fictional corpus epitomizes such practice of "theorizing in the flesh" since it offers a sustained theoretical study in the construction of identity in general and of gender identity in particular.

Tales Told under the San Fernando Hill

Lawrence Scott

1. The Architect and His Wife

"He's in the orchid house, madam," the old nurse, Justine, called from the courtyard where she sat overlooking the gulf, sewing and tending the memories of her madam's daughters.

"Leave him, Justine, with his toothbrush. Soon he'll even forget that, and I'll have to keep them alive." Emilia Estafan continued to mend her husband's old khaki pants, seeing him as Justine had described, cleaning the leaves of his precious orchids with his old toothbrush, in case blight crinkled their leaves and stunted their growth.

When Carlos Estafan, the architect of San Fernando, was not in his office at his drawing board, level with the sill of the Demerara window overlooking the wharf with the sloops waiting to be loaded with sugar, he would spend what seemed like an eternity in his orchid house. It seemed like this to his wife, Emilia, whom he had married when she was sixteen. So, now that her daughters themselves had married and left home, she was still a young woman with a whole life to live, while he seemed more and more like an old man.

Emilia never let that thought enter too deeply into her imagination, otherwise she would have to go and confess to the parish priest, Father Boniface, the terrifying fantasies which were unleashed in her mind; things she had not thought it possible that she could imagine, that anyone could imagine. Where did these imaginings bloom? How, out of nothing? How, with the kind of mother and father she had had, could she imagine such . . . ? She hated to think of them, and then of course it made her think of them even more. Days, they became inescapable; obsessions, like some dark flower, some deadly night shade growing as black as purple in her brain.

"Bless me Father, for I have sinned."

"My daughter?"

"Father, it's a month since my last confession."

"My daughter?"

"Father, they've come again. Last night it was the boy first of all, in the garden under the bougainvillea arbor, as brown and as smooth as a young deer, his mouth wet; so wet and smooth, I could feel his hot breath smelling of guavas on my neck where he stood naked as the day he was born; standing there, looking up at my window with the moonlight on his face; his face like an angel's; his limbs and torso as natural to the garden as the limbs of the orange trees and the bark of the cedars."

The priest wondered at the woman's flight in words.

"I felt the walls of the house dissolve and the garden rise up, carrying him into my room, into my bed. First it was the boy. But then, the girl, Father. I had not known that desire until she was in my arms like one of my daughters at first, and then, Father, that other desire. Then they were together again and stayed in the garden together and played till I could watch it no longer, the unspeakable things they did with each other, that I had to leave the window and kneel at the *prie-dieu* and ask the Blessed Thérèse, the Little Flower, to intercede on my behalf. It used to work when I was small, Father. I think it did. It does not seem to now. Nothing seems to work now. And I'm a grown-up woman now, Father. Why did it work then, the way of perfection?"

"My child?"

"My husband, Father. He remembers nothing. What must I do about the boy, Father? And, what about the girl?"

"My daughter, there are other penitents in the line, you must stop and say ten Hail Marys for the forgiveness of those souls still in purgatory. Keep praying to the Little Flower."

"Yes, Father."

MEANWHILE, Carlos Estafan had continued all that afternoon in the shade of the orchid house where the angel hair fern grew in the moist soil between the pebbles of the pathways. He continued to scrub the fleshy leaves of the epiphytes with his old toothbrush. All of his life now was consumed in this horticulture.

Justine was still at her lookout in the courtyard. Her sewing had fallen from her lap and she had nodded off into the daydreams of a woman who had come as far as this on her own, tending her madam's affairs and her madam's daughters as if they had been her own. Somewhere in her humming, with which she had comforted those little girls in their growing, was a lamentation that came into her voice and sounded like the surf of the sea, swelling and breaking on the shore.

2. The Women of the Legion of Mary

"Who it is? So long they have Father in there listening, when so many people want to confess."

"Is Mistress Estafan, Mistress Redhead. You didn't see Father call her out of her pew when he come inside the Church?"

Mrs. Nunez said, "She don't have to line up."

"I bet I know what she have to confess. People that have she color skin have only one thing to confess, pride and greed."

"That is two things," Mrs. Nunez chipped in. "And is color of skin that determining sin now? You know life tell me that all kind of people capable of all kind of things, what you calling sin. I believe that some of them is not even sin."

"That is what I have to say, you can believe what you like." Mistress Redhead took a kerchief out of her bosom, emitting the odor of talcum powder and bay rum, to wipe her black brow and fan herself in the heat.

"You think is only pride and greed they have to confess. They must have ordinary sins like other people." Mrs. Nunez, a coco 'panol, winced a little at what she saw might be an implied attack on her own mixed blood by the black woman. She had also heard her berating the Venezuelan girls who came from down the main, "Them red skin girls think they pretty," and who dance "those lewd dances," as Mistress Redhead like to put it, in the clubs on the wharf of San Fernando. Mrs. Nunez did not want to be confused with those girls, though she was proud of her Venezuelan ancestry, her father coming to the island to work the cocoa in the Montserrat hills. She knew what people said that some of them were not real girls only play-play girls, them boys that does like to dress up like girls.

"Ordinary sins? Sin is not ordinary, child, sin is . . . ," and Mistress Redhead broke off and turned her eyes to the life-size crucifix above the high altar, leaving Mrs. Nunez to imagine what sin could be if it was not ordinary.

Mistress Redhead, as she examined her conscience before entering the confessional box, thought that sin was like life, that part of your life which did not go so good. How could sin be the same for her as for Mistress Estafan? While Mistress Estafan lived on the *morne*, the highest peak before the summit of San Fernando Hill, in a house reaching beyond itself with turrets and balconies, grand staircases and bay windows, decorated with fretwork and the lace of lattice, its terraces falling away to lawns and sunken gardens under orange trees, Mistress Redhead lived behind the Radio City Cinema in Rushworth Street, not far from Paradise Cemetery, in a small gingerbread house, a miniature conception of grandeur, at least on the outside. While it was not the lowest part of town, it was still too near to the market in Mucurapo Street where life was such a confusion day and night that it would be impossible for her to imagine what sin meant there.

Mistress Redhead had long ago got rid of her husband. She kept Eldridge's name, Redhead, because of her children, but, now, she unassailably raised her head as she walked down the street and made sure she was known as Mistress Redhead. Though she knew that people knew why she threw Eldridge out of the house—for philandering and adultery with those same Venezuelan young girls who hung out of the balcony above Chen's shop on the corner of Mucurapo and Coffee Street, giggling behind those silly fans Chen had imported from Hong Kong, and she herself had heard the rumor that those girls got up to all kind of things with themselves. But, Mistress Redhead did not want to think about that. It was bad enough to think of Elridge with one of them, or two of them or whatever number it was.

She felt it deeply and the memory of Elridge Redhead's skin was like velvet to her touch.

And as if Mrs. Nunez knew what was in Mistress Redhead's thoughts, she expressed what was going on in her own head, thinking aloud. "You know they say some of them girls is not really girls at all. Them is play-play girls, them soft face boys from down the main in pretty shirts and tight pants who like to wine they bamsie in the street, as they swing that purse they have in their hand." The line of a calypso ran through her head, "Norman is that you . . ." Mrs. Nunez lowered her voice, holding back from literally bursting out into full voice for the rendition of the calypso. She had gone beyond her thoughts with talking them aloud.

"What you talking about girl?" The terrible thought was that Elridge had not only gone with one or two or three of them girls from the balcony of Chen's shop but that one of them might not have been a girl at all. Elridge!

She chose to return to her previous thread of thought, her honor and dignity. This was not the sin of pride, she thought, this was dignity to deport herself in this way now.

Was her sin envy, as she tried to raise her self-esteem and her income with the piano lessons she gave bright boys and girls from the convent and the Catholic college? Was it envy that made her house shine with polish and new linoleum, bright waxened flowers in the green cut glass vase on the center table, placed expertly on the crocheted doily mat? Or, was it dignity?

Mistress Redhead examined her conscience. She grew philosophical. She was a teacher in the school built against the walls of the church of Notre Dame de Bon Secours where Indian children, smart in mathematics, smelling of coconut oil, labored their way out of the sugarcane fields where their parents cut cane. Sin and history, thought Mistress Redhead. Did one absolve the other?

She had kept her eyes fixed on the crucifix where the nails fastened the hands and feet of her savior to the wood of the cross.

Could she hold Mistress Estafan responsible for that crime? On Good Friday, in the service of the mass of the Pre-Sanctified, they used to say the Jews were responsible. Then she had read what terrible things the Nazis had done to the Jews. Then you see, the logic led her to herself and her own people and Mistress Estafan's part in the whole thing; the calamitous holocaust of the Middle Passage, that long procession of charnel galleons. History and poetry lifted Mistress Redhead's pride. She found beautiful lines in difficult books for difficult subjects in Mr. Sealey's bookshop in the arcade on Penitence Hill. Mistress Redhead's grandfather had the story almost firsthand, and she wondered if he, in his time, had gone up to the great house on the *morne* and killed those whom she found in there at the time, whether that would've been a sin to crucify her savior, or an act to liberate her people? Mistress Redhead scared herself with her speculations.

The fleeting thought from her conversation with Mrs. Nunez flickered to bring her down from the heights of her philosophical speculation. Eldridge with one of them buller boys? She had never ever spoken the word and she looked about her as if her thought might have been heard. My God! Things had become worse in this world.

"*Morne*," she gathered herself, reflecting aloud, sounding her sadness with a moan. "While it means a little hill, also means sadness in classical French," Mistress Redhead said melancholically to Mrs. Nunez as she moved off to kneel in the confessional to confess her sins to Father Boniface.

"What you say Mistress Redhead? Where you does get these things from? I en't catch what you say, nuh." Mrs. Nunez fixed her mantilla on her head and resumed her posture for prayer, but was too distracted by Mistress Redhead and her ideas of other people and things. She kept seeing those pretty boys from down the main wining their bamsie in the High Street as if is carnival. And is not only the boys from down the main, is all of them, young black fellas, Indians, French creole, Syrian, Chiney, the lot. She might be happier if she minded her own business, Mrs. Nunez thought quietly to herself.

3. The First Kiss

When the Estafan house on the *morne* was silent, and Emilia and Carlos were asleep at siesta time, and Justine was resting on her iron bed in the servant's room off the courtyard, and this world seemed like on another planet to Rushworth Street and Mucurapo Street in downtown San Fernando, the children stole into the garden to play. These were Carlos and Emilia's nephews who lived on the *morne* in the neighboring houses surrounded by guava trees which bore enormous fragrant fruit full of pink seeds on which maggots like to feed. The boys scraped out the seeds and the maggots and filled the pink cup of pulp with brown sugar, to gorge themselves on the confection.

In the silence of the early afternoon, before Carlos went back to his drawing board in his office overlooking the wharf and the sloops loaded with sacks of sugar, and Emilia went to her Legion of Mary Praesidium Meeting at five o'clock, Guillaume and Pierre played in the hot and silent garden. They crept up from their houses next door under the guava trees and played in the orchid house, in the mango orchard among the anthuriums and under the bougainvillaea arbors at the bottom of the terraces where the giant cacti unfurled their dangerous tendrils. They played in the grotto of the Madonna Dolorosa and the shaded courtyard of this mysterious garden belonging to their uncle and aunt; a forbidden place.

Le Petit Morne was a hill of cousins. Beneath the hill, the traffic in the town of San Fernando droned like a swarm of bees punctuated by the blare of car horns and the high voices of Chutney music over the tassa drums.

In the presbytery, next to the church, Father Boniface snored the sleep of a priest exhausted by the sins of the town.

The boys should have been in their rooms, resting as their mothers thought, if not actually sleeping. They should have been reading comic books quietly: Batman, Captain Marvel, Wonderwoman and Superman; a pantheon of Americana.

But this, this prowling around the garden in the heat of the afternoon was illicit.

They were cousins. They were friends. They fought and played and grew together, their bodies changing, their sex flourishing without any idea of the sins that plagued Mistress Redhead or their aunt Emilia Estafan.

In the hot and still afternoon, they did not think of the fires of hell or of mortal sin. Those thoughts and fears would come in the night, if they came at all, and they would have to go to sleep in their parents' bed and be given hot cocoa to drink with vanilla mixed in to soothe and quieten their fear. They would have to be given the rosary and be told to say an act of contrition and make a firm purpose of amendment, sent off to sleep folded in the wings of their guardian angels until Father Boniface could absolve them in the morning before the six o'clock mass, for they had arrived at the age of reason, made their First Communions, and were just about to be confirmed.

But really they had just been children as any enlightened person would know; boys together, fascinated by the little pleasure growing between their legs and the pleasure they gave themselves and each other if they touched those little totees, if they stroked them with soft and gentle fingers, licked them with sticky tongues. All boys have known these peccadilloes with each other and joked boastfully of them when they are drunk men. "Man, and you rub totee when you was a boy!"

These were not sins. These were not nails to be driven into the hands of Mistress Redhead's savior on the cross.

Cockerels crowed in the afternoon, defying the prescribed dawn, three times even, suggesting a denial and betrayal the boys did not understand.

Then in the loft above the servants' quarters where Justine was sleeping; in this loft where chickens liked to roost so that the floor was soft with molted feathers, nests of warm eggs, the boys lay in the stillness of the hot afternoon, drawn here by their play and innocence.

Guillaume and Pierre lay on their backs and looked up at the low ceiling in which they saw little dots of light in the darkness; like the stars at night in an immense sky. Constellations, galaxies! Their eyes smarted from flecks of dust falling, held in the gossamer cobwebs.

Justine snored and dreamt her old woman's dreams in the room below. She dreamt of cane fields and a mother's ambition that her daughter would not break her back with that labor.

"Let me lie on top of you," Guillaume whispered.

They had never done that before and Pierre felt that he could not breathe.

"Let me kiss you," Guillaume whispered again, "as if you were a girl."

"But, I'm a boy," Pierre protested, then let himself slip into an idea of himself as a girl as Guillaume positioned himself.

"Let me kiss you anyway. Pretend." And he put his lips on Pierre's and then having never learnt this, they began to feel the tips of their tongues in each other's mouths and soon they were going deeper with their sighs.

"This is like in the films," Pierre said breathlessly, enjoying the pretense. "Like Lana Turner with Rock Hudson."

"Like Burt Lancaster and Deborah Kerr in *From Here to Eternity.*"

"On the beach in see-through swimming costumes which Father Boniface says is immoral."

"Does he?"

"He told me that in confession."

Without much thought, the boys had undressed each other in what now was truly a kind of passion, Pierre's boys' clothes discarded. Their brown bodies were stuck with white chickens' feathers in the dim light of stars, glowing with the aura of the Hollywood screen.

4. The Architect's Tumor

"Those children, again," said Emilia to Carlos as their breakfast was ending and he was peeling a ripe banana to put out on the tray for the birds. He was not listening to her and felt that he had now enough excuses which she could use for his lack of attention and not feel that he had neglected her, but just that he could not help it. Doctor Maillot had told Emilia on the phone that Carlos was seriously ill.

"You said something?" Carlos cut open grapefruits and ripe mangoes for the birds' platter, and already the blue tanagers, the yellow-breasted keskidee, the palm tanagers, and the blue streaks of the blue jeans were darting in for their morning feed.

"Guillaume and Pierre, your nephews, I am worried. Yesterday after siesta, I saw them crawling out of the loft above Justine's room covered with feathers. They were naked and were washing the feathers off their bodies at the standpipe by the orchid house. What do you make of that?"

"Unsure of who they are they're pretending to be birds, but it didn't work out. You sure it's not one of your dreams?"

"Dreams? What dreams? Why don't they know who they are?"

"Do we really know who we are?"

Immediately he said this, she saw his back disappearing into his study where she knew he would be cloistered for an hour with his stamps before he went into the orchid house. Horticulture came after philately, then came architecture at his drawing board overlooking the wharf.

Dreams: what did he know of her dreams? They weren't dreams, they were thoughts, or, yes, daydreams, when she was on her own overlooking the garden as she had been doing at the end of siesta and seen Pierre and Guillaume emerging from the loft encrusted with birds' feathers. Or, they were visions. Father Boniface said they were bad thoughts. She did see the boys, she couldn't help seeing them if they were in her garden when she looked out of her bedroom window. What had they to do with the boy and girl whom she saw doing their unspeakable acts; his breath hot on her neck, his body wet like a young deer? And she? Who was she, the girl who came into her bed and lay in her arms bringing that desire?

Only confession gave respite to the laryngitis Emilia continued to suffer because of her inability to speak out about the world of her dreams and feelings.

Justine found it hard to hear and so to understand what was going on for her madam, but she guessed from the look on her face that it was the distress she had seen there ever since her last daughter Giaconda had got married and left the house, leaving her alone with her husband. Justine watched the confusion on her young madam's face. It was not something she had ever allowed herself to experience. She preferred to keep herself to herself. She would be content with the married girls coming back to visit and in time bringing their own children to her. That would be sufficient, she told herself. Hers was the Nurse's story.

5. The Women of the Legion of Mary

"You hear the news? Mistress Estafan's husband dead," Mrs. Nunez announced.

"Is so?" Mistress Redhead said. "I didn't know he was sick. To tell you the truth I never really see him. I sure he must be there in the front pew with she Sunday mass, but I never really see him, is always she I see, and then she used to have three daughters but they gone and get married. So long she not come to meetings. So, she on she own now. Well, that is something in the big house, all on she own. But she is a young woman. She could married again."

"They say they find one big tumor growing in Mr. Estafan brain. Is that he dead of?"

"An ordinary death."

"What you mean, an ordinary death?"

"Well, he en't dead of anything really special, like say, a lingering and gradually debilitating disease which eventually send him mad so that he roam the streets and bring shame on the family and town."

"You have an imagination, yes, Mistress Redhead, and you could speak some words sometimes. Trouble with all you teachers. I think he dead of quite a grand death, a tumor. Some people does dead just so, you know. Nothing, they just die. But a tumor?"

"Is so I want to die. Drop my neck so like a fowl, and when they feel my pulse I done gone already." She laughed.

"You feeling lucky? You know what some people does say about death, that your whole life at the moment of your death, that it all come back from the time you is a tiny child to whenever it catch you, old, young, middle age, anyhow. You believe that? But you will have an extraordinary death, Mistress Redhead. I feel so for sure."

"It sound like it could happen. But Father Boniface say you have to live every moment as if you going to die at any time. He comes like a thief in the night, is what the gospel say. You mustn't go back in your house to fetch your coat. When death call, you just have to go."

"Is so I want it. I 'fraid suffering, and I en't have no coat. And they say in the end, Mr. Estafan had to suffer, and she, his young wife, because she younger than he, had to sit by the bed for days with her daughters, while he suffered there with a tumor growing inside his head. He had tubes coming out of his head and mouth. He was in a coma. They say people does hear when they in a coma. You have to be careful what you say, because they could suddenly wake up like Lazarus, I suppose, and if you not saying something you want them to hear, it could be really embarrassing." Mrs. Nunez went on with her anxiety. She would not like people to be hearing the thoughts she did not care to express, like telling Mistress Redhead about the play-play girls in their pretty shirts and tight pants.

The women talked of suffering, dying, and death. Sins were again confessed, nails driven into the savior were released with forgiveness and Father Boniface's absolution.

6. Rita Hayworth's Kiss

The next time that Emilia Estafan spotted her two nephews emerging from the loft above Justine's room she could not run to her husband in shock to say that they had transformed themselves into birds. She remained transfixed at the windowsill of her bedroom looking down into the courtyard, as one of them, whom she thought must be Pierre, because the other one still looked like Guillaume, was finding it difficult to get out of the window to the loft. What in fact she saw emerging from the window gradually was what looked to her like a giant chrysalis. The two small feet in silver shoes encrusted with sequins dangled from beneath a profusion of chiffon and tulle and hooped crinolines. Emerging out of this confection as the body lowered itself from the window sill was her nephew Pierre. She gave herself the advice she had eventually got from Father Boniface to make a distinction between fantasy and reality and to check what her desire led her to believe. She would have liked to believe that this was a giant chrysalis at the moment of becoming a butterfly.

She watched in fascination as the other boy eventually lowered himself on to the courtyard. Pierre was now standing in the full-length evening dress she recognized as one her daughter Esmeralda had worn to a dance on Old Year's night for her debut. It had been relegated to a trunk of old clothes that Emilia hoped would one day become the dressing-up box when her grandchildren came to stay. Well, it seemed it had already come into use as a masquerade for one of her nephews. Guillaume seemed naked next to Pierre, in just his shorts, as she saw them disappear into the orchid house. Not having Carlos to talk to, she remembered what he had said when she had told him about them covered with chicken feathers. Pierre must be unsure of who he is. She wanted to creep down and peep at her nephews and see what they were doing, but that felt incorrect and so she decided to return to her own siesta and leave the garden to the children.

The garden left to the children at siesta was alive with the plaintive cry of the cigale singing for rain. In the intervals of that lamentation, the garden was a continual moan of the doves. The season was just itself changing its dress from the dry season into the wet season and the pouis and immortelles had dropped their dresses to the ground where the yellow and orange petals ringed the trees. The wide umbrellaing branches of the flamboyant trees drenched in red and yellow were like the crinolined skirts prepared for a drag queen's ball.

In the shadows of the orchid house in the cool of its shade Pierre danced the dance of the seven veils he had seen Rita Hayworth dance in the film *Salome,* discarding his various skirts as Guillaume looked on bewildered but unmistakably attracted to his cousin whom he held in his arms at the discarding of the last veil as s/he swooned. At that moment he kissed him on the mouth.

"Gosh, is that what it's like to be a girl?"

"Boy. I don't know."

The boys stood almost naked in front of each other, laughing.

7. The Parish Priest

So, as well as the daily masses, the nuns' confessions, the confessions of the laity, benediction, visits to the sick and dying, Father Boniface had on top of all his priestly work, his works of mercy, the momentous funeral of Carlos Estafan, the architect of San Fernando who had built the church, the town hall, the technical college, the boys college and the extension to the convent for the nuns of Cluny. The town was a monument to the man who loved to sit in his orchid house and clean the leaves of his orchids with an old toothbrush.

But on this day of days, Father Boniface had time in between everything else, like carrying communion for old Mrs. Espinet on Penitence Hill, to escape to Rushworth Street for his weekly visit to Mistress Redhead.

He entered her backyard through a gate cut into the blue galvanized fence which led past the soursop trees and the fowls and ducks which Mistress Redhead had running about and feeding on scraps. He entered the clacking yard and climbed the broken-down backstairs onto the back verandah where she always met him dressed in her housecoat all ready, so as not to waste any time.

"Elizabeth." Here he allowed himself to call her by her first name, never in the parish, always then, Mistress Redhead.

"Hans," she dropped the Father Boniface and allowed him to kiss her on the cheek while still on the open back verandah, the yard shaded by the almond trees from the road.

Entering the house out of the blinding sun and oppressive humidity of the wet season was like entering a dark and soothing cave which felt like velvet and shimmered with the watery satin and taffeta antimacassars on Mistress Redhead's proudly upholstered chairs and couch. The curtains were drawn and orange lamps lit up the darkness as they both entered Mistress Redhead's small bedroom with the big brass bed and the varnished bureau. Here they were both in another world. "I say you not coming today."

"You know I had to come. How could I not come. You know, the delay with the visits to the sick and . . ."

"Well you here now, come, let me take you things."

You could say that this rendezvous had grown out of the spiritual talks Father Boniface had had to give Mistress Redhead when she came to confession with the worry of what she wanted to do to her husband in revenge for going with those girls who hung over the balcony of Chen's shop at the corner of Mucurapo and Coffee Street. Or, the revenge when she desired to avenge her people's history with the sacrifice of Mistress Estafan; something her grandfather did not do.

Father Boniface was a white man, one of those Dutch missionaries, and though Mistress Redhead knew it contradicted everything she thought about white people on the *morne*, she could not now resist this man who had offered her so much spiritual comfort and had not even thought to ask for any of this which she now gave him, in the arms of her soft and perfumed body. It first happened on the night they had to clear up after the harvest festival and he had dropped her off at home with the remainder of the prizes for the bran tub and hoop-la. He had come in for a little drink of mauby which was her speciality, and then she gave him one of her finest rums, and one thing led to another and he ended up spending the night and being late for the five o'clock mass.

Life was good to them because it never occurred to Mistress Redhead that these visits, these moments in the cool shadows of her bedroom, were nails to be driven into the savior. And though it wasn't long before rumor spun out a tale to keep all the ladies and the gentlemen of the parish astonished, Father Boniface continued to come through the gate in the blue galvanized fence, through the backyard with the ducks and fowls, to comfort Mistress Redhead and to indulge an acknowledged weakness in himself which had grown out of his loneliness.

Before he left that morning it was on Mistress Redhead's mind to ask him what he thought of play-play girls. Did they really exist? But she decided against it, putting the thought out her mind, allowing the flavor of their mutual indulgence to linger. Then, a thought crept into Mistress Redhead's head. If Hans could leave his priesthood for her, he might like Elridge leave it for them girls or boy-girls on Chen's balcony.

8. The Architect's Widow

And, in a similar way, Emilia Estafan indulged a weakness of hers to believe that her daydreams were true. She continued to live in the big house at the summit of the *morne* on her own with Justine who had now drawn completely the curtains of her cataracts so that her big ears which sprouted hairs were her only real line of communication to the world around her as she used to say, "Is only these I have now," cupping her ears to press them toward where she heard her companions speaking to her.

But Emilia's daydreams were suddenly shattered when she realized that the boy whom she saw as wet as a deer and who at times floated up to her windowsill was Ram the yard boy, and the young girl with whom he did unspeakable things was her niece, Yvonne.

While her nephews continued to emerge out of Justine's loft stuck with feathers or in Rita Hayworth get-ups, her niece was having a dangerous liaison with the yard boy. Yes, the sin of impurity, definitely a nail in the cross through the hands and feet of the savior. But the real danger for Emilia with the liaison was the miscegenation; this young brown deer wet and trembling, *tupping,* one of those words which astonished Father Boniface, and made him think that Emilia Estafan had something in common with Mistress Redhead's imagination and flight with words, her fair niece.

When she turned to her *prie-dieu* to kneel and speak to the Little Flower, it seemed to be a daydream after all. Prayer had worked this time. Or, had it?

Still, the next day the young wet deer came floating up to her window from the garden into her bed, his hot breath with the scent of guavas on her neck, and following stealthily the young girl to cradle herself in her arms, bringing that other desire.

9. Justine's Last Words

Justine thought that her cataracts were a blessing in disguise. Whatever life had dealt her she thought of as a blessing. It was her nature. But her ears burnt, not with words spoken about her, she had been long forgotten, shuffling around in alpagats while younger women came to do the housework, but with the screams of delight which came from her Madam's bedroom at siesta time. She thought maybe she had imagined the death of the master, Carlos Estafan. Was he not buried in Paradise Cemetery?

Well, maybe even those cries of delight which she heard at siesta time coming from her madam's bedroom were not nails to be driven into the hands and feet of the savior, but a sign of the freeing of her madam's larynx. She no longer carried, she noticed, that look of distress on her face.

"Is time I dead, yes," she said. "I swear it. I swear point blank upon a pitchpine board. I swear, I swear. Yea, Lord." Then, she laughed out loud, her mending falling to the ground, her blind eyes watering with her joy.

The children had loved to hear her swear in this way in her Barbadian accent which she had lost a little with her journey to Trinidad. They would cry out, "Say it again, Nurse!" But that time had gone with the girls growing up, getting married and leaving. They were not her girls anymore.

THESE TALES were first heard in the quiet tones of the confessional, in the gossip on the pews of the parish church, through the whisperings in a secret garden, and in the dimly lit bedroom of illicit lovers behind the

Radio City Cinema near Paradise Cemetery. They were heard from an old woman as she looked out from a courtyard above the sea. They were heard while, for some, their childhood disappeared, their youth bewildered them, their middle age filled them with doubt and then joy. For others, their loneliness filled them with desire and in their old age they were prepared for death, as a welcome relief from the darkness of cataracts and the discomfort of burning ears, no longer the nurse who could see the excitement and enjoy the cries of her madam's daughters at play.

4

Symptoms and Detours

The Body of Vodou

Corporeality and the Location of Gender in Afro-Diasporic Religion

Roberto Strongman

RECENT SCIENTIFIC experiments in the area of perception and cognition present further evidence that the relationship between the self and the body is not a universal given, but imagined and constructed. Out-of-body experiments conducted by two research groups using slightly different methods expanded upon the "rubber hand illusion." In that illusion, people hide one hand in their lap and look at the rubber hand set on a table in front of them. As a researcher strokes the real hand and the rubber hand at the same time with a stick, people have the sensation that the rubber hand is their own. When a hammer hits the rubber hand, the subjects recoil or cringe. According to the August 2007 issue of *Science,* two different research teams led by H. Henrik Ehrsson and Bigna Lenggenhager created whole-body illusions with similar manipulations, this time through the use of virtual-reality technology.[1] The subjects wore goggles connected to two video cameras placed six feet behind them and, as a result, saw their own backs from the perspective of a virtual person located behind them. When the researcher stroked the subject's chest and moved the second stick under the camera lenses simultaneously, the subjects reported the sense of being outside of their own bodies, looking at themselves from a distance where the cameras were located. The scientists infer from these experiments that they now understand how the brain combines visual and tactile information to compute and determine where the self is located in space. These experiments help us to understand that the location of the self vis-à-vis the body can and is culturally constructed through the senses. The body and its self need not be coterminous. The self need not reside inside the body, but may be imagined or placed externally. In different ways, current scientific discourse coincides with Afro-Diasporic philosophy in its exposure of subjective inwardness as an illusion.

The Western philosophical tradition clearly presents the concept of a unitary soul within the hermetic enclosure of a body. In *Sources of the Self*, Charles Taylor presents a genealogy of the Western self in which Descartes marks the most important milestone. He writes, "The internalization wrought by the modern age, of which Descartes' formulation was one of the most important and influential, is very different from Augustine's. It does, in a very real sense, place the moral sources within us. Relative to Plato, and relative to Augustine, it brings about in each case a transposition by which we no longer see ourselves as related to moral sources outside us, or at least not at all in the same way. An important power has been internalized."[2] It is important to place Taylor's claims concerning Descartes in the historical context of the Enlightenment. The theocentric philosophical tradition delineated by Plato and Augustine is characterized by man's search for an identity that lies beyond himself, in the Divine without. The intense secularization of the Enlightenment disrupts this theocentrism by foregrounding the individual, a move that brings about the internalization of identity. This sense of inwardness, however, is dependent upon a clear demarcation between the new boundaries of the self and the body. In the following passage, Descartes reasons how even if the mind or soul might be within the body, the two remain distinct parts of the individual:

> In order to begin this examination, then, I here say, in the first place, that there is a great difference between mind and body, inasmuch as body is by nature always divisible, and the mind is entirely indivisible. For, as a matter of fact, when I consider the mind, that is to say, myself inasmuch as I am only a thinking thing, I cannot distinguish in myself any parts, but apprehend myself to be clearly one and entire; and although the whole mind seems to be united to the whole body, yet if a foot, or an arm, or some other part, is separated from my body, I am aware that nothing has been taken away from my mind. And the faculties of willing, feeling, conceiving, etc. cannot be properly speaking said to be its parts, for it is one and the same mind which employs itself in willing and in feeling and understanding. But it is quite otherwise with corporeal or extended objects, for there is not one of these imaginable by me which my mind cannot easily divide into parts and which consequently I do not recognize as being divisible; this would be sufficient to teach me that the mind or soul of man is entirely different from the body, if I had not already learned it from other sources.[3]

Clearly, Descartes's concern is to negate the full absorption of the soul by the body in the process of subjective internalization. The two remain distinct entities, even if one resides within the other. Apart from remarking on Descartes's famous *Cogito* in his description of the "I" as the "thinking thing," we should note his concern for divisibility and indivisibility as tests for integrity. Descartes believes that the possibility of the body to be separated into parts implies that it is of a different nature than the indivisible mind/soul. In fact, Western philosophy will not be able to develop a discourse for the parts of the mind until the twentieth century with Freud's "The Ego and the Id" and by Sartre, who in *L'être et le néant* claims that "alterity is, really, an internal negation and only a conscience can constitute itself as an internal negation."[4] Nevertheless, through his reasoning, Descartes crystallizes the notion of a self within a body, establishing this self as internal, unitary, and inseparable from the body.

In the twentieth century, a strong Western philosophical current attempts to amend the internal subject posited by Descartes. Bataille, for example, posits the divine as self inside the body: "By 'internal experience' I mean that which normally is called 'mystical experience': ecstasies, rapture, as a form of mediating emotion."[5] Bataille here suggests that even though inwardness initially required secularization, once it is established it can become sacramental once again without forcing the self to exit the body. Similarly, Michel Serres in *Variations sur le corps* uses an aesthetic discourse to claim that the body's internalization of the self does not imply a rejection of the profound and transcendental mystery of artistic appreciation. While Bataille and Serres are interested in recuperating the Divine for the internal self, for Sartre "all other conceptualization of alterity will end up presenting it as in-itself, in other words, to establish between it and Being an external relationship, which would require the presence of a witness to verify that the other is different from that which is in-itself."[6]

In *Caliban's Reason*, Paget Henry explains that Afro-Diasporic philosophy does not exist as a tradition isolated from other manifestations of culture. Henry's argument implies the need to investigate Afro-Diasporic religion as a repository of philosophical information that can overcome the imposition of Western philosophical discourses on colonized peoples. In fact, a thorough study of Afro-Diasporic religions reveals how—unlike the Western idea of the fixed internal unitary soul—the Afro-Diasporic self is removable, external, and multiple. In his study of the Akan conceptual scheme, Kuame Gyekye presents a tripartite plan of the self composed of the *honam* (the material body), the *okra* (the immaterial soul), and the *sunsum* (the quasi-material spirit),[7] and Kwasi Wiredu explains Gyekye's systematization of Akan personhood by comparing it with Descartes's mind/body binarism:

One thing, in any case, should be absolutely clear: Neither the okra nor the sunsum can be identified with the immaterial soul familiar in some influential Western philosophical and religious thinking (with all its attendant paradoxes). This concept of the soul is routinely used interchangeably with the concept of mind while the concept of okra and sunsum are categorically different form the Akan concept of mind (adwene), as our previous explanation should have rendered apparent. Thus Descartes (in English translation) can speak indifferently of the soul or the mind and appear to make sense. In Akan to identify either the okra or the sunsum with adwene would be the sheerest gibberish.[8]

The multiplicity of the self displayed in the Akan scheme is prevalent in Western African societies and has been noted by the Haitian Vodou scholar Guérin Montilus in his study of Adja philosophy:

> The Vodu religion of the Adja taught these same Africans that their psychic reality and source of human life was metaphorically symbolized by the shadow of the body. This principle, represented by the shadow, is called the *ye*. There are two of these. The first is the inner, the internal part of the shadow, which is called the *ye gli;* that is, a short *ye*. The second, the external and light part of the same shadow, is called the *ye gaga;* that is, the long *ye*. The first *ye gli,* is the principle of physical life, which vanishes at death. The second, *ye gaga,* is the principle of consciousness and psychic life. The *ye gaga* survives death and illustrates the principle of immortality. It has metaphysical mobility that allows human beings to travel far away at night (through dreams) or remain eternally alive after the banishment of the *ye gli*. After death, the *ye gaga* goes to meet the community of Ancestors, which constitutes the extended family and the clan in their spiritual dimensions.[9]

This multiplicity of the self found in African philosophy survives in the Caribbean Diaspora. The African duality of the immaterial self—the *okra* and *sunsum* of the Akan and the *ye gli* and *ye gaga* of the Adja—becomes the *tibonanj* and the *gwobonanj* in Haitian Vodou. Margarite Fernández Olmos and Lizabeth Paravisini-Gebert thus define these two elusive terms: "The head, which contains the two elements that comprise the soul—the ti bònanj or ti bon ange (the conscience that allows for self-reflection and self-criticism) and the gwo bònanj or gros bon ange (the psyche, source of memory, intelligence, and personhood)—must be prepared so that the gros bon ange can be separated from the initiate to allow the spirit to enter in its place."[10] Here we begin to see that there is a cooperative relationship between the *tibonanj* and the *gwobonanj*. Alfred

Métraux further expounds on this cooperation: "It is the general opinion that dreams are produced by the wanderings of the Gros-bon-ange when it abandons the body during sleep. The sleeper becomes aware of the adventures of the Gros-bon-ange through the Ti-z'ange who remains by him as a protector and yet never loses sight of the Gros-bon-ange. He wakes the sleeper in case of danger and even flies to the rescue of the Gros-bon-ange if this faces real danger."[11] For the self to achieve altered states of consciousness—in trance possessions, dreams, or death—the *tibonanj* allows the *gwobonanj* to become detached from the person. In the case of trance possession, the *gwobonanj* surrenders its place and its authority to the *mèt tet*, "the main spirit served by that person and the one s/he most often goes into trance for."[12]

Karen McCarthy Brown further explains the multiple concept of the self in Vodou by presenting this notion of the *mèt tet*, roughly translated as "the master of the head": "The personality of the *mèt tet* and that of the devotee tend to coincide, an intimate tie hinted at in the occasional identification of the "big guardian angel" (*gwo bònanj*), one dimension of what might be called a person's soul, with the Vodou spirit who is his or her *mèt tet*."[13] Here we see how the *gwobonanj* is the central element of the self in Vodou. Not only is it the seat of individuality but it also maintains links between *mèt tet* and the *tibonanj*, two aspects of the self that are not directly connected to each other. These links are broken after the death of the individual, in the Vodou ceremony of *dessounin*. We can summarize the roles of the two most important aspects of the self by saying that the *gwobonanj* is consciousness, while the *tibonanj* is objectivity. The *gwobonanj* is the principal soul, experience, personality, the personal soul or self.[14] The *tibonanj* is described as the anonymous, protective, objective conscience that is the truthful and objective, the impersonal spiritual, component of the individual,[15] whose domain also encompasses moral considerations and arbitration.[16] The *tibonanj* is a "spiritual reserve tank. It is an energy or presence within the person that is dimmer or deeper than consciousness, but it is nevertheless there to be called upon in situations of stress and depletion."[17]

The complex relationship between the *gwobonanj* and the *tibonanj* has at times not been correctly understood by Western scholars, who have disseminated erroneous information, further muddying our collective understanding of the self in Vodou. For example, Desmangles ascribes to the *tibonanj* characteristics that most scholars attribute to the *gwobonaj*: "The ti-bon-anj is the ego-soul. It represents the unique qualities that characterize an individual's personality."[18] Comparisons to Western philosophy underscore his confusion: "The Vodou concept of the ti-bon-anj in heaven seems to correspond to the Roman Catholic doctrine of the soul, for Vodouisants believe that it 'appears' before Bondye to stand before the heavenly tribunal where it is arraigned for its misdeeds, and must suffer the appropriate penalties."[19] Similarly, Wade Davis ascribes to the *tibonanj* attributes that most scholars use to define the *gwobonanj:* "The Ti bon ange [is] the individual, aura, the source of all personality and willpower."[20] Furthermore, Davis says that the *tibonanj* travels during sleep,[21] while most scholars agree that it is the *gwobonanj* who does so.[22]

In addition to the *gwobonanj,* the *tibonanj,* and the *mèt tet,* there remain three components of Vodou concept of personhood. The *nam* is the "spirit of the flesh that allows each cell to function"[23] or "the animating force of the body."[24] The *zetwal* is the "celestial parallel self, fate"[25] and the "spiritual component that resides in the sky"; it is "the individual's star of destiny."[26] The *kòr kadav* is "the body itself, the flesh and blood,"[27] "the dead body of a person," and "a material substance separable from these various animating spiritual entities."[28]

The phenomenon of trance possession needs to be explained through the multiplicity of the self in Vodou. The projection of Western philosophical concepts by anthropologists onto Vodou has been responsible for inaccurate understandings of trance possession: "The symptoms of the opening phase of the trance are clearly pathological. They conform exactly in their main features, to the stock clinical conception of hysteria."[29] Even as Métraux inaccurately equates trance possession with the already questionable notion of "hysteria," he does provide one of the clearest definitions of this phenomenon during the 1950s, the early period of serious scholarly investigation of Vodou. Métraux's work helps us to locate the seat of selfhood in the corporeal head of the individual. In Haitian Kreyòl, *tèt* has an interesting double meaning. It is a noun referring to the anatomical "head," and in its function as a reflexive prefix attached to personal pronouns, it also means "self." This synecdoche becomes important as it establishes the head as a referent for selfhood, in a part-for-whole metaphor. It also presents the head as the physical location for the multiple parts of the self. Writing in the interstices between African and European philosophies, Métraux describes trance possession using an ambiguous language implying penetration and hovering. This vacillation between metaphors for possession continues in the following quote: "The relationship between the loa and the man seized is compared to that which joins a rider to his horse. That is why a loa is spoken of as mounting or saddling his *chual* (horse). . . . It is also an invasion of the body by a supernatural spirit; hence the often-used expression: 'the loa is seizing his horse.'"[30] Métraux's use of in/out metaphors for the phenomenon of possession is a Western importation. The rider metaphor popularized by early scholars of Vodou such as Zora Neale Hurston in *Tell My Horse* (1938) and Katherine Dunham in *Island Possessed* (1969) articulates the language used by the initiates themselves.

Afro-Diasporic religions operate under a transcorporeal conceptualization of the self that is radically different from the Western philosophical tradition. Unlike Descartes's unitary soul, the immaterial aspect of the Afro-Diasporic self is multiple, external, and removable. These various subjectivities rest upon a concave corporeal surface reminiscent of a saddle or a calabash.

What are the possible implications for gender in a modular system in which the self can be substituted for temporarily by a subjectivity of another gender? Some of these gender implications of Afro-Diasporic transcorporeality are evident in René Depestre's novel *Hadriana dans tous mes rêves*. In this, Hadriana—a white French woman living in Haiti—is turned into a zombi on her wedding day and becomes the leader of a Vodou community. Martin Murno sees in Hadriana's whiteness "obvious traces of Depestre's francophilia."[31] But he also concedes that there might be an element of resistance in Depestre's idealization of Hadriana's beauty by claiming that Hadriana might embody a "reversal of colonial eroticization of its tropical other."[32] Her aborted marriage begins a non-heteronormative characterization of Hadriana that continues throughout her spiritual evolution. At the outset of the text, Hadriana is associated with Nana Buruku, a *lwa* that is often represented as embodying a primordial androgynous gender. "The people of Jacmel, unable to accept that a heart attack brought Nana down to the foot of the altar, used their necrophilic imagination to reinsert their daughter into a fairy tale. Her body's disappearance from the sepulcher was the catalyst for such a leap from the fear of death into fantasy."[33]

At the end of the novel, she is associated with a male deity of spring: "I was Simbi-the-Spring. The gods of Vodou ordered me take a handful of emigrants from Jacmel to Jamaica."[34] The regendering seen in Hadriana's transmutation into various deities is also evident in the powerful trance ·a *Mambo* experiences at another point in the text: "From the first notes of the dance, Saint James the Greater—the first in the family of the Oguns—mounts Brévica Losange as his horse. In that manner possessed, the Mambo improvises a song in harmony with the drums."[35]

This female Vodou priestess's identification with one of the most virile of *lwas* demonstrates how the substitution of the *gwobonanj* by the *mèt tet* of another gender can have as a result the Vodouisant's corporeal regendering.

In addition to her association with Nana Buruku and Simbi-la-Source, Hadriana is constantly associated with yet another *lwa*: Gédé, whose domain is life and death. Although his demeanor is humorous, he is known for speaking harsh truths. His portrayal as an undertaker in enhanced by his top hat. His eyeglasses have only one lens, implying vision in this world and the next. His walking cane is a phallus, acquiring a transcorporeal aspect in the hands of his female devotees. Hadriana's death is presented as the responsibility of this *lwa*: "A man with a resemblance to Baron-Samedi invites those Gédés at his side to take the casket from the apostolic hands that carry it."[36] Hadriana's inert body becomes the very representation of death, and therefore that of Gédé: "Twenty meters around the spectacle, the musicians, in unison, impose the general fever of the drum: the crowd stops dancing to mimic the corpse-like ugliness of Hadriana Siloé, making the square a settlement of death's kingdom."[37] Hadriana's identification with this mortuary and highly sexual deity is evident in a description of a Vodou ceremony that foregrounds Gédé's transgression of the binarisms of death/life, masculinity/femininity, terrestrial/celestial, sacred/profane:

> On the contrary, drums and wind instruments change Madame Losange's song into a sunny season of the night: their musical fury alternates in each of the living death and birth, cries of agony and exclamations of orgasmic triumph. The musical volcano reduced to ashes the legendary obstacles between Thanatos and Eros, beyond the prohibitions against the sperm of black males and the eggs of white females. The explosion of Gédés, enlivened by the warm blood, puts the souls and the bodies, the tumescent penises and the vaginas, in cosmic harmony with the crazy hope of rescuing Nana Siloé from death and light again, among us, the star of her life in her flesh.[38]

The transcorporeality found in the religious tradition of Vodou enables the assumption of cross-gender subjectivities in the secular arena. Depestre makes use of irony not only by having Hadriana's death take place at the wedding altar, but also by having the wake take place during carnival. Troupes of revelers parade by Hadriana's dead body. The contrast between feast and funeral highlights a reversal of gender norms in the Caribbean carnival tradition of the *mariage burlesque*: "I stopped in front of a group of men disguised as women. In order to simulate an advanced state of pregnancy, they placed pillows under their satin dresses. They had breasts and buttocks fit for Venus Kallipygos. Supported by staffs, the cross-dressers chatted with people dressed in white clothes."[39] Édouard Glissant presents this tradition as one of the few places in which West Indian society is able to critique patriarchal heteronormativity:

> There is an occasion in Martinique in which men and women meet in order to give a symbolic representation of their relationship. This is the tradition of the burlesque marriages during carnival, a critique of family structure. The man has the role of the wife (often pregnant) and the woman that of the husband; an adult has the role of an infant in a crib. It is not surprising that the burlesque marriage is one of the rare forms still alive of that great popular and collective questioning that can be none other than the Martinican carnival.[40]

Glissant's Martinican context prevents him from considering Haitian Vodou as yet another site in which West Indian societies are able to question the dictates of gender and sexual norms. However, this Martinican perspective enables us to consider the ways in which this transcorporeality extends beyond the religious and permeates the entire structure of West Indian society, even of those segments that have become greatly Europeanized as a result of departmentalization.

That the representation of West Indian society in Depestre is suffused with exoticism has not gone unnoticed by literary critics. In an effort to redeem Depestre's work, Martin Munro reminds us, "Exoticism is not, not always, a product of the hegemonic gaze. The processes of mass exile from the Caribbean have rendered the dualistic center-periphery concept of hegemony ever more redundant."[41] In other words, we could read Depestre's exoticism as stemming from a deep nostalgia and as catharsis for the loss and separation from his native Haiti as a result of his exile in France.

Likewise, unlike the Western idea of the body as the enclosure of the soul, the *kòr kadav* is an open vessel that finds metaphoric and aesthetic expression in the *Kwi, govi,* and *kanari* containers of Haitian Vodou. As Thompson explains, one of the most arresting sights for a newcomer into an Afro-Diasporic religious setting is the collection and assortment of ritual containers: "The close gathering of numerous bottles and containers, on various tiers, is a strong organizing principle in the world of vodun altars. That unifying concept, binding Haitian Rada altars to Dahomean altars in West Africa, precisely entails a constant elevation of a profusion of pottery upon a dais, an emphasis on simultaneous assuagement (the liquid in vessels) and exaltation (the ascending structure of the tiers)."[42]

In fact, some of the most striking art objects of the African diaspora are anthropomorphic receptacles, as noted by Falgayrettes-Leveau in his exhibit book *Réceptacles:* "The Kuba and their kin in Zaire have privileged in an almost codified, yet refined, manner the representation of the head in crafting the most beautiful of their receptacles: the cups for drinking palm wine."[43] These cephalomorphic receptacles emblematize the function of the head—and, through synecdoche, the body—as an open container. This association of the head with such ritual containers is evident in the use of a specific receptacle called *pò tets*, literally "container heads": "This part of the initiation also involves the preparation of the pò tets, as containers for the new selves, repositories for ingredients symbolic of the new union of spirit and human being: hair, sacrificial food, herbs, and oils. When the initiates join the community for their presentation as ounsis, they walk with these pots balanced on their heads and place them in the altar, as symbol of their entering the community as initiated ounsi."[44] This representation of the head as an open vessel becomes evident in the association between the material body and various types of ritual containers in Depestre's *Hadriana:* "I was overcome by violent internal convulsions. All my bones vibrated until they almost cracked. I was in a nightmare inside a nightmare. I was a stolen soul. They separated my *tibonanj* from my *gwobonanj.* They had enclosed the first in a calabash to take it by mule back to a penitentiary of souls in the mountains of Haut-Cap-Rouge. The second, arm tied behind his back, was flagellated like an ass in the opposite direction. All links were broken between my two forms of being."[45] Here it is possible to see Depestre's important depiction of the African multiple self. Through this quote we also become aware of the ways in which aspects of the self might be removable without producing the individual's death. It is also significant how Depestre presents the calabash as one of the receptacles that may be used as a substitute for the human body.

Davis explains how the separation of the corporeal and immaterial aspects of the self that Depestre describes constitute the phenomenon of zombification: "The spirit zombie, or the zombie of the ti bon ange alone, is carefully stored in a jar and may later be magically transmuted into insects, animals, or humans in order to accomplish the particular work of the bokòr. The remaining spiritual components of man, the n'âme, the gros bon ange, and the z'étoile, together form the zombi cadaver, the zombi of the flesh."[46] This very detached description of the process of zombification is consistent with Davis's clinical view of zombification as purely the result of neurotoxin poisoning.[47] However, for Depestre, zombification has much more emotive connotations associated to loss of autonomy and spiritual imprisonment: "This place of detention was prepared to receive the bottled up souls of people condemned to a privation of their spiritual liberty. The practice consisted in bottling up the imaginary of individuals who have become living dead. The bottles that you will see are little forgotten things in glass, crystal, metal, ceramic, leather, wood, and stoneware!"[48] Through these passages we see that Depestre, like Davis, conceives the *tibonanj* as the principal soul and the seat of individuality. However, this view is incongruent with the work of other scholars who believe that "the famous zombies are people whose Gros-bon-ange has been captured by some evil hungan, thus becoming living-dead."[49] Moreover, apart from zombification, there are various forms of spiritual embottlement, all of which involve the capturing of the *gwobonanj,* not the *tibonanj.* For instance, when the individual willingly decides to bottle up part of his self, it is the *gwobonanj:* "A certain amount of immunity against witchcraft may be obtained by requesting an hungan to extract the Gros-bon-ange from the body and to enclose it in a bottle. The soul, removed from its bodily envelope, may either be hidden or buried in a garden or entrusted to the hungan for safekeeping."[50] While this procedure protects the *gwobonanj,* it does not prevent bodily damage to the material body from which it proceeds. This creates a potentially dangerous scenario in which people who have sustained severe bodily injury—either through spells or accidents—will beg to have their *gwobonanj* liberated from the bottle, in order to end their corporeal suffering through death.

The *gwobonanj* must be ritually removed from the person's head shortly after death through the ceremony of *desounnin,* in which "the Oungan calls the spirit, or in some cases the name of the dead, then removes the lwa and puts it in a pitcher or bottle, called a govi. In death, the link between the spirit and its human vessel must be broken, so that the individual's spirit can move beyond death, and beyond revenge, joining the ancestors under the waters in the mythical place called Ginen (Guinea)."[51] Then, a year and a day after death, the *gwobonanj* is called up from the water in a ceremony referred to as *rele mò nan dlo* (calling the dead from the water) and installed in a *govi* clay pot.[52]

Depestre and Davis are correct in their assessment of zombification as constituting the embottlement of one part of the self. However, they are mistaken by saying that this part is the *tibonanj,* since this and other types of spiritual embottlements involve the containment of the *gwobonanj.* Beyond noticing these important discrepancies, what is important for us to consider here is how, regardless of what aspect of the self is bottled up, according to all of these authors, any type of hermetic enclosing of the self is seen as potentially dangerous or associated with death. The fact that one of the most dreaded Afro-Diasporic states of being should be so similar to the Cartesian view of the hermetically sealed soul points to the contestatory and critical relationship between these two philosophical traditions. Curiously, the zombified body of Haitian Vodou bears striking similarities to the body without organs that Gilles Deleuze and Félix Guattari elaborate in *L'Anti-Oedipe:* "Death instinct, that is his name. Since the desire desires also that, death, because the body full of death is an immobile motor, because life's organs are the working machine. The body without organs is not the witness of an original nothingness, not any more than the remains of a lost totality. It is not a projection; it has nothing to do with the body itself or the image of the body. It is the body without an image. Him, the unproductive . . . the body without organs is anti-production."[53] In this sense, both the Western and the African view of personhood can be seen to coincide. By presenting the most abject state of being as that of the body that is deprived of its immaterial elements—organs, *gwobonanj*—both traditions present an image of the exploited, enslaved, unremunerated, and incomplete worker. Descartes's body-as-clockwork and Vodou's *kòr kadav* are more similar than previously thought.

One of the *gwobonanj* kept by the *bokòr* is that of a same-sex-loving male artist: "There is a queer painter imprisoned in the seltzer water syphon."[54] While Fanon famously insisted there is no homosexuality in the West Indies,[55] other French West Indian writers such as Depestre and Frankétienne present same-sex desire as intrinsic to the region. Frankétienne's Kreyòl novel *Adjanoumelezo* utilizes the voice of Gédé—the jocular Vodou *lwa* of life, death, overflowing sexuality, and bawdiness—to speak openly about the important role that queers play in Vodou: "Papa Gédé draws cosmograms with small fine letters for his pleasure on sheets of paper. He plays with words. He sows words. He solders words, He hems words. He dresses words and phrases in decorative lace. Papa Gédé has no problem or shyness to say that which he sees, hears or feels."[56] Gédé's lack of shame allows the articulation of an erotics of women-loving-women that turns *madevinez* from derogatory epithet into passionate poetic embellishment: "The smell of the divinity along the celestial route of the rainbow, dyke-route, dyke-mouth, open up the path as if cutting through the middle of a pineapple."[57]

Similarly, Gédé's voice in Franketienne's *Adjanoumelezo* locates the source of sexual desire of men for men in the phallus of Dambala, the snake god. Paralleling his earlier beautification of *madevinez,* Franketienne explains the effeminacy of the *masisi* as divine in nature, coming about through male devotion to Lasirenn. Franketienne writes, "Wow! Wow! Wow! I am hot. I take a deep breath opening my mouth like the crab to exclaim hip! hip! hurrah! I am sucking on the head of a serpent. I am twisting the serpent's meat. I am eating the cock's vein. I am groping the tailbone. The mermaid calls the faggot sweet things, honey, cherry and mounts him. Oh boy! Oh boy! Oh boy!"[58] In fact, Franketiénne's spiralist word play leads us to the origins of the word *Masisi* in the Fon language of Benin and Togo: "Mami Wata is about fertility, femaleness, and beauty. Mostly women become Mamisis; men who become Mamisis are particularly good-looking and often dress and plait their hair like women."[59] The African counterpart of the Haitian Lasirenn is Mami Wata, whose initiates, *Mamisis*—read: *Masisis*—embody the femininity of the deity. The Fon term for initiates of the sea goddess becomes in Haiti a referent to male homosexuality.

While Franketienne's *Adjanoumelezo* honors the full pantheon of Vodou laws—"Dambala's horse is on at the crossroads, torn apart. In order to go higher and farther, we ask Legba to open the barrier for us. We glide and descend into the fire of Ogun. We are troubling Simbi's water"[60]—Géde and Lasirenn occupy a primordial role in the narrative, the first because of this unbridled sexuality and the second because of her associations with same-sex-loving male initiates.

In Anne Lescot and Laurence Magloire's film *Des hommes et des dieux,* *masisis* owe their desire not to Lasirenn, but to Ezili Dantò—the eternal mother spirit and a *lwa* whom some consider to be a lesbian.[61] With the backdrop of marketplaces, hair salons, Vodou temples, sacred waterfalls, and dance clubs in Haiti, this groundbreaking film gives voice to a range of Haitian *masisis,* most of whom explain their same-sex desire as stemming from their spiritual connection to Dantò.[62] There is Blondine, who sells tobacco snuff in the Port-au-Prince street market, as passersby mock him for his effeminate demeanor, appearance, and trade. He is tired of the insults in Haiti and would like to move to the Dominican Republic someday. He says that "Lwa gate'm" (the *lwa* spoiled me) and that his father accepts his orientation as "bagay mistik" (something sacred). There is Denis, whom we see at an *ounfò* (Vodou temple) singing to Dantò, "Maman kote ou ye?" (Mother, where are you?). There is Innocente, who also feels he has been the victim of prejudice because "moun pa eklere" (people are uneducated). His public humiliations have lessened a great deal since he became an *oungan,* or Vodou priest. His family accepts him because it is "bagay mistik" caused by Ezili. He has adopted his sister's child, acting out of the maternal instinct with which Erzulie has gifted him. All these men use Kreyòl terms to name their lived experience: *masisi, madevinez, en kache.* None use "gay," "lesbian," or "the closet."

However, class divisions in Haiti become clear when the interviewees with a higher degree of education and better command of French come on the screen. Fritzner, an *oungan,* says that people are born like this, and that placing the origin of same-sex desire on Dantò is rubbish. In his Frenchified Creole, he uses French terms to define same-sex desire: "homosexuelle," "homo," and "lesbienne." Speaking in French, Érol also speaks of "homos" and "héteros." He explains that queer men say that they have been "appellé par Erzulie" (called by Ezili) in order to avoid Western taboos and find safety in the refuge of "la religion de la tolerance" (the religion of tolerance). According to his reasoning, men who love men choose Dantò, rather than her choosing them. They know that she is a mother who accepts her children just the way they are. She will not turn them away. However, his reason does not prevent him from accepting that in the phenomenon of trance possession something quite transcendental occurs with respect to gender. He acknowledged that when men lend their bodies to Dantò, these male bodies are transformed by the femininity of the goddess. Similarly, he believes that Ogun is able to "change l'esprit de femme en homme" (transform the spirit of a woman into a man's).

While the film exposes the hardship of being part of a sexual minority in a country not always friendly to difference, its narrative is not one of tragedy, but of joy in the face of adversity and of the hope of overcoming difficulties. For instance, the dancers at the *kompa* club underscore the health dangers of casual sex in the country with the highest incidence of HIV infection in the Western Hemisphere. Nevertheless, there is catharsis for this anxiety, and the homophobia, at the ritual bathing at the St. Jacques waterfalls.

The film is to be commended for giving voice to men from a wide range of social classes and professions. However, the film is not always sensitive to issues of language when it translates *masisi* and *madevinez* in the subtitles using First World terminologies. Furthermore, the film should be critiqued for its foregrounding of the troubling issue of causality: What makes these men gay? Perhaps a more helpful question would have been; What accounts for the large numbers of people who are non-heteronormative in these religions? Such a question would have likely yielded a fruitful exploration on the non-binary quality of Vodou, a multiplicity beyond the dualism of maleness and femaleness, and an elucidation of how the phenomenon of possession allows cross-gender identifications.

Unlike the Western idea of a unitary self that is fixed within the body, the African Diasporic philosophical-religious tradition conceives the body as a concavity upholding a self that is removable, external, and multiple. Allowing for a wider range of subjectivities than the more rigid Western model, the modular African Diasporic discourse of personhood becomes a vehicle for the articulation of noncompliant identities that are usually constrained by normative heteropatriarchy. Haitian literary works like René Depestre's *Hadriana dans tous mes rêves* and Frankétienne's *Adjanoumelezo* and filmic ones like Lescot and Magloire's *Des hommes et des dieux* illustrate this modular and transcorporeal view of the African Diasporic self in their representations of trance possession, uses of ritual containers, and the phenomenon of zombification.

Notes

1. Ehrsson, "Experimental Induction"; Lenggenhager et al., "Video Ergo Sum."
2. Taylor, *Sources of the Self,* 143.
3. Descartes, *Discourse on Method,* 105–6.
4. Sartre, *L'être et le néant,* 666. Unless otherwise stated, all translations are my own.
5. Bataille, *L'expérience intérieure,* 15.
6. Sartre, *L'être et le néant,* 666.
7. Gyekye, *African Philosophical Thought,* 89.
8. Wiredu, *Cultural Universals and Particulars,* 129.
9. Montilus, "Vodun and Social Transformation," 2.
10. Fernández Olmos and Paravisini-Gebert, *Creole Religions,* 118.
11. Métraux, "Concept of the Soul," 85.
12. McCarthy Brown, "Afro-Caribbean Spirituality," 10.
13. McCarthy Brown, *Mama Lola,* 112–13.
14. Deren, *Divine Horsemen,* 44.
15. Ibid.
16. Agosto de Muñoz, *El fenómeno de la posesión,* 52.
17. McCarthy Brown, *Vodou in Haitian Life and Culture,* 9.
18. Desmangles, *Faces of the Gods,* 67.
19. Ibid., 69.
20. Davis, *Serpent and Rainbow,* 185.

21. Ibid., 182.

22. McCarthy Brown, "Afro-Caribbean Spirituality," 9; Montilus, "Vodun and Social Transformation," 4.

23. Davis, *Serpent and Rainbow*, 185.

24. McCarthy Brown, "Afro-Caribbean Spirituality," 8.

25. Ibid., 9.

26. Davis, *Serpent and Rainbow*, 185.

27. Ibid., 185.

28. McCarthy Brown, "Afro-Caribbean Spirituality," 9.

29. Métraux, "Concept of the Soul," 120.

30. Ibid.

31. Munro, *Exile and Post-1946 Haitian Literature*, 127.

32. Ibid.

33. Depestre, *Hadriana dans tous mes rêves*, 99.

34. Ibid., 207.

35. Ibid., 77.

36. Ibid., 92.

37. Ibid., 68.

38. Ibid., 79.

39. Ibid., 59–60.

40. Glissant, *Discours antillais*, 1981, 299.

41. Munro, *Exile and Post-1946 Haitian Literature*, 134.

42. Thompson, *Flash of the Spirit*.

43. Falgayrettes-Leveau, "Avant-Propos," 32.

44. Fernández Olmos and Paravisini-Gebert, *Creole Religions*, 118–19.

45. Depestre, *Hadriana*, 175.

46. Davis, *Hadriana*, 186.

47. Davis, *Passage of Darkness*.

48. Depestre, *Hadriana*, 175.

49. Métraux, "Concept of the Soul," 87.

50. Ibid., 86.

51. Dayan, *Haiti, History and the Gods*, 261.

52. McCarthy Brown, "Afro-Caribbean Spirituality," 8.

53. Deleuze and Guattari, *L'Anti-Oedipe*, 15.

54. Depestre, *Hadriana*, 176.

55. Fanon, *Peau noire, masques blancs* (1995), 146.

56. Frankétienne, *Adjanoumelezo*, 12.

57. Ibid., 249.

58. Ibid., 513.

59. Rosenthal, *Possession, Ecstasy, and Law*, 118.

60. Frankétienne, *Adjanoumelezo*, 60.

61. René and Houlberg, "My Double Mystic Marriages," 299.

62. Magloire and Lescot's representation of *masisi* culture is a palliative to its depiction in "Imagine Heaven," the introduction to *Sacred Arts of Haitian Vodou*. In this introductory essay, Donald Cosentino uses Susan Sontag's "Notes on Camp" to make a facile connection between Vodou trance and gay balls when he says that "trance possession may also be seen as a kind of voguing of the

divinities" (55). However, this is an erroneous interpretation. Trance is more than putting on clothes and it is certainly not drag. The concept of "realness" popularized in Jenny Livingston's film *Paris Is Burning* is dependent on impersonation, passing, parodying, and cross-dressing, but this is certainly not the case of trance possession in Vodou—as Consentino suggests. The transcendental and life-transforming act of a Haitian *masisi* being ridden by a *lwa* cannot be compared with black gay men in Brooklyn enacting a simulacrum of fashion runway shows. This conflation of the sacred and profane obfuscates what is at the core of both events.

Helen in Her Yellow Dress

Dressing, Undressing, and Cross-Dressing in the Literature of the Contemporary Caribbean

Lizabeth Paravisini

THERE IS a scene in Derek Walcott's *Omeros* (1990) in which the expatriate Major Plunkett walks into his bedroom and surprises his maid Helen trying on a bracelet belonging to his wife Maud. The Major, turned momentarily into a *voyeur-malgré-lui,* is bewildered before the multiple levels of transgression embedded in the mesmerizing tableau he sees reflected in his mirror—by the possibility of theft, the crossing of boundaries by a maid who "kept the house // as if it were her own,"[1] the sexual titillation and intimacy of this mimicry of dressing, and, most particularly, by the threat of class cross-dressing that the gesture implies. For Helen, a poor black woman in the freshly postcolonial society of Saint Lucia, the appropriation of a white woman's jewelry represents a challenge to an established colonial order that signals its class and race distinctions in part through the means of dress codes and restricted access to certain types of adornments.

The blurring of colonial social categories signaled by Helen's transgressive gesture turns the bedroom—the most intimate of spaces—into a liminal and potentially subversive space where colonial, racial, and class binaries are destabilized. Witnessing her transgression leaves the Major at her mercy, aroused and complicit, forced to acknowledge her power. Outside the bedroom—where it is harder to escape these social categories—the bracelet is replaced by a yellow dress of Maud's that Helen appropriates (claiming it had been offered as a gift) and in which she weaves in and out of the text. It becomes a symbol of Helen's class-cross-dressing presence in the text—the central prop in the performance of her quest for a fluid identity in her native Saint Lucia. Helen's moments of transgressive dressing—and of the undressing inherent in the voyeuristic moments against which it resonates—could be read as rehearsals for the dress's final appearance in the text. Toward the end of the poem, in the small bedroom she shares with Achille, Helen helps him don her yellow dress as he prepares to emerge into the streets of his village of Gros Ilet as a cross-dressed female warrior to perform the *paille-banane* traditional Boxing Day dance in the capital city of Castries.

Helen's yellow dress—as it moves from class to cultural to gender cross-dressing in *Omeros*—functions as a destabilizing element in Walcott's approach to the binaries of race, gender, class, and culture that have been the legacy of colonial history in the Caribbean. Mercurial and protean, the dress serves as my point of departure for a discussion of ways in which a number of Caribbean texts written within the last two decades— Walcott's *Omeros*, Jamaica Kincaid's *The Autobiography of My Mother* (1997), and José Alcántara Almánzar's "Lulú or the Metamorphosis" (1995)—address the implications of class, cultural, and gender cross-dressings as acts of political appropriation that subvert power relations in postcolonial societies. The incidents of cross-dressing narrated in these texts reveal asymmetries in the class, race, and gender binaries in their respective societies through which we can glimpse the characters' search for hybrid identities in the interstices created by their breach of accepted gender norms. These breaches, as the readings of the texts that follow will show, draw upon the erotic as a symbolic and social system that can be both empowering and destructive, depending on the nature of the infringement of the codes. Cross-dressing, as presented in Walcott's and Kincaid's texts, can serve as a "creative tool for subverting social and racial stereotypes and creating individual identity"[2]; it can also, as in Alcántara Almánzar's work, show the limits of such textual subversions, as the cross-dressed body becomes an emblem of criminality and defiance, emerging from the text as dangerous and degenerate and, therefore, expendable. I link these tensions, in my conclusion, to the work of the Jamaican artist Ebony Patterson, whose work explores the liberating possibilities of dancehall as "the belly of Jamaican society that reaffirms, reflects and assigns labels as it relates to social norms or behaviors deemed deviant within Jamaican society."[3]

The trajectory of Helen's yellow dress in *Omeros* is inscribed by Walcott into the narrative of Saint Lucians' resistance to the vestiges of colonial control, a struggle articulated in the text through challenges to the validity of well-established colonial binaries as sites of signification. Building on the "time-honored conflation of women's bodies and the clothes they wore,"[4] Walcott will allow the complex web of correspondences between Helen's clothing, her resistant bearing, and other characters' gazes to open a hybrid space in which he can rehearse different versions of her identity,

not all of which are centered on colonial dichotomies. She is the perennial object of other characters' gaze. Described first from the perspective
of the poet's gaze, Helen enters (and eventually will exit) the text in the
traditional Saint Lucian madras head-tie, proud and queenly against the
background of bad-tempered tourists and locals in the uniforms of servitude of a tourist industry that has rejected her "'cause she dint take no
shit/from white people and some of them tourist" (33). Her first appearance in the text in her yellow dress is described from the perspective of
the Plunketts, who glimpse her as "that ebony girl in her yellow dress"
whose future—which the Major identified with that of her island—felt
"sinister" (29). Helen in her traditional madras dress is inscribed into a
history of servitude; Helen in her yellow dress is power-bound, a "maid
turn[ed] into the mistress" (64) behaving as if she owned her employers. "'There's our trouble,'" Maud remarks when she sees Helen "in the
same yellow frock Maud had altered for her" (29), a disturbing garment
insofar as it allows Helen to usurp the privileges of women like Maud in
the public spaces of Britain's former empire. As Walcott writes:

> This was the distress
> of the pale lemon frock, which Helen claimed Maud gave
> her but forgot. He stayed out of it, but that dress
>
> had an empire's tag on it, mistress to slave.
> The price was envy and cunning. (64)

The first sight of Helen in her yellow dress, with its subtle reminding
of the colonial mistress/slave binaries, is used by Walcott to show precisely how those binaries no longer can predict how interactions between
characters can develop in post-independence societies (and their literary
texts). The Saint Lucia through which Helen parades with her (perhaps
stolen) yellow dress is no longer the colony of a powerful nation in which
"the metonymy of clothing and identity [had] prompted the passing of
sumptuary laws to prevent dressing above one's class."[5] It is, on the contrary, a space in which these relationships are developing under as yet
unclear rules now that "the/Empire was ebbing" (30).

Walcott shows the post-independence awareness of the shifts in what
had seemed fixed binaries through the Major's abject recognition of
Helen's complete indifference to the sexual tensions her presence creates
between him and Maud.[6] Helen's "cold smile" (93) manifests her rejection of an erotic desire rooted in obsolete notions of imperial otherness,
which the Major will seek to sublimate through Homeric interpretations

that move erotic desire into a safer symbolic realm. The Major—as if doing penance for reverting to imperial covetousness in his desire for Helen—decides to write her/the island a proper history built (ironically enough) on placing on her/the island a burden of Homeric significance ("its Homeric association//rose like smoke from a siege" [31]). As a historian, Major Plunkett remains prey to cultural binaries that defeat his efforts in advance. As Rhona Dick has argued, "History for Plunkett is a tale of safe stereotypes of good and bad . . . in which he allies himself with a genealogical view of inherited heroism," fearing that "if the colonialists are declared 'bastards' his inheritance, which is his identity, will be lost."[7] Looking beyond "factual fictions" for the truth behind history, however, Major Plunkett finds only a mirror to his own erotic desire—the desire of Great Britain and France for Saint Lucia and its surrounding islands, on the one hand, and his own desire for Helen, on the other. He comes to learn "that History earns its own tenderness/in time; not for a navel victory, but for//the V of a velvet back in a yellow dress" (103). When he had caught Helen trying on Maud's bracelet, "he had closed his eyes at her closeness, a pleasure/in that passing scent which was both a natural odour/and pharmacy perfume" (96). The encounter, he later recognizes, had brought to the fore the limitations of the writing of academic history in fostering a true understanding of the past ("the passionless books/did not contain smell, eyes, the long black arm, or his/knowledge that the island's beauty was in her looks" [96]). The sexual desire explicit in the encounter also brings into question the sincerity of the Major's commitment to the island and its people. Betrayed by sexual desire, he ponders the lasting power of the desire of empire. "No. My thoughts are pure," he claims. "They're meant to help her people, ignorant and poor./But these, smiled the bracelet, are the vows of empire" (97).

Helen parades through the text in her yellow dress not only as a reminder to the Major of the futility of his own desire—of "the deep humiliation//he suffered for her and the lemon frock" (103)—but also as the "looming specter of class and race insurgency" that seeks to destabilize the "disciplined class, gender, and race distinctions" of colonialism in a post-independence society.[8] Helen and the yellow dress that becomes "her sign" are markers for an emancipatory élan that identifies Helen as a character committed to defining her life in her own terms—even within the narrow constraints of a poor former colony in which her employment options are circumscribed by the new servitude of the tourist industry. The dresses she tries on, discards, and returns to—the traditional madras costume in which she serves food to tourists, the dress she irons to parade her beauty through Gros Ilet's Friday-night jump-up, and above all, the yellow dress that draws to her the Major's desire and Maud's ire—rehearse a number of possible identities that will coalesce once she chooses a life with Achille and Hector's yet unborn child. At a pivotal point in the text, she removes her yellow dress before Walcott describes a masturbation scene that signals her self-sufficiency, turning the small bedroom she shares with Achille into the most emancipatory space in the poem. It is only then that the yellow dress can be relinquished to Achille and reassigned to a role with a deeper cultural significance when he cross-dresses as a female warrior to go into mock-battle as a *paille-banane* female warrior. The *paille-banane* dance—"an act of liberation and affirmation," a "performance to keep alive traditions that seemed to have been forgotten and to reinforce the link with the ancestral memory of Africa"[9]—is rooted in a quintessentially carnivalesque cross-dressing whose object is the debunking of those binary categories to which empire clings with such tenacity. Androgynous and ambiguous, the cross-dressed Achille, in his commitment to maintaining African-derived traditions, can help people "laugh // at what they had lost in the *paille-banane* dancers" (273).

The incorporation of Helen's yellow dress (through which she performed her own class-cross-dressing ritual) into Achille/Saint Lucia's yearly gender-cross-dressing tradition, however, adds a new level of significance to the power of this appropriated garment to "alter the identities imposed on [the formerly colonized] by colonial norms."[10] The dress itself is altered, creolized, Africanized, by the addition of bells and "small circular mirrors [that] necklaced the split bodice / that was too small for his chest" (275). It is also inalterably transformed by its appropriation into a dance whose central purpose is that of reliving the trauma of the Middle Passage, of recalling "the hold / closing over their heads, the bolt-closing iron, / over eyes that never saw the light of this world, // their memory still there although all the pain was gone" (277).

When Jamaica Kincaid published *The Autobiography of My Mother,* she signaled her novel's dialogue with Walcott's *Omeros* in a number of ways: through her dedication of the work to Walcott, through her homage to Helen in the creation of her indomitable protagonist, through the rearticulation of Walcott's erotic scenes of voyeurism and masturbation, through the use of the bedroom as a safe space for the rehearsal of possible gender identities, and through Xuela's obsession with class cross-dressing and the emancipatory possibilities of cross-dressing. The relationship between the two texts is underscored, moreover, in Kincaid's laying bare of the complexities and contradictions of a number of binaries that we have come to associate with postcolonial Caribbean literature and which feature prominently in *Omeros:* the correlations of sexuality and power, the legacy of colonialism and racism in the Caribbean and its impact on the relationships between women of different races and classes, and the self-loathing and self-destructiveness of the colonized so brilliantly described in Frantz Fanon's *Black Skin, White Masks.*

Kincaid, in the development of her intertextual connections between her novel and Walcott's poem, uses the conflation of clothing and character that Walcott deployed so effectively through Helen's yellow dress as the means of telegraphing to the reader the connections between the characters and their links to colonial control. Through this conflation, which stems primarily from the characters' understanding of clothing as visual markers of race and class status, Kincaid shows the possibilities of using clothing as "a vehicle for social critique, a metaphor for resistance to social regulation,"[11] a path away from the gender and class binaries of her postcolonial society. She does this from the opening chapter of the novel, in which her infant character Xuela is dropped off by her father (together with his soiled laundry) to be taken care of by his laundress. Her father emerges from his entrance into the text as a handsome, ambitious, and vain man whose mimicry of the ways of the colonizers—seen primarily through his interest in the colonizers' clothes—will lead him to greed, insensitivity, brutality, and betrayal. His choices of clothing—impeccable, finely tailored, well-ironed, and spotless—become a sign of the many ways in which he adheres to the beliefs of the people who have subjugated him.[12] In this pursuit he has assumed a series of deceiving masks—masking through class cross-dressing being Xuela's favorite image for his mimicry of the English—which in time become so fixed that his true self can no longer emerge from behind them as the clothes become his skin. Nowhere is this clearer than in his donning the policeman's uniform that "came to define him" (90) and which brought such fear to those around him (22). The young Xuela, whom he retrieves from the laundress's house in his uniform, is presciently aware of the significance of a garment through which he seeks to fix a new identity and erase his colonial and racial otherness; it was "too bad he had not thought of changing his clothes," she notes, "it was too bad that I had noticed he had not done so, it was too bad that such a thing would matter to me" (25). Later, as he grew richer, his finely tailored white linen suits replace his policeman's skin, as a new layer representative of his deeper collusion with the colonial enterprise. In contrast, the painful absence of her mother is poignantly signaled by the merest glimpse of the hem of her gown in dreams, the ethereal hem a constant reminder that she, at least, will never be defined by her clothing.

Xuela is a character partly defined by her consciousness of the meanings of dressing in a colonial setting. Her entrance into school is marked by the indelible memory of "the feel of the cloth of my skirt and blouse—coarse because it was new—a green skirt and beige blouse, a uniform, its colors and style mimicking the colors and style of a school somewhere else" (12). Kincaid, like Walcott before her, will explore the signifying possibilities of clothing choices primarily through what they tell us about relationships between women of different classes and races in a postcolonial setting. In *The Autobiography of My Mother*, Maud's bracelet becomes a poisoned necklace given to Xuela by her light-skinned and upwardly mobile stepmother, an ornament that fortunately fails to dazzle the child, thereby saving her life.

It is through several reiterations of Helen's yellow dress, however, that Kincaid explores most effectively the relationship between dress, class, gender, race, and the legacy of colonialism. Xuela's refusal to accept the restrictions imposed upon her by colonial society are seen best through her relationship with Madame LaBatte, the light-skinned wife in the middle-class couple with whom she is sent to live by her father so she can further her education.[13] Barren and unhappy, Madame LaBatte wants Xuela to provide the child she herself has been unable to conceive. Her attempts at seducing Xuela into this sexual/maternal surrogate role manifest themselves through her offering of a series of garments that Xuela rejects, as she had rejected her stepmother's poisonous necklace. There is much of the archetypal fairy-tale narratives of offers of poisoned clothing and jewelry in these rejections, which bring to bear on the novel all the deep psychological significance of the folk tradition and appear here in the service of a bitter critique of colonialism.

When Xuela meets Madame LaBatte, the latter is wearing "a white dress made of a coarse cloth decorated with embroidery stitching of flowers and leaves; I noticed this," the character tells us, "because it was a dress people in Mahaut would have worn only to church on Sundays" (63–64). The dress—to an astute clothes-reader like Xuela—appears as a mirror to Madame LaBatte's own inner defeat, and is therefore tainted and unacceptable. Kincaid's inversion of the relationship between Helen and Maud works at a multiplicity of levels. Not only is Madame LaBatte, unlike Maud, actively encouraging a sexual relationship between her husband and Xuela, but she is also depicted as pressing gifts of clothes on the latter (there is no question here of a stolen dress): "One day, without any preparation, she gave me a beautiful dress that she no longer wore," Xuela explains (68). On another occasion, after Xuela had consummated her sexual relationship with Monsieur LaBatte, Madame LaBatte celebrates the event with another gift of clothes: "She then bathed me and gave me another dress to wear that she had worn when she was a young woman. The dress fit me perfectly, I felt most uncomfortable in it, I could not wait to remove it and put on my own clothes again" (75). The offerings of garments, like the necklace before it, are acts imbued with the notion of casting spells that would bind the other in relationships of threat or control (78).

Melissa Mowry, writing about prostitution and pornography in seventeenth-century England, suggests that the control of class cross-dressing was "one means by which democracy might be kept in check."[14] The point-counterpoint relationship between Walcott's and Kincaid's texts suggests, in turn, ways in which we can read Helen, and later Xuela, as what Mowry calls "emblems of democratic, class transgression" in the "site of social discipline" that is colonial society.[15] What makes possible their role as transgressive emblems is the erotic—the voyeuristic desire that places women like Helen and Xuela in the slippery sexual terrain that allowed for class mobility for women of color in colonial societies. Both Walcott and Kincaid inscribe their heroines in voyeuristic scenes of eroticized dressing/undressing in which they are observed by other characters, as well as in scenes of masturbation in which we, the readers, become the voyeurs. Both types of scenes help elucidate why their performance of class cross-dressing is acceptable—even justified in their historical context—and how, in turn, they are both self-sufficient enough to escape the complexities and constraints of such archetypical traps of colonial sexuality. In both cases, the act that signals the escape is the surrender of the class cross-dressing through which control could have been exercised, acts that take place in the characters' small, confined bedrooms and mark their rejection of the grander bedrooms of colonial sexual mastery. In Helen's case, the yellow dress is surrendered to Achille in his cross-dressing performance as a female *paille-banane* dresser. In Xuela's case, she purges herself of both the child she conceived with Monsieur LaBatte and of the clothing through which Madame LaBatte wished to reward her for the child, through a painful abortion followed by a period of penance in which she dresses in the clothes of a dead man and learns to know herself (99).

For Xuela, gender cross-dressing allows for a temporary escape from the lure of a class cross-dressing that would require a surrender of her body to the demands of colonized sexual performance. Dressing as a man places Xuela outside the conventions of her society—indeed, it allows her to temporarily "disappear" from her social milieu—opening a space in which she can carve a new role for herself, different from that pre-scribed by her father and the LaBattes while simultaneously rehearsing new modes of expression for the exceptionality that is the salient mark of her character. In Xuela's case, her pivotal period of gender cross-dressing (during which she not only renounces the possibility of motherhood but also temporarily forsakes her education and class through her work as a laborer) both "reveals how gender is symbolically constructed and strikes at the heart of the social imperative to categorize individuals by rank."[16]

Xuela seeks to define herself outside rank and other colonial categories—tainted as they are by oppression and racism—and trusts only her naked-ness to encapsulate her true identity. In an illuminating scene, during which Kincaid has her protagonist confront the wife of her lover Roland, her blue dress made from stolen Irish linen is ripped from her neck to her waist, revealing her nakedness underneath, her breasts "like two small pieces of unrisen dough, unmoved by the anger of this woman" (172–73).

José Alcántara Almanzar's 1992 short story "Lulú or the Metamor-phosis"[17] follows in nuanced detail its male-to-female transgendered character as he/she prepares for his/her cross-dressed appearance at a public carnival fête in the guise of a rumba dancer. The gender binary embodied by the protagonist's self-betraying body is mirrored in the story's structure, which, instead of offering a linear, chronological narra-tive, alternates between the details of Lulú's painstaking transformation in the intimacy and solitude of his small bedroom and the events that unfold after she leaves the house, glorious in her metamorphosis—"with a joyous expression on her face that makes her look radiant, as if she were floating in space" (101)—only to be violently attacked by a band of revelers dressed in piratical costumes as Sir Francis Drake and his crew. The multiple binaries in which Lulú is trapped—of gender, race, and class—force her into constant transgressive acts against which her soci-ety rises to reimpose the raucous masculinity exemplified by the piratical crew that initiates the attack against her. These binaries are also asserted by the official, institutional violence exemplified by the policeman who *"grabbed her by the arm as he continued hurling blows at the dancer's soaked body, thrusting her into the line of prisoners heading for the station in a forced march"* (101).

Both Alcántara Almanzar and the critics who have commented on the story root the work in the Dominican Republic's gender and social binaries.

In this "stunning" story, Peter Piatkowski writes, Alcántara Almanzar "maps out a day-in-the-life of our heroine," detailing "the struggle and duality that Lulú faces not only emotionally, but physically as well."[18] Williams Siemens, in a review of the work, refers to the story's "masterful play on order and chaos."[19] In an interview with H. J. Manzari, Alcántara Almanzar underscores the binary systems at the core of his tale when he speaks of the work in the context of his society's sometimes violent reaction to those who challenge "the dualities of human existence: the squalid, the grotesque, and the scandalous."[20] He locates himself as a transgressive writer in this respectability/scandal binary by citing people's response to the tale of his cross-dressing transgendered protagonist: "Scandalous to the point that people who know me tell me 'you are nothing like your stories, you're a decent person, you don't use foul language, but your stories are filled with outrageous things.' To which I answer: 'Well, they say that the writer undresses himself as he writes.'"[21]

The authorial undressing to which Alcántara Almanzar alludes is evident in the challenge he offers to Dominican notions of masculinity in his compassionate portrayal of his transgendered protagonist. Although structurally his narrative remains within the bounds of the binaries it explores, there is in its characterization of the transgendered Lulú a side-stepping of those binaries to allow for the textual exploration of hybrid identities. The process of transformation, the narrative tells us, is a painful but necessary progression toward bodily "truth," despite the expression of centuries of denial and hostility implicit in the violent attack on Lulú.[22]

I would like to focus on just one aspect of this complex narrative—the dress that sums up Lulú's dreams and aspirations as a cross-dressing/transgendered subject in the homophobic milieu Alcántara Almanzar describes above, one in which her reality would be described as "squalid" or "grotesque" precisely because it awakens anxieties about the lack of fixedness of sexual identity. We meet Lulú—coquettish and playful, even in his male attire—in her flirtatious mode as she sells the sweets for which she is known, her "tiny ass imprisoned in tight blue jeans" (93). The "ceremony" that will transform him into a rumba dancer has as its most important prop a dress modeled on musical cinema's (not colonial) models of mulatto femininity. The flashy, somewhat over-the-top *rumbera* dress the narrator describes is linked to expressions of cultural authenticity (and dramatic insouciance) through musical performance.

Lulú's transgendered aspirations are defined within the constraints of a genre/gendered performance bound by race in Hispanic-Caribbean musical traditions. A dark-skinned man seeking a female identity, he cannot project this self onto "a sassy Spaniard or a little Dutch girl" (95). Lulú models her forthcoming gender performance, instead, on the flamboyant—almost gaudy—stars of popular flamenco (Lola Flores) or rumba, the African-derived variety of Latin rhythms whose female performers include Celeste Mendoza (Cuba), Tongolele (Mexico), and Xiomara Alfaro (Cuba) and who are associated in cinema with the career of Brazilian dancer Carmen Miranda and the Latin big-band sound of Xavier Cugat. Stars known for their highly stylized and outlandishly flashy performances, singer/dancers like Flores and Miranda radiated an exuberant form of femininity rooted in a display of racial otherness that emerges in the text as an appropriate role for a dark-skinned man enacting his decidedly female metamorphosis. What Lulú seeks, as Alcántara Almanzar poignantly describes it, is an emancipatory moment in which his character can display his true gender identity with an abandon that he can experience only in the confines of his small room. When Lulú gets the opportunity for performing this true identity, the performance hovers between liberation and loss of control:

> Her body was moving without restraint; the feet drew sparks from the mosaics; the legs, lengthened by the high heels, dashed to and fro furiously, as if deranged; the hips contorted; the bracelet-laden arms whirled, tracing circles in the air; the head gaily followed the rhythm of the music. In the midst of the frenzied uproar, she danced with eyes closed, seemingly enthralled in a brutal trance. She advanced and retreated, shook the bare shoulders, got down on her knees and up again, now completely barefoot. Her two massive feet, finally liberated from the high heels, took hold of the pavement, Zigzagging, filling her with pleasure. (97)

Lulú's intense pleasure, which occurs just before the pirate crew erupts onto the stage to disrupt her performance, parallels the pleasure she had experienced in the intimacy of her bedroom through masturbation, a pleasure cut short then by memories of previous humiliations and threats of violence. Lulú's performance, aborted by violence, had also failed because of the incompleteness of her transformation, which is recognized and rejected by others because it is understood as an attempt at gender metamorphosis—a transgendering—and not a "harmless" instance of carnival cross-dressing. Surrounded as she is by men cross-dressed as nuns who also participate in the attack against her, she becomes an abomination because her transformation seeks to be a reality and not a carnival performance. Ultimately, her performance fails precisely because the character cannot dismiss the doubts about the reception of her performance that stem from memories of past threats of violence. Transgender, as Wendy Castro writes, "is a loaded concept that implies a mode of reflexive performativity intent on dismissing gender binaries."[23] In a brilliant paragraph that weaves together Lulú's painstaking application of makeup and his/her memories of moments of threat and rupture in his/her public life, we see these binaries piling their weight on the character, undermining the possibilities of a successful performance: the afternoon he/she ran into Ciro and "he wouldn't return her greeting, wouldn't or was ashamed to, since he looked the other way and went on selling his peanuts, ignoring the cashew-nut paste she had made just for him" or the day in which she was "chased by some thugs yelling 'faggot,' 'queer freak,' throwing orange rinds and food scraps at her" (100). Lulú's performance is undermined by the beers he/she drinks before emerging from the house, beers he consumes to placate his/her doubts about his performance and possible transcendence into a mark of real acceptance by his/her society. When she finally emerges into the street—out of the sanctuary of her small apartment—she is only *falsely majestic, betrayed by trips and burps, by the convulsive swishing of her hips, the agitated flailing of her excessively bejeweled arms, the nervous contortions of her head, the troubled and searching eyes* (94).

Alcántara Almanzar's tragic tale finds its pathos precisely in the gap between the transformative magic that can transpire in the intimacy of the bedroom and the violence with which these transformations are often greeted in our societies. Timothy S. Chin has written about the responsibility that literature and the arts bear for either condoning or decrying such violence: "Given the alarming persistence of anti-gay violence in contemporary Caribbean societies and the reproduction in literature and popular culture of ideologies that condone or legitimate such violence, we clearly need a critical practice that goes beyond simple dichotomies—us/them, native/foreign, natural/unnatural—a practice that can not only affirm but also critique 'indigenous' cultures in all of their varied and inevitably contradictory forms."[24] "Lulú or the Metamorphosis" engages this responsibility openly. In so doing, this work seeks to breach the divide between the text and our daily socio-reality in ways that bring it closer to the work of writers such as Mayra Santos Febres—who in *Sirena Selena* (2000) narrates the transformation of a golden-voiced fifteen-year-old gay street hustler into the cross-dressed bolero-singing diva Sirena Selena—or painters like Ebony Patterson—who in works like *Gangstas for Life* and the *Doiley Boyz* series (2009) addresses cross-dressing as a ritual of masking that helps the subject navigate the vexed terrain of postcolonial identity in Jamaica.

In April 2007, two years before Patterson produced *Gangstas for Life* and the *Doiley Boyz* series, a cross-dressing man was severely beaten by a mob in Falmouth's Water Square in Trelawny, Jamaica. The man had been spotted waiting for transportation, wearing "heavy make-up, high-heeled shoes, a long pair of shiny earrings, a black leather jacket over a snug black-and-white blouse, a tight-fitting pair of jeans, a black wig, a pair of sunglasses and a handbag slung over his broad shoulders."[25] The news had spread quickly, and soon "scores of angry residents" converged on the square and began attacking the man as he cried out for the police. During the attack, "the wig the man was wearing fell off and wads of newspaper stuffed in a brassiere to lift the man's chest dislodged, while a cosmetic kit containing lipsticks of varying colours was thrown from a bag he was carrying, much to the amusement of the large crowd who stood watching."

> "B***y boy fe dead," persons among the mob shouted.
>
> The sentiments were echoed by the rest of the riled-up crowd. "Falmouth no pet no b***y boy. We no want none a them bout here," one woman yelled.
>
> After the mob dispersed, the victim was whisked off in a police service vehicle, much to the disapproval of the crowd who rushed upon the vehicle demanding the man's release.
>
> "If you ever did see him. Him dress hotter than you and me," one young girl was overheard telling her friend.
>
> "Nu worry man, we gi him a proper [beating]," one man said proudly.[26]

The beating had been the second in western Jamaica in a month.

The social anxieties surrounding cross-dressing in the Caribbean of the 1990s, as my readings of Walcott, Kincaid, and Alcántara Almanzar show, were exacerbated in the Jamaica of the early twenty-first century. In 2004 Human Rights Watch reported that "political and cultural factors, including religious intolerance of homosexuality, Jamaican popular music, and the use of antigay slogans and rhetoric by political leaders, also promote violence and discrimination based on sexual orientation and gender identity."[27] In January 2004, at the Rebel Salute concert in St. Elizabeth, Jamaica, Capleton and Sizzla sang almost exclusively about gay men: "kill dem, battybwoys haffi dead, gun shots pon dem . . . who want to see dem dead put up his hand."[28] Derogatory terms for gay men ("chi-chi men" and "battybwoys") have been used by other internationally known Jamaican reggae and dancehall singers like Elephant Man,

Bounty Killer, Buju Banton, Beenie Man, TOK, and others who have urged their audience in their music to shoot, burn, rape, stone, drown, and shoot homosexuals. Politicians embraced these homophobic songs, incorporating them into their campaigns for office. During the 2001 elections, Human Rights Watch reported, the Jamaican Labour Party (the main opposition party) used as its campaign song "Chi Chi Man," a song that celebrates the burning and killing of gay men. The ruling People's National Party, for its 2002 campaign, used as its campaign slogan the phrase "Log On to Progress," which alluded to a popular song and dance ("Log On") advocating the kicking or stomping of gay men.[29] The church has been instrumental in the intensification of homophobia in Jamaica. Evangelical Christianity is particularly strong on the island, and it advocates the reading of the Bible for its strong anti-homosexuality message. As a result, pastors preach vehemently against homosexuality as a sin, often invoking cultural arguments, such as Jamaican society's intolerance, as reasons to support the continued criminalization of homosexuality.[30]

The return of Portia Simpson-Miller as prime minister in 2012 made many hope for change as she "made a courageous stand before she took office in January, speaking out against discrimination on the basis of sexual orientation and gender identity and suggesting a review of Jamaica's anti-buggery law."[31] However, in July 2012, Boris Dittrich, advocacy director for the Lesbian, Gay, Bisexual, and Transgender (LGBT) Rights Program at Human Rights Watch, declared that in Jamaica "homophobia is so bad that human rights defenders advocating the rights of LGBT people are not safe."[32]

The 2007 Trelawny attack and the many that followed it should be seen in the dual context of both the intensification of homophobia just described and the opening of spaces that defy the gender binary on which such homophobia is based, such as Jamaica's dancehall. Dancehall—the popular variant of reggae that has dominated Jamaican music production since the 1980s—is both a genre associated with anti-gay lyrics and a space where the culture's "stereotypical ideologies of homosexual practices" can be challenged.[33] This opening was explored by the Jamaican artist Ebony Patterson in 2009 with *Gangstas for Life* and the *Doiley Boyz* series. The works, which raise questions about masculinity and representation in dancehall culture, use "images [that] are deconstructed into stereotypical homosexual beauties, with bleached faces, red glossed lips, glitter and feminine motifs" that "challenge practices of the emasculation of young black males and question stereotypical standards of beauty amongst genders."[34]

In *Untitled Yutez* (part of the *Doiley Boyz* series), Patterson gives us a richly suggestive and highly transgressive view of dancehall culture as it relates to Jamaican culture in general and its homophobia in particular. It also provides us with a nuanced counter-text to Alcántara Almanzar's bleak representation of the violence that awaits those who dare cross the gender divide through the development of a cross-dressed, transgendered persona. In *Untitled Yutez*, Patterson explains, she was seeking to unveil "the dichotomy between Jamaican stereotypical ideologies of homosexual practices and its parallels within dancehall culture, where skin bleaching (whitening) has become trendy and fashionable primarily among young black males."[35] Dancehall, arguably an unsafe space for those not complying with Jamaica's strict heterosexual codes, emerges here as a space akin to the bedroom in the texts I have discussed above, where cross-dressing males can escape their ascribed bounded roles and rehearse identities impossible outside its confines. Donna Hope echoes Patterson's reading of the liberating potential of dancehall, calling it "a cultural dis/place of ongoing dialogue, confrontation, and contestation with the rigid sociopolitical, gendered, and classed hierarchies of Jamaica."[36]

Patterson, in an interview with Oneika Russell, discussed her own strong personal connection to dancehall as "my generation's music" and her concern for the negative light in which it is presented in Jamaica, precisely because of its association with widespread homophobic sentiment on the island.[37] Her work is anchored in the contradictions she finds between the practices of dancehall, as she has observed them, and the focus of critics of dancehall on its sometimes violent messages. The art historian Veerle Poupeye has observed, quoting Brathwaite, that in Jamaica the role of the artist has evolved into that of "a crucial social mediator" (171) that bridges the gap between high and popular art by "creating a continuum between elite and folk . . . in keeping with the egalitarian ethos of the period."[38] Patterson describes her artistic role in the same vein, explaining that she sees herself "as some kind of Dancehall mediator or cultural mediator in some ways."[39] In her work on dancehall, her mediating influence is deployed through her representations of cross-dressed male bodies against backgrounds of domesticity that suggest a redefinition of notions of masculinity in Jamaican culture. As Poupeye describes the work, Patterson "probes the contradictory interplay between the hardcore masculine posturing of the 'gangsta' and the feminized personal aesthetic that is now the norm among males in the dancehall culture and exemplified by such practices as skin bleaching,

Untitled Yutez, from the *Doiley Boyz* series, Ebony G. Patterson, 2009. Mixed media drawing with shelf, toy guns, crayons, and other objects. Collection of the artist. (Image courtesy of the artist and Monique Meloche Gallery)

eyebrow shaping, and the wearing of flamboyant clothing and 'bling' jewelry and accessories."[40]

    Untitled Yutez is a complex, challenging work that brings a multiplicity of elements to bear on the question of gender identity in Jamaican dancehall. Its cross-dressed subjects—set as they are against a background of pseudo–William Morris wallpaper—seem to dare both the world of Victorian domesticity that still holds considerable sway over Jamaican middle-class culture and the violence that has been perpetrated against homosexuals in the defense of anachronistic Victorian notions of propriety. The work's iconography borrows from portraiture (I am thinking of Jan van Eyck's 1434 *The Arnolfini Portrait*), paintings of the Madonna and Child with their golden halos (here made out of gold doilies), the wall-mounted chromolithographs with a shelf for votive offerings common throughout the Catholic, Santería, and Vodou-practicing Caribbean (the votives here replaced with crayons and multicolored plastic guns), and a heavy sprinkling of kitsch.

The subjects of *Untitled Yutez,* in their implied invitation to dance, appear to encourage/provoke the viewer into an acceptance of a restaging of masculinity made possible by the rising popularity of male dancers in dancehall culture; their invitation, conveyed through their poses, gestures, and facial expressions, is in and of itself a subversion of the abject roles assigned to homosexuals and cross-dressers in Jamaican society,[41] as we see from the depiction of the victim of the Trelawny attack discussed above. This invitation should be seen in the context of what Donna Hope sees as the "the empowering and liberating potential of selective manifestations of a 'dancehallized' identity which is transmitted from within the disempowering and socially darkened spaces of Kingston's depressed communities."[42] These "ideo-spatial transgressions and gendered representations," Hope adds, "reflect dancehall culture's propensity to traffic in ambivalent representations of self and personhood, which often resist efforts to homogenize."[43] The implied invitation—especially if we read the crayons and plastic toys as votive offerings—could also be read as one to erase what Poupeye calls dancehall's "conflation of sexuality and violence, its glorification of the gun, and its intolerance of difference, such as its notorious homophobia."[44]

As I approach the end of my discussion, I would like to return to the work's connection to the emancipatory possibilities of cross-dressing within the bounds of protected, domestic spaces that I explored in the writings of Walcott, Kincaid, and Alcántara Almanzar. I would like to return, in short, to Helen in her yellow dress in that small bedroom she shared with Achille.

Ebony Patterson has spoken about the allure of the domestic as a realm associated with the feminine—hence, the use of doilies and wallpaper in her work as emblems of femininity that help her "reshape" the masculine through its immersion in the domestic and familial. These doilies, and particularly the wallpaper (so reminiscent of William Morris "Thistle" and "Acanthus" designs), inscribe this domesticity in the social and racial structures of the Victorian empire and the impact it had on so-cial mores among its colonial subjects. Helen's appropriation of Maud's yellow dress, and Xuela's refusal of Madame LaBatte's many offerings of dresses, constituted clear textual challenges to such mores, especially as they hypocritically made women like them prey to the unwanted sexual advances of colonial males. The cross-dressing subjects of Patterson's work, encased in the preciousness of their equally Victorian floral dresses, seem to appeal to the viewer to extricate them from such Victorian con-fines. Like the characters in Kincaid's novel, they are threatened by the possibility of these flower-patterned clothes becoming their skins. Only their bleached white faces remain as a testament to their resistance.

For them, as for Helen in her yellow dress, Xuela in her laborer's clothes, and Lulú in her aborted metamorphosis, the domestic space—the intimacy of the bedroom—has been the space of emancipation and appro-priation from which they have emerged cross-dressed (sometimes doubly so) to face what our societies have made out of the debris of their colonial histories. Of all their *sorties* it can be said, as the Major and Maud said upon seeing Helen in her yellow dress, "There's our trouble" (29). Of all of them it should be said that, as class and gender cross-dressed creations, they represent a clear challenge to colonial binaries whose time, like the Major's interpretations of Caribbean history, has passed.

Notes

1. Walcott, *Omeros*, 64. Further references to this book will be given in parentheses in the text.

2. Guth, "Charles Longfellow and Okakura Kakuzō," 606.

3. Patterson, "Journey of Self-Discovery."

4. Mowry, "Dressing Up and Dressing Down," 79.

5. Castro, "Stripped," 111.

6. These binaries are explored in all their complexities in Smith, *Sex and the Citizen*.

7. Dick, "Remembering Breen's Encomium," 111.

8. Mowry, "Dressing Up and Dressing Down," 80.

9. Zoppi, "*Omeros*, Derek Walcott," 518.

10. Guth, "Charles Longfellow and Okakura Kakuzō," 606.

11. Ibid., 632.

12. Kincaid, *Autobiography*, 108. Further references to this novel will be given in parentheses in the text.

13. Omise'eke Tinsley explores the remnants of these relations in her *Thieving Sugar*. Here I owe a debt to Spelman, *Inessential Woman*.

14. Mowry, "Dressing Up and Dressing Down," 80.

15. Ibid., 80.

16. Hindmarch-Watson, "Lois Schwich," 81.

17. Alcántara Almanzar, "Lulú or the Metamorphosis." Further references to this short story will be given in parentheses in the text.

18. Piatkowski, "Our Caribbean."

19. Siemens, "Review of *Remaking a Lost World*," 374.

20. Manzari, "Afternoon with José Alcántara Almánzar."

21. Ibid., 954–55.

22. See Rinaldo Walcott, "Reconstructing Manhood," for an insightful discussion of further ramifications of these binaries.

23. Castro, "Stripped," 119.

24. Chin, "'Bullers' and 'Battymen,'" 140.

25. Hines, "Mob Beats Cross-Dresser."

26. Ibid.

27. "Homophobia in Jamaica."

28. Younge, "Chilling Call to Murder."

29. "Homophobia in Jamaica."

30. Jamaican critics like Carolyn Cooper and Joan Morgan have argued against the misreading of singers like Buju Banton and others by critics unfamiliar "with the metaphorical qualities of the Jamaican vernacular." See Chin, "'Bullers' and 'Battymen,'" for an illuminating analysis of the controversy.

31. "Jamaica: Combat Homophobia."

32. Ibid.

33. Patterson, "Journey of Self-Discovery."

34. Ibid.

35. Ibid.

36. Hope, *"Passa Passa,"* 125. Archer, "Accessories/Accessaries," offers a different reading, arguing that Patterson's paintings, "like surveillance identikits, . . . reveal yet another layer to the narrative of mimicry and masking already explored, one that requires an inverse reading of the mask—not about putting on but rather taking off. . . . It is a striptease that confounds racial categorization and brings new complexity to Fanon's psychoanalysis of black skin and white masks as well as our understanding of the legacy of slavery, so far acknowledged but not yet compensated for" (110). Whereas here I focus quite specifically on the "dressing" (or "putting on") aspects of the work, Archer sees the clothing as much less relevant to Patterson's meaning than the process of "taking off" or "undressing" she identifies in the analysis.

37. Patterson and Russell, "Mi Did Deh Deh."

38. Poupeye, "What Times Are These?," 171.

39. Patterson and Russell, "Mi Did Deh Deh."

40. Poupeye, "What Times Are These?," 180.

41. Guth, "Charles Longfellow and Okakura Kakuzō," 606.

42. Hope, *"Passa Passa,"* 127.

43. Ibid.

44. Ibid., 172.

Defying Binarism

Cross-Dressing and *Transdressing* in Mayra Santos Febres's *Sirena Selena vestida de pena* and Rita Indiana Hernández's *La estrategia de Chochueca*

Odile Ferly

Mayra Santos Febres's *Sirena Selena vestida de pena* relates the story of a teenager rescued from the street and drug addiction to make a career as a transvestite bolero singer.[1] Using the trope of passing, and blurring the line between reality and illusion through the portrayal of an androgynous, racially mixed protagonist symbolically represented as a mermaid, this tale deconstructs binaries of gender, sexuality, class, and race, thereby calling into question common understandings of self-hood. Similarly, in Rita Indiana Hernández's *La estrategia de Chochueca* the young, lower-middle-class protagonists overtly display their disenchantment and dissent with their milieu through a disregard for social norms and an escape into narcotics.[2] Here too the novel revisits the neat dichotomies of identity categories in order to challenge the conservatism that still permeates Dominican society and the premises of the national discourse.

In the nineteenth-century Cuban classic *Cecilia Valdés*, a beautiful, transgressing *mulata* is harshly punished for aspiring to marry her white lover.[3] Even though she could pass for white, the protagonist is recognized by most characters as mulatto, and in fact the author, Cirilo Villaverde, seems particularly keen on fixing her ethnicity. Villaverde's abolitionist views notwithstanding, this cautionary tale thus appears to uphold the notion of strictly exclusive alternatives, that is, *either* white *or* black. Despite her visible predominantly white ancestry (seven of her eight great-grandparents), Cecilia is classified purely on the basis of her black parentage; blacks—lumped together with mulattoes—and whites become sealed-off categories. The dynamics of polarity on which society relies for its organization are thus preserved. This in turn guarantees the perpetuation of a (post)slavery system aligning class with race.

Such a dualistic model has of course no biological ground, and seems to bear little relevance to the Hispanic Caribbean context, given the actual racial continuum found in its population. Indeed, Cecilia's social class weighs as much as her ancestry in determining her ethnic categorization. The author himself points to the imbrication of race and class in nineteenth-century Cuba, with his remark that society tolerates interracial marriages between white men and *mulatas,* even darker ones, when these are wealthy. Money therefore has whitening powers.[4]

Unlike nineteenth-century passing narratives, the turn-of-the-millennium fiction examined here argues in *favor of* the dismantlement of the binary mind-set that underlies conventional conceptions of identity. Although several characters also pass across race, class, and age, ostensibly gender passing is the primary focus of Santos Febres's novel. Gender categories are most strikingly unsettled through the narrative voice, which oscillates throughout between masculine and feminine perspectives in relation to the main character, Sirena Selena.[5] Not surprisingly, seeing and being seen are central to this novel focusing on a performer and the world of show business. Voyeurism is pervasive, drawing attention to what Elaine Ginsberg calls the "specularity" of identity and passing, that is, "the cultural logic" whereby "the physical body is the site of identic intelligibility," or the logic that erroneously grounds identity in the visible.[6] Sirena is introduced in male attire, "on a business trip" with his mentor, Martha, and initially referred to in the masculine form. Gender switches soon occur within a single sentence: "As a young *man, Selena* was nervous" (11, translation and emphasis mine; "De jovencito *la* Selena iba nervioso"). Viewed as male, Sirena emerges as an abused underage prostitute; by contrast, her female impersonation (Selena) yields the image of a confident, glamorous diva.

Reality and illusion are blurred throughout the text. For instance, the Dominican businessman Hugo Graubel exclaims at Sirena's rehearsal, "If I didn't know that it was an illusion, I would never know Sirena's *secreto.* She looks so fabulous," to which Martha retorts, "She is fabulous" (36). Both characters thus evidence their awareness of the imposture as much as their eagerness to hold the illusion as genuine. In another voyeuristic scene, in which Hugo spots Sirena in a bikini on the beach, the *mise en abîme* of the interplay between illusion and reality becomes dizzying: "[S/he looked] like a tomboy trying to be *un hombrecito* on the beach, but showing her femme side with her little jumps and squeals"

(43). Here, is Sirena an effeminate male adolescent, a tomboy trying to project masculinity, a *femme* lesbian, or truly a hermaphrodite? The sight of Sirena arouses in Hugo a desire fraught with ambiguity: "He desired *her* that way, so tiny, such a little street *boy*. He recognized her as the woman of his dreams" (43, emphasis mine). As will be shown, the nature of Hugo's desire resists classification, challenging sexual as well as gender binaries.

Sirena's claim early on in the novel that Martha "helped to transform him into who he really was" (4) conflates truth and fantasy. The notion of transformation, seemingly at odds with that of a core self implied in "who he really was," underscores the malleability of identity: it is shaped, rather than inherent. Toward the end, Sirena insists again on the idea of self-generation (and here too specularity, or lack thereof—*cegar/ dazzling*—is paramount): "*She* was the hired star. Paid to dazzle the guests. And eager to dazzle them, this time. This was the opportunity to dazzle even *himself* and believe to be a lady coming down a mar-ble staircase" (169, translation and emphasis mine; "*Ella* era la estrella contratada. *Le* pagaban por cegar a los invitados. Y esta vez sí quería cegarlos. Esta era su oportunidad de cegarse a *él mismo* y creerse una señora bajando una escalera de mármol"). The emphatic term "ella" combined with the alliteration in *a* makes Sirena conspicuously feminine, thus ostensibly designating her imposture as cutting across class—her intrusion in this aristocratic setting—not gender barriers. The ambigu-ous neutrality of the following two sentences—achieved chiefly through the use of "le" and the absence of subject pronouns in Spanish—barely announces the abrupt shift to the masculine form: "él mismo." So, for once in the novel, Sirena perceives himself as an illusion. Yet maintain-ing this illusion, or rather "turning for good into his own image" (110, translation mine), is for Sirena the "enabling fantasy"—to borrow from Marjorie Garber—that allows him to escape a sordid reality of drugs, prostitution, and various forms of exclusion.[7]

Crucially, however, outside of her stage role of bolero diva, in most in-stances, as on the beach clad in a bikini and a shirt, Sirena seems content with a hermaphroditic, sexually ambiguous appearance. Quite unlike Martha, the teenager becomes uneasy in a fixed gender, as when appearing unequivocally male on the plane in the opening scene.[8] Arguably, Sirena Selena's *natural* state is that of a subject alternatively choosing to be male or female, or else remain ambiguously gendered, at any given moment. Hence the recurrent depiction of the protagonist as a (fallen) angel—angels are thought to be genderless—and "niña marimacha," or tomboy. For pubescent Sirena, gender identification seems optional, and Martha notes how easily Sirena can "change between bodies without major trauma" (90).

Garber argues in *Vested Interests* that the transvestite figure functions as a third point, *neither* male *nor* female, to signal a "category crisis" often marking "displacements from the axis of *class* as well as from *race* onto the axis of gender,"[9] an observation that particularly fits Martha in the novel, as will be shown later. Echoing this notion of "third point," Peres Alós and Kahmann further argue that heteronormativity is *predicated on* two mutually exclusive genders, since a third gender would invalidate the categories of hetero- and homosexuality.[10] Luis Felipe Díaz concurs when he notes in his own analysis of the novel that hierarchies of power rely on clear-cut dichotomies, particularly so in relation to gender.[11] Yet, rather than adhering to a single alternative or third gender that would be static, Santos Febres's characters have a gamut of genders at their disposal, which results for most in shifting gender identifications and/or sexual orientations.[12]

Indeed, indeterminacy characterizes Sirena, and this applies not only to the protagonist's gender and sexuality but also to her age (a fifteen-year-old passing for eighteen), class, profession (prostitute/artist), and ethnicity. Interestingly, while the Dominican teenager Leocadio, whose story parallels that of Sirena, is repeatedly described as "yellow," or a light-skinned mulatto, Sirena's "light cinnamon" complexion is only discreetly mentioned. Sirena's mulatto ethnicity thus appears neutral, unmarked, neither black nor white. In fact, the transvestite's very identity seems escapable, unstable, as reflected in the stage name Sirena Selena. By definition half-woman and half-fish, a *sirena,* or mermaid, evokes monstrosity as well as fluidity and mystery: Ulysses and his crew were captivated by the mermaids' songs, just like Sirena's audience, especially Hugo. As for the term *selena,* it relates to the moon, which, according to Van Haesendonck, was a "bisexual symbol" in Ancient Greece.[13] For Leocadio—who figures as a burgeoning Sirena[14]—gender roles, and perhaps sexuality too, are likewise dynamic concepts: "There are many ways to be man or woman. . . . Sometimes you can be both without having to cease being either" (258, translation mine).

Such ambiguity, however, is not restricted to adolescent characters. Martha literally performs gender bending through makeup, plastic surgery, hormone treatment, and cross-dressing. There are recurring mentions in the text of her body and the financial cost of its remodeling. Although consistently referred to in the feminine, biologically Martha is in fact half-female and half-male, and hopes to be reconciled with her whole body through transsexual surgery. Thus, for Martha, ultimately gender should be fixed: her heteronormativity and compliance with patriarchal gender dynamics—she calls a long-term lover "husband" and expects to be kept by him—may well be an attempt to crystallize her gender by reinforcing what she perceives as femininity. So for Martha, unlike Leocadio and Sirena, indeterminacy causes anxiety. In this respect it is significant that the novel should focus on her as a preoperative transsexual, that is, a character still in the process of shaping her gender identity. Indeed, as illustrated by La Billy, a former drag queen turned travel agent who no longer cross-dresses, gender and sexual identification can actually fluctuate over time.

Blurred gender and/or sexuality equally characterize most of the protagonists in civilian clothes, as illustrated by Migueles, and by Hugo, who views Sirena as his double. This supports Garber's contention that the transvestite figure often signals another displacement across ethnicity or class, or any form of trespassing. Neither Migueles nor Hugo is explicitly bisexual, but both alternate heterosexual with homosexual practices. Migueles projects the image of a "fully-fledged, macho man" (197, translation mine; "un hombre hecho y derecho"), while occasionally prostituting himself with male tourists, which triggers his uncertainties around sexual identity. Not unlike Martha, then, Migueles strives to reinforce a binary conception of self.

As for Hugo, he regards his heterosexuality as a lifelong masquerade. The denial of the homoerotic dimension of his desire manifests itself in his claim to heterosexuality through his marriage with Solange and in his relations with transvestites rather than overtly male partners. His complex sexual identity, however, remains indefinable. At the climax of his orgasm with Sirena, for instance, Hugo cries out "sirenito" ("little merman"), thereby not only enraging his young companion for marking him as unquestionably male, but also revealing his own intention to blur illusion and reality. Hugo, then, performs sexual passing: despite his attraction to the transvestite's femininity, he resents the flawlessness of Sirena's gender impersonation.

In fact, with Martha's claim to have forgotten the "choreography of masculinity" (117, translation mine)—an assertion that echoes Judith Butler in *Gender Trouble*—the novel posits gender roles and gender itself as performance; consequently, everybody somehow passes. Indeed, every character evidences a propensity to pass across all types of social boundaries: each plays a part. As Martha argues, "It's all about image," a matter of "choreography and acting" (23, translation mine). She herself poses as a respectable, white, professional woman. On the other hand, Sirena becomes increasingly engrossed in the role of glamorous diva who never "[steps] out of character" (83) even without makeup.

A more conventional passing character, Solange, crosses class boundaries. Having ascended to Dominican aristocracy by marrying Hugo at sixteen, she never overcomes the downfall of her bourgeois family. She longs for anonymity in Miami, where nobody could verify her plebeian origins. Like Hugo, Solange is repeatedly depicted as the transvestite's alter ego. This proliferation of the protagonist's doubles functions of course to further challenge what Homi K. Bhabha calls a "plenitudinous" conception of the Self.[15] In a scene toward the end of the novel, Solange walks down the stairs with gestures that mirror Sirena's moments before. The latter claims that Solange is "a swindler like me, a girl dressed as woman who believes she's at the top" (168, translation mine), while Solange, comparing herself to Sirena, admits, "Sirena wasn't exactly a woman, as she herself wasn't when she [got] married" (240, translation mine). So Solange's very "womanhood" is exposed as transvestism: this deflates any essentialist understanding of identity.

All of the characters actually see—consciously or not—at least part of their identity as malleable, often deliberately using the strategy of passing for personal advancement. As Martha puts it, referring to the drag queens, "We all wanted to be something else, to be somewhere else. . . . The trick has always been to deny our dark reality." The racial overtone of this remark aside, particularly interesting here is the idea of identity as not only performance but also performativity—that is, "a reiteration of norms which precede, constrain, and exceed the performer and in that sense cannot be taken as the fabrication of the performer's 'will' or 'choice.'"[16] Here the transvestites' sociocultural bovarysm (their desire to be other socially or culturally) appears dictated by a compulsive adherence to prevailing norms with social, cultural, and ethnic ramifications.

Besides unsettling binary identity categories at the individual level, the novel challenges conventional definitions of collective identities, which are all too often conceived as pure, immutable, and impermeable. Bhabha contends that postcolonial perspectives expose culture as "constructed through a process of alterity."[17] This is illustrated by Martha's extensive use of Spanglish and the insertion of a chapter (XXXV) reporting directly in English the views of a Canadian tourist in Santo Domingo, which both attest to the North American cultural domination of Puerto

Rico and most of the Caribbean. This acculturation process can be further assessed through the countless Western icons of popular culture idolized by the Puerto Rican drag queens—Bette Midler, Sophia Loren, Diana Ross, Josephine Baker, and others—or through Martha's difficulty to comprehend that a Cuban transvestite might not wish to imitate Marilyn Monroe. Yet at the same time, Sirena and Martha are steeped in local popular culture, epitomized by bolero and humor. Cultures and collective identities are thus revealed to be in a process of perpetual elaboration and mutual influences.

Racial binaries too disappear in a Caribbean context of intense miscegenation. Most characters in the novel are mulatto, and many—for instance, Martha and her fellow Marilyn fans—suffer from a lactification complex. Martha's ambivalent ethnic identification is perhaps most evident during her show, when she tells her audience, "As the saying goes, . . . we've all got some African blood running in our veins. . . . Look how proudly I carry this nose, these full lips and these sweet, shapely hips" (139). Martha's ostentatious black pride rhetoric is undermined by her efforts to refashion her body through plastic surgery (detailed in chapter XI), targeting areas that alter not only her gender identification but her phenotype too: her hair, straightened and bleached, her chemically lightened skin, and, first and foremost, her nose, which she found "very coarse, very broad" (52) and had reshaped into "a small, pinched" (53) nose. That Martha's aesthetic canons are in fact highly racialized becomes obvious when she likens her ideal nose to that of "a rich girl, . . . the daughter of senators," adding that with such a nose she looked "like someone else, someone I should be, someone I was inside since I was a little girl" (53), which echoes Sirena's claim that Martha "helped to transform him into who he really was" (4). Yet the reference to a senator's daughter also points to the imbrication of race and class in Caribbean societies, a reality that gives material motivations to the characters' desire to pass for white: in Martha's words, "to deny the dark reality." With her internalized Negrophobia and her compliance with heteronormativity and traditional gender roles, Martha emerges as far more conformist than first meets the eye. She too understands identity as somewhat static; only, she claims a right to (re)define herself. By contrast, holding a less rigid conception of identity, Sirena and Leocadio hardly seem troubled by blurred gender or ethnicity, and they display little racial anxiety: their desire for social mobility does not quite translate into a whitening complex. Instead, they move freely up and down the gender spectrum and racial continuum.

Beyond the individual level, the distinction between wealthy (Puerto Rican) and poor (Dominican) Caribbean nations is muddled by the interactions between poor or modest Puerto Ricans (Sirena, Martha) and affluent Dominicans (Hugo and his circle). National boundaries too collapse in this age of global capital: Martha dreams of establishing a multinational of gay and transvestite bars across "this wanton Caribbean" (12). Similarly, she expresses solidarity with the Dominican Republic, "this *other* godforsaken island, floating as well as it could in its ample ocean" (14, emphasis mine), the word "other" binding the two islands under a same title, despite the apparent socioeconomic and political differences due to Puerto Rico's commonwealth status.

In addition, Martha and Sirena are eminently transnational characters who do not hesitate to go overseas to carry out their business. For Sirena Selena, this is only the first destination, as she intends to head north, thus joining many of her compatriots in the diaspora. And indeed, in the light of a U.S. immigration policy that favors nationals from industrialized countries and bearing in mind Santos Febres's characterization of the Caribbean as a "transvestite dressed as First World,"[18] emigration and border crossing can be regarded as the ultimate form of tres/passing and transgressing in the novel. In this respect, it is worth recalling that Sirena's debut is staged in the Dominican Republic to circumvent legal age restrictions in Puerto Rico. So the interrelatedness of (border) crossing, tres/passing, and cross-dressing is explicit.

Sirena Selena thus foregrounds a dynamic conception of individual and communal identity. Despite their differing responses to it, the characters understand their selves as mutable: even Martha believes she can redefine herself. Culture is likewise represented as changing, albeit largely, in the Caribbean context, through unequal power relations that lead to acculturation. Finally, the region is shown to be in constant redefinition, as a result of internal and external migratory movements, what Santos Febres calls "translocation." Critics have noted that the text certainly supports an identification of Puerto Rico with the elusive, passing protagonist, thus calling into question the collective identity of the island, which passes for First World despite its sociopolitical and economic reality.[19]

Whereas *Sirena Selena* is structured around the concepts of passing and cross-dressing, Rita Indiana Hernández's first novel, *La estrategia de Chochueca*, relies on the notions of trespassing—to be understood at once in the sense of transgressing and in its etymological meaning of dying—and what will be called *transdressing*. In addition to the ethnic and social hierarchies, gender roles, and sexual norms defied by passing and cross-dressing, *transdressing* involves the infringement of taboos around death. The novel revolves around the eccentric Chochueca, a real-life Dominican figure particularly familiar to the capital city, who would request the deceased's clothes at their wakes. By wearing a dead person's clothes, Chochueca evidences his little respect for the sacred nature of death as well as his disdain for conventions that stigmatize such clothes. His apparent insensitivity to the relatives' suffering is shocking, as the seventeen-year-old narrator Silvia reports: "What a nerve, Chochueca, everybody is weeping, biting their lips with grief, pulling their hair out" (46). Against public opinion, however, Silvia sanctions Chochueca's behavior and expresses her admiration: "This is your magic, Chochueca, making a dead person's shoes walk" (46). Chochueca stands on the threshold between this and the afterworld, and his state could be a metaphor for his extreme deprivation: "He had long departed from this world" (46). A dead man among the living, the boundary he crosses is perhaps the scariest of all. This may explain Silvia's fascination, indeed her obsession, with the character.

The text establishes a parallel between Chochueca's strategy and the actions of Silvia and her friends, who could be seen as heirs to Chochueca in their scorn for social conventions. When Octaviano and Robin pawn stolen concert speakers which Silvia is asked to return on their behalf, Octaviano's uncle Saturnino recalls the time the youth opened tombs to rob dead people of their watches, thereby explicitly connecting them with Chochueca. He adds, "This is no joking matter" (14). More than the violation of the law, it is the overt irreverence for death that particularly scandalizes Saturnino. So the text connects the notion of transgressing to those of trespassing and *transdressing*: from this world to the next for Chochueca, from what is acceptable to what is not for the youth.

As in *Sirena Selena*, many lines become blurred in this novel: those between wealth and poverty, drunkenness and sobriety (or being on drugs and being clean), what is legal and what is illicit, as well as the distinction between social progress and decline, or between fallacious political rhetoric and socioeconomic reality. Moreover, the boundaries between bisexuality, homosexuality, and heterosexuality collapse. Here, however, transgression has wider implications than in Santos Febres, where, despite allegorical undertones conflating Sirena and Puerto Rico, the infringement of social norms through passing and cross-dressing remains largely restricted to the individual. In *La estrategia de Chochueca*, trespassing and *transdressing* aspire not only to greater individual freedoms but also to societal transformation, which makes the characters Silvia and her acolytes Franco, Julia, Salim, and Amanda more subversive than Santos Febres's drag queens. The facile Manichaeism and polarity on which most conservative value systems are grounded—including the dominant ideology in the Dominican Republic—are thereby undermined.

While it remains unclear whether or not Chochueca would only ask for men's clothes, for Silvia and in particular Franco, *transdressing* definitely involves cross-dressing. Thus, one day Franco hosts a party wearing eye makeup and "a little green chiffon skirt" (39). As Juan Duchesne Winter points out, the novel is quite emphatic on "an *other* sexuality" (8, his italics). The characters are not simply homo-, hetero-, or even bi-; rather, they resort to a whole range of sexual practices. Indeed, they all display carefree attitudes toward sex. Salim acknowledges openly, "What I like is screwing" (39). As for Julia, once she moves in with Franco, she shares "the bed, men, the bathroom, and Genoa salami sandwiches" with him (35–36). The casual enumeration equating "bed" and "men" with "salami sandwiches" trivializes the characters' sexual behaviors, thereby deriding the strict moral codes around sexuality. Similarly, Silvia shares Salim's attraction to Amanda: "[Salim] began to touch [Amanda], and I together with him from my seat . . . , like a cold pain as her soft, pink lips under my thumb which was Salim's, the cheese-like back, the belly under the hand under the blouse, the hand that slides and dies, already seemed like two slugs, almost dripping, and I, meanwhile, was stirring the ice cubes in my glass" (40). This highly homoerotic scene is paralleled by another toward the end, where Silvia this time dances with Amanda and kisses her, "eating the delicious eternity of her tongue" (66). Yet it is clear that Silvia is attracted to Amanda in particular, not to women in general: her desire is not confined to one sexual category. This sexual freedom among the group troubles others: "as if, with our habit of getting into the toilet in threesomes, of kissing each other on the mouth, men and women, of laughing uproariously, we splashed our onlookers with an unbearable substance" (18). Thus, the social and sexual transgressions of Silvia and her friends, their preference for love triangles over couples, dispose of the clear-cut binaries so fundamental to "hierarchies of power," as argued by Luis Felipe Díaz. The youth thereby defy the conservative values inherited from dictator Trujillo (1930 to 1961) that prevailed into the 1990s, notably through Trujillo's successor Balaguer.

In a society that holds sexism and womanizing as integral components of "true masculinity"—a view widely promoted by Trujillo—Franco's overt homosexuality and cross-dressing stand in defiance. In this sense it is highly ironic that this character should be the namesake of Spain's fascist dictator, a figure emulated by Trujillo. The extent of Franco's courage can be assessed when compared to one of his lovers, Leo. Far from giving up the pretense to heterosexuality, Leo feeds into the myth of male hyper(hetero)sexuality, much like Santos Febres's Migueles. Indeed, while he boasts of the size of his genitals, he takes pride in his girlfriend's virginity. Franco, on the other hand, makes Leo papaya milkshakes and is openly affectionate toward him, thereby adopting a nurturing and loving behavior conventionally associated with the "feminine." His attitude, it is suggested, motivates the vicious homophobic attack he suffers from a lover, an act on which the novel closes.

Franco, however, is not alone in challenging the dominant ideology. Silvia's acts of subversion are more subtle, but just as meaningful. Besides her sexual behavior that disrupts hegemonic binaries, she too performs a small act of cross-dressing, when at the end of the novel she visits Franco at the hospital and emerges from the bedroom in his clothes. It is also Silvia who underscores the transgressive role of lunatics and transvestites such as Chochueca and Franco, when she muses on the hidden face of the city, the one not divulgated in tourist brochures, that of early morning, of "ill-knotted ties and transvestites eating a mango while holding their breasts, the blind city burning, falling apart, undoing its intolerable perfection" (49). Through such sociopolitical statements, Silvia demystifies the dominant rhetoric regarding the political, economic, and cultural state of the country, as well as the national identity discourse.

The subversive political message of the novel is clear from the opening, when Silvia rejoices in finding herself alone "in this crappy underdevelopment" (13). Silvia's observation is an indictment against the fallacy of the progress rhetoric promulgated by Trujillo, evidenced, for instance, in the post-hurricane reconstruction of the capital city, renamed Ciudad Trujillo in 1936. This ostentatious act, Rodríguez points out, was intended to portray the dictatorship as a turning point in Dominican history, one that initiated a phase of modernization for the country and of regeneration for its people. This remodeling came with the imposition of a new set of values that recuperated the mid-nineteenth-century discourse of *hispanidad,* an ideology that emphasizes the Spanish lineage of the Dominican people in ethnic, religious, linguistic, and cultural terms.[20] In the same vein, the celebrations of the centenary in 1944 were marked by the introduction in schools of history textbooks in which Trujillo was cast as the architect of national regeneration, "el Padre de la Patria Nueva" (the Father of the New Fatherland). Such rhetoric around progress is undermined when Silvia describes the piles of garbage lying around the city, or the country's squalid health facilities. Clearly, Silvia sees the nation's trajectory as one of regression, not progression.

Silvia's opening remark brings to mind Edmundo Desnoes's novel *Memorias del subdesarrollo* (Memories of underdevelopment), where the narrator-protagonist constantly refers to Cuba—and by extension the Caribbean—as underdeveloped, and to his compatriots as unsophisticated. Both characters therefore seem to share similar views on their respective homelands. Unlike Desnoes's antihero, however, Silvia does not speak out of a Eurocentric mind-set. On the contrary, she subverts the values of *hispanidad,* which denies the African ancestry of the Dominican people by seeking to define them as essentially white, slightly mixed with Amerindian blood. Silvia remarks how her Nordic appearance and Salim's blackness make their association odd, if not unthinkable, to passers-by. The latter automatically assume the pair to be a tourist seduced by an unscrupulous Afro-Dominican, which speaks to the divide along color lines in Dominican society. Silvia counters this latent racism by "performing" her Dominicanness, putting on a heavy local accent, thereby stating emphatically that a fair complexion does not preclude being Dominican, and that conversely Africanness too is an integral part of the national identity. She thus dismantles the racial tenets of the hegemonic Hispanist discourse. As in Santos Febres's novel, Hernández's text underscores the ethnic composition of the population across the spectrum: Silvia is white, Salim black, while Franco is half–East Asian.

Finally, Silvia's expression "crappy underdevelopment" echoes the phrase "this other godforsaken island" with which Martha also refers to the Dominican Republic, linking it to Puerto Rico in a denunciation of the poverty and oppression that plague the neighboring nations. By focusing on passing characters who cross divides they experience as injustices, Santos Febres's novel deflates binary dichotomies that often give ground to the most blatant social iniquities, thereby undermining the very foundations on which most societies are organized. In Hernández's text, Silvia expresses her solidarity with Chochueca, and there is an implicit alliance between the youth and the indigent man. The text further operates a demystification of sociopolitical rhetoric and taboos around sex and death. Arguably, this refutes Duchesne Winter's contention that the "Chochueca strategy" merely consists in "taking on cool poses for the sake of dignity and creativity, with no authority or paternal eye to challenge" and is therefore not truly transgressive.[21] Whereas in *Sirena Selena* the eponymous protagonist aspires to emigrate to the United States, apparently little concerned with transforming Puerto Rican society, in *La estrategia de Chochueca* the stakes seem higher, for the characters' transgressions question the very national identity articulated by the hegemonic discourse of the Trujillo era.

In a memorable ball scene in *Cecilia Valdés*, an "invisible line" divides mulatto dancing couples from couples composed of *mulatas* with white partners. The narrator observes that segregation occurs naturally, as if by tacit agreement. So the interracial couples are clearly marked as transgressive, and the classic novel appears to condemn them. Quite on the contrary, in the millennial novels examined above, passing and trespassing are transformative, to borrow Valentine's qualifier of transgender. Both texts unsettle dichotomous conceptions of self, to consider instead the multitude of intermediate positions available on the identity spectrum, while simultaneously exposing identity categories themselves as constructs. Silvia and her friends, as well as Martha and her "sisters in drag," disrupt the conservative binarism of their respective societies, thereby dismantling hierarchies of gender, sexuality, class, and ethnicity. Nevertheless, the drag queens' way of life does not challenge Puerto Ricanness in the fundamental way in which Chochueca's disciples subvert the sense of community that Dominicans widely share—or imagine. Indeed, through *transdressing, La estrategia de Chochueca* erodes the polarities at the core of *trujillista* ideology, questioning the monolithic Hispanist discourse, notably in its heteronormative and racialist dimensions, and in its claims to national regeneration.

Notes

1. Santos Febres, *Sirena Selena vestida de pena*. Further page references to this novel will be given in parentheses in the text. Most references are to Stephen Lytle's English translation. The others, translated by myself and indicated as such, are to the original Spanish edition.

2. Hernández, *La estrategia de Chochueca*. Further references to the Spanish original will be given in parentheses in the text. All the translations are mine.

3. Although her father initially attempted to make her pass for white, Cecilia is recognized by most of her fellow characters as mulatto. So the author does not seem interested in exploring the construct of race, which arguably distinguishes the novel from passive narratives.

4. See Villaverde, *Cecilia Valdés*, part 1, chapter 9 (170). As Fanon notes sarcastically in relation to 1950s Martinique in *Peau noire, masques blancs*, "one becomes white once endowed with a certain number of millions" (35). Nevertheless, the union of mulatto *men* with white women remains unacceptable in *Cecilia Valdés*.

5. The terms "masculine" and "feminine" are preferred to "male" and "female" here because they designate both grammatical categories and social notions

of gender. This is particularly significant, as gender is conveyed in the Spanish text via the gendered nouns, articles, adjectives, and personal pronouns. Sirena is perceived at times as feminine and at times as masculine by the other characters. Thus, while fully aware of Sirena's biological gender, Hugo almost consistently regards her as female in order to legitimate his own desire, an aspect discussed below.

6. Ginsberg, "Introduction," 2, 3.

7. Garber, *Vested Interests*, 6.

8. In "Sliding Significations," Cutter makes a similar argument regarding Nella Larsen's Clare in *Passing*.

9. Garber, *Vested Interests*, 17, her italics.

10. See Alós and Kahmann, "La ruptura con el *continuum* sexo-género-deseo," 4, 5; and Díaz, "La narrativa de Mayra Santos."

11. This recalls the dynamics of race in (post)slavery societies, where a clear distinction is drawn between blacks and whites as polar opposites, so as to preserve the binary model.

12. The anthropologist David Valentine has observed this phenomenon within the transgender community, especially among the disenfranchised. See his *Imagining Transgender*.

13. Van Haesendonck, "*Sirena Selena vestida de pena* de Mayra Santos Febres," 81.

14. More than a mere double, for Jossianna Arroyo, Leocadio is Sirena's consciousness: "If Sirena is gestuality and performativity, . . . Leocadio figures in the novel as a kind of 'consciousness'" ("Sirena canta boleros," 45). Translation mine.

15. Bhabha, *Location of Culture*, 46.

16. Butler, *Bodies That Matter*, 134.

17. Bhabha, *Location of Culture*, 175.

18. See interview by Güemes, "Las ciudades de América Latina." See also the articles by Barradas and Van Haesendonck in *CENTRO Journal* 15, no. 2 (Fall 2003). To Barradas the tourism industry imposes a form of transvestism on the area, while Van Haesendonck views Puerto Rico's political status as transvestism.

19. See articles by Arroyo, Barradas, Delgado-Costa, and Van Haesendonck in the special issue of *CENTRO Journal* (15, no. 2 [Fall 2003]) dedicated to the novel.

20. Nestór E. Rodríguez, *Escrituras de desencuentro*, 26–33.

21. Duchesne Winter, "Bajo la mirada de dios y de los perros," 10. Translation mine.

Broadcasters and Butterflies

Sexual Transgression as Cultural Critique in Dutch Caribbean Writing

Isabel Hoving

THE FIGURE of an adolescent transvestite, says Mayra Santos Febres, struck her as the best representation of the Caribbean one can imagine. The Caribbean *is* transvestism—it can be understood *as,* and *in,* the spectacular strategy of survival of transvestism, which lets its opaque, untranslatable body flaunt its tragic desire for an alterity and multiplicity that cannot be expressed in the linearity of dominant colonial discourse.

But to what extent does Santos Febres's intriguing description of the region, which is deeply rooted in the flamboyant Hispanophone Caribbean, where, in the late 1920s, subversive writers celebrated cannibalism as an alternative Caribbean epistemology, and where literary experiment and subversion have long blossomed freely, apply to the modest strips of land that were once colonized by the Dutch? At first sight, the answer is sobering. Surinamese (migrant) literature,[1] which will be the focus of this essay, seems hardly interested in the celebration of such transgression. Even if the best-known Surinamese comedian on Dutch television weekly performs as a transvestite,[2] the literary cast of transvestite and transgender characters is modest indeed. Nevertheless, some of these characters can be said to represent Dutch-Caribbean experience.

Listen to the unhappy protagonist in a recent Surinamese migrant novel, who feels affinity with his transvestite colleague Roy Bandman, when he reflects on his *own* position as an ethnic outsider: "How could Bandman live in the knowledge that he did not belong anywhere?"[3] Poor Roy Bandman—while he is being pictured as the tragic outsider par excellence, he is not even granted the small comfort of belonging to a community of intriguing transvestite or transgender literary characters, in his own Dutch part of the Caribbean. He might have been comforted to hear about Carlos Seinpaal, a well-educated, middle-class, mercurial black man, whose name means "semaphore," and who is the subject of a short portrait by the white Dutch social scientist and journalist John Jansen van Galen, a frequent visitor to Surinam.[4] Carlos, who by the end of the portrait has undergone a sex change and lives as a ridiculed recluse in Surinam, sees herself as "a broadcasting station of sorts," and she explains, "I use the echo. I receive the echoing response." Sensitive to the many sexist and racist responses to her appearance, she "analyzes society without taking part in it" (576). In stark, short sentences, she announces, "I am not a mixer, I am not a cocktailmaker." During the course of her life, she has defined herself respectively as a Surinamese man (in the Netherlands), as black (in the United States), and as Dutch (in Surinam). Just like Bandman, this sensitive transsexual expresses her society's general condition; its way of alienating and excluding people, as in Bandman's case; its racism and sexism. Their "presence . . . marks the trouble spot, indicating the likelihood of a crisis somewhere, elsewhere."[5] Though the transsexual Seinpaal refuses to embrace the hybridity that is usually associated with transgender people, transsexuals and transvestites, she does criticize the tenacious racial and sexual identity politics that mark Surinamese society. Perhaps we should read her resistance to metaphors of hybridity not just as the transsexual's insistence on the unambiguous reality of the feminized body,[6] but also as an echo of dominant, middle-class Surinamese standards: as the quest for a stable identity, instead of the foregrounding of difference. In this respect, sardonically, we could follow Santos Febres's lead and compare middle-class Surinam to the transsexual, or the transvestite during performance; they are all opposed to mixing genders, fascinated by the extreme, identitarian stereotype: Woman; Man.

However, the standards of the middle class do not organize all reflection about transvestism in Surinam. The anthropologist and cultural theorist Gloria Wekker explains that the Creole gender system in the lower Surinam classes is much less rigid and hierarchical. The African-Surinamese concept of identity would be multiple and dynamic and both men and women would have a certain freedom to behave in ways that are traditionally linked to the opposite sex.[7] This relative flexibility can be explained with the help of the African American religion Winti, which informs the Surinamese concept of the self. Winti is characterized by "the belief in personified supernatural beings, that can occupy a human being and rule out his consciousness, after which they can reveal past, present and future and heal illnesses of a supernatural character."[8] People who are occupied by *winti* may display the behavior that belongs to this god even if they are not in trance. However, people may also have characteristics that are associated with a *winti,* without ever being visited by him or her.[9] Male and female *winti* may visit both women and men. In addition, the *kra* (soul) and *dyodyo* (protective divine parents) of human beings have both a male and a female aspect.[10] Thus, women from the working classes might say that a transvestite man has a prominent female *winti,* such as the mother goddess Aisa.[11] Wekker observes that at certain women's parties one will almost always encounter men that are dressed and behave like women; in addition, the most popular theater plays at a certain college would stage transvestites. Within this worldview, the transvestite would hardly count as radical and subversive.[12] Most Surinamese writers dealing with the issue, however, adopt middle-class values, which are based on fixed, stable gender binaries. We can conclude that there are at least three different discourses in which the transvestite can be framed in Surinamese writing: as the transgressive figure that marks a crisis in society (Garber); as the more radically liberating transgressor, who effectually deconstructs binarism (Santos Febres); and as the representation of traditional, indigenous beliefs, which are different from colonial or nationalist discourse (Wekker). It remains to be seen which of these discourses will be mobilized, in a particular literary work, and how that will be done.

In this essay I will discuss the ways in which Surinamese (migrant) writing uses transvestism to explore its own social and cultural crises. After a short discussion of a few of the handful of sexually ambivalent or transgressive characters in three recent novels and stories, I will devote the rest of the essay to one particular novel that does not *present* transvestism but *relates* to it: Cándani's *Huis van as.* This oblique reference shows that Surinamese (migrant) writers may not always define society's racial and sexual dualism as the main social problem, so that subversion of that binarism, through the figure of the transvestite or transgender character, will not be their main concern.

Throwing Out the Transvestite

As the beginning of an answer, we can point out that Bandman and Seinpaal share their destiny as the antennae of the crises in Surinamese society with a handful of other sexually marginalized characters in Dutch-Caribbean (migrant) literature who serve to mark the crisis in the postcolonial condition, or migrant experience. As Marjorie Garber explains, the "apparently spontaneous or unexpected or supplementary presence of a transvestite figure in a text (whether fiction or history, verbal or visual, imagistic or 'real') that does not seem, thematically, to be primarily concerned with gender difference or blurred gender indicates *a category crisis* elsewhere, an irresolvable conflict or epistemological crux that destabilizes comfortable binarity, and displaces the resulting discomfort onto a figure that already inhabits . . . the margin."[13] In Surinamese (migrant) writing, this strategy is almost painfully clear: the few transvestites, transsexuals, or other sexual border crossers are, after having functioned as the markers and mediators of the plight of the story's straight heroes and heroines, left to their own devices: loneliness, exclusion, death. One might suspect that Surinamese (migrant) writers do not feel any affinity with Mayra Santos Febres's sharp analysis of the tragic transvestite nature of the Caribbean condition as a whole—the impulse of their writing is toward the exclusion and erasure of the transsexual, transgender person, and transvestite, and the restoration of balance and wholeness.

The novel in which the transvestite Roy Bandman figures, which was written by a Surinamese-born, Netherlands-based writer, shows that this restorative literary project is nevertheless ambivalent. The story is set in a remote village in an unnamed Caribbean nation easily recognizable as Surinam, a small society of Amerindians, maroons, Creoles, Hindustani, and Chinese. When Bandman at a certain moment realizes that his transvestism is discovered, he prepares to commit suicide. The sympathetic main protagonist, a preacher of maroon-Creole background, comes to the rescue: to explain Bandman's nightly appearance as a woman, in the graveyard just outside his house, he invents a story about a dead sister by whom Bandman would be haunted. The maroon leader believes the tale, and Bandman is saved—on the condition that, in the future, he will hide behind a fence around his house. The potentially subversive, (post)colonial act of transvestism is thus intentionally *masked* as indigenous (in the tale of the haunting sister) and can thus claim—wrongly, but effectively—a traditional form of respect.[14] This narrative solution downplays the potentially subversive nature of the act of transvestism.

This literary occurrence of transvestism can serve as an example of a more general strategy in Dutch-Surinamese (migrant) novels by women writers.[15] Ethnic and political relations are imagined as gendered. The wish to heal the painfully fragmented community is represented as a (collective) sexual desire; inevitably, there will also be a reflection on productive and unproductive sexualities. In this aspect, these women writers respond to the nationalists who, as Paul Gilroy observed,[16] tend to define the crisis in black communities as a crisis of black masculinity, which should be solved by restoring the traditional heterosexual family, that is, by reinstalling the father as the authoritarian patriarchal head of the family and reducing women to the role of mothers of the nation's sons. Many women writers seek the solution in the evocation of *less* patriarchal ways to explore or heal the rupture: from the imagination of a more vulnerable, or hybrid, masculinity (in older men—de Noré, Cándani; in an ethnically mixed foundling—Roemer) to the forceful re-creation of new genealogical ties by producing interracial babies, and/or the refusal to procreate (Rahman, Roemer).

Central in these literary responses is, again and again, the concern with the tragic separations imposed by (post)colonialism (especially between "races," ethnicities). In the most significant literary texts, the (post)colonial separations are often unmasked as perverted in the first place,[17] and transgressions of the boundaries are imagined as both healing (aimed at reconnection) and perverted (often mimetic in nature, and therefore obeying the same logic as the colonial system that created the divisions). Thus, the transgressions lay bare the perversion in the system, while (defiantly) admitting to their own perversity. In these stories, the central act of sexual transgression is often performed by an outright social outcast, who is hardly tolerated—the transvestite, the homosexual, the pedophile.

This is clearly the case in a story by the Surinam-born, Amsterdam-based writer Karin Amatmoekrim. The sexual transgression of the pedophile who is the center of her narrative lays bare the violence in the imposition of gender roles and colonial racist religious discourse. The pedophile's desires, understood as a longing for purity, are presented as a caricature of the Christian command to embrace purity and innocence; they also mimic the motherly patriarchal, colonial insistence on the pedophile son's immaturity.

Another case is the first novel by the Dutch writer Annette de Vries, whose father is from Surinam, where she grew up. *Scheurbuik* (Scurvy, 2002) presents a Dutch-Surinamese woman who seeks reconciliation to the country of her birth. This reconciliation takes place mainly through the reconnection with an old friend, who is dying of leukemia. This friend, a gay dancer, a paradigmatic border-crosser, balancing between life and death, masculinity and femininity, Surinam and Holland, advises the heroine to create a syncretic diasporic identity. De Vries's ethics is clear: reconnection can only occur when transgression and illness are embraced. Remarkably, it is nevertheless the gay border-crosser, who, lonely, wise, has to die, to allow the heterosexual heroine to live her full, reconciled life. The three examples discussed so far make us pause. Even if the cultural critique produced in these imaginations of sexual transgression is profound, the fact that the transgressive forces themselves (the transvestite, the pedophile, the gay dancer) are eliminated suggests that the novels' ethical project of reconnecting frustrates their critical project of questioning society's binary social structure.

Now I want to move on to a novel in which the tensions around the issue of identity take on an even more complicated pattern, to the point where identity and binarism do not seem relevant issues any longer.

Reading for the "Trans" 1: Tracing an Oedipal Transgression

The stories I have discussed so far are organized according to the logic of abjection—the transgressive markers of crisis have to be gotten rid of once they have served their goal. In some novels, the border-crossers signify a more permanent alienation that is shared by all citizens of the postcolonial nation, suggesting that the crisis to be faced is much more than just a personal rite of passage. The latter is the case in the Hindustani Dutch writer Cándani's second novel, *Huis van as* (2002).[18]

A clear example of the novel's effort to implicate sexual transgression as the *permanent* marker of a structural, shared crisis is found in the following scene. A man intervenes in a row between two women who accuse each other of adultery. Women should not curse each other out: "Everyone has a problem in their home, he said. Everyone has a reason for shame."[19] The fact that this intervention is timidly reported by a seven-year-old boy, who is probably the fruit of an incestuous relationship himself, opens the possibility of reading this as a reference to a shared transgression of sexual norms, within a postcolonial context. Such a reading is all the more encouraged when we consider that this line echoes a much-quoted statement in a famous novel on colonial transvestism and transgender positions, *Cereus Blooms At Night*, by Trinidadian-Canadian writer Shani Mootoo, in which the reference is to the shared, hidden practice of transvestism and also, implicitly, to the colonial condition itself: "You are not the first or the only one of your kind in this place. You grow up here and you don't realize almost everybody in this place wish they could be somebody or something else?"[20]

This is not the only moment where the two novels show affinities. The abundance of sensual references to nature is another similarity; so is the way in which the daughter-figure, involved in incest, is placed on the side of paradisiacal nature itself. Another affinity can be found in the literary devices of doubling and mirroring, so that many characters become each other's mirrors, or fuse; this device is also prominent in Trinidadian-

British Lawrence Scott's *Aelred's Sin*. Both Mootoo's and Scott's work (especially his novel *Witchbroom*) have been discussed within the context of transvestism and transgenderism, as projects of subversion. Inspired by these two examples from the Anglophone Caribbean, I would like to move outside the frame of Surinamese (migrant) writing and try, for the sake of my argument, to test another comparative reading. To what extent can we say that Cándani's Hindustani-Dutch migrant novel shares a project comparable with these two Anglophone Caribbean novels, which are reputedly much more subversive than their Surinamese counterparts? Are these three novels all involved in a radical deconstruction of alienating binary gender and racial oppositions through the lens of sexual transgression, but opting for different means to do so? Can we suggest that, even if *Huis* does not present transvestites or transsexuals, it does offer characters and moments that are transgressive, and that question and subvert social binarism every bit as much as other novels in which transvestism is the central theme? Let us try to test this bold thesis and see where such a reading strategy (a reading for the *trans-* of subversive transgression, even in a novel without transvestites, transgender people, or transsexuals) leads us in the case of Cándani's poetic, evocative novel. It is undeniable that the sexual transgression in this story is serious: the novel's naive narrator, a Hindustani Surinamese girl who returns for a visit to Surinam from the Netherlands after seven years, discovers that her own father fathered a son with her adored bosom friend, Señorita, when the latter was only thirteen years old. Furthermore, it is quite possible that the bosom friend was her father's illegitimate daughter—which would make him both the father and the grandfather of his illegitimate son. The novel relates the daughter's reluctant inquiry into these hidden family stories, intertwining the search with her growing despair about her position as an outsider—to her own family, to Surinam, to life itself.

As in other Caribbean novels on these themes, the narrative links transgressive sexual behavior to postcolonial poverty, lack of education, and alcoholism. In this case, however, we are invited to think of incest as a *solution* to these disasters. By picturing the events through the eyes of the returning daughter, the novel offers an unexpected view of the violent, oppressive incestuous relation: it suggests that it is the twelve-year-old Señorita who seduces a man her father's age, to escape the violence of her own abusive, alcoholic biological father. The readers are assured that this relationship turns into a genuine love relation that lasts until the narrator's father's death; it cannot even be defined as incestuous, for until the very last moment, the father is not aware of the fact that the girl he loves might be his own daughter. The crisis addressed is thus not primarily the individual male sexual violence in Caribbean society. However, patriarchal social structures in themselves *are* criticized as the cause of the father's transgression, and of that of the girl he loves; and it is also the cause of the narrator's problems. The narrator's alienation from life itself is the result of her blind decision to let her overly protective father guide her, as patriarchal structures seemed to demand ("With every step I took, I belonged more and more to you [the father]. Less and less I belonged to myself" [94]). Señorita's decision to seduce her friend's father sprang from her wish to live a life other than her mother's, escaping the female destiny of being bullied by parents-in-law, trapped in a loveless marriage; she even states that she wanted to be loved to be able to love herself. More important still, the novel is organized around the tragic consequences of decolonization: the nation is split by the departure of many citizens, who are accused of abandoning and forgetting those who stay behind (62). As the novel understands exclusion and isolation as the most destructive conditions imaginable, independence is depicted as a cruel machine that drove some into isolation by fleeing overseas, while condemning others to isolation because they were left behind. In spite of what one might expect, the novel does not consider the father's transgressive sexual behavior as the novel's main transgression. The main transgression, rather, lies in the father's decision to migrate to the Netherlands to escape the effects of his deeds, thus forcing both girls into a life-killing isolation. Tellingly, the father legitimizes his (sexually motivated) departure by his dissatisfaction with independence. His flight from Surinam is the migrant's anxious effort at distancing himself from the suffocating, corrupt sexual politics and gender politics in the former colony, including his own scandalous behavior—an effort that echoes Césaire's evocation of the Caribbean island as the corrupted maternal body.

This reading could be developed in an allegorical reading, which takes as its point of departure the earlier moment when the father, in his youth, loses himself for three days in the depths of the forest during a hunting party. When he returns, he has turned wild and does not speak anymore; his real self has stayed in the forest, it is said, and what returned was a body inhabited by another (98). The father begins to travel, until he finally dies in a car accident. The corrupted father can be said to embody Surinam itself when he was young, and the alienation from Surinam when older. Another argument for such a reading is suggested by the fact that the alienated, heartbroken father recognizes himself in the simple

Señorita, who is represented as life itself—she is that very authenticity he has lost during his mythical three days in the tropical forest. Señorita is closely linked to the half-cultivated sensual Surinamese landscape of the meadows next to the house. She pops up, mysteriously, at the very beginning of the story, when the prodigal daughter contemplates the fields around her former home. She recognizes the rampant plants she had once planted herself and that have now gone wild; butterflies welcome her, smells surround her, the wind opens the door of the old home, until she feels she is being watched. From the heart of this friendly, forgotten, exuberant nature, Señorita appears as a mirage, a mirror image, as nature's soul itself—or as the soul the narrator has lost (7–9). It is Señorita who tells the narrator the names of the flowers she has forgotten (31).

I will leave the connection between Señorita and the lush landscape aside for the moment, and elaborate on the oedipal narrative that seems to dominate the story, which is clearly marked by the narrator's oedipal desire for the father. A reconnection to the father—and therefore also Surinam—would offer the narrator a full subject position, marked by gender, sexuality, and nationality. Remarkably, the novel pictures the *migrant*'s life in the privileged zones of Western Europe as sterile—instead of that of the impoverished inhabitants of the marginal spaces in Surinam, who struggle with poverty, alcoholism, and broken families. To the narrator, life and fullness are directly connected to the non-normative love, childbirth, and humiliation one finds in the deprived areas of Surinam—and in Señorita (87). Feeling excluded, she just longs to be marked by life, love, and suffering, disregarding social norms. She desperately wants to "become one with everything, in the way I could be one with Señorita in the old times" (28). As she realizes only now, she never knew the father she followed and loved blindly. She now learns that she cannot relate to her father if she does not acknowledge his hidden sexual history; she cannot embrace Surinam if she does not embrace its hidden histories of incest. Señorita functions as the mirror that shows her that incest is at the heart of her desire for the father—and this, in my view, is the transgressive moment of the narrative, especially because Señorita refuses to obey the prohibition. The narrator wavers between a narrative according to the logic of the imaginary—her intense need for reconnection makes her see the world as organized around the binary opposition of closeness/isolation only, so that adultery and incest become meaningless words—and a narrative according to the logic of the symbolic, where adultery and incest *do* count as transgressions she has to condemn. Without the alienation caused by these taboos, one cannot enter the symbolic order. But the narrator, sick with the desire of reunion, has trouble accepting this.

On the one hand, then, we discern a radical resistance against the (neo)colonial patriarchal family values that destroy the (in this novel) essential value of intimacy, which is tied to the imaginary. In the desire for closeness, there is no such thing as transgressive love, for there are no boundaries to transgress; there is only the sterility of distance, contrasted to the fullness of intimacy and connectedness. On the other hand, the novel obeys a heterosexual, oedipal logic. This second—or first—pattern checks the story's subversiveness, and forms an obstacle to the emergence of transgender characters, transvestites, or lesbian love. The crisis addressed by the incestuous girl Señorita is that of postcolonial isolation. She embodies both the bliss of connectedness and the horrifying transgression of incest that is nothing but the extreme consequence of the desire for connectedness, which originates in the traumatic divisions caused by colonialism.

Reading for the "Trans" 2: In the Very Heart of Binarism

I have suggested that this Dutch-Surinamese migrant novel would be less subversive than its Anglophone counterparts, since, by refraining from portraying queer, transgender, and transvestite characters, it does not explode dominant heterosexual, oedipal patterns. However, is it not possible to recognize the transvestite in Señorita? The girl's seductive behavior is modeled after an adulterous woman she spied upon, but especially after the movie stars and fictional heroines whom she imitates when having sex. "I played how they would play. Looking drunkenly and deeply into the man's eyes. I talked with fingers, because I did not have the beautiful words" (43). This young FTF-transvestite[21] understands that femininity is but a role to play; without words, she grasps the essence of the notion of simulacrum, through which, according to Severo Sarduy, we can understand transvestism.[22] As Sarduy argues, simulacra work without referring to the original Platonic Idea, or an inner essence. For Marjorie Garber, this is the reason to suggest that "the transvestite marks the entry into the Symbolic."[23] Indeed, not as a transvestite during performance (who sees femininity as *real*), but as a transvestite who reflects on her performance, Señorita understands very well that femininity and masculinity are nothing but performances, social codes. Señorita's acceptance of the coded nature of the symbolic order makes her much more part of that order than the narrator, who is the real outsider.

However, close scrutiny suggests that a play with performance is not the novel's main concern. Rather, there is an imaginary logic at work in Cándani's narrative, especially because it is presented through the eyes of the focalizing narrator, who longs for seamless reconnection. The story displays an infinite mirroring and doubling of all characters, without ever referring to a stabilizing, foundational power: many characters seem to melt into each other, functioning as each other's mirrors or shadows. When Cándani's narrator walks towards her bosom friend Señorita for the first time after seven years, it is "as if I was walking towards myself" (9). She sees her as a clay puppet, made "to create the woman I had loved to be myself" (13), and remembers how she learned to imitate her friend's voice to the point where even her friend's mother was fooled. On the other hand, she also complains, "Her full life mirrored my own empty life" (45–46). Sometimes the two girls melt into one ("the girl with whom I formed one whole" [9]; "She lies so close as if her breathing passes through my lungs" [77]), and then again they are each other's mirrors: one represents the uneducated, poor, sexually transgressive, but authentic and full life of postcolonial Surinam, the other the educated, rich, sexually experienced but unmarked, alienated, empty life of the migrated Surinamese. The game of mirroring does not stop here. Sometimes the narrator seems to take on her father's position. Sometimes she even positions herself as Señorita's lover, as if claiming the son's oedipal right to love the woman his father loves ("My heart desires her skin. . . . Father, my father has loved the magnificent skin of b-e-a-u-t-i-f-u-l-l-a-d-y" [35–36]).

The equations keep proliferating. For Señorita's grandmother, her own son (Señorita's father) and the narrator's father are both her own sons—she has breastfed both (101). Does that mean that Señorita's desire for her friend's father is in principle already an incestuous desire, as both fathers can be considered brothers, or more? And do all women collapse into one? Indeed, the narrator sees Señorita and herself in Señorita's grandmother, who again mirrors all women, as all women in Surinam will become grandmothers one day (84). What should we make of the fact that Señorita's name, given her by her inadequate father, by mistake, is an empty name? And what of the fact that the narrator deconstructs that name (see above)? Her son Anjana's name means "the unknown," but it is also his father (who is also the father of one or possibly both young women) who is described as "the unknown." A last important example of mirroring lies in Señorita's identification with her great-aunt, who committed suicide when she found herself pregnant as the result of incest. When Señorita was born, her grandmother (the deceased's sister) said "that her sister had returned" (38).

The hut where the suicide is committed, and where all significant and transgressive actions of the narrative take place, including its natural surroundings (where meaningful patrilineal names are lacking), can be read in Lacanian fashion as the timeless imaginary space where the protagonists are caught in endless mirroring. We might understand this imagination as the utopian space where transgressive (incestuous) desires can be satisfied, where girls can immerse themselves in love relationships that stay outside the logic of patriarchy. The imaginary is, as Kaja Silverman explains, "that order of the subject's experience which is dominated by identification and duality. . . . [It makes it] possible to discover correspondences and homologies."[24] In contrast to the symbolic order, it is the place where one is not yet fully alienated from one's own needs.[25] Following Silverman's and Spivak's insistence that the imaginary is a register that coexists with the symbolic order throughout our life, we might recognize this narrative space as a Caribbean space of utopian transgression, where feminine and masculine roles are abated—the pre-pubescent girl is not yet a woman when she seduces the man, the man has renounced his active masculinity, just as the lovers in *Cereus* are a transgender boy who is no longer a girl, and a transvestite man who has renounced his masculinity—though in Cándani's novel the gender roles are not subverted or reversed. Safely situated in a space outside the realm of the Law, in the very heart of binarism and duality, we discover a utopian play with binary gender patterns. But it is fulfilling within that space only, as the players turn out to be victims or losers as soon as they emerge in the symbolic order.

There are two reasons, then, why we could question the social subversiveness of this transvestite play with binary codes. The first reason is that my effort to read Señorita as a transvestite shows that the novel reveals only *some* of the insights embodied by the transvestite (for example, the insight that gender roles are performances), and not the radical insight into the very real violence of a rigid gender system that comes with the literal transgressions of gender boundaries. The second reason why the transvestite would not be subversive lies in the more general observation that the play with binary-crossing offers no solution for any social or political (post)colonial crisis.

An anthology on postcolonial and queer theory quotes Hardt and Negri: "The postmodernist and postcolonialist [and queer?] theorists who advocate a politics of difference, fluidity, and hybridity in order to challenge the binaries and essentialism of modern sovereignty have been outflanked by the strategies of power."[26] The transvestite, border-crosser, often functions as the very embodiment of the concept of hybridity, but that concept has been exhaustively discussed as possibly counterproductive, as it is tenaciously steeped in a dialectic that leads to synthesis, instead of taking its distance from, or questioning, binarism.[27] But as many Caribbean theorists such as Édouard Glissant have argued, the divisions of the postcolonial condition cannot be healed—and certainly not by the dream of hybridization. The history of colonialism and slavery has ruptured the continuity of genealogy that supported the community. As a result, the Caribbean has become an area of incommensurable, untranslatable differences that cannot be known according to the logic of legitimacy. The opacity of the postcolonial world is not *knowable*. It is precisely this insight, also presented in Cándani's novel, that opens the possibility for a new way of reading. This reading allows us to recognize a different narrative in Cándani's novel, and to understand what cultural work the novel's transgressive character is accomplishing. Indeed, the subversion of social categories is not its main effect. But it performs another kind of cultural critique. In the section below, I will venture a non-psychoanalytical, non-binary reading, and a move away from the tenacious binarism of the (post)colonial imaginary.

Reading for the "Trans" 3: Beyond Hybridity

When Santos Febres looks at Glissant for another imagination than the one that obeys the logic of legitimacy, she finds it in his poetics of relation, which has close affinity with the logic of illegitimacy represented by her own notion of the transvestite. Santos Febres takes care to point out that Glissant's relationality represents "a synthesis that is not achieved through reunion but through expansion."[28] With this term a sudden link is established between Cándani's narrative and Deleuzian-Glissantian theory.

My psychoanalytical reading above neglected the prominence of nature in the narrative. Much more than a mere setting, it is an agent in its own right. Though I have proposed to read this celebration of nature as an allegorical story of the migrant's longing for her *reunion* with the lost nation, I would now prefer to approach it as the narrative of joyful *expansion*, in the Glissantian sense, where a young girl realizes her desires by entering a multiplicity of relationships, with the human and nonhuman alike. Rather than understanding the endless game of mirroring and doubling as a play within the imaginary, I propose to see the game as an effort to *pluralize* the body. To a certain extent, this desire for multiplicity is already implicit in Santos Febres's definition of the transvestite, as quoted at the start of this essay, but in feminist Deleuzian approaches this plurality receives much more emphasis; Moira Gatens, for example, defines the body as "a nexus of variable interconnections, a multiplicity."[29] The novel allows us to distinguish two alternative views on Señorita's erotic behavior: the narrator, still taking the paternal Law seriously, is shocked to see her sensual friend dismiss it; the friend, not very interested in the laws, as she has already accepted that all laws are mere codes, prescribing performances, is seduced by the possibilities of "becoming" in itself. To stay with Deleuzian terms, Señorita can be seen to inhabit the plane of immanence, the plane of becoming, while the narrator is situated on the plane of transcendence. For the narrator, desire obeys a Lacanian psychoanalytical logic: it is, as Elizabeth Grosz explains, "that yearning to fill in, to reproduce a lost plenitude,"[30] whereas for Señorita, desire seems to be something else: "Instead of a yearning, desire is an actualization, a series of practices, action, production, bringing together components, making machines, making reality."[31] Now we can understand why Señorita, in spite of her own worries about her isolation and lack of education, seems both a more passionate and a more pragmatic personality than the nostalgic, desperately longing narrator. In the Deleuzian view, "desire does not take for itself a particular object whose attainment it requires; rather, it aims at nothing in particular above and beyond its own proliferation or self-expansion."[32] One remembers that Señorita desired the father to be able to love *herself*. Her desire is aimed at *loving*—it did not emerge as the desire for a particular love object.

This reading emerges when we respect the novel's careful evocation of Señorita as a sensual body. Señorita is a beautiful, sensual appearance, a tender body that haunts the narrator, who loves to sleep with her in the same bed. The girl is a living part of the sparkling, scented landscape that surrounds her house, which is also significant and moving to the narrator, who observes it continuously, with the same intensity with which she observes her friend. In feminist appropriations of Deleuzian theory,[33] we find a radical redefinition of subjectivity by a return to its material basis: the human body itself. As Claire Colebrook explains, "The body *is* in its modes of practice, self-representation, and engagement."[34] The body should be seen in the Deleuzian terms of *becoming*, so that the human can be seen as *"nothing other than* an interpretation of its own body (a becoming-other than the body)."[35] In Cándani's novel, this emphasis on the corporeal becoming of human subjectivity helps us to see that

Señorita is not just imagined as a girl in lush surroundings, but as a sensual organism within a sensual network of plant and animal life, which is imagined as the place of becoming itself. It is here that the narrator becomes aware, again and again, of the fact that the girl is not her projection, her dream twin, her creation, but "a woman" in her own right—a description I wish to read as a synonym for a sexual, desiring subject. Explaining Moira Gatens's political, feminist reading of the Deleuzian-Spinozist notion of subjectivity, Colebrook states that Gatens sees "the sexual subject as an effect of *doubling,* whereby the subject occurs as a relation to its image. . . . It is the doubling of the material body *as* an ideal body. It is the material becoming other than itself; and this becoming also occurs in relation to an other body."[36] Indeed, Señorita seduces the narrator's father by imitating the pictures of beautiful women she has seen; if we explain this imitation as an instance of doubling, which is then repeated in the very many other instances of doubling (Señorita as the incestuous great-aunt who killed herself, Señorita as the narrator, Señorita as the Surinamese landscape), an image emerges of a girl who is constantly becoming in relation to other bodies.

My point is that the significance of this narrative does not lie in showing that gender identities are mere performances. There is still reason to see Señorita as a transvestite, but not because she presents the shocking visual spectacle to a large audience, but because, well aware of the coded nature of gender and sexuality, she adopts the small gestures of seduction we can also find in the landscape surrounding her: the butterfly touch. Here we see the affinity not just with *Cereus*'s "insect aesthetics," but also with the approach to transvestism in Sarduy, which is based on studies of animal mimesis: when the writer and a friend meet a group of transvestites like "phosphorescent bands of recently opened chrysalises," he is "brushed, as if by lethal elytra, by the sharp, starched organzas of pleated skirts, the poisoned flowers clutched in skinny yellowish hands, and also the cheap, sickeningly sweet perfume."[37] This is not a transvestism of the gaze, but a transvestism of the touch and smell. It is not meant to subvert, but to relate, seduce, and, in Señorita's case, heal separation and loneliness. In the touch we find a discourse of healing that is very closely related to Glissant's poetics of relation. It offers an intimate way of knowing that is not intellectual, but that, in Cándani's work, represents another healing model of postcolonial or migrant being: in her first novel, *Oude onbekenden* (Old unknowns, or Old un-acquaintances), the young female protagonist, a migrant, realizes a desired return by entering into love relationships with Surinamese men, urged by a desire to relate to their bodies; it is an effort to pluralize herself, to relate, to expand.

To recapitulate, the narrative offers the subtle interweaving of different narratives of sexual transgression, which work with and against each other. First, we have the identitarian oedipal account of the narrator, who judges the events under the denominator of perverted transgression, emphasizing the decay that is the result of the transgression (an evaluation that is expressed in the title, House of ashes), but nevertheless jealous of the transgressors. In this narrative the incestuous transgression emerges, Garber-wise, as the sign of a category-crisis (between generations, between [neo]colonial classes, between nationalities) that threatens the narrator's own conventional existence. Second, and closely related, the narrator evokes an imaginary logic that she projects on Señorita, and creates a space for her own dreams of reunion. Third, there is the narrative of desire suggested by Señorita, which is not based on oedipal norms, but on an ethics of becoming. Señorita's narrative should be understood, in my eyes, as a continuation of Santos Febres's notion of the transvestite, as Señorita is marked by the transvestite's desire of multiplicity and alterity, but refuses (in the Deleuzian-Glissantian sense) the tragedy in this desire. This refusal becomes visible in her refusal of the division between the imaginary and the symbolic, an attitude that becomes visible in her pragmatic desire of a "normal" social life, schooling, and the like, without renouncing her distance to patriarchal norms. Señorita's narrative is not organized around an identity in crisis, but concerned with the affirmative nature of identity and becoming.[38]

But this is not all. In the fourth place, we can discern a place-bound, spiritual discourse that is expressed, first, in Señorita's grandmother's mild tolerance, based on her belief that Señorita is her returned sister, and, second, in nature itself. Nature functions as an alternative discourse, with its own ethics. The narrator visits her father's grave: "Silent and quiet he lies, and smells of the earth that has received him. More peaceful than when he would lie in God's arms, where he would have to give account. A scent, a breath he is now, together with all the others here, the plants, the wind, in the sun and the rain" (106). One recognizes in this quote, and in other references in the novel to a desire to escape social constraints and to become one with life itself (27, 78, 103), the generalized ideal of deliverance from the confinements of human social life (which occurs in both Hinduism and Buddhism).[39] The novel translates this ideal into a valorization of nature as the vital space where life unfolds freely, unhampered by loveless prohibitions or a binary logic.

The image of the butterfly embodies this freedom, which could be called transgressive if it was not based on the dismissal of boundaries as futile, within a natural discourse. On the one hand, we can see this discourse, which celebrates nature's boundless plurality and mobility, as related to the Hindustani critique of creole dominance in the definition of the decolonizing nation of Surinam since the 1950s. Hindustani critics emphasized the cultural *diversity* of the nation, adopting the Dutch model of pillarization, striving for Hindustani institutions.[40] On the other hand, the novel's plea for plurality is also geared *against* the Hindustani ethnic institutions, especially patriarchal marriage. Diversity and hybridity in themselves do not necessarily lead to freedom. Nor do images of hybridity, such as the transvestite, necessarily signify subversion. All forms of diversity and hybridity may turn into confining institutions in their turn. At the very end of the story, the narrator explicitly embraces a non-binary ethics of radical multiplicity, relationality, and expanding potentiality that is associated with mobility. Señorita's little son sends her a drawing of his new cat, while telling her about his new friends: "A new player. Time goes by, brings with it new lives" (108). Movement, not the frozen framework of oedipal logic, is the vitalizing principle. When she looks at the whirling leaves, she muses, "Even the dead, I think, do not persist in lying still" (108).

Nor do the many images of sexual transgression, in Dutch-Caribbean writing. The different, conflicting images keep marking the moments of pain and violence in the postcolonial and migrant experience, sometimes questioning binarism, sometimes reinforcing it, while they check and challenge each other. Different, sometimes incommensurable, postmodern, Caribbean postcolonial, new materialist, nationalist, and traditional Surinamese or other spiritual or religious notions are evoked, in an ongoing literary reflection that tries to relate them to each other in a *syncretic* way,[41] respecting their irreconcilable differences. The explorations of these varied discourses serve different social aims: historiography, healing, cultural critique, social comment, ethical innovation, and sometimes subversion. But, as these discourses are not always organized around binaries of race, gender, and class, the transvestite is not necessarily subversive, nor is s/he the only image of sexual transgression to perform a cultural critique. Apparently, these Surinamese (migrant) writers diagnose the social crisis not so much as an effect of binarism, but rather as an effect of the isolation, divisions, failed relations and responsibility. The task at hand, then, is the search for new ways of reconnection—or new ways to relate to the irreparable dividedness of postcoloniality, in the

Glissantian way. The admirable courage of this new Surinamese (migrant) writing shows itself more in the radical images used to explore those (im) possibilities, than in their subversive use of spectacular transvestism.

Notes

1. In this essay I will refer to novels written by writers who were born and bred in Surinam and are still living there, novels by writers who were born in Surinam but have migrated to the Netherlands, and novels by Dutch immigrant writers from a Surinamese family background. Though I depart from the assumption that, in spite of their many differences, there is a continuity between the works of these writers, I will try to specify each writer's background as well as I can.

2. The Surinamese-Dutch comedian Jörgen Raymann has his own weekly television show, in which "Auntie Es," an elderly Surinamese woman, is one of his most popular impersonations.

3. Goudzand Nahar, *Hele dagen*. 156. All translations of Dutch texts are mine.

4. Galen, *Kapotte plantage*. Further references to this book will be given in parentheses in the text. I am grateful to Michiel van Kempen for guiding me to this fascinating short text.

5. Garber, *Vested Interests*, 17.

6. Ibid., 355.

7. Wekker, *Gouden munt*, 78, 100.

8. Qtd. in ibid., 82.

9. Ibid., 83–84.

10. Ibid., 86–89.

11. Ibid., 100.

12. See also Wekker, *Politics of Passion*.

13. Garber, *Vested Interests*, 17.

14. This characteristic trait of the postcolonial condition is what Spivak calls catachresis (*Critique*, 14; *Teaching Machine*, 59–61, 280–81).

15. The overwhelming majority of the writers at the start of the twenty-first century are female.

16. Qtd. in Smyth, "Sexual Citizenship," 145.

17. Robert Young, in *Colonial Desire*, has theorized the white obsession with illegitimate sexuality in racial theories.

18. Cándani (1965) was born in Surinam and migrated to the Netherlands in 1990. The Hindustani represent more than a quarter of the Surinamese population.

19. Cándani, *Huis van as*, 69. Further references to this novel will be given in parentheses in the text.

20. Mootoo, *Cereus Blooms at Night*, 258.

21. Female-to-Female.

22. Sarduy, *Written on a Body*, 97.

23. Garber, *Vested Interests*, 354.

24. Silverman, *Subject of Semiotics*, 157.

25. Ibid., 162.

26. Qtd. in Hawley, *Postcolonial, Queer,* 9; his comment.

27. See Werbner and Modood, *Debating Cultural Hybridity.*

28. Santos Febres, "The Caribbean and Transvestism," 165, in this volume.

29. Gatens, "Feminism as 'Password,'" 61.

30. Grosz, "Thousand Tiny Sexes," 171.

31. Ibid., 171.

32. Ibid., 172.

33. Represented by new materialist, often Australian, feminist scholars such as Moira Gatens, Elizabeth Grosz, Claire Colebrook, and Rosi Braidotti.

34. Colebrook, "Radical Representations," 86.

35. Ibid., 86.

36. Ibid., 86.

37. Sarduy, *Written on a Body,* 94.

38. Colebrook, "Radical Representations," 90.

39. I would not argue for a Hindu or Buddhist reading of the narrative's ethics, in spite of, for example, the reference to the Ramayana (76) or Siddharta (78), or the clay dolls the girls play with when young (the image of the clay body being a sign of transience in Hindu death lyrics, as Els Moors explains [114]). The novel's ethics is much more syncretic.

40. Choenni and Kanta, *Hindostanen,* 107.

41. Syncretism respects the incommensurability of the components of an assemblage, which are not seen as opposed. In this sense it differs from the notion of synthesis that is at the heart of the concept of hybridity, and that conceptualizes difference as binarism, and therefore resolvable (Becquer and Gatti).

Bibliography

Abramson, Julia. "Review of *Célanire Cou-Coupé*." *World Literature Today* 75, no. 2 (Spring 2001): 306.

Aching, Gerard. *Masking and Power: Carnival and Popular Culture in the Caribbean*. Minneapolis: University of Minnesota Press, 2002.

Agard-Jones, Vanessa. "Le jeu de qui? Sexual Politics at Play in the French Caribbean." In *Sex and the Citizen: Interrogating the Caribbean*. Ed. Faith Smith. Charlottesville: University of Virginia Press, 2011. 181–98.

Agosto de Muñoz, Nélida. *El fenómeno de la posesión en la religión "Vudu."* Río Piedras: Instituto de Estudios del Caribe, 1976.

Alcántara Almanzar, José. "Lulú or the Metamorphosis." In *Remaking a Lost Harmony: Short Stories from the Hispanic Caribbean*. Ed. Margarite Fernández Olmos and Lizabeth Paravisini-Gebert. Fredonia: White Pine Press, 1995. 93–101.

Alexander, M. Jacqui. "Erotic Autonomy as a Politics of Decolonization: An Anatomy of Feminist and State Practice in the Bahamas Tourist Economy." In *Feminist Genealogies, Colonial Legacies and Democratic Futures*. Ed. M. Jacqui Alexander and Chandra Talpade Mohanty. London: Routledge, 1997.

———. "'Not Just (Any) Body Can Be a Citizen': The Politics of Law, Sexuality and Postcoloniality in Trinidad and Tobago and the Bahamas." *Feminist Review* 48 (Autumn 1994): 5–23.

———. *Pedagogies of Crossing: Meditations on Feminism, Sexual Politics, Memory and the Sacred*. Durham, NC: Duke University Press, 2005.

Alós, Anselmo Peres, and Andrea Cristiane Kahmann. "La ruptura con el *continuum* sexo-género-deseo: Algunos apuntes acerca de la obra *Sirena Selena vestida de pena*, de Mayra Santos-Febres." *Espéculo: Revista de estudios literarios* 29 (June 2005). http://www.ucm.es/info/especulo/numero29/sirena.html (accessed 13 May 2012).

Amatmoekrim, Karin. "Decaloog van een oude vrouw" [An old woman's Ten Commandments]. In *Nieuwe Surinaamse en Antilliaanse verhalen* [What we should not talk about: New Surinamese and Dutch-Antillian stories]. Haarlem: In de Knipscheer, 2007. 127–37.

Anderson, Linda. "Autobiographical Travesties: The Nostalgic Self in Queer Writing." In *Territories of Queer Desire: Refiguring Contemporary Boundaries*. Ed. David Alderson and Linda Anderson. Manchester: Manchester University Press. 68–81.

Anzieu, Didier, et al. *L'épiderme nomade et la peau psychique*. Paris: Editions Apsygée, 1990.

Archer, Petrine. "Accessories/Accessaries; or, What's in Your Closet?" *Small Axe* 32 (July 2010): 97–110.

Arenas, Reinaldo. *Antes que Anochezca*. 1992. Barcelona: Tusquets Editores, 2005.

Arnold, A. James. "*Créolité*: Power, Mimicry, and Dependence." *Review: Literature and Arts of the Americas* 37, no. 68 (2004): 19–26.

———. "The Erotics of Colonialism in Contemporary French West Indian Literary Culture." In *Sisyphus and Eldorado: Magical and Other Realisms in Caribbean Literature*. Ed. Timothy J. Reiss. Asmara: Africa World Press, 2002. 68–81.

Arroyo, Jossiana. "Sirena canta boleros: Travestismo y sujetos transcaribeños en *Sirena Selena vestida de pena*." *CENTRO Journal* 15, no. 2 (Fall 2003): 38–51.

Bakhtin, Mikhail. *Rabelais and His World*. Trans. Hélène Iswolsky. New York: John Wiley and Sons, 1984.

Balzac, Honoré de. *Sarrasine*. 1830. In *Sarrasine, Gambara, Massimilla Doni*. Ed. Pierre Brunel. Paris: Gallimard, 1995. 33–78.

Barradas, Efraín. "*Sirena Selena vestida de pena* o el Caribe como travestí." *CENTRO Journal* 15, no. 2 (Fall 2003): 52–65.

Barringer, Tim, Gillian Forrester, and Barbaro Martinez-Ruiz, eds. *Art and Emancipation in Jamaica: Isaac Mendes Belisario and His Worlds*. New Haven, CT: Yale Center for British Art, 2007.

Bataille, Georges. *L'expérience intérieure*. Saint-Amand: Gallimard, 1943.

Bayley, Bruno. "Donna Hope on Masculinities in Jamaican Dancehall." Interview. *Gay Lesbian Bisexual Trans-gender and Queer Jamaica*. http://glbtqja.wordpress.com/2011/04/11/donna-hope-on-masculinities-in-jamaican-dance hall/ (accessed 15 March 2012).

Becquer, Marcos, and José Guatti. "Elements of Vogue." *Third Text* 16/17 (1991): 65–81.

Bejel, Emilio. "Cuban CondemNation of Queer Bodies." In *Cuba, the Elusive Nation: Interpretations of National Identity*. Ed. Damián J. Fernández and Madeline Cámara Betancourt. Gainesville: University Press of Florida, 2000. 155–74.

———. *Gay Cuban Nation*. Chicago: University of Chicago Press, 2001.

Belisario, Isaac Mendes. *Sketches of Character, in Illustration of the Habits, Occupation, and Costume of the Negro Population, in the Island of Jamaica, Drawn after Nature, and in Lithography*. Kingston, Jamaica, 1837.

Benítez-Rojo, Antonio. *Mujer en traje de batalla.* Santafé de Bogotá, Colombia: Alfaguara, 2001.

———. *The Repeating Island: The Caribbean and the Postmodern Perspective.* Trans. James Maraniss. 2nd ed. 1992; Durham, NC: Duke University Press, 1996.

Berlant, Lauren, and Elizabeth Freeman. "Queer Nationality." In *Fear of a Queer Planet: Queer Politics and Social Theory.* Ed. Michael Warner. Minneapolis: University of Minnesota Press, 1993.

Bhabha, Homi K. *The Location of Culture.* London: Routledge, 1994.

———. *Nation and Narration.* London: Routledge, 1990.

Boehmer, Elleke. *Colonial and Postcolonial Literature: Migrant Metaphors.* Oxford: Oxford University Press, 2005.

Bolin, Anne. "Transcending and Transgendering: Male-to-Female Transsexuals, Dichotomy and Diversity." In *Third Sex, Third Gender: Beyond Sexual Dimorphism in Culture and History.* Ed. Gilbert H. Herdt. New York: Zone Books, 1996. 447–73.

Bornstein, Kate. *My Gender Workbook: How to Become a Real Man, a Real Woman, the Real You, or Something Else Entirely.* New York: Routledge, 1998.

Boullosa, Carmen. *They're Cows, We're Pigs.* New York: Grove Press, 1997.

Boyce Davies, Carol. *Black Women, Writing and Identity: Migrations of the Subject.* New York: Routledge, 1994.

Boyle, Elizabeth. "Vanishing Bodies: 'Race' and Technology in Nalo Hopkinson's *Midnight Robber.*" *African Identities* 7, no. 2 (2009): 177–91.

Braidotti, Rosi. *Transpositions: On Nomadic Ethics.* 2006; Cambridge: Polity Press, 2011.

Brathwaite, Edward Kamau. *Contradictory Omens: Cultural Diversity and Integration in the Caribbean.* Mona, Jamaica: Savacou Publications, 1974.

Burton, Richard D. E. *Afro-Creole: Power, Opposition and Play in the Caribbean.* Ithaca, NY: Cornell University Press, 1997.

———. *La Famille Coloniale: La Martinique et la Mère Patrie, 1789–1992.* Paris: L'Harmattan, 1994.

Butler, Judith. *Bodies That Matter: On the Discursive Limits of "Sex."* London: Routledge, 1993.

———. *Gender Trouble: Feminism and the Subversion of Identity.* 1990. New York: Routledge, 1999.

———. *Undoing Gender.* New York: Routledge, 2004.

Calcagno, Francisco. *Diccionario biográfico cubano.* New York: Ponce de León, 1878.

———. *Don Enriquito: Novela histórica Cubana.* Habana: "El Pilar" de M. de Armas, 1895.

Cándani. *Huis van as.* Haarlem: In de Knipscheer, 2002.

———. *Oude onbekenden.* Haarlem: In de Knipscheer, 2001.

Cante, Richard C. "Pouring on the Past: Video Bars and the Emplacement of Gay Male Desire." In *Queer Frontiers: Millennial Geographies, Genders, and Generations*. Ed. Joseph A. Boone, Martin Dupuis, et al. Madison: University of Wisconsin Press, 2000. 143–65.

Carlisle, David Brez. *Human Sex Change and Sex Reversal: Transvestism and Transsexualism*. Lewiston, NY: Edwin Mellen Press, 1998.

Carr, Brian. "At the Thresholds of the 'Human': Race, Psychoanalysis, and the Replication of Imperial Memory." *Cultural Critique* 39 (Spring 1998): 119–50.

Carter, Angela. *Nights at the Circus*. London: Vintage, 1994.

Case, Sue-Ellen. "The Final Frontier: A Roundtable Discussion" (moderated by Tania Modleski). In *Queer Frontiers: Millennial Geographies, Genders, and Generations*. Ed. Joseph A. Boone, Martin Dupuis, et al. Madison: University of Wisconsin Press, 2000. 316–39.

Castro, Wendy Lucas. "Stripped: Clothing and Identity in Colonial Captivity Narratives." *Early American Studies* (Spring 2008): 104–36.

Certeau, Michel de. *The Writing of History*. Trans. Tom Conley. New York: Columbia University Press, 1988.

Césaire, Aimé. *Et les chiens se taisaient*. In *Les armes miraculeuses*. 1946; Paris: Gallimard, 1970.

Chamoiseau, Patrick. *Biblique des derniers gestes*. 2002; Paris: Gallimard, 2003.

———. *Écrire en Pays Dominé*. Paris: Gallimard, 1997.

———. *L'esclave vieil homme et le molosse*. Paris: Gallimard, 1997.

———. *Texaco*. Paris: Gallimard, 1992.

Chancy, Myriam J. A. *Searching for Safe Spaces: Afro-Caribbean Women Writers in Exile*. Philadelphia: Temple University, 1997.

Chevannes, Barry. *Learning to Be a Man: Culture, Socialization and Gender Identity in Five Caribbean Communities*. Barbados: University of the West Indies Press, 2001.

Chin, Timothy S. "'Bullers' and 'Battymen': Contesting Homophobia in Black Popular Culture and Contemporary Caribbean Literature." *Callaloo: Gay, Lesbian, Bisexual, Transgender Literature and Culture* 20, no. 1 (1997): 127–41.

Choenni, Chan E. S., and Kanta Sh. Adhin, eds. *Hindostanen: Van Brits-Indischeemigranten via Suriname tot burgers van Nederland*. Den Haag: Sampreshan, 2003.

Cixous, Hélène. "The Laugh of the Medusa." In *New French Feminisms: An Anthology*. Ed. Elaine Marks and Isabelle de Courtivron. Amherst: University of Massachusetts Press, 1980. 245–64.

Cliff, Michelle. *Abeng*. 1985; London: Penguin, 1991.

———. *Claiming an Identity They Taught Me to Despise*. Watertown, MA: Persephone Press, 1980.

———. *If I Could Write This in Fire*. Minneapolis: University of Minnesota Press, 2008.

———. *No Telephone to Heaven.* 1987; New York: Penguin/Plume, 1996.

Cobham, Rhonda, and Honor Ford-Smith. Introduction to *Bellywoman Bangarang,* by Sistren and Honor Ford-Smith. Amherst, MA: Unpublished, 1990. iv–xxxiv.

Colebrook, Claire. "From Radical Representations to Corporeal Becomings: The Feminist Philosophy of Lloyd, Grosz, and Gatens." *Hypatia* 15, no. 2 (2000): 76–93.

Collier, Gordon. "Spaceship Creole: Nalo Hopkinson, Canadian-Caribbean Fabulist Fiction, and Linguistic/Cultural Syncretism." In *A Pepper-Pot of Cultures: Aspects of Creolization in the Caribbean.* Ed. Gordon Collier and Ulrich Fleischmann. Amsterdam: Rodopi (*Matatu* 27–28), 2003. 443–56.

Condé, Maryse. *Célanire cou-coupé.* Paris: Laffont, 2000. *Who Slashed Célanire's Throat? A Fantastical Tale.* Trans. Richard Philcox. New York: Atria, 2004.

———. "Order, Disorder, Freedom, and the West Indian Writer." *Yale French Studies* 83, no. 2 (1993): 121–35.

Connell, R. W. *Masculinities.* 2nd ed. Cambridge: Polity Press, 2005.

Conner, Randy P., and David Hatfield Sparks. *Queering Creole Spiritual Traditions: Lesbian, Gay, Bisexual, and Transgender Participation in African Inspired Traditions in the Americas.* New York: Harrington Park Press, 2004.

Cooper, Carolyn. "Enslaved in Stereotype: Race and Representation in Post-Independence Jamaica." *Small Axe* 16 (September 2004): 154–69.

———. *Noises in the Blood: Orality, Gender and the "Vulgar" Body of Jamaican Popular Culture.* Basingstoke: Macmillan, 1993.

Core, Philip. *Camp: The Lie That Tells the Truth.* London: Plexus, 1984.

Cosentino, Donald J. "Imagine Heaven." In *Sacred Arts of Haitian Vodou.* Ed. Donald Cosentino. Los Angeles: UCLA Fowler Museum of Cultural History, 1998. 25–55.

Craft, William. *Running a Thousand Miles for Freedom; or, The Escape of William and Ellen Craft from Slavery.* London: William Tweedie, 1860.

Crichlow, Wesley. *Buller Men and Batty Bwoys.* Toronto: University of Toronto Press, 2004.

The Cuba Commission Report: A Hidden History of the Chinese in Cuba. 1876. Introduction by Denise Helly. Baltimore, MD: Johns Hopkins University Press, 1993.

Cuadra, Ivonne. "Entre la historia y la ficción: El travestismo de Enriqueta Faber." *Hispania* 87, no. 2 (2004): 220–26.

Cutter, Martha J. "Sliding Significations: Passing as a Narrative and Textual Strategy in Nella Larsen's Fiction." In *Passing and the Fictions of Identity.* Ed. Elaine K. Ginsberg. Durham, NC: Duke University Press, 1996. 75–100.

Dabydeen, David. *Hogarth's Blacks: Images of Blacks in Eighteenth-Century English Art.* Manchester: Manchester University Press, 1987.

Dalby, Jonathan. "Women and Infanticide in Nineteenth-Century Rural France." In *Engendering History: Caribbean Women in Historical Perspective.* Ed.

Verene Shepherd, Bridget Brereton, and Barbara Bailey. New York: St. Martin's, 1995. 337–68.

Dash, J. Michael. "Postcolonial Caribbean Identities." In *African and Caribbean Literature*. Ed. Abiola Irele and Simon Gikandi. Cambridge: Cambridge University Press, 2004. 2: 785–96.

Davis, Wade. *Passage of Darkness: The Ethnobiology of the Haitian Zombie*. Chapel Hill: University of North Carolina Press, 1988.

———. *The Serpent and the Rainbow*. New York: Simon and Schuster, 1986.

Davy, Kate. "Fe/male Impersonation: The Discourse of Camp." In *Critical Theory and Performance*. Ed. Janelle G. Reinelt and Joseph R. Roach. Ann Arbor: University of Michigan Press, 1992. 236–47.

Dayan, Joan. *Haiti, History and the Gods*. Berkeley: University of California, 1995.

De la Cruz, Sor Juana Inés. *Carta atenagórica*. N.p.: Red Ediciones, 2011.

Deleuze, Gilles, and Félix Guattari. *L'Anti-Oedipe*. Paris: Éditions de Minuit, 1972.

Delgado-Costa, José. "Fredi Velascues le mete mano a *Sirena Selena vestida de pena*." *CENTRO Journal* 15, no. 2 (Fall 2003): 66–77.

Depestre, René. *Hadriana dans tous mes rêves*. Paris: Gallimard, 1988.

Deren, Maya. *Divine Horsemen*. New York: Chelsea House, 1970.

Derrida, Jacques. *L'écriture et la différence*. Paris: Seuil, 1967.

Descartes, René. *Le Discours de la méthode: Pour bien conduire sa raison, et chercher la vérité dans les sciences*. Leyde: Imprimerie de Ian Maire, 1637. *Discourse on Method and Meditations on First Philosophy*. Ed. David Weissman. New Haven, CT: Yale University Press, 1996.

Des hommes et des dieux. Directed by Anne Lescot and Laurence Magloire. Digital LM Film Production, 2002.

Desmangles, Leslie G. *The Faces of the Gods: Vodou and Roman Catholicism in Haiti*. Chapel Hill: University of North Carolina Press, 1992.

Desnoes, Edmundo. *Memorias del subdesarrollo*. Madrid: Mono Azul Editora, 2006.

Díaz, Luis Felipe. "La narrativa de Mayra Santos y el travestismo cultural." *CENTRO Journal* 15, no. 2 (Fall 2003): 24–37.

Dick, Rhona. "Remembering Breen's Encomium: 'Classic Style,' History and Tradition in Derek Walcott's *Omeros*." *Journal of Commonwealth Literature* 35, no. 2 (2000): 105–15.

"Do We Want Cuba?" Philadelphia *Manufacturer*, 16 March 1889.

Dubey, Madhu. "Becoming an Animal in Black Women's Science Fiction." In *Afro-Future Females: Black Writers Chart Science Fiction's Newest New-Wave Trajectory*. Ed. Marleen S. Barr. Columbus: Ohio State University Press, 2008. 31–51.

Dubois, W. E. B. *The Souls of Black Folk*. 1903. Ed. Brent Hayes Edwards. Oxford: Oxford University Press, 2007.

Duchesne Winter, Juan. "Bajo la mirada de dios y de los perros." Prologue to *La estrategia de Chochueca*, by Rita Indiana Hernández. San Juan: Isla Negra, 2003. 7–10.

Dunham, Katherine. *Island Possessed*. 1969; Chicago: University of Chicago Press, 1994.

Dynes, Wayne R., ed. *Encyclopedia of Homosexuality*. New York: Garland, 1990. 189.

Easton, Lee, and Kelly Hewson. "Returning to Repair: Resolving Dilemmas of the Postcolonial Queer in Lawrence Scott's *Aelred's Sin*." *Ariel* 35, nos. 3–4 (July–October 2004): 81–97.

Egglestone, Ruth Minott. "A Philosophy of Survival: Anancyism in Jamaican Pantomime." *Society for Caribbean Studies Annual Conference Papers* 2 (2001). http://www.caribbeanstudies.org.uk/papers/2001/olv2p5.pdf.

Ehrsson, H. Henrik. "The Experimental Induction of Out-of-Body Experiences." *Science* 317, no. 5841 (24 August 2007): 1048.

Elia, Nada. "'A Man Who Wants to Be a Woman': Queerness as/and Healing Practices in Michelle Cliff's *No Telephone to Heaven*." *Callaloo: Gay, Lesbian, Bisexual, Transgender Literature and Culture* 23, no. 1 (Winter 2000): 352–65.

Ellis, Nadia. "Out and Bad: Toward a Queer Performance Hermeneutic in Jamaican Dancehall." *Small Axe* 35 (July 2011): 7–23.

Eshun, Kodwo. "Further Considerations on Afrofuturism." *CR: The New Centennial Review* 3, no. 2 (Summer 2003): 287–302.

Espinosa, Norge. "Vestido de Novia." In *Antología de la Poesía Cubana*, tomo IV. Ed. Ángel Esteban and Álvaro Salvador. Madrid: Editorial Verbum, 2002. 479–89.

Esquemeling, John. *Bucaniers of America*. 2 vols. London: Wm. Crooke, 1684.

Falgayrettes-Leveau, Christiana. "Avant-Propos." *Réceptacle*. Paris: Éditions Dapper, 1997.

Fanon, Frantz. *Peau noire, masques blancs*. Paris: Le Seuil, 1952. *Black Skin, White Masks*. Trans. Charles Lam Markmann. New York: Grove Press, 1967 and 1968.

Farley, John. *Kingston by Starlight*. New York: Three Rivers Press, 2005.

Feinberg, Leslie. *Transgender Warriors: Making History from Joan of Arc to Dennis Rodman*. Boston: Beacon Press, 1996.

Fernández Olmos, Margarite, and Lizabeth Paravisini-Gebert. *Creole Religions of the Caribbean: An Introduction from Vodou and Santería to Obeah and Espiritismo*. New York: New York University Press, 2003.

Ferris, Lesley. "Introduction: Current Crossings." In *Crossing the Stage: Controversies on Cross-Dressing*. Ed. L. Ferris. London: Routledge, 1993. 1–18.

Fick, Carolyn. *The Making of Haiti: The Saint-Domingue Revolution from Below*. Knoxville: University of Tennessee Press, 1990.

Forbes, Curdella. *From Nation to Diaspora: Samuel Selvon, George Lamming and the Cultural Performance of Gender*. Mona, Jamaica: University of the West Indies Press, 2005.

Forfreedom, Ann. "Lesbos Arise!" *Lesbian Tide,* May/June 1973, 4.

Foucault, Michel. *Discipline and Punish: The Birth of the Prison.* 1975. Trans. Alan Sheridan. London: Penguin Books, 1991.

———. "Technologies of the Self." In *Ethics: Subjectivity and Truth. Vol. 1: Essential Works of Foucault, 1954–1984.* Ed. Paul Rabinow. 3 vols. New York: New Press, 1997. 223–51.

Fouchard, Jean. *The Haitian Maroons: Liberty or Death.* New York: Edward W. Blyden Press, 1981.

Franco, Pamela. "The Invention of Traditional Mass and the Politics of Gender." In *Trinidad Carnival: The Cultural Politics of a Transnational Festival.* Ed. Garth L. Green and Philip W. Scher. Bloomington: Indiana University Press, 2007. 25–47.

Frankétienne. *Adjanoumelezo.* Port-au-Prince: Imprimerie des Antilles, 1987.

Freeman, Elizabeth. Introduction to "Queer Temporalities." Special issue, *GLQ* 13, nos. 2–3 (2007): 159–76.

Frydman, Jason. "Jamaican Nationalism, Queer Intimacies, and the Disjunctures of the Chinese Diaspora: Patricia Powell's *The Pagoda.*" *Small Axe* 34 (March 2011): 95–109.

Fuente, Alejandro de la. *A Nation for All: Race, Inequality and Politics in Twentieth-Century Cuba.* Chapel Hill: University of North Carolina Press, 2001.

Fuss, Diana. "Interior Colonies: Frantz Fanon and the Politics of Identification." *Diacritics* 24, nos. 2–3 (Summer–Autumn 1994): 19–42.

Galen, John Jansen van. *Kapotte plantage: Suriname, een Hollandse erfenis* [Broken plantation: Surinam, a Dutch heritage]. Amsterdam: Balans, 1995.

Garber, Marjorie. *Vested Interests: Cross-Dressing and Cultural Anxiety.* New York: Routledge, 1992.

———. *Vice Versa: Bisexuality and the Eroticism of Everyday Life.* 1995; New York: Simon and Schuster, 1996.

Gatens, Moira. "Feminism as 'Password': Re-thinking the 'Possible' with Spinoza and Deleuze." *Hypatia* 15, no. 2 (2000): 59–75.

Gaudio, Rudolph P. "Male Lesbians and Other Queer Notions in Hausa." In *Boy-Wives and Female Husbands: Studies in African Homosexualities.* Ed. Stephen O. Murray and Will Roscoe. New York: Palgrave, 1998. 115–28.

Gibson, Margaret. "Guiltless Credit and the Moral Economy." *J- Spot: A Journal of Social and Political Thought* 1, no. 3 (June 2001): 1–10.

Gilbert, Helen, and Joanne Tompkins. *Post-colonial Drama: Theory, Practice, Politics.* London: Routledge, 1996.

Gillespie, Carmen. "'Nobody Ent Billing Me': A U.S./Caribbean Intertextual, Intercultural Call-and-Response." In *Sex and the Citizen: Interrogating the Caribbean.* Ed. Faith Smith. Charlottesville: University of Virginia Press, 2011. 37–52.

Gilroy, Paul. *The Black Atlantic: Modernity and Double Consciousness.* London: Verso, 1992.

Ginsberg, Elaine K. "Introduction: The Politics of Passing." In *Passing and the Fictions of Identity*. Ed. Elaine K. Ginsberg. Durham, NC: Duke University Press, 1996. 1–18.

Glass, Honey. "Queer." *Sight and Sound* 10 (1997): 38.

Glave, Thomas. "Between Jamaica(n) and (North) America(n): Convergent (Divergent) Territories." *Black Renaissance/Renaissance Noire* 6, no. 11 (Fall 2004): 120–37.

———. "Whose Caribbean? An Allegory, in Part." *Callaloo* 27, no. 3 (2004): 671–81.

Glissant, Édouard. *Le discours antillais*. 1981; Paris: Gallimard, 1997. *Caribbean Discourse: Selected Essays*. Trans. Michael Dash. Charlottesville: University of Virginia Press, 1989.

———. *Introduction à une poétique du divers*. Paris: Gallimard, 1996.

———. *Poétique de la relation*. Paris: Gallimard, 1990. *Poetics of Relation*. Trans. Betsy Wing. Ann Arbor: University of Michigan Press, 1997.

González Echevarría, Roberto. *La ruta de Severo Sarduy*. Hanover, NH: Ediciones del Norte, 1987.

Gopinath, Gayatri. *Impossible Desires: Queer Diasporas and South Asian Public Cultures*. Durham, NC: Duke University Press, 2005.

Gordon, Leah. *Kanaval: Voudou, Politics and Revolution on the Streets of Haiti*. London: Soul Jazz Publishing, 2010.

Goudzand Nahar, Henna. *Heledagen in de regen* [Whole days in the rain]. Breda: De Geus, 2005.

Green, Sharon. "Sistren Theatre Collective: Struggling to Remain Radical in an Era of Globalisation." *Theatre Topics* 14, no. 2 (September 2004): 473–95.

Grosz, Elizabeth. "A Thousand Tiny Sexes: Feminism and Rhizomatics." *Topoi* 12 (1993): 167–79.

Gruschka, Andreas. "Critical Pedagogy after Adorno." In *Critical Theory and Critical Pedagogy Today*. Ed. Ilan Gur-Ze'ev. Haifa: Faculty of Education, University of Haifa, 2003. 241–60.

Güemes, César. "Las ciudades de América Latina son travestis con ropaje de Primer Mundo." Interview with Mayra Santos Febres. *La Jornada* (Mexico City), 4 October 2000. http://www.jornada.unam.mx/2000/10/04/03an1clt .html (accessed 15 April 2012).

Guth, Christine M. E. "Charles Longfellow and Okakura Kakuzō: Cultural Cross-Dressing in the Colonial Context." *Positions* 8, no. 3 (2000): 605–36.

Gyekye, Kuame. *An Essay on African Philosophical Thought: The Akan Conceptual Scheme*. Philadelphia: Temple University Press, 1995.

Halberstam, Judith. *Female Masculinity*. Durham, NC: Duke University Press, 1998.

———. *In a Queer Time and Place: Transgender Bodies, Subcultural Lives*. New York: New York University Press, 2005.

Hammond, Nicholas. "'All dressed up . . . ': L'Abbé de Choisy and the Theatricality of Subversion." *Seventeenth-Century French Studies* 21 (1999): 165–72.

Haraway, Donna. *Simians, Cyborgs, and Women*. New York: Routledge, 1991.

Hardt, Michael, and Antonio Negri. *Commonwealth*. Cambridge, MA: Belknap/ Harvard University Press, 2009.

Harris, Joseph. *Hidden Agendas: Cross-Dressing in Seventeenth-Century France*. Tübingen: Gunter Narr Verlag, 2005.

Hausman, Bernice L. *Changing Sex: Transsexualism, Technology, and the Idea of Gender*. Durham, NC: Duke University Press, 1995.

Hawley, John, ed. *Postcolonial, Queer: Theoretical Intersections*. Albany: State University of New York Press, 2001.

Hayles, N. Katherine. *How We Became Posthuman: Virtual Bodies in Cybernetics, Literature, and Informatics*. Chicago: University of Chicago Press, 1999.

Helly, Denise. *Idéologie et ethnicité: Les Chinois Macao à Cuba, 1847–1886*. Montréal: Presses de l'Université de Montréal, 1979.

Henke, Holger. "Jamaica's Decision to Pursue a Neoliberal Development Strategy: Realignments in the State-Business-Class Triangle." *Latin American Perspectives* 26, no. 5 (September 1999): 7–33.

Hennessy, Rosemary. *Profit and Pleasure: Sexual Identities in Late Capitalism*. New York: Routledge, 2000.

Henry, Paget. *Caliban's Reason: Introducing Afro-Caribbean Philosophy*. New York: Routledge, 2000.

Herbert, John. *Fortune and Men's Eyes*. New York: Grove Press, 1967.

Hernández, Rita Indiana. *La estrategia de Chochueca*. 1999; San Juan: Isla Negra, 2003.

Hewson, Kelly. "An Interview with Earl Lovelace." *Postcolonial Text* 1, no. 1 (2004). http://postcolonial.org/index.php/pct/article/viewArticle/344/802.

Highway, Tomson. "The Rez Sisters." In *Postcolonial Plays: An Anthology*. Ed. Helen Gilbert. London: Routledge, 2001. 394–418.

Hindmarch-Watson, Katie. "Lois Schwich, The Female Errand Boy: Narratives of Female Cross-Dressing in Late-Victorian London." *GLQ* 14, no. 1 (2007): 69–98.

Hines, Horace. "Mob Beats Cross-Dresser: Melee in Falmouth; Wig, Form-Fitting Blouse Ripped Off." *Jamaica Observer*, 28 April 2007.

Hodge, Merle. "The Shadow of the Whip: A Comment on Male-Female Relations in the Caribbean." In *I Am Because We Are: Readings in Black Philosophy*. Ed. Fred Lee Hord and Jonathan Scott Lee. Amherst: University of Massachusetts Press, 1995. 189–94.

"Homophobia in Jamaica and Its Role in Driving the HIV/AIDS Epidemic." *Human Rights Watch*. http://hrw.org/reports/2004/jamaica1104/.

Honoré, Brian. "The Midnight Robber: Master of Metaphor, Baron of Bombast." *TDR* 42, no. 3 (Autumn 1998): 124–31.

Hope, Donna P. "*Passa Passa*: Interrogating Cultural Hybridities in Jamaican Dancehall." *Small Axe* 21 (October 2006): 125–39.

Hopkinson, Nalo. *Brown Girl in the Ring*. New York: Warner Books, 1998.

———. *Midnight Robber.* New York: Warner Books, 2000.

———. *The New Moon's Arms.* New York: Warner Books, 2007.

———. "The Profession of Science Fiction, 60: Sometimes It Might be True." *Foundation: The International Review of Science Fiction* 33, no. 91 (Summer 2004): 5–10.

———. *The Salt Roads.* New York: Warner Books, 2003.

———. *Skin Folk.* New York: Warner Books, 2001.

Hopkinson, Nalo, and Alondra Nelson. "Making the Impossible Possible: An Interview with Nalo Hopkinson." *Social Text* 71, no. 20 (Summer 2002): 97–113.

Hulme, Peter. *Colonial Encounters: Europe and the Native Caribbean, 1492–1797.* London: Routledge, 1986.

———. "Expanding the Caribbean." In *Perspectives on the "Other America": Comparative Approaches to Caribbean and Latin American Culture.* Ed. Michael Niblett and Kerstin Oloff. Amsterdam: Rodopi, 2009. 29–49.

———. "Polytropic Man: Tropes of Sexuality and Mobility in Early Colonial Discourse." In *Europe and Its Others.* Ed. Francis Barker, Peter Hulme, Margaret Iversen, and Diana Loxley. Colchester: Essex University Press, 1985. 17–32.

Hurston, Zora Neale. *Tell My Horse: Voodoo and Life in Haiti and Jamaica.* 1938. New York: Harper, 1990.

Hussey-Whyte, Donna. "A Pink Wig Found with 'Dudus,'" *Jamaica Observer,* 23 June 2010.

"Jamaica: Combat Homophobia." *Human Rights Watch,* 18 July 2012. http://www.hrw.org/news/2012/07/18/jamaica-combat-homophobia.

Jamaican Cultural Development Commission. *Jonkonnu—Meet the Characters.* http://www.jcdc.org.jm/jonkonnu_characters6.htm.

Jarrett, Gene. "A Song to Pass On: An Interview with Thomas Glave." *Callaloo* 23, no. 4 (2000): 1227–40.

"John Herbert." http://www.canadiantheatre.com/dict.pl?term=Herbert%2C%20John (accessed 3 June 2007).

Kempen, Michiel van, and Wim Rutgers. *Noordoostpassanten: 400 jaar Nederlandse verhaalkunst over Suriname, de Nederlandse Antillen en Aruba.* Amsterdam: Contact, 2005.

Keyssar, Helene. *Feminist Theatre.* London: Macmillan, 1984.

Kincaid, Jamaica. *The Autobiography of My Mother.* New York: Plume, 1997.

Kristeva, Julia. *Revolution in Poetic Language.* Trans. Margaret Waller. New York: Columbia University Press, 1984.

Lacan, Jacques. *Le Séminaire de Jacques Lacan, Livre XI, "Les quatre concepts fondamentaux de la psychanalyse."* Paris: Seuil, 1973.

———. "What Is a Picture?" In *The Four Fundamental Concepts of Psycho-analysis.* Ed. Jacques-Alain Miller. Trans. Alan Sheridan. New York: Norton, 1998. 105–19.

Larsen, Nella. *An Intimation of Things Distant: The Collected Fiction of Nella Larsen.* Ed. Charles Larson. New York: Anchor Books, 1992.

Lenggenhager, Bigna, et al. "Video Ergo Sum: Manipulating Bodily Self-Consciousness." *Science* 317, no. 5841 (24 August 2007): 1096–99.

Lewis, Linden. "Caribbean Masculinity: Unpacking the Narrative." In *The Culture of Gender and Sexuality in the Caribbean.* Ed. Linden Lewis. Gainesville: University Press of Florida, 2003. 94–128.

Lim, Eng-Beng. "Glocalqueering in New Asia: The Politics of Performing Gay in Singapore." *Theatre Journal* 57, no. 3 (2005): 383–405.

Lockwood, Lee. *Castro's Cuba, Cuba's Fidel.* 1967. Boulder, CO: Westview, 1990.

Lokaisingh-Meighoo, Sean. "Jahaji Bhai: Notes on the Masculine Subject and Homoerotic Subtext of Indo-Caribbean Identity." *Small Axe* 7 (March 2000): 77–92.

Lorde, Audre. "Age, Race, Class, and Sex: Women Redefining Difference." In *Gender through the Prism of Difference.* Ed. Maxine Baca Zinn, Pierrette Hondagneu, and Michael A. Messner. New York: Oxford University Press, 2005. 245–50.

Ludmer, Josefina. "Las tretas del débil." In *La sartén por el mango.* Ed. P. E. González and E. Ortega. Río Piedras: Ediciones Huracán. 47–54.

Lumsden, Ian. *Machos, Maricones, and Gays: Cuba and Homosexuality.* Philadelphia: Temple University Press, 1996.

Malefant, Charles. *Des colonies et particulièrement de celle de Saint-Domingue.* Paris, 1814.

Mani, Lata. "Contentious Traditions: The Debate on Sati in Colonial India." *Cultural Critique* 7 (1987): 119–56.

Manzari, H. J. "An Afternoon with José Alcántara Almánzar (Interview)." *Callaloo: Gay, Lesbian, Bisexual, Transgender Literature and Culture* 23, no. 3 (2000): 953–60.

Mardorossian, Carine M. *Reclaiming Difference: Caribbean Women Rewrite Postcolonialism.* Charlottesville: University of Virginia Press, 2005.

"Marking World Day of Social Justice, Transgender Citizens, Supported by SASOD, Move to the Courts to Challenge Guyana's Law against 'Cross-Dressing.'" 22 February 2010. http://sasod.blogspot.com/2010/02/marking-world-day-of-social-justice.html (accessed 10 April 2012).

Marshall, Peter. *Cuba Libre: Breaking the Chains?* Boston: Faber and Faber, 1987.

Martí, José. *Inside the Monster: Writings on the United States and American Imperialism.* Ed. Philip S. Foner. Trans. Elinor Randall, Luis A. Baralt, Juan de Onís, and Roslyn Held Foner. New York: Monthly Review Press, 1975.

———. *Lucía Jerez o Amistad funesta.* 1885; La Habana: Letras Cubanas, 1997.

———. "Mi raza." In *Obras completas,* vol. 2, *Cuba: Política y revolución, 1892–1893.* Havana: Editorial Nacional de Cuba, 1963. 298–300.

———. "A Terrible Drama: The Funeral of the Haymarket Martyrs." In *Inside the Monster: Writings on the United States and American Imperialism.* Ed. Philip S. Foner. Trans. Elinor Randall, Luis A. Baralt, Juan de Onís, and Roslyn Held Foner. New York: Monthly Review Press, 1975. 287–324.

———. "A Vindication of Cuba." In *Our America: Writings on Latin America and the Struggle for Cuban Independence.* Ed. Philip S. Foner. Trans. Elinor Randall, Juan de Onís, and Roslyn Held Foner. New York: Monthly Review Press, 1977. 234–41.

Martínez-Alier, Verena. *Marriage, Class and Colour in Nineteenth-Century Cuba: A Study of Racial Attitudes and Sexual Values in a Slave Society.* Cambridge: Cambridge University Press, 1974.

Martínez-Fernández, Luis. "The 'Male City' of Havana: The Coexisting Logics of Colonialism, Slavery and Patriarchy in Nineteenth-Century Cuba." In *Women and the Colonial Gaze.* Ed. Tamara L. Hunt and Micheline R. Lessard. London: Palgrave, 2002. 104–16.

Maysles, Philip. "Dubbing the Nation." *Small Axe* 11 (2002): 91–111.

McCarthy Brown, Karen. "Afro-Caribbean Spirituality: A Haitian Case Study." In *Vodou in Haitian Life and Culture: Invisible Powers.* Ed. Claudine Michel and Patrick Bellegarde-Smith. Basingstoke: Palgrave, 2006. 1–26.

———. *Mama Lola: A Vodou Priestess in Brooklyn.* Berkeley: University of California Press, 1991.

McClintock, Anne. *Imperial Leather: Race, Gender and Sexuality in the Colonial Contest.* New York: Routledge, 1995.

———. "'No Longer in a Future Heaven': Gender, Race and Nationalism." In *Dangerous Liaisons: Gender, Nation, and Postcolonial Perspectives.* Ed. Anne McClintock, Aamir Mufti, and Ella Shohat. Minneapolis: University of Minnesota Press, 1997. 89–112.

McDowell, Deborah. "Transferences: Black Feminist Discourse: The 'Practice' of 'Theory.'" In *Feminism Beside Itself.* Ed. Diane Elam and Robyn Wiegman. New York: Routledge, 1995. 93–119.

Métraux, Alfred. "The Concept of the Soul in Haitian Vodu." *Southwestern Journal of Anthropology* 2, no. 1 (Spring 1946): 84–92.

Milne, Lorna. "The *Marron* and the *Marqueur*: Physical Space and Imaginary Displacements in Patrick Chamoiseau's *L'esclave vieil homme et le molosse.*" In *Ici-Là: Place and Displacement in Caribbean Writing in French.* Ed. Mary Gallagher. New York: Rodopi, 2003. 61–81.

Misrahi-Barak, Judith. "Beginner's Luck among Caribbean-Canadian Writers: Nalo Hopkinson, André Alexis and Shani Mootoo." *Commonwealth* 22, no. 1 (Autumn 1999): 89–96.

Mohanty, Chandra Talpade. *Feminism without Borders: Decolonizing Theory, Practicing Solidarity.* Durham, NC: Duke University Press, 2003.

Montero, Oscar. "The Signifying Queen: Critical Notes from a Latino Queer." In *Hispanisms and Homosexualities.* Ed. Sylvia Molloy and Robert McKee Irwin. Durham, NC: Duke University Press, 1998. 161–74.

Montilus, Guérin C. "Vodun and Social Transformation in the African Diasporic Experience: The Concept of Personhood in Haitian Vodun Religion." In *Haitian Vodou: Sprit, Myth, and Reality*. Ed. Patrick Bellegarde-Smith and Claudine Michel. Bloomington: Indiana University Press, 2006. 1–6.

Moors, Els. "De ondraaglijke zwaarte van het bestaan. Het proza van zeven Surinaamse schrijfsters uit de 21ste eeuw." *OSO. Tijdschrift voor Surinamistiek* 32, no. 1 (2004): 110–21.

Mootoo, Shani. *Cereus Blooms at Night*. Vancouver: Press Gang, 1996.

Morris, Mervyn. "Important Production." *Daily Gleaner,* 9 March 1978, 4–5.

Mowry, Melissa. "Dressing Up and Dressing Down: Prostitution, Pornography, and the Seventeenth-Century English Textile Industry." *Journal of Women's History* 11, no. 3 (1999): 78–103.

Muñoz, José Esteban. *Disidentifications: Queers of Color and the Performance of Politics*. Minneapolis: University of Minnesota Press, 1999.

Munro, Martin. *Exile and Post-1946 Haitian Literature: Alexis, Depestre, Ollivier, Laferriere, Danticat*. Liverpool: Liverpool University Press, 2007.

My Beautiful Launderette. Directed by Stephen Frears. Channel Four Films, 1985.

Naipaul, V. S. *Miguel Street*. New York: Vanguard Press, 1960.

New, Caroline. "Sex and Gender: A Critical Realist Approach." *New Formations* 56 (2005): 54–70.

Newton, Esther. *Mother Camp: Female Impersonators in America*. Englewood Cliffs, NJ: Prentice-Hall, 1972.

Noble, Bobby (Jean). "Zoom, Zoom, Boy-hood Imaginaries, and the Trans-Formations of Manhood." Paper presented at the Gay and Lesbian Studies Association Annual Conference, Toronto, 2003.

O'Callaghan, Evelyn. "Naipaul's Legacy: 'Created in the West Indies'—For Export," *Lucayos* 1 (2008): 106–17. http://www.cobses.info/ojs/index.php?journal=lucayos&page=article&op=viewFile&path[]=9&path[]=9 (accessed 10 April 2012).

Opoku-Agyemang, Naana Jane. "Gender-Role Perceptions in the Akan Folktale." *Research in African Literatures* 30, no. 1 (Spring 1999): 116–39.

Pancrazio, James J., ed. *Enriqueta Faber: Travestismo, documentos e historia*. Madrid: Editorial Verbum, 2008.

Paris Is Burning. Directed by Jennie Livingston. Miramar Films, 1990.

Parker, Andrew, Mary Russo, Doris Sommer, and Patricia Yaeger, eds. *Nationalisms and Sexualities*. New York: Routledge, 1992.

Patterson, Ebony. "A Journey of Self-Discovery." http://www.artitup.zoomshare.com/1.shtml (accessed 17 January 2009).

Patterson, Ebony G., and Oneika Russell. "Mi Did Deh Deh: A Candid Conversation between Two Contemporary Jamaican Artists." *Small Axe,* 11 August 2009. http://smallaxe.net/wordpress3/vocabularies/2009/08/11/mi-did-deh-deh-ebony-patterson-oneika-russell/ (accessed 31 August 2009).

Pellegrini, Ann. "After Sontag: Future Notes on Camp." In *A Companion to Lesbian, Gay, Bisexual, Transgender, and Queer Studies*. Ed. George E. Haggerty and Molly McGarry. Malden: Blackwell, 2007. 168–93.

Pellón, Gustavo. "Severo Sarduy's Strategy of Irony: Paradigmatic Indecision in *Cobra* and *Maitreya*." *Latin American Literary Review* 11, no. 23 (1983): 7–13.

Piatkowski, Peter. Review of *Our Caribbean*. *Feminist Review*, 11 September 2008. http://feministreview.blogspot.com/2008/09/our-caribbean-gathering-of-lesbian-and.html (accessed 19 January 2009).

Piñera, Virgilio. *La vida entera (Antología poética 1937–1977)*. Madrid: Huerga y Fierro, 2005.

Pirates of the Caribbean. Directed by Gore Verbinski. Walt Disney Pictures in association with Jerry Bruckheimer Films, 2003.

Poupeye, Veerle. "What Times Are These? Visual Art and Social Crisis in Postcolonial Jamaica." *Small Axe* 29 (July 2009): 164–84.

Povinelli, Elizabeth, and George Chauncey. "Thinking Sexuality Transnationally: An Introduction." *Gay and Lesbian Quarterly* 5, no. 4 (1999): 439–52.

Powell, Jessica Ernst. "Fabricating Faber: The Literary Lives of a Nineteenth-Century Transvestite in Cuba." PhD diss., University of California–Santa Barbara, 2006.

Powell, Patricia. *The Pagoda*. New York: Alfred A. Knopf, 1998.

———. *A Small Gathering of Bones*. Oxford: Heinemann, 1994.

Prater, Tzarina T. "Transgender, Memory, and Colonial History in Patricia Powell's *The Pagoda*." *Small Axe* 37 (March 2012): 20–35.

Price, Richard, and Sally Price. "Shadowboxing in the Mangrove." *Cultural Anthropology* 12, no. 1 (1997): 3–36.

Propp, Vladimir. *Morphology of the Folk Tale*. Austin: University of Texas Press, 1968.

Prosser, Jay. *Second Skins: The Body Narratives of Transsexuality*. New York: Columbia University Press, 1998.

Purdom, Judy. "Mapping Difference." *Third Text* 32 (1995): 19–32.

Puri, Shalini. *The Caribbean Postcolonial: Social Equality, Post-Nationalism, and Cultural Hybridity*. New York: Palgrave, 2004.

Raiskin, Judith. *Snow on the Cane Fields: Women's Writing and Creole Subjectivities*. Minneapolis: University of Minnesota Press, 1995.

Ramraj, Ruby S. "Nalo Hopkinson's Colonial and Dystopic Worlds in *Midnight Robber*." In *The Influence of Imagination: Essays on Science Fiction and Fantasy as Agents of Social Change*. Ed. Lee Easton and Randy Schroeder. Jefferson, NC: McFarland, 2008. 131–38.

———. "Nalo Hopkinson: Transcending Genre Boundaries." In *Beyond the Canebrakes: Caribbean Women Writers in Canada*. Ed. Emily Allen Williams. Trenton, NJ: Africa World Press, 2008. 135–53.

Ramsdell, Catherine. "Nalo Hopkinson and the Reinvention of Science Fiction." In *Beyond the Canebrakes: Caribbean Women Writers in Canada*. Ed. Emily Allen Williams. Trenton, NJ: Africa World Press, 2008. 155–72.

Raymond, Janice. *The Transsexual Empire: The Making of the She-Male*. Boston: Beacon Press, 1979.

Rechy, John. "The Outlaw Sensibility in the Arts: From Drag and Leather to Pose, the Mythology of Stonewall, and a Defense of Stereotypes." In *Queer Frontiers: Millennial Geographies, Genders, and Generations*. Ed. Joseph A. Boone, Martin Dupuis, et al. Madison: University of Wisconsin Press, 2000. 124–32.

Reckord, Michael. "Sistren Play Brethren Superbly." *Sunday Gleaner,* 12 September 1993, 3D.

Reddock, Rhoda. "Interrogating Caribbean Masculinities: An Introduction." In *Interrogating Caribbean Masculinities: Theoretical and Empirical Analyses*. Ed. Rhoda Reddock. Mona, Jamaica: University of the West Indies Press, 2004. xiii–xxxiv.

René, Georges, and Marilyn Houlberg. "My Double Mystic Marriages to Two Goddesses of Love: An Interview." In *Sacred Arts of Haitian Vodou*. Ed. Donald Cosentino. Los Angeles: UCLA Fowler Museum of Cultural History, 1998. 287–99.

Rey, Terry. "The Virgin Mary and the Revolution in Saint Domingue: The Charisma of Romaine-la-Prophétesse." *Journal of Historical Sociology* 11 (1998): 341–69.

Richard, Nelly. *Masculine/Feminine: Practices of Difference(s)*. Durham, NC: Duke University Press, 2004.

Rodríguez, Juana María. *Queer Latinidad: Identity Practices, Discursive Spaces*. New York: New York University Press, 2003.

Rodríguez Juliá, Edgardo. *Caribeños*. San Juan: Instituto de Cultura Puertorriqueña, 2002.

Rodríguez, Néstor E. *Escrituras de desencuentro en la República Dominicana*. Mexico: Siglo Veintiuno/Estado de Quintana Roo, 2005.

Rohmer, Sax (pseud. of Arthur Sarsfield Ward). *The Insidious Dr. Fu-Manchu: Being a Somewhat Detailed Account of the Amazing Adventures of Nayland Smith in His Trailing of the Sinister Chinaman*. 1913. Mineola: Dover, 1997.

Roscoe, Will. *The Zuni Man-Woman*. Albuquerque: University of Mexico Press, 1991.

Rosenfeld, Kathryn. "Drag King Magic: Performing/Becoming the Other." In *The Drag King Anthology*. Ed. Dona Troka, Kathleen Lobesco, and Jean Noble. New York: Harrington Park Press, 2002. 201–20.

Rosenthal, Judy. *Possession, Ecstasy, and Law in Ewe Voodoo*. Charlottesville: University of Virginia Press, 1998.

Ross, Andrew. *Real Love in Pursuit of Cultural Justice*. New York: New York University Press, 1998.

Routon, Ken. "Trance-Nationalisms: Religious Imaginaries of Belonging in the Black Atlantic." *Identities: Global Studies in Culture and Power* 3, no. 3 (2006): 483–502.

Rubin, Henry. *Self-Made Men: Identity and Embodiment among Transsexual Men.* Nashville: Vanderbilt University Press, 2003.

Said, Edward. *Orientalism.* New York: Vintage, 1979.

Saint-Méry, Médéric Louis Élie Moreau de. *Description topographique, physique, civile, politique et historique de la partie française de l'Isle Saint-Domingue. Avec des observations générales sur la population, sur le caractère & les mœurs de ses divers habitans; sur son climat, sa culture, ses productions, son administrations &c, &c. Accompagnées des détails les plus propres à faire connaître l'état de cette colonie à l'époque du 18 Octobre 1789; Et d'une nouvelle carte de la totalité de l'Isle.* 2 vols. Philadelphia: Chez l'auteur, 1797–98.

Salkey, Andrew. "Anancy and Jeffrey Amherst." In *The Penguin Book of Caribbean Short Stories.* Ed. E. A. Markham. London: Penguin, 1996. 11–13.

Sandoval, Chela. *Methodology of the Oppressed.* Minneapolis: University of Minnesota Press, 2000.

Santner, Eric L. *On Creaturely Life: Rilke, Benjamin, Sebald.* Chicago: University of Chicago Press, 2006.

Santos Febres, Mayra. "Caribe y travestismo." In *El artista caribeño como guerrero de lo imaginario.* Ed. Rita De Maeseneer and An Van Hecke. Madrid: Iberoamericana, 2004. 37–44.

———. *Sirena Selena vestida de pena.* Barcelona: Mondadori, 2000. *Sirena Selena.* Trans. Stephen Lytle. New York: Picador, 2000.

Sarduy, Severo. "Copy/Simulacrum." 1982. In *Written on a Body,* by Severo Sarduy. Trans. Carol Maier. New York: Lumen, 1989. 1–2.

———. *De donde son los cantantes.* 1967. Ed. Roberto González Echevarría. Madrid: Cátedra, 1997. *From Cuba with a Song.* Trans. Jill Levine. Los Angeles: Sun and Moon, 1994.

———. "Writing/Transvestism." In *Written on a Body,* by Severo Sarduy. Trans. Carol Maier. New York: Lumen, 1989. 33–37.

———. *Written on a Body.* Trans. Carol Maier. New York: Lumen, 1989.

Sartre, Jean-Paul. *L'être et le néant: Essai d'ontologie phénoménologique.* Mésnil-sur-l'Estrée: Gallimard, 1943.

Sawicki, Jana. "Foucault, Feminism and Questions of Identity." In *A Cambridge Companion to Foucault.* Ed. Gary Gutting. Cambridge: Cambridge University Press, 1994. 286–313.

Scher, Philip W. "Copyright Heritage: Preservation, Carnival and the State of Trinidad." *Anthropological Quarterly* 75, no. 3 (2002): 469–70.

Scott, Lawrence. *Aelred's Sin.* London: Allison and Busby, 1998.

———. *Witchbroom.* London: Allison and Busby, 1992.

Sedgwick, Eve Kosofsky. "Paranoid Reading and Reparative Reading; or You're So Paranoid, You Probably Think This Introduction Is About You." In *Novel*

Gazing: Queer Readings in Fiction. Ed. Eve Kosofsky Sedgwick. Durham, NC: Duke University Press, 1997. 2–33.

———. *Tendencies.* Durham, NC: Duke University Press, 1993.

Serres, Michel. *Variations sur le corps.* Saint-Amand-Montrond: Éditions Le Pommier, 1999.

Sharpe, Jenny. "Dub and Difference: A Conversation with Jean 'Binta' Breeze." *Callaloo: Gay, Lesbian, Bisexual, Transgender Literature and Culture* 26, no. 3 (Summer 2003): 607–13.

Sharpe, Jenny, and Samantha Pinto. "The Sweetest Taboo: Studies of Caribbean Sexualities: A Review Essay." *Signs: A Journal of Women in Culture and Society* 32, no. 1 (2006): 247–74.

Sheller, Mimi. *Citizenship from Below: Erotic Agency and Caribbean Freedom.* Durham, NC: Duke University Press, 2007.

———. *Consuming the Caribbean: From Arawaks to Zombies.* London: Routledge, 2003.

Siemens, William L. "Review of *Remaking a Lost World: Short Stories from the Hispanic Caribbean.*" *World Literature Today* 70, no. 2 (1996): 374.

Sifuentes-Jáuregui, Ben. *Transvestism, Masculinity and Latin American Literature: Genders Share Flesh.* Basingstoke: Palgrave MacMillan, 2002.

Silverman, Kaja. *The Subject of Semiotics.* New York: Oxford University Press, 1983.

Sistren. "Can I Call You Sister?" Interview with Owen "Blacka" Ellis. *Sistren* 15, nos. 1–2 (1993): 34–35.

Sistren Theatre Collective. *Muffet Inna All a Wi.* Kingston, Jamaica: Unpublished, 1986.

Sives, A. "Changing Patrons, from Politician to Drug Don: Clientelism in Downtown Kingston, Jamaica." *Latin American Perspectives* 29, no. 5 (September 2002): 66–89.

Sklodowska, Elzbieta. *Espectros y espejismos: Haití en el imaginario cubano.* Madrid: Iberoamericana, 2009.

Smith, Faith, ed. *Sex and the Citizen: Interrogating the Caribbean.* Charlottesville: University of Virginia Press, 2011.

Smith, Karina. "Demystifying 'Reality' in Sistren's *Bellywoman Bangarang.*" *Kunapipi* 26, no. 1 (2004): 66–77.

Smith, Paul Julian. "Cuban Homosexualitites: On the Beach with Néstor Almendros and Reinaldo Arenas." In *Hispanisms and Homosexualities.* Ed. Sylvia Molloy and Robert McKee Irwin. Durham, NC: Duke University Press, 1998. 248–68.

Smyth, Heather. "Sexual Citizenship and Caribbean-Canadian Fiction: Dionne Brand's 'In Another Place, Not Here' and Shani Mootoo's 'Cereus Blooms At Night.'" *ARIEL: A Review of International English Literature* 30, no. 2 (1999): 141–60.

Solomon, Alisa. "It's Never Too Late to Switch: Crossing toward Power." In *Crossing the Stage: Controversies on Cross-Dressing*. Ed. Lesly Ferris. London: Routledge, 1993. 144–54.

Sommer, Doris. *Foundational Fictions: The National Romances of Latin America*. Berkeley: University of California Press, 1991.

Sontag, Susan. "Notes on 'Camp.'" *Against Interpretation and Other Essays*. New York: Farrar, Straus and Giroux, 1966. 275–92.

Spelman, Elizabeth V. *Inessential Woman: Problems of Exclusion in Feminist Thought*. Boston: Beacon Press, 1988.

Spivak, Gayatri Chakravorty. "Can the Subaltern Speak? Speculations on Widow Sacrifice." In *Marxism and the Interpretation of Culture*. Ed. Cary Nelson and Lawrence Grossberg. London: Macmillan, 1988. 271–313.

———. *A Critique of Postcolonial Reason: Toward a History of the Vanishing Present*. Cambridge, MA: Harvard University Press, 1999.

———. *Outside in the Teaching Machine*. New York: Routledge, 1993.

Stone, Sandy. "The 'Empire' Strikes Back: A Posttranssexual Manifesto." In *Body Guards: The Cultural Politics of Gender Ambiguity*. Ed. Julia Epstein and Kristina Straub. New York: Routledge, 1993. 280–304.

"Tallulah Bankhead." http://www.corpse.org/issue_12/foreign_desk/appert.html (accessed 28 May 2007).

Tapia y Rivera, Alejandro. *Póstumo el transmigrado y Póstumo el envirginado*. 1892. San Juan: Publicaciones Gaviota, 2008.

Taylor, Charles. *Modern Social Imaginaries*. Durham, NC: Duke University Press, 2004.

———. *Sources of the Self: The Making of Modern Identity*. Cambridge, MA: Harvard University Press, 1989.

Thomas, Deborah. *Modern Blackness: Nationalism, Globalization, and the Politics of Culture in Jamaica*. Mona, Jamaica: University of the West Indies Press, 2004.

Thompson, Robert Farris. *Flash of the Spirit African and Afro-American Art and Philosophy*. New York: Random House, 1983.

Tinsley, Omise'eke Natasha. *Thieving Sugar: Eroticism between Women in Caribbean Literature (Perverse Modernities)*. Durham, NC: Duke University Press, 2010.

Towle, Evan B., and Lynn M. Morgan. "Romancing the Transgender Native: Rethinking the Use of the Third Gender Concept." *GLQ* 8, no. 4 (2002): 469–97.

Trotz, Alissa. "This Case Is about and for All of Us." *Starbroek News*, 1 March 2010. http://www.stabroeknews.com/2010/features/03/01/this-case-is-about-and-for-all-of-us/ (accessed 10 April 2012).

Trotz, Maya. "Interview with Lady Saw." July 2003. http://www.jouvay.com/interviews/ladysaw.htm (accessed 15 April 2012).

Valentine, David. *Imagining Transgender: An Ethnography of a Category.* Durham, NC: Duke University Press, 2007.

Van Haesendonck, Kristian. *"Sirena Selena vestida de pena* de Mayra Santos-Febres: ¿transgresiones de espacio o espacio de ansgresiones?" *CENTRO Journal* 15, no. 2 (Fall 2003): 78–97.

Vázquez, Andrés Clemente. *Enriqueta Faber: Ensayo de novela histórica.* Habana: Impr. y papelería "La Universal" de Ruiz y hermano, 1894.

Veal, Michael E. *Dub: Soundscapes and Shattered Sounds in Jamaican Reggae.* Middletown, CT: Wesleyan University Press, 2007.

Villaurrutia, Xavier. *Obras.* 2nd ed. Mexico City: Fondo de Cultura Económica, 1966.

Villaverde, Cirilo. *Cecilia Valdés o La loma del ángel.* 1839/1882. New York: Anaya Books, 1971.

Vries, Annette de. *Scheurbuik.* Amsterdam: Atlas, 2002.

Walcott, Derek. "The Caribbean: Culture or Mimicry?" *Journal of Interamerican Studies and World Affairs* 16, no. 1 (February 1974): 3–13.

———. *Omeros.* London: Faber and Faber, 1990.

Walcott, Rinaldo. "Reconstructing Manhood; or, The Drag of Black Masculinity." *Small Axe* 28 (March 2009): 75–89.

Walker, Karyl, and Kimmo Matthews. "Cops Tailed 'Dudus' for Hours before Pulling Over Car." *Jamaica Observer,* 23 June 2010.

Waters, Mary-Alice, ed. *Our History Is Still Being Written: The Story of Three Chinese-Cuban Generals in the Cuban Revolution, Armando Choy, Gustavo Chui, Moisés Sío Wong.* New York: Pathfinder, 2005.

Watson-Aifah, Jené. "A Conversation with Nalo Hopkinson." *Callaloo* 26, no. 1 (2003): 160–69.

Weatherston, Rosemary. "An Interview with Cherríe Moraga. Queer Reservations; or Art, Identity, and Politics in the 1990s." In *Queer Frontiers: Millennial Geographies, Genders, and Generations.* Ed. Joseph A. Boone, Martin Dupuis, et al. Madison: University of Wisconsin Press, 2000. 64–83.

Weheliye, Alexander G. "'Feenin' Posthuman Voices in Contemporary Black Popular Music." *Social Text* 71, no. 2 (Summer 2002): 21–47.

Wekker, Gloria. *Ik ben een gouden munt: Ik ga door vele handen, maar ik verlies mijn waarde niet. Subjectiviteit en seksualiteit van creoolse volksklasse vrouwen in Paramaribo.* Amsterdam: Vita, 1994.

———. *The Politics of Passion: Women's Sexual Culture in the Afro-Surinamese Diaspora.* New York: Columbia University Press, 2006.

Werbner, Pnina, and Tariq Modood, eds. *Debating Cultural Hybridity: Multi-Cultural Identity and the Politics of Anti-Racism.* London: Zed Books, 1997.

Whittle, Stephen. "Gender Fucking or Fucking Gender? Current Cultural Contributions to Theories of Gender Blending." *In Blending Genders: Social Aspects of Cross-Dressing and Sex Changing.* Ed. Richard Ekins and Dave King. London: Routledge, 1996. 196–214.

Wiegman, Robyn. *American Anatomies: Theorizing Race and Gender.* Durham, NC: Duke University Press, 1995.

Williams, Eric. *Capitalism and Slavery.* Richmond: William Byrd Press, 1994.

———. *From Columbus to Castro: The History of the Caribbean, 1492–1969.* New York: Vintage, 1970.

Williams, Walter L. *The Spirit and the Flesh: Sexual Diversity in American Indian Culture.* Boston: Beacon Press, 1986.

Wilson, Gladstone. "The Sistren Theatre Collective (Jamaica)." In *Alternative Media: Linking Global and Local.* Ed. Peter Lewis. Paris: UNESCO, 1993. 41–49.

Wiredu, Kwasi. *Cultural Universals and Particulars: An African Perspective.* Bloomington: Indiana University Press, 1996.

Wynter, Sylvia. "Jonkonnu in Jamaica: Towards an Interpretation of Folk Dance as a Cultural Process." *Jamaica Journal* 4, no. 2 (June 1980): 34–48.

Young, Robert J. C. *Colonial Desire: Hybridity in Theory, Culture and Race.* London: Routledge, 1995.

Younge, Gary. "Chilling Call to Murder as Music Attacks Gays." *Guardian,* 26 June 2004.

Zabus, Chantal. *Tempests after Shakespeare.* Basingstoke: Palgrave Macmillan, 2002.

Žižek, Slavoj. *Looking Awry: An Introduction to Jacques Lacan through Popular Culture.* Cambridge, MA: MIT Press, 1991.

———. *The Ticklish Subject: The Absent Centre of Political Ontology.* London: Verso, 1999.

Žižek, Slavoj, Eric L. Santner, and Kenneth Reinhard. *The Neighbor: Three Inquiries in Political Theology.* Chicago: University of Chicago Press, 2005.

Zoppi, Isabella Maria. "*Omeros,* Derek Walcott and the Contemporary Epic Poem." *Callaloo* 22, no. 2 (1999): 509–28.

Contributors

ROBERTO DEL VALLE ALCALÁ is a lecturer in English at the University of Alcalá in Spain. He specializes in cultural and literary studies in the English- and Spanish-speaking worlds, and has published in journals such as *Culture, Theory and Critique, Key Words: A Journal of Cultural Materialism,* and *Psikeba: Revista de Psicoanálisis y Estudios Culturales,* among others.

LEE EASTON has been collaborating with Kelly Hewson for more than a decade, exploring a mutual interest in the intersection of postcolonial and queer reading strategies. In addition to this collaboration, which has produced several articles on the scholarship of teaching and learning, Lee has also coedited a collection of essays on science fiction and social change. With Richard Harrison, he is coauthor of *Secret Identity Reader: Essays on Sex, Death, and the Superhero.* Lee Easton is Associate Dean, Faculty of Humanities and Social Sciences, at the Sheridan Institute of Technology and Advanced Learning in Oakville, Ontario.

ODILE FERLY is Associate Professor of Francophone Studies at Clark University. She is the author of *A Poetics of Relation: Caribbean Women Writing at the Millennium* (2012), a pan-Caribbean study of recent women's fiction from the Francophone and Hispanophone regions. She has also published articles on the literary representation of the Haitian community in Guadeloupe and on the depiction of the continental Caribbean by Antillean authors. Ferly's current research focuses on cultural politics in the French Caribbean.

MARIA CRISTINA FUMAGALLI is the author of *Caribbean Perspectives on Modernity: Returning Medusa's Gaze* (2009) and *The Flight of the Vernacular: Seamus Heaney, Derek Walcott and the Impress of Dante* (2001), editor of *Agenda: Special Issue on Derek Walcott* (2002–2003) and coeditor of *Surveying the American Tropics: A Literary History from New York to Bahia* (2012). She is currently working on a new monograph entitled *On the Edge: The Border between Haiti and the Dominican Republic,* for which she received the support of the AHRC and a Leverhulme Research Fellowship. She has published numerous articles on Caribbean literature and culture and contributed chapters and essays to many edited collections.

KELLY HEWSON teaches postcolonial literature, film studies, and composition at Mount Royal University. A former judge of the Caribbean-Canadian Region of the Commonwealth Writers' Prize and co-organizer of the Prize in Calgary in 2003, she has published interviews with Austin Clarke, Earl Lovelace, and Derek Walcott, and coauthored an article on Lawrence Scott. She enjoys a rich writing and teaching partnership with Lee Easton from which they have produced work on various topics such as reading representations of race in American film, cosmopolitanism, and film, the U.S.-Canada border, the Canadian student film spectator, theories of affect and transformative pedagogies, and, most recently, resiliency thinking.

ISABEL HOVING is affiliated with the Department of Film and Literary Studies of Leiden University, where she teaches postcolonial theory, cultural analysis, gender studies, and ecocriticism. She is the author of a study on Caribbean migrant women writers, *In Praise of New Travellers* (2001). She has coedited books on (Dutch) migration, Caribbean literatures, African literature and art, and has just completed a monograph on the intersections of postcolonial theory and ecocriticism. She is on the editorial board of *Thamyris/Intersecting: Place, Sex, and Race* and *Ecozon@: The European Journal on Literature, Culture and the Environment.* In addition to her academic work, she is an award-winning youth writer.

WENDY KNEPPER is a Lecturer in English at Brunel University where she teaches postcolonial and modernist literatures. Her publications include *Patrick Chamoiseau: A Critical Introduction* (2012) and contributions to the *Journal of Commonwealth Literature, PMLA, Small Axe,* and numerous essay collections. Currently, she is working on the Palgrave critical introduction to Caribbean Literature and a book-length project about contemporary Caribbean biopolitics and in/justice in the context of globalization studies and recent debates about world literature.

BÉNÉDICTE LEDENT is Professor at the University of Liège, in Belgium, where she teaches English language and postcolonial literatures, especially those of the African diaspora. She is the author of *Caryl Phillips* (2002) and has coedited several collections of essays, most recently *Caryl Phillips: Writing in the Key of Life* (2012, with Daria Tunca) and *New Perspectives on the Black Atlantic* (2012, with Pilar Cuder-Domínguez). She has contributed essays to edited collections and to several journals including *Commonwealth, Kunapipi,* and *Moving Worlds.*

CARINE M. MARDOROSSIAN is Associate Professor of English at the University at Buffalo, where she specializes in Caribbean, postcolonial, and feminist studies. Her articles have appeared in *Small Axe, Callaloo, Journal of Caribbean Literatures, Signs,* and *College Literature,* as well as in numerous anthologies. She has just completed her second book, entitled *Framing the Victim: Rape, Masculinity, and Agency in the Contemporary United States,* and is now working on an ecocritical study of Caribbean fiction.

SHANI MOOTOO was born in Ireland in 1957 to Trinidadian parents. She grew up in Trinidad and at the age of twenty-four relocated to Canada, where she currently lives. Her novels, poems, paintings, photographs, and videos boldly explore the interconnections of gender, sexuality, and race. Her literary career began in 1993 with the publication of *Out on Main Street,* a selection of short stories. Three years later she published her first novel, *Cereus Blooms at Night,* which was shortlisted for the Scotia Bank Giller Prize, the Ethel Wilson Fiction Prize, the Books in Canada–First Novel Award, and was long-listed for the Man Booker Prize. In 2001 she published her first collection of poems, *The Predicament of Or,* followed, in 2005, by a novel, *He Drown She in the Sea.* Her most recent novel, *Valmiki's Daughter,* was long-listed for 2009's Scotia Bank Giller Prize.

MICHAEL NIBLETT is a Research Fellow at the Yesu Persaud Centre for Caribbean Studies at the University of Warwick. He is the author of *The Caribbean Novel since 1945* (2012) and coeditor with Kerstin Oloff of *Perspectives on the "Other America": Comparative Approaches to Caribbean and Latin American Culture* (2009). He has written a number of articles on Caribbean and world literature, and he is coeditor of a forthcoming special edition of the *Journal of Postcolonial Writing,* titled *Postcolonial Studies and World Literature.*

Kerstin Oloff is a Lecturer in Latin American Studies at the University of Durham. She is the coeditor with Michael Niblett of *Perspectives on the "Other America": Comparative Approaches to Caribbean and Latin American Culture* (2009). She has published articles, interviews, and reviews in edited collections and academic journals (including *Revista Hispánica Moderna, Latin American Research Review,* and *La Habana Elegante*).

Lizabeth Paravisini is Professor of Caribbean culture and literature at Vassar College. She has authored several books, among them *Phyllis Shand Allfrey: A Caribbean Life* (1996), *Jamaica Kincaid: A Critical Companion* (1999), *Creole Religions of the Caribbean* (2003, with Margarite Fernández Olmos), and *Literature of the Caribbean* (2008). She has also coedited collections of essays, the latest of which is *Displacements and Transformations in Caribbean Cultures* (2008; with Ivette Romero-Cesareo). In addition to book chapters, she has also published numerous articles and translations in such journals as *Callaloo, Journal of West Indian Literature, Obsidian,* and *Revista Mexicana del Caribe,* to mention just a few.

Mayra Santos Febres is a Puerto Rican novelist, poet, essayist, and literary critic born in 1966. In 1984 she began publishing poetry in a variety of international periodicals and journals, including *Página Doce* (Argentina), *Casa de las Américas* (Cuba), *Revue Noire* (France), and *Review: Latin American Literature and Arts* (USA). Her first two collections of poetry, *Anamu y manigua* and *El orden escapado,* were published in 1991 to great critical acclaim. In 1996 she won the Juan Rulfo Award for her short story "Oso blanco." *Sirena Selena vestida de pena,* her first novel published in 2000, has been translated into English, French, and Italian and was short-listed for the Rómulo Gallegos Prize. Her more recent books include *Nuestra Señora de la noche* (2006) and *Tratado de medicina natural para hombres melancólicos* (2011). Santos Febres holds a PhD from Cornell University and is currently professor at the University of Puerto Rico–Río Piedras.

Paula K. Sato is an Assistant Professor of French at Kent State University. Her publications include an essay on the Orient and Orientalism in Severo Sarduy's *Écrit en dansant* (From Cuba with a song), which appeared in *L'Orient dans le roman de la Caraïbe* (The Orient in the Caribbean novel; Mounia Benalil, ed., 2007); an essay on the counter-Gothic strategies of Meiling Jin, which appeared in *Asian Gothic: Essays on Literature, Film and Anime* (Andrew Hock Soon Ng, ed., 2008); and a comparative study of Aimé Césaire, Charlotte Brontë, and Jean Rhys, which appeared in the special issue of *Canadian Review of Comparative Literature* titled *Discourses on Trans/National Identity in Caribbean Literature* (Jacqueline Couti, ed., 2011).

LAWRENCE SCOTT is from Trinidad and Tobago. His latest novel, *Light Falling on Bamboo* (2012), was inspired by the paintings, life, and times of Michel Jean Cazabon, Trinidad's most famous nineteenth-century painter. His novel *Aelred's Sin* (1998) was awarded a Commonwealth Writers' Prize (Best Book in Canada and the Caribbean). His first novel, *Witchbroom* (1992), was short-listed for a Commonwealth Writers' Prize in 1993 (Best First Book). This was followed by *Ballad for the New World* (1994), including the Tom-Gallon Award–winning short story "The House of Funerals" (1986). His novel *Night Calypso* (2004) was also short-listed for a Commonwealth Writers' Prize (Best Book Award), long-listed for the International IMPAC Dublin Literary Award (2006), and translated into French. It was the One Book One Community choice in 2005 by the National Library of Trinidad and Tobago. He is the editor of *Golconda: Our Voices Our Lives* (2009), an anthology of stories and poems from the sugar belt in Trinidad. Over the years, he has combined teaching with writing. He lives in London and Port of Spain, and his website is www.lawrencescott.co.uk.

KARINA SMITH is a Senior Lecturer in the School of Communication and the Arts at Victoria University (Melbourne, Australia). She has published on Sistren Theatre Collective's work in *Kunapipi, Situation Analysis, MaComère, ThirdSpace, Modern Drama,* and *Theatre Research International,* as well as in *Compelling Confessions: The Politics of Personal Disclosure* (2011), edited by Suzanne Diamond, and *MLA Options for Teaching Series: Teaching Anglophone Caribbean Literature* (2012), edited by Supriya M. Nair. She is currently working on a monograph with CaribVic (The Caribbean Association of Victoria) about the Caribbean community's stories of migration to Victoria, Australia.

ROBERTO STRONGMAN is Associate Professor in the Department of Black Studies at the University of California, Santa Barbara. His interdisciplinary approach encompasses the fields of religion, history, and sexuality in order to further his main area of research and teaching: Comparative

Caribbean Cultural Studies. His transnational and multilingual approach to the Caribbean cultural zone is grounded in *La Créolité*, a movement developed at *L'Université des Antilles et de La Guyane* in Martinique, where he studied as a dissertation fellow. His articles have appeared in *Journal of Haitian Studies*, *Journal of Caribbean Studies*, *Journal of Caribbean Literatures*, *Callaloo*, *Kunapipi*, *Wadabagei*, and the *Journal of Latin American Cultural Studies*. Dr. Strongman is currently preparing his first book, *Black Atlantic Transcorporealities*, for publication.

CHANTAL ZABUS holds the "Institut universitaire de France" Chair of Comparative Postcolonial Literatures and Gender Studies at the University Paris 13-Sorbonne Paris Cité. She is the author of *Between Rites and Rights: Excision in Women's Experiential Texts and Human Contexts* (2007); *The African Palimpsest* (1991; rpt. 2007); and *Tempests after Shakespeare* (2002). Her most recent book, *Out in Africa: Same-Sex Desire in SubSaharan Literatures and Cultures*, is currently under review. She has edited several volumes, including *Fearful Symmetries: Essays and Testimonies on Excision and Circumcision* (2009) and, with Silvia Nagy-Zekmi, *Colonization or Globalization? Postcolonial Explorations of Imperial Expansion* (2010) and *Perennial Empires: Postcolonial, Transnational and Literary Perspectives* (2011). She is currently working on an edited volume (with David Coad), *Transgender Experience: Found in Transition* (2013). Her personal website can be accessed at www.zabus.eu.

Index